TRAJECTORIES IN THE STUDY OF RELIGION

TRAJECTORIES IN THE STUDY
OF RELIGION
Addresses at the
Seventy Fifth Anniversary
of the
American Academy of Religion

Ray L. Hart, Editor

Scholars Press
Atlanta, Georgia

TRAJECTORIES IN THE STUDY OF RELIGION
Addresses at the
Seventy Fifth Anniversary
of the
American Academy of Religion

BL21
.T73

©1987
Scholars Press

Library of Congress Cataloging in Publication Data

Trajectories in the study of religion.

(Scholars Press studies in religious and theological scholarship)
Major addresses delivered at the 75th anniversary meeting of the American Academy of Religion, held Dec. 8-11, 1984, in Chicago.
1. Religion—Congresses. 2. Theology—Congresses. I. Hart, Ray L. II. Series.
BL21.T73 1987 200 86-20272
ISBN 1-55540-064-7 (alk. paper)

Printed in the United States of America
on acid-free paper

CONTENTS

PREFACE

This volume comprises the major addresses delivered at the 75th Anniversary meeting of the American Academy of Religion, held December 8–11, 1984, at the Palmer House Hotel in Chicago: the Plenary Addresses, the Scholars Press Associates Lectures, and the 75th Anniversary Lectures. I regret that two addresses are lacking owing to unavailability of mss., the Plenary Address by Dr. William J. Bennett, then Chairman of the National Endowment for the Humanities, now U.S. Secretary of Education ("Relentless Suboptimization and the Art of Soulcraft"), and the 75th Anniversary Lecture by Father Gustavo Gutiérrez ("Liberation Theology: The Continuing Challenge"). Of all the lectures printed here, only one was not actually delivered at the 75th meeting. Owing to what proved to be his terminal illness, Prof. Dr. Eric Voegelin was unable to be present. Our joy in publishing his last words, on which he worked heroically with waning energies, only partially mitigates profound sadness at his passing.

In the course of the 75th Anniversary year, the officers immersed themselves in such recorded histories of the AAR as are extant. We debated among ourselves whether the time were ripe to launch a full-scale history of the organization, and concluded that the 100th Anniversary will offer that properly auspicious occasion. The 75th Anniversary Banquet was seized as the moment to honor our Founding and Guiding Parents. From the Banquet program and for posterity we list below names and committees that have figured prominently in our heritage. A brief history of the AAR and an overview of the 75th Anniversary Meeting are offered in the essay by Professor Leo O'Donovan.

As the NABI Self-Study Committee gave birth to a new name and a new reality for our learned society in 1963, the American Academy of Religion, and set its agenda for twenty years, so in 1984 the AAR Task Force on Governance and Development was constituted to envisage the next twenty-five. We believe that matters of such moment have been set in motion that they will claim the energies and loyalties of every scholar in the field. May coming generations be so invigorated that they look back on us as the sleepy ones!

The work of the 75th Anniversary celebration was shared by many hands. For planning and execution thanks are due the Program Committee and its Sub-Committee on the 75th Anniversary (Catherine Albanese, Ray L. Hart, James Wiggins, Charles Winquist), and most especially for the energies and wisdom of our Executive Director, Professor James Wiggins, and his staff (notably, Ms. Helen Sessler), and my secretary, Ms. Jean Harte. The celebration could not have been the success it was without the close cooperation of all program unit officers at both the national and regional levels. But of course the efforts of these individuals and the rationale for our learned society as such is for the sake of substantive scholarly work, the tip of the iceberg of which is manifest (for this occasion) in this volume. To each contributor I express for the Academy our gratitude for the timely submission of mss. and correction of proofs. And for the record we may note those who were invited to contribute to the 75th celebration and thus to this volume but were unable to do so because of conflicting schedules: Jorge Luis Borges, Hayden White, Jacques Derrida, Octavio Paz, Julia Kristeva, Umberto Eco, Edmond Jabés, and Michel Foucault.

No funds for the 75th Anniversary and its related projects were derived from the operating budget of the Academy (the latter supported by member dues). We note, and are deeply grateful for, financial support of 75th Anniversary projects by several friends of religion in higher learning. The Henry Luce Foundation made possible the genuinely international character of our enterprise, subvening the participation by distinguished scholars from abroad. The Exxon Education Foundation subvened curricular revision and formation, the initial work of our new standing Committee on Education and the Study of Religion, and the publication of associated volumes. An anonymous AAR member contributed generously to new publications and research projects. The Lilly Endowment subvened the work of the Task Force and, for an initial period, the enhancement of central office staff for development projects. In all, approximately $175,000 was sought and obtained for these projects, a favorable augury.

Before I turn to—I was about to say "weightier matters," but it really is only—a personal response to the 75th Anniversary, permit me an observation that risks the jejune: the importance of *little* moves by many people in places often unmarked and unnoticed in such a field of inquiry as ours. One remembers the jejune game of "May I?" and the fact that, in that game, Baby Steps and Duck Waddles were as important to winning as Giant Steps. One remembers the words of a youth writing his mother from the trenches of WWI, Franz

Rosenzweig: "No one need live a moment longer than he enjoys living simply for the sake of tasks—they will be taken care of, if not by oneself by the next person. The thing is simply to live in the conviction that one cannot tell what good may come of it."

* * *

When I reflect on an ostensibly big event in a piece of time, I find crowding in on that reflection the reverie of timepieces. The event were one thing (one imagines) were it anticipated, endured, and looked back upon through the measurement of sun-dials, shadows, hour-glasses; another through an electronically driven "watch," without moving "hands." And why *do* we still call our timepieces *watches* when the segments of day and night have long since ceased to be discriminated by "watches" (as in the biblical three watches of the night)? A wisdom in our language chimes with that in time: stand watch.

Could one have counseled in advance the some 4,000 scholars (including AAR & SBL) attending the 75th, one might have said: stand watch on your first impressions. Who knows what they severally were, and how they are now interlaced with "results"? It can be said of large events what Winston Churchill said of reading great books: stand watch over timing. "It is a great pity to read a book too soon in life. The first impression is the one that counts; and if it is a light one, it may be all that can be hoped for. A later and second perusal may recoil from a surface already hardened by premature contact."

My impression . . . .

An event of this sort rightly glories in continuity of surface: look at how long we've been at it, this thing of importance! But such a celebration should also occasion a rupture of plane, should offer relief from the "vague average," surcease from the ceaseless everydayness of things falling out. One sought an occasion which might surprise us with a consciousness of the sought that had guided our unruptured seeking—an occasion that, if thus effective, could not fail reflexively to radicalize the "we" of seeking in the study of religion(s), the sought. In the permutations of time, are seeker and the sought commensurable? I believe Mircea Eliade had such a problematic in mind when, at a high moment at the 75th Anniversary Banquet, he mused anecdotally the question whether the scholar of religion ever changes his/her mind as a result of (another's) scholarship. That question interrogates the question of the relationship between the scholarly seeker and the scholarly sought, at bottom a question of *political* commensurability, the *polis* of the seeker and that of the sought.

The surface permutations were clearly in evidence: from our origins among a small band of WASP scholars, the *polis* of scholarly seekers has expanded to include women (although they were *proportionately* higher *ab origine!*), Blacks, Jews, Roman Catholics, Buddhists, Muslims, Hindus, *et al*; from Protestant Christianity and its scriptures, the *polis* of the sought now coincides with the religions of the world—their scriptures and their suffusion of human culture.

One pauses to harken to Hegel: *results* are not to be regarded without their *becoming*—for their becoming establishes the kind of being that results have. Did we get certain kinds of scholarly seekers "in," then expand the sought to include their subject matters? Or was there an intrinsic *nisus* in the sought itself which diversified its seekers? Do we understand the *becoming* of the study of religion(s)? What *displacements* would such an understanding have in the *meaning of the results*?

The potency for radical displacement was more or less successfully evaded (not by design, heaven forfend, of course). Such is the texture of academic intratemporality that the problematic of the becoming of religious studies could only rumble beneath and occasionally pierce the surface of celebration. Like scholars *überhaupt*, scholars of religion(s) negotiate only at a distance both with what is "out there" and with what is "in here." What is out there (beyond the walls of academe) currently and one suspects for a long time to come is a powerful assault on humanism ("secular, godless humanism"), and is our "out there" not the context of the humanities? But to this mindless there is added, currently and one suspects for a long time to come, a mindful assault *within* the humanistic enterprise upon the bias that has sourced venturing, at least in the west's adventure: upon the *I* or the *we* of seeking. Did we understand the becoming of religious studies, we might ascribe this latter assault not only to a currently fashionable school of thinking in the west but as well to the reflexive effect of expansion in the sought (to include, in instance, a-, anti-, or differently humanistic religious sensibilities in the east).

As the AAR's 75th Anniversary was once our anterior future and had to be imagined in order to heave into an ever so brief present, so now it is the posterior beckoning a new anterior future, that of the 100th. I am not a prophet, or the son of two, but I believe our posterior future offers a scrutiny of signs for the anterior. That scrutiny requires an enlivening of imagination not overly exercised by the anticipation of results. The question of the scholarly seeker and the scholarly sought in matters religious has been stirred in the Try-Pot, and what shall be rendered of the human and the sacred when the ship makes port on the 100th cannot be envisaged from any top gallant.

In what has become a Bultmannian cliché (itself a variant on

Hegel), the meaning of an event is a function of the future to which it gives rise. The results of the 75th will be known in the anterior beginnings of the 100th, when it is seen what posterior becomings were authorized and nourished.

Ray L. Hart
President, American Academy of
Religion, 1984–85

University of Montana

Leaders in the 75 Year Journey of the American Academy of Religion

In 1909 Professor Ismar J. Peritz of Syracuse University conceived a new organization for professors of Bible. At the annual meeting of the SBLE that year he convened a gathering of Professors, Irving Wood, Smith College; Raymond C. Knox, Columbia University; and Olive Dutcher, Mount Holyoke College. That "founding four" generated the "Association of Biblical Instructors in American Colleges and Secondary Schools", the first program of which was held the following year. At the December 1922 meeting the members voted to change its name to the "National Association of Biblical Instructors" with care aforethought for the acronym NABI. In 1933 after years of persistent urging by Professor Peritz a twice annual journal, the *Journal of the NABI*, was launched, the name of which was changed in 1937 to the *Journal of Bible and Religion* when it became a quarterly publication. In December 1963, upon recommendation of a Self-Study Committee supported by a Danforth Foundation grant, the name of the organization was changed to the "American Academy of Religion." That committee helped establish the agenda for twenty years and in January, 1964 the new corporation was legally created. Two years later the name of the journal was changed to the *Journal of the American Academy of Religion*. In 1984 with the support of a grant from the Lilly Endowment a Task Force on Governance and Development made a series of proposals that the Board of Directors in an unprecedented special meeting in September 1984 received and adopted. It is hoped that the efforts to implement these proposals will benefit the Academy in ways comparable to what has emerged since 1964 from the farsighted proposals of the 1963 Self-Study Committee.

PRESIDENTS

1910–1925	Charles Foster Kent *Yale University*	1956	A. Roy Eckhart *Lehigh University*
1926	Irving F. Wood *Smith College*	1957	Robert M. Montgomery *Ohio Wesleyan University*
1927	Eliza H. Kendrick *Wellesley College*	1958	H. Neil Richardson *Boston University*
1928	Walter W. Haviland *Friends Select School*	1959	Lauren E. Brubaker, Jr. *University of South Carolina*
1929	Ralph K. Hickok *Wells College*	1960	Lionel A. Whiston, Jr. *Eden Theological Seminary*
1930	Irwin R. Beiler *Allegheny College*	1961	Robert V. Smith *Colgate University*
1931	Laura H. Wild *Mt. Holyoke College*	1962	Fred D. Gealy *Methodist Theological* *School of Ohio*
1932	Chester Warren Quimby *Dickinson College*	1963	Clyde A. Holbrook *Oberlin College*
1933	James Muilenburg *University of Maine*	1964	Ira J. Martin, III *Berea College*
1934	Elmer W. K. Mould *Elmira College*	1965	James L. Price *Duke University*
1935	Florence M. Fitch *Oberlin College*	1966	William Hordern *Lutheran Theological*
1936	S. Ralph Harlow *Smith College*		*Seminary*
1937	Frank G. Lankard *Drew University*	1967	John Priest *Florida State University*
1938	Mary E. Andrews *Goucher College*	1968	J. Wesley Robb *University of Southern*
1939	William Scott *Randolph-Macon* *Woman's College*	1969	*California* Jacob Neusner *Brown University*
1940	B. Harvie Branscomb *Duke University*	1970	Claude Welch *University of Pennsylvania*
1941	Katharine H. Paton *Baldwin School*	1971	James Burtchaell *Notre Dame University*
1942–43	Edgar S. Brightman *Boston University*	1972	Robert Michaelsen *University of California,*
1944	Floyd V. Filson *McCormick Theological* *Seminary*	1973	*Santa Barbara* Charles Long *University of Chicago*
1945	Mary Ely Lyman *Sweet Briar College*	1974	Christine Downing *Rutgers University*
1946	J. Paul Williams *Mt. Holyoke College*	1975	William May *University of Indiana*
1947	Rolland E. Wolfe *Western Reserve University*	1976	Preston Williams *Harvard University*
1948	Dwight M. Beck *Syracuse University*	1977	Schubert Ogden *Southern Methodist*
1949	Selby Vernon McCasland *University of Virginia*	1978	*University* John Meagher
1950	Virginia Corwin *Smith College*	1979	*University of Toronto* Langdon Gilkey
1951	Mary Francis Thelen *Randolph-Macon Woman's* *College*	1980	*University of Chicago* William Clebsch *Stanford University*
1952	Charles S. Braden *Northwestern University*	1981	Jill Raitt *Duke University*
1953	Carl E. Purinton *Boston University*	1982	Gordon Kaufman *Harvard University*
1954	W. Gordon Ross *Berea College*	1983	Wilfred Smith *Harvard University*
1955	Arthur C. Wickenden *Miami University*	1984	Ray L. Hart *University of Montana*

JOURNAL EDITORS

1933–1937 Ismar J. Peritz
*Syracuse
University*

1937–1960 Carl E. Purinton
Boston University

1960–1969 A. Roy Eckhart
Lehigh University

1969–1979 Ray L. Hart
*University of
Montana*

1979–1984 Robert P.
Scharlemann
*University of Iowa
and University of
Virginia*

EXECUTIVE DIRECTORS

1964–72   Harry Buck
Wilson College

1973–75   Robert Spivey
*Florida State
University*

1976–79   John Priest
*Florida State
University*

1979–82   Charles Winquist
*State University of
California at
Chico*

1982–   James B. Wiggins
*Syracuse
University*

NABI SELF-STUDY COMMITTEE 1963

Robert V. Smith (Chair)
Colgate University

Dwight Beck
Syracuse University

Harry M. Buck
Wilson College

Robert Eccles
DePauw University

Clyde A. Holbrook
Oberlin College

AAR TASK FORCE ON GOVERNANCE AND DEVELOPMENT—1984

John Dillenberger
Graduate Theological Union

Ray L. Hart (Co-Chair)
University of Montana

Charles Long
*University of North Carolina
at Chapel Hill and Duke
University*

Wendy O'Flaherty
University of Chicago

Schubert Ogden
*Southern Methodist
University*

James B. Wiggins (Co-Chair)
Syracuse University

Editor's Preface to "Quod Deus Dicitur," by Eric Voegelin

Professor Voegelin was born in Germany and educated in Austria (Dr. rer. pol., University of Vienna, 1922, at the age of 21) On a two-year Rockefeller Fellowship he came to the United States and studied with John Dewey at Columbia, Alfred North Whitehead at Harvard, and John R. Commons at Wisconsin. In 1938, after being dismissed from his position at the University of Vienna by the Nazis he returned to the U.S.A. and taught briefly at Harvard, Bennington College, and the University of Alabama before settling into an enormously productive sixteen years at Louisiana State University. In 1958 he returned to Germany where he founded the Institute of Political Science and taught at the University of Munich until 1969. From 1969 until his death he was Research Professor at the Hoover Institution at Stanford University.

When I invited Professor Voegelin to deliver a Plenary Address at the 75th Anniversary meeting of the American Academy of Religion, he accepted reluctantly and tentatively, owing to the precarious state of his health. And when it became apparent that he could not be present, I urged him to prepare his address for publication. I am told by his wife, Lissy, and his friend and Assistant, Paul Caringella, that, true to the end to his character of iron resolve, he took himself out of the hospital (1) to die at home and (2) to finish his last work. The first and last work of Eric Voegelin, as for Plato, was the ascent of the soul to God.

Of these pages, Caringella has written: "Eric Voegelin began dictating "Quod Deus Dicitur" on January 2, 1985, the day before his eighty-fourth birthday. He revised the last pages on January 16th; further revisions were made on January 17th and in the afternoon of January 18th, his last full day before his death on Saturday the 19th at about eight in the morning.

"When the dictation reached Anselm's prayer, Voegelin provisionally inserted pertinent pages from an earlier manuscript, with minor adjustments. He similarly adapted at the beginning of Sec. 5 a paragraph from his "Response to Professor Altizer" (*JAAR* 43: 1975, p. 770f.) His discussion of Hesiod's *Theogony* and Plato's *Timaeus* in the last pages and in the planned conclusion is based on the full analytical treatment in the last 30-odd pages of the unfinished fifth and last volume of his *Order and History*.

"Voegelin had spoken of dictating three or four more pages (which usually meant seven or eight manuscript pages) to bring the paper to its conclusion. I have included the five texts which he intended to comment upon and which mark the direction he wanted to take."

Toward the end of the essay, the material in brackets contains Paul Caringella's notes on the direction the commentary upon each of the five texts was intended by Voegelin to take.

To Mrs. Voegelin's Dedication, I wish to add my own profound gratitude to Paul Caringella for his help in bringing Voegelin's last words to press. I express as well my deepest thanks for the assistance of Gregor Sebba, University Professor (Emeritus) at Emory University, who, alas, also died shortly after his review of this manuscript. He and his eminent translator wife, Helen Sebba, were dear and lifelong friends of the Voegelins.

————R.L.H.

QUOD DEUS DICITUR

ERIC VOEGELIN*

The question raised by the title of this lecture has received its specific form through Thomas Aquinas in his *Summa Theologiae,* I.2.3.

This question does not permit a simple answer as if its divine topic were an entity with properties about which one can advance propositions of the kind that apply to things in the external world. We are not facing God as a thing but as the partner in a questing search that moves within a reality formed by participatory language. Moreover, we ourselves are part of the questioned reality that we are linguistically intending as if it were an external object about which we could talk as if we were cognitive subjects facing objects of cognition. The noetic search for the structure of a reality that includes divinity is itself an event within the reality we are questioning. Hence, at every point in the process, we are faced with the problem of an inquiry into something experienced as real before the inquiry into the structure of its reality has begun. The process of our *intellectus* in quest of our *fides,* a process that also can be formulated as our *fides* in quest of our *intellectus,* is a primary event.

* * *

The event of the quest is an historical process. The world of symbols compactly symbolizing reality at any given historical point has to submit to the pressure of noetic analysis, with the result that the ground of reality hitherto symbolized as "the gods" has to die in its symbolized form, to be replaced by new symbols symbolizing the "God" whose presence beyond the gods endows them with their claim to necessary being.

*Dedication: This last work of Eric Voegelin would never have reached paper but for the understanding and devotion of Paul Caringella, who took down the dictation from an almost inaudible voice under the saddest circumstances. For this my husband wanted to thank him by dedicating the work to him; unfortunately fate and death stepped in and prevented him from doing what he so much liked to do. But knowing his heart and mind so well I can speak for him now, to thank our friend Paul for the love he has given us ever since we have known him. Lissy Voegelin.

The two great civilizational contexts in Western history representative for this structure of the search are (a) the emergence of the "God" from the polytheistic symbolism in Hellenic culture and (b) the emergence of the "God" from the tension between doctrinal and mystical theology in the Christian societies since antiquity.

The linguistic complications arising from the paradoxic structure of the process have never noetically been sufficiently analyzed. The language of the supposedly analytical discourse on the questions of divinity has stabilized, by cultural consensus, on a level of compactness which does not sufficiently distinguish between the paradoxic structure of the divine-human encounter in the search on the one side, and the symbols arising in reflection on the culturally concrete expression of the search on the other. This unsatisfactory state of analysis causes the debate to be conducted in terms of the well-known reflective dichotomies of theological discourse. The symbols dominating reflective language on the fringe of compactness and differentiation can be summarized in the list of:

1. Philosophy and Religion
2. Philosophy and Theology
3. Natural Theology and Revelatory Theology
4. Faith and Reason
5. Reason and Revelation
6. Science and Religion
7. Natural Theology and Supernatural Theology

Each of these dichotomies furnishes the occasion for indefinite debate on the compact level, without ever penetrating to the fundamentally paradoxic structure of thought that is peculiar to the participatory relation between the process of thought and the reality in which it proceeds.

* * *

In the article in the *Summa* on the question whether God exists, to which the title of this lecture refers, Thomas has attained a certain degree of clarity about its paradoxic structure. The question concerning *quod Deus dicitur* is not raised arbitrarily but presupposes a scriptural article of faith. This article is the formula of the *ego sum qui sum* of Exodus 3:14. If there were no symbol of faith already in historical existence there would be no question. This article of faith is part of the procedure of noetic questioning regarding its meaning. The "question of God" cannot be made intelligible unless the question of God is part of the reality to be explored. The symbol of the divine *ego sum* is part of the exploratory consciousness which approaches the symbol of faith as the answer to an inquiry arising from the particular experiences of reality. For the *ego sum* of the scripture symbolizes the necessary pole of a reality which in its phenomenal particularity is experienced only as contingent. The experienced tension between contingency and necessity is the structure in reality which is at issue in the question of divinity.

This structure is then pursued by Thomas into the five well-known experiences of contingent reality. In the first of the tensions experienced, reality is in motion and the motion requires a mover. On this particular level one can only proceed from one particular movement to its particular mover and would proceed indefinitely without reaching an explanation of the phenomenon of movement. In order to become intelligible, the process of particular movement requires a first mover (*primum movens*). And in this noetic process of analysis Thomas identifies the first mover as the something (*hoc*) in which "omnes intelligunt *Deum*," as the something, the *hoc*, that all understand to be God. The *Deus* of this proposition is the answer responding to the structure of the noetic question.

The same type of argument then is applied to the *causa efficiens*. In a series of efficient causes it makes no more sense to proceed indefinitely; one arrives at sense only through the symbolism of a first uncaused cause; and here again Thomas formulates this first cause to be "quam omnes *Deum* nominant," the cause that all call God. The same symbolizing procedure applies to the other so-called proofs for the existence of God: The necessary cause of all other things is "quod omnes dicunt *Deum*;" and when an ultimate cause of goodness and perfection in all things has to be symbolized, again "hoc dicimus *Deum*." Finally, the procedure is applied to the end of all reality: There is something intelligibly intelligent (intelligens) by which all natural things are ordered to an end, and that intelligibly intelligent (intelligens) is the *hoc* that "dicimus *Deum*." There is no divinity other than the necessity in tension with the contingency experienced in the noetic question.

*   *   *

The Thomasic analysis touches the paradoxic structure of the tension between the compact symbols of faith and the operation of the noetic intellect. However, it is hampered in its clear formulation by the compactness of the reflective symbols Thomas has to use in his historical situation. They are the symbols of a truth of revelation in the tradition of the Judaic-Christian faith, and the philosophical symbols deriving from the culturally different context of Hellenic civilization. In order to clarify some of these complications it will be helpful to refer briefly to the advances of analysis in the Cartesian and post-Cartesian enterprises.

Consider, for instance, the formulation given to the problem by Leibniz in his *Principes de la nature et de la grâce*. The "metaphysical" analysis of Leibniz assumes the principle of sufficient reason (raison suffisante) as the explanation for all that happens in reality. The quest of the sufficient reason culminates in the two questions: (a) Why is there something rather than nothing, and (b) Why are the things as they are? On this level of symbolization Leibniz arrives at formulations closely resembling those of Thomas. The experience of contingent reality implies a non-contingent reason for what is experienced as contingent. "Et cette dernière raison des choses est appelée *Dieu*."

Though the formulation of Leibniz resembles that of Thomas, one should be aware of its post-Cartesian aura. What comes to the fore now is the inherence of the answer in the event of the question. And that imaginative characteristic which goes beyond the simple assumption of a revelatory symbol is due to the Cartesian insight of the answer as being contained in the act of doubting and desiring. The experienced transition from an apparently certain cogito ergo sum to an imaginatively doubting and desiring ego is the meditative source of the understanding that there is no ego without a comprehending reality to be symbolized as the perfection toward which the imaginative ego strives. An ego that doubts and desires to go beyond itself is not the creator of itself but requires a creator and maintainer of its doubting existence, and that cause is the "God" who appears in the analyses of the *Third Meditation* and the *Principles*. There is no doubting contingency without the tension toward the necessity which makes the doubt evident as such.

This advance into the imaginative structure of the noetic question, however, is still handicapped by another compact element in the Thomasic analysis, that is, by the construction of a meditative analysis as a syllogistic proof. Even Descartes and Leibniz still want to understand the analysis as a proof for the existence of the God of Revelation, an assumption shown to be untenable by Kant in the *Critique of Pure Reason*. Since, however, Kant's positive analysis of the imaginative question was insufficient, it fell to Hegel to recognize, against the criticism of Kant, "the so-called proofs for the existence of God as descriptions and analyses of the process of the *Geist* itself. . . . The rising of thought beyond the sensual, the thought transcending the finite into the infinite, the leap that is made by breaking from the series of the sensual into the supersensual, all this is thought itself, the transition is *only thought itself*." (*Enzyklopaedie* 1830 §50)

In this passage from Hegel one can discern the historical strata of the analysis. They are (a) the Thomasic argument (with its ultimate ground in Aristotle), (b) the Cartesian advance to the argument as an imaginative event, (c) the Kantian criticism of its syllogistic structure, and (d) a new clarity about the process of noetic analysis. What makes the Hegelian insight, however, still unsatisfactory is the tendency to raise the paradoxic structure, as revealed in the reflective dimension of consciousness, into an ultimate solution of the problem of divinity. This hypostatisation of reflective consciousness obscures the fact that the noetic movement itself, the divine-human encounter, is still an active process in tension toward the symbols of faith. The hypostatisation of the reflective symbols leads to the deformative construction of the process of thought into the finished thought of a System of conceptual science.

* * *

The difficulties the modern thinkers have with their inadequate positive analyses of the consciousness of reality stem from the inadequate distinction between the process of noetic analysis and the reflective symbols describing the historical process of analysis. The experiential point of the confusion is formulated by Thomas (*ibidem* I.2) as the difference between the *Deus in se* and the *Deus quoad nos*. In faith we are living in the tension between contingency and divine necessity while in the reflective symbols the necessary and the contingent poles of the tension are reflectively hypostatised into transcendent and immanent entities. That the divine necessity is not a thing known by its properties is clearly seen by Thomas as the source of the difficulties, but he does not determine with equal clarity the difficulty, seen already by Plato in the *Phaedrus* and the *Timaeus*, that arises from the intentionalist structure of language: our inclination to think in thingly propositions about experiences which are not experiences of things. The primary structure of the divine-human encounter must be distinguished from the reflective symbolization of the poles of the tensional encounter as thingly entities. Thomas goes only so far as to distinguish between the a priori of the divine necessity and the a posteriori of its proof from the effect in the contingent experiences, losing thereby certain qualities of the analysis achieved by Anselm of Canterbury, as well as by the Hellenic philosophers. It will therefore be proper to state the reflective problem of the syllogistic construction in its principal points.

The "ontological proof" rejected by Thomas did not in his time yet exist in this symbolic form. The word *ontologia* appears in the seventeenth century in Clauberg's *Elementa philosophiae sive Ontosophiae* (1647) (or perhaps in Goclenius' *Lexicon Philosophicum*, 1613) and finds acceptance among philosophers through its use in the eighteenth century by Leibniz, Wolff and Kant. The *Meditations* of Descartes are not yet encumbered by the term and that is perhaps the reason why they still could be close to the earlier quest of Anselm (which Descartes might not have known) because they rely for the dynamics of the questing movement on the tension of perfection-imperfection. In the *Critique of Pure Reason* Kant applies the symbol "ontological proof" to the Cartesian *Meditations* as a term already in general use.

The data just given point to an area of discourse that moves rather on the fringe of exact experiential analysis; they suggest the attempt to establish "ontology" as a more precise synonym for "metaphysics" and thereby to establish metaphysics as the polemical alternative to theology. The term "metaphysics" itself was introduced by Thomas into Western philosophy in his commentary on the Aristotelian *Metaphysics* on the basis of the development of the term by the Arabic philosophers. We are touching the problem of the reflective deformation of experiential reality through reflective symbolisms conditioned by concrete historical situations.

That is not to say that there is not a real experiential problem at the basis of the deformation, nor that this problem was not seen and formulated by Thomas himself. The distinction of the "priora simpliciter" of faith from the "posteriora" of its reality gained from its effects makes it possible to deny the priora which do not permit its properties to be known as if they were the properties of a thing. And since the thingly properties are not known except through their effects, the priora of faith can be denied as to their reality. The experiential basis of this consequence is presented by Thomas in the scriptural symbolism "Dixit insipiens in corde suo: Non est Deus." The deformative confusion in the "heart" of the insipiens (in the English translation: of the fool) is the experiential source which brings the problem of the non-thingly structure of divine symbols to attention. It is the *cor suum* in man which is the experiential place of a hypostatising position or negation of divinity.

* * *

Hegel's analysis, in spite of the deformative reflective construction, comes close to the understanding of the noetic process as it had been experienced by Anselm of Canterbury at the beginning of scholasticism. In the *Proslogion*, Anselm's analysis is explicit about the limits of the noetic quest. In the second part of his work, in *Proslogion* XIV, he acknowledges that the God found by the truth of reason is not yet the God whom the seeker has experienced as present in the formation and re-formation of his existence. He prays to God: "Speak to my desirous soul what you are, other than what it has seen, that it may clearly see what it desires." And in *Proslogion* XV he formulates the structural issue with classic exactness: "O Lord, you are not only that than which a greater cannot be conceived, but you are also greater than what can be conceived." This is the limit of the noetic conceptual analysis disregarded by Hegel. One should note that in the section on Anselm of Canterbury in his *Geschichte der Philosophie*, Hegel deals extensively and competently with the "ontological proof", but does not mention the second part of the *Proslogion* with its analogical exploration of the divine light beyond human reason. The noetic quest of Anselm thus assumes the form of a Prayer for an understanding of the symbols of faith through the human intellect. Behind the quest, and behind the *fides* the quest is supposed to understand, there now becomes visible the true source of the Anselmian effort in the living desire of the soul to move toward the divine light. The divine reality lets the light of its perfection fall into the soul; the illumination of the soul arouses the awareness of man's existence as a state of imperfection; and this awareness provokes the human movement in response to the divine appeal. The illumination, as St. Augustine names this experience, has for Anselm indeed the character of an appeal, and even of a counsel and promise. For in order to express the experience of illumination he quotes John 6:24: "Ask, and you will receive, that your joy may be full." The Johannine words of the Christ, and of the Spirit that counsels in his name, words meant to be understood in their context, express the divine movement to which Anselm responds with the joyful counter-movement of his quest (XXVI). Hence, the latter part of the *Proslogion* consistently praises the divine light in the analogical language of perfection. Anselm's Prayer is a *meditatio de ratione fidei* as he formulates the nature of the quest in the first title of the *Monologion*. The praying quest responds to the appeal of reason in the *fides*; the *Proslogion* is the *fides* in action, in pursuit of its own reason. St. Anselm, we must therefore conclude, clearly understood the cognitive structure as internal to the Metaxy, the in-between of the soul in the Platonic sense.

The meaning of the Metaxy in this context can perhaps be most clearly understood in the Myth of the *Phaedrus*. In this Myth Plato ranks the Olympian gods together with their human followers as the beings within the cosmos who are endowed with souls and therefore are concerned with their immortality. The Olympians, who already enjoy the status of immortals, have only to preserve it by appropriate action; while the human souls who desire immortality have yet to rise to it by an effort that is, in various degrees, handicapped by their mortal bodies whose passions drag them down. Neither the preserving actions of the gods, however, nor the desirous efforts of their human attendants can achieve their goal through processes within the cosmos. For the source of immortality is the extra-cosmic divine reality beyond the heaven (*exo tou ouranou*) that surrounds the cosmos, and the intra-cosmic beings who have souls must rise to this source by means of the noetic "wings" that enable them to ascend to the truth of the Beyond. This ascent of the souls is not everyday business. Ordinarily, so Plato lets the Myth tell us, the gods and their followers will attend to their intra-cosmic affairs, and only on festive occasions will they rise to the superheavenly region (*hyperouranios topos*). And there, from the roof of the cosmos, they will contemplate the *ousia ontos ousa* that is visible only to the *nous*, the guide of the soul.

*   *   *

But in what sense can Anselm at all connect the term "proof" with a noetic quest in response to the movement of the Spirit, a quest which he correctly recognizes as a Prayer? The key to the answer is given in the fact that the term does not occur in the *Proslogion* itself but only in the discussion with Gaunilo. There is no reason why the term should be used in the *Proslogion*; for when a believer explores the rational structure of his faith the existence of God is not in question. In his answer, however, Anselm must use the term "proof" because Gaunilo acts the rôle of the fool, of the insipiens, who says "there is no God" and assumes that the explorer of faith is engaged in a "proof" for the assertion that God exists. The noetic reflection of the spiritualist acquires the character of an affirmative proposition concerning the existence of God only when confronted by the *insipiens* who advances the negative proposition that God does not exist. The symbolism of the noetic quest threatens to derail into a quarrel about proof or non-proof of a proposition when the fool enters the discussion. The existence of God can become doubtful because, without a doubt, the fool exists.

The fool cannot be dismissed lightly. The folly of responding to the divine appeal by denial or evasion is just as much a human possibility as the positive response. As a potentiality it is present in every man, including the believer; and in certain historical situations its actualization can become a massive social force. But who, or what, is a fool?

The philological situation is clear. When Anselm and Gaunilo speak of the *insipiens*, their language draws on Psalm 13 (14) in the translation of the Vulgate: "The fool (*insipiens*) says in his heart 'There is no God'." The *nabal* of the Hebrew text is translated by the Vulgate as *insipiens* and further translated, by both the Standard Version and the Jerusalem Bible, as *fool*. This last translation is perhaps not the best, for the English word *fool* derives from the Latin *follis*, meaning a bellows or wind-bag, and has retained from its origin an aura of wind-baggery, silliness, lack or weakness of judgment, that will neither suggest the fundamental corruption of existence, nor the spectrum of corruptive symptoms, intended by *nabal*. The fool of the Psalm is certainly not a man wanting in intellectual acumen or worldly judgment. Such alternative translations as the impious, the profane, the reckless, or the worthless man, which all have been tried and all have their merits, show the difficulty of rendering the richness of meaning peculiar to a symbol as compact as *nabal*. However, since a more satisfactory translation and one better fitting into contemporary usage seems to me impossible, I shall retain the established "fool" and only take care to make its meaning clear.

In Psalm 13 (14), the *nabal* signifies the mass phenomenon of men who do evil rather than good because they do not "seek after God" and his justice, who "eat my people as they eat bread" because they do not believe in divine sanction for acts of unrighteousness. The personal contempt of God will manifest itself in ruthless conduct toward the weaker man and create general disorder in society. The situation envisaged by the Psalm seems to be the same as the contempt of God and his prophets characterized by Jeremiah 5:12ff and, as early as the eighth century B.C., by Isaiah 32. In these Israelite contexts, the contempt, the *nebala*, does not necessarily denote so differentiated a phenomenon as dogmatic atheism, but rather a state of spiritual dullness that will permit the indulgence of greed, sex, and power without fear of divine judgment. The contemptuous folly, it is true, can rise to the radical "There is no God", but the phrase does not appear to have been experienced as a noetic challenge. The fool stands against the revealed God, he does not stand against a *fides quaerens intellectum*. This further component, characteristic of the Anselm-Gaunilo debate, must be sought rather in the philosophers' tradition that has entered Christian theology. It is Plato who describes the phenomenon of existential foolishness, as well as the challenge it presents to the noetic quest, for the case of Sophistic folly, the *anoia*, in *Republic* II and *Laws* X.

In Greek society, the potentiality of responding to the divine appeal by rejecting it has expressed itself in a series of negative propositions which circumspectly cover the whole range of the experience. In both the *Republic* (365b–e) and the *Laws,* Plato presents these propositions as triadic set:

(1) It seems that no gods exist;
(2) Even if they do exist, they do not care about men;
(3) Even if they care, they can be propitiated by gifts.

Though Plato does not give a specific source for the set but refers to it only as being in general use in his intellectual environment, it probably is a Sophistic school product, for it has the same structure as the set of propositions preserved in Gorgias' essay *On Being*:

(1) Nothing exists;
(2) If anything exists, it is incomprehensible;
(3) If it is comprehensible, it is incommunicable.

The sets suggest that, in the Sophistic schools, the contempt of the gods had grown into a general loss of experiential contact with cosmic-divine reality. The triadic patterns of negative propositions appear to have developed as an expression for the resultant contraction of man's existence. The mass acceptance of this pattern aroused Plato so strongly as a challenge to his noetic quest of the divine ground that he devoted the whole Book X of the *Laws* to its refutation. The details of the refutation, resulting in the positive propositions that the gods exist, that they do care about man, and that they cannot be made accomplices in human criminality by offering them bribes from the profits of crime, are not our present concern. But we must consider his analysis of the noetic challenge and the language developed for its articulation.

The sophistic argument for the negative triads apparently rested on a radical denial of divine reality experienced as present in either the order of the cosmos or the soul of man. In order to be plausible in the Hellenic culture of the fourth century B.C., the denial had to be couched in the form of a counter-myth to the symbolization of divine order in reality by the cosmogonic myth of the Hesiodian type. The form actually assumed by the argument apparently was a cosmogony in which the gods of the myth are replaced by the elements in the material sense as the "oldest" creative reality. At any rate, Plato considers the negative triads invalidated on principle, if he can refute the assumption that all reality originates in the movement of material elements. Against this assumption he argues: there is no self-moving matter; all material movements are caused by movements of other matter; the patterned network of cause and effect must be caused in its turn by a movement that originates outside the network; and the only reality we know to be self-moving is the Psyche. Hence, in a genetic construction of Being, the elements cannot function as the "oldest" reality; only the divine Psyche, as experienced by the human psyche, can be "oldest" in the sense of the self-movement in which all ordered movement in the world originates. The argument sounds quite modern in its recourse to the reality of the psyche, and of its experiences, against constructions which express the loss of reality and the contraction of the self—though the modern constructors do not have to deform a Hesiodian myth for their purpose but must replace the divine ground of Being by an item from the world-immanent hierarchy of being as the ultimate "ground" of all reality. But the argument is neither modern nor ancient; it rather is the argument that will recur whenever the quest of divine reality has to be resumed in a situation in which the "rationalization" of contracted existence, the existence of the fool, has become a mass phenomenon. The argument, of course, is not a "proof" in the sense of a logical demonstration, of an *apodeixis*, but only in the sense of an *epideixis*, of a pointing to an area of reality which the constructor of the negative propositions has chosen to overlook, or to ignore, or refuse to perceive. One cannot prove reality by a syllogism; one can only point to it and invite the doubter to look. The more or less deliberate confusion of the two meanings of the word "proof" is still a standard trick employed by the negators in the contemporary ideological debates; and it has played an important rôle in the genesis of the "proofs" for the existence of God ever since the time of Anselm.

That the negative propositions are not a philosopher's statement concerning a structure in reality, but express a deformation of the "heart", is the insight gained by Plato. The Sophistic folly, the *anoia*, is not merely an analytical error, it is a *nosos*, a disease of the psyche, requiring the psychological therapy which in the *Laws* he grants to the extent of five years. In *Republic* II, he further develops the language that will describe the existential disease inasmuch as he distinguishes between the falsehood in words and the falsehood, or lie (*pseudos*), in the soul itself. The "ignorance within the soul" (*en te psyche agnoia*) is "truly the falsehood" (*alethos pseudos*), while the falsehood in words is only "the after-rising image" (*hysteron gegonon eidolon*). The false words, therefore, are not an "unmixed falsehood" as is the "essential falsehood" (*to men de to onti pseudos*) in the soul. The verbal falsehood, the "rationalization", we may say, is the form of truth in which the diseased soul expresses itself (*Republic* 382). As the distinctions show, Plato is struggling to find the analytical language that will fit the case under observation, but he has by far not completed the task of developing the concepts of a "pneumopathology," as Schelling has called this discipline. He does not yet have, for instance, a concept like the *agnoia ptoiodes*, the "scary ignorance" of Chrysippus that has become the "anxiety" of the moderns; nor does he have the Chrysippian *apostrophe*, denoting the inversion of the movement, the *epistrophe*, that leads the prisoner in the Cave up to the light; nor Cicero's characterization of the disease of the mind, of the *morbus animi*, as an *aspernatio rationis*, a rejection of reason. Still, he has seen the crucial point that the negative propositions are the syndrome of a disease that affects man's humanity and destroys the order of society.

In the analysis of the disease and its syndrome, Plato created a neologism of world-historic consequences: when dealing with the propositional sets he used, for the first time in the history of philosophy as far as we know, the term "theology". In the *Republic*, Plato speaks of the negative propositions as *typoi peri theologias*, as types of theology (379a), and opposes to them the positive counter-propositions as true types. Both types, the negative as well as the positive, are theologies, because they both express a human response to the divine appeal; they both are, in Plato's language, the verbal mimesis respectively of man's existence in truth or falsehood. Not the existence of God is at stake, but the true order of existence in man; not the propositions stand against each other but the response and the non-response to the divine-appeal: the propositions, positive or negative, have no autonomous truth. The truth of the positive propositions is neither self-evident, nor a matter of logical proof; they would be just as empty as the negative ones, if they were not backed by the reality of the divine-human movement and counter-movement, of the Prayer answering the appeal in the soul of the proponent; and Plato provides this truth by his magnificent analysis and symbolization of the experiences. Hence the verbal mimesis of the positive type, as it has no truth of its own, can be no more than a first line of defense or persuasion in a social confrontation with the verbal mimesis of the negative type. Even more, the positive propositions derive an essential part of their meaning from their character as a defense against the negative propositions. As a consequence, the two types of theology together represent the verbal mimesis of the human tension between the potentialities of response or non-response to divine presence in personal, social, and historical existence. If the fool's part in the positive propositions is forgotten, there is always the danger of derailing into the foolishness of believing the truth of these propositions to be ultimate. But the assumption of ultimacy would make them indeed as empty of the experiential truth in the background as the fools pretend them to be.

* * *

The experiential truth in the background of Plato's analysis is not a matter of simple statements. It would have to include Plato's own analytical achievements in his struggle for clarifying problems initiated by predecessors as well as the meanings that have remained compact in Plato's work. An adequate presentation of the issues would require therefore more than one volume on Hellenic philosophy, literature and art extending from Homer and Hesiod to Neoplatonism. In the present context I can do no more than point to a few of the important phases in the process of differentiating experiences and symbolizations.

A central issue is the differentiating transition from the polytheistic language of the gods to the language of the one divinity beyond the gods. The experiential tension in Plato's cultural situation is suggested by changes in the Invocations of the gods preceding an analysis of structure in reality. In the *Timaeus*, for instance, Socrates invites Timaeus to be the next speaker to engage in an imaginative creation of the likely language that will symbolize the structure and to open his speech with an Invocation of the gods. That the imaginative analysis is to be a Prayer is presupposed. In his answer Timaeus agrees that everybody who has any sense will call upon "God" before an undertaking, small or great. A likely discourse concerning the All (*to pan*) will have to invoke the gods and goddesses (unless we are utterly demented): Pray that all we say may in the first place be approved by them and secondly by ourselves. Let us take it for granted therefore that we have duly invoked the divinities and let us invoke ourselves so as to expound most clearly our views concerning the All. (27c) The Invocation has become restricted in its language and does not name the "God" invoked. The symbolic elaboration invoking the one "God" is reduced to a mental invocation implied in the act of beginning. The "gods" have not disappeared and are not quite replaced by the one "God".

In order to sense the cultural tension in this mental Invocation of "God" without naming him, one should be aware of the decline in the *fides* in the many gods as it appears, for instance, in the parodistic Invocation in Aristophanes' *Thesmophoriazusae* with their feminist touch: Pray to the gods, to the Olympians and Olympianesses, to the Pythians and Pythianesses, to all the Delians and Delianesses. (330–333) The Platonic one "God" is the divinity experienced as present beyond the many gods who, as the Invocation of Aristophanes shows, are experientially dying. The noetic analysis creates a newly differentiated form of Prayer beyond the earlier Invocations of muses and the gods. What is differentiating in the noetic experience is the Oneness of divinity beyond the plurality of the gods.

This differentiation of the Oneness of divinity, then, requires a change in the language of reality from the being-things in the plural to the singular of the one "Being." In the earlier language of Hesiod the reality of things is still expressed by the plural *ta eonta*, the gods being compactly things covered by the same term as the things of the external world. In the language of Parmenides this experiential revelation of Oneness is marked by the transition from the plural *ta eonta* to the singular *to eon*. By this change of language the "being-things" begin to be differentiated from a "Being" that comprehends all things. In the work of Parmenides the transition is so radical that the "being-things" lose something of their status as real in relation to the overshadowing "Being" in the singular. The revelatory pressure of the Being beyond the being-things was apparently experienced so intensely that the structure of a cosmic whole of reality in the tension of Being and things could only be insufficiently symbolized in language. Hence, in the *Timaeus* Plato had to go beyond *to eon* by coining the symbol *to pan* in the sense of a one All that comprehends (*periechein*) the being-things. The *to pan*, the intelligible order of the universe, is now symbolized as the cosmos in tension between the order (*taxis*) imposed by a Demiurge and the disorder (*ataxia*) of a spatio-temporal *chora* on which it is imposed. Reality becomes an ordered Oneness accessible to mathematical analysis.

The symbolization of this experience, however, does not result for Plato in a System. The structure of divinity experienced remains mysterious. There is a Demiurge who orders a disorderly reality but he orders it according to a paradigm of order which itself is a god; moreover, the cosmos organized according to the paradigm, in its turn, is the unique or one-born (*monogenes*) divine copy of the paradigm. The order of the paradigm is the ultimate reality comprehending all being-things in the one cosmos. In Plato's experience this one-ness of the All was of such revelatory importance that he coined for it the term *monosis* (3lb), a term that disappeared in later philosophical language. The symbol "order" acquires the differentiated meaning of oneness excluding a plurality of universes, leaving open the mystery of disorder in the order of the All.

An important component in Plato's struggle for a language of the one God beyond the gods—all too frequently neglected—are the experiences of divinity unfolding in the Invocations of Hesiod's *Theogony*. For Hesiod, the source of the truth about reality, to be sure, are divine figures, the Muses. But the Muses are not the Olympian gods; they are generated by Zeus, far from the Olympians, in his union with Mnemosyne. The source of truth is trans-Olympian and the Zeus who generates the Muses is himself a god who has been born though he does not die. Moreover, what the Muses sing about the reality that includes the gods is sung primarily not to men but to the gods themselves, and especially to a Zeus who seems to be not quite conscious of his position and powers as the divine ordering force in reality. For Hesiod, Zeus is no god unless there is a divine reality Beyond the gods. In these Hesiodian symbolizations we recognize the first intimations of the comprehending (*periechon*) Beyond that ultimately becomes the *epekeina* of Plato.

* * *

(Ed. Note: If the reader has not referred to the Editor's Preface, s/he should do so before proceeding.)

[1. The All-enfolding "divine" of Anaximander and how it is be spoken of according to Aristotle in *Physics* 4, 203b7:]

> *Of the* apeiron *there is no beginning* (arche) *. . . but this seems to be the beginning of all the other things and to enfold* (periechein) *all things and steer all, as all those say who do not postulate other causes, such as mind or love, above and beyond the* apeiron. *And this is the divine* (to theion); *for it is immortal*

(athanaton) and indestructible (anolethron), as Anaximander says. . . (Translation from Kirk, Raven & Schofield, The Presocratic Philosophers, 2nd ed., 1983, p. 115.)

[2. The Prayer in Plotinus V, 1, 6 invoking God before attempting the search for the proper language in which to speak of the One and of the mystery of its emanation, which can only be spoken of in dream-like metaphors such as the perfume metaphor Plotinus chooses ("perfumed things"):]

> Let us speak of it in this way, first invoking God himself, not in spoken words, but stretching ourselves out with our soul into prayer to him, able in this way to pray alone to him alone. (Translated by H. A. Armstrong, Plotinus, Vol. V, Loeb's Classics, 1984.)

[3. The Prayer in Plato's *Timaeus*, this time invoking the *"theos soter"* (48d) as Plato begins the attempt to find the proper language for speaking about the non-thing-like pole in the tension between the forming divine and the receptive but resistant unformed *chora* (Space):]

> And, as before, so now, at the commencement of our account we must call upon God the Savior to bring us safe through a novel and unwonted exposition to a conclusion based on likelihood, and thus begin our account once more. (Translated by R. G. Bury, Plato, Vol. IX, Loeb's Classics, 1929, pp. 111 and 113.)

[Again the language must become dreamlike and metaphorical. (Timaeus 48e-53c, esp.51b-c).]

[4. The "mental Prayer" (*das mentale Gebet*) of Goethe:]

> Das mentale Gebet, das alle Religionen einschliesst und ausschliesst und nur bei wenigen, gottbegünstigten Menschen den ganzen Lebenswandel durchdringt, entwickelt sich bei den meisten nur als flammendes, beseligendes Gefühl des Augenblicks; nach dessen Verschwinden sogleich der sich selbst zurückgegebene unbefriedigte, unbeschäftigte Mensch in die unendlichste Langeweile zurückfallt.
> The Mental Prayer which encompasses and excludes all religions and which only in a few god-favored men permeates their whole way of life, develops in most men only as a flaming, enrapturing feeling of the moment; once this has vanished, man, returned to himself, unsatisfied, unoccupied, at once falls back into the most interminable boredom. (Goethe, West-Östlicher Divan, Noten und Abhandlungen, "Ältere Perser," Leipzig, Insel-Verlag 1912, p. 142.)

[5. The manifestation of the equivalent Christian experience and expression of the "divine":

(a) The *pleroma* and *theotes* in Colossians 2:9:]

> For in him the whole fulness (pleroma) of divine reality (theotes) dwells bodily.

[(b) The "Tetragrammatic" name of the "divine" in Thomas, *Summa Theologiae* I.13.11.1:]

> *Dicendum quod hoc nomen* Qui est est *magis proprium nomen Dei quam hoc nomen* Deus, *quantum ad id a quo imponitur, scilicet ab esse, et quantum ad modum significandi et consignificandi, ut dictum est. Sed quantum ad id ad quod significandum, imponitur nomen est magis proprium hoc nomen* Deus, *quod imponitur ad significandum naturam divinam. Et adhuc magis proprium nomen est* Tetragrammaton, *quod est impositum ad significandam ipsam Dei substantiam incommunicabilem, et, ut sic liceat loqui, singularem.*
>
> "He who is" is more appropriate than "God" because of what makes us use the name in the first place, i.e. his existence, because of the unrestricted way in which it signifies him, and because of its tense, as we have just said. But when we consider what the word is used to mean, we must admit that "God" is more appropriate, for this is used to signify the divine nature. Even more appropriate is the Tetragrammaton, which is used to signify the incommunicable and, if we could say such a thing, individual substance of God.

(Translated by Herbert McCabe, O. P., Thomas Aquinas, *Summa Theologiae*, Vol. I, "The Existence of God," Part I: Questions 1–13, Image Books, 1969, p. 226.)

THE EXPANDING WORLD OF METAPHOR
NORTHROP FRYE*

Let us start with literature, and with the fact that literature is an art of words. That means, in the first place, a difference of emphasis between the art and the words. If we choose the emphasis on words, we soon begin to relate the verbal structures we call literary to other verbal structures. We find that there are no clearly marked boundaries, only centres of interest. There are many writers, ranging from Plato to Sartre, whom it is difficult, or more accurately unnecessary, to classify as literary or philosophical. Gradually more and more boundaries dissolve, including the boundary between creators and critics, as every criticism is also a recreation. Sooner or later, in pursuing this direction of study, literary criticism, philosophy, and most of the social sciences come to converge on the study of language itself. The characteristics of language are clearly the essential clue to the nature of everything built out of language.

The developments in linguistics and semiotics in the last quarter-century have shown us how language both expresses and structures our consciousness in time and space. I speak of these developments only in passing, because there are many scholars who can speak about them with more authority than I can. In this area of study a word is primarily a signifier, related arbitrarily, or more precisely by convention, to what it signifies. What makes a word a word is its difference from other words, and what gives words a public meaning for a community is the disentangling of them from the associations of those who use them, including the author. Jacques Derrida in particular has emphasized that this attitude to language is one in which writing or printing is logically prior to the spoken word. In oral discourse the words are still, in a manner of speaking, unborn, still attached to an enclosing presence or speaking personality.

We can also, however, turn to the other emphasis on the *art* of

*University Professor at the University of Toronto (Massey College), Dr. Frye presented this lecture to a Plenary Session of the 75th Anniversary meeting of the American Academy of Religion in Chicago, December 8, 1984.

words, where we begin with a practical common-sense distinction in which, say, Keats and Shelley are poets and not philosophers, and Kant and Hegel philosophers and not poets. Again there are no definable boundaries, and no one asserts that there are, but we do have, in practice, a distinctive area in which literature has the same kind of integrity that music has when distinguished from songs of birds or noises in the street. The painter René Magritte painted a highly representational picture of a pipe and gave it the title "This is not a Pipe", and one can see very well what he means. The centre of the art of words is poetry, and from here on I shall be speaking of poetry.

In poetry, accidental resemblances among words create sound-patterns of rhyme, alliteration, assonance and metre, and these have a function in poetry that they rarely have outside it. The function of these sound-patterns is to minimize the sense of arbitrariness in the relation of word and meaning, to suggest a quasi-magical connection between the verbal arrangement and the things it evokes. Puns and different or ambiguous associations bound up in a single word seem to be structural principles rather than obstacles to meaning. Above all, in poetry we are in the area of figurative language, where the status of the word as a word is called to our attention, and the relation of that word to its context has to be given special treatment. Of course we use figurative language everywhere, but in poetry what seems to be dominant in importance is not so much the relation of signifiers to signifieds as the *resonance* among the signifiers.

The poet may be very remote in time, place, language and cultural context from his reader. Hence there are two directions in the study of poetry. One is an attempt to determine, so far as is humanly possible, what a poem meant in its own original context; the other tries to see what the qualities in it are that make it still communicable to us. The critical reader of a poem is one of a large number of people who have read it, hence he cannot dream of any definitive criticism of it, for the simple reason that he is not all those other people. He is a spokesman for a community of readers, and fails if he replaces the poem with himself. But his reading is only his, and it may range in motivation from devoted discipleship to a kind of ritual murder of his poet. We might say that the reader invents his text, the word "invention" having its double meaning of something subjective that we make up ourselves and something objective that we find outside us. An invention comes out of an inventors's mind, but an invention that works must have some roots in the external world. It is normally best to begin reading our poem in a mood of Leibnitzian optimism that the words chosen for that poem are the best of all possible words.

So far, there is not much difference between the role of the reader of poetry and that of any other reader. But the poem (one might have to modify the statement in regard to prose fiction) seems to be radically an *oral* production, an utterance. This utterance is not a direct address to the reader; it is broadcast, like a radio program, and is separate from both reader and poet. Poets have always said that they did not feel that they were making their poems; they felt more like mothers bringing an independent life to birth. The written poem comes into being partly because of this independence. If there is anything to be said for Marshall McLuhan's axiom that the content of any given medium is the form of a previous medium, then the content of written poetry is the form of oral poetry, which seems invariably to precede it historically. The subordinate and secondary status assigned to writing, of which so many post-structural critics complain, is derived from a literary convention, but within literature the convention is rooted in the facts of literary experience.

The source of the convention is the fact that the poem, like a musical score, but unlike other types of verbal structure, is being referred back to an actual performance. If we want to know what a poem "really means", we have to read the poem itself aloud. The poet may be replaced by a reciter, as Homer is by Ion in Plato, or the oral reader may not be present at all, except as a minor element in a silent reader's response. But, except in poetry where literature is encroaching on the visual arts (as in concrete poetry, shape poems, and typographical designs like those of E. E. Cummings), there is always a priority of utterance to writing. This convention is closely related to another convention within poetry itself that the spoken words are actually being sung or played as a musical composition. Thus Milton says halfway through *Lycidas*, "But now my oat proceeds", "oat" meaning a reed, or a kind of rustic oboe, and at the end "Thus sang the uncouth swain to th' oaks and rills". The impossibility of singing and playing a wind instrument at the same time does not bother Milton. The written text of a poem is a kind of charm or spell: a spell that, so to speak, knows and repeats the *names* of the poem, and has the power to summon an absent present into reappearance.

II

Of all figures or rhetorical devices that emphasize the relation of signifiers to one another, the simplest and most direct is the metaphor, the figure that tells us that one signifier *is* another signifier, even if each term keeps its own conventional relation to a signified. That is, the metaphor is usually presented in some variant of the grammatical model "A is B". Stock examples of such metaphors may be found in Jacob's prophecy (Genesis 49) concerning the tribes of Israel: "Joseph is a fruitful bough", "Naphtali is a hind let loose", "Issachar is a strong ass", and the like.

Such metaphors are curiously self-contradictory. First, they assert, or appear to assert, that A is B. But they also imply that A is quite obviously not B, and nobody could be fool enough to imagine that it was. The metaphor is totally illogical, for logic preserves the common-sense principle that A is always A, never B, and the only metaphors that make logical sense are tautologies with one term, such as "Elizabeth II is Queen of England". Accepting the assertion "A is B" as a statement of fact we call "taking a metaphor literally". I have often enough attacked this addled use of the word "literal", but as soon as we raise the question of "literal meaning", as that phrase is generally used, each term is related to a separate signified meaning and the metaphorical link between them vanishes. So our first problem is, what is the point of saying that A is B when anyone can see that A is not B?

Let us first try to put the question into some form of historical perspective. We notice that a typical metaphor, such as "Joseph is a fruitful bough", identifies some aspect of human personality or consciousness ("Joseph") with some aspect of the natural environment ("fruitful bough"). If we were to think of a permanent relationship of this sort which we might in some contexts have to "take seriously", we should come to the conception of a god, or, at least, a nature-spirit. The god is an early form of socially postulated metaphor, but the god has many mutations and derivations, such as the totemic animal in totemic societies. The Bible does not accept gods or nature-spirits, but still "Joseph is a fruitful bough" is a development of the same mode of thinking that elsewhere identifies Neptune with the sea or Baal with the fertility of the land.

Metaphor, then, arises in a state of society in which a split between a perceiving subject and a perceived object is not yet habitual, and what it does in that context is to open up a channel or current of energy between human and natural worlds. The gods are not simply projections of the human mind on nature: they are evocations of powers of nature as well. The starting-point of metaphor, then, seems to be what I propose to call, taking a term from Heidegger, ecstatic metaphor, the sense of identity of an individual's consciousness with something in the natural world. I say an individual, but of course a social or group consciousness is what is almost always primarily involved. If we look at the cave-drawings of animals in Altamira or Lascaux, and think of the fantastically difficult conditions of lighting and positioning in which they were done, we can get some sense of the titanic will to identify that they represent. We can distinguish certain aspects that seem more reasonable to us, such as the magical wish to evoke by art a supply of animal food, but the will to identify is what is in the centre. Similarly, the chief "primitive" use of music seems to have been ecstatic, designed to merge the consciousness with another kind of being, like the Dionysus cult in Greece that has given us the word "enthusiasm", and the school of prophets in the Old Testament whom King Saul briefly joined (I Samuel 10:5–6).

Such forms of ecstatic identification survive in modern religion, and have left many traces in literature. In drama, for example, we require the actor to be ecstatically identified with his role. But gods suggest a more stabilized social relationship of a sort that produces cults, statues, temples, myths, prayers and sacrifices. Any such metaphor as "Neptune is the sea" is the base line of a triangle with its apex pointing to the group of worshippers who acknowledge the identity. The sense of a subjective consciousness separated from the physical world seems to become continuous around the time of the earliest civilizations, although some would put it much later. In proportion as it does so, the ecstatic response becomes individualized: the social conditioning is of course still there, but its workings in the individual mind become harder to trace. Along with this goes the specifically "literary" response to metaphor: the sense of it as assumed, as putting something in a way that does not assert or deny anything about the "real" world. Poetry thus becomes a form of play, to use Francis Bacon's term, or, as we should now say, there is an ironic distancing between literature and experience. I am not sure that the modern phrase is an improvement on Bacon.

Literature thus becomes detached from the kind of commitment that we call "belief". In the poetry of the Christian centuries Jupiter and Venus are readily absorbed, the more readily because they are not believed in. Of all works of Classical literature, the one that had the most pervasive influence over the next thousand years was probably Ovid's *Metamorphoses*. The metamorphosis, in Ovid, is typically a story of the disintegrating of metaphor, the breaking down of some conscious personality into a natural object, as when Daphne becomes a laurel tree or Philomela a nightingale. When Jupiter assumes the form of a bull or a swan for one of his amours, the original story may have actually identified the god and the animal; but in the age of poetry he is merely putting on a disguise to fool Juno, usually without success.

A literary age tends to think of ecstatic forms of identification as primitive and something to be outgrown, as modes of behavior that would seem hysterical in our society. Such terms as Lévy-Bruhl's *participation mystique* suggest an attitude of keeping them at arm's length. We are afraid of losing our sense of the distinction between fiction and fact, like Don Quixote at the puppet show, and the tendency of younger readers to identify with (or, in the fashionable euphemism, relate to) some figure in a book or movie or rock band they admire we think of as immature. Yet it seems clear that one of the social functions of literature is to keep alive the metaphorical way of thinking and of using words. So our next problem is, why should it be kept alive?

I have often reverted to the lines from *A Midsummer Night's Dream* in which Duke Theseus summarizes the three types of people who, from his point of view, take metaphor, as we say, literally or seriously:

> The lunatic, the lover and the poet
> Are of imagination all compact.

We see that the word "imagination" already contains the twofold emphasis it still has in the contrast between "imaginary" and "imaginative". Theseus' emphasis is on the whole on the pathological side: lunatics, lovers and poets for him are people disturbed emotionally who see things which are not there. He goes on to say that lunatics see more devils than hell can hold, and that the poet's eye moves from heaven to earth and from earth to heaven, suggesting that the poet is essentially a lunatic on a good trip. The inclusion of the lover is particularly interesting, because sexual love is a throwback to ecstatic metaphor. The sexual drive is symbolically toward a union of two people in one, or, as Sir Thomas Browne says, "United souls are not satisfied with embraces, but desire to be truly each other". He goes on to say, however, "which being impossible, their desires are infinite, and must proceed without a possibility of satisfaction". It seems to Browne, as perhaps to most of us, safer to stay with embraces.

The association of lover and poet is what enables John Donne to write such poems as "The Extasie"and "The Canonization", which begin with a celebration of sexual union and end with images of books and sonnets. It also accounts for the hundreds, if not thousands, of poems bewailing the cruelty and indifference of a poet's mistress. Few poets in medieval or Renaissance times would set up as poets without declaring themselves head over heels in love: a poet not a lover is conventionally a rather poor creature. The same convention assumes that poetry is the normal result of frustration in love: Eros is the presiding genius of the awakening of the imagination, and poetry is written as what biologists now call a displaced activity, the baffling of love by a lady's cruelty. But Eros is still the driving force of the poetry, and Eros does not care how casual or inappropriate any given metaphor may be: he only wants to get as many images copulating as possible.

Behind the lover, the practical and rather commonplace mind of Theseus sees nothing but lunatics. But even in this paper we have already seen that many of the most intense forms of human experience take some form of ecstatic metaphor. The hypothetical nature of literature, its ironic separation from all statements of assertion, was as far as I got in my *Anatomy of Criticism*, published nearly thirty years ago. The literary imagination seemed to me then, as in large part it does now, to be primarily a kind of model-thinking, an infinite set of possibilities of experience to expand and intensify our actual experience. But the *Anatomy* had led me to the scripture or sacred book as the furthest boundary to be explored in the imaginative direction, and I then became increasingly fascinated with the Bible, as a book dominated by metaphor throughout, and yet quite obviously not content with an ironic removal from experience or assertion. Clearly one had to look at other aspects of the question, and reconsider the cultural context of metaphor, as something that not only once had but may still have its roots in ecstatic experience.

I had noticed, for example, that many of the central Christian doctrines (e.g., Christ is God and man) were grammatically expressible only in metaphor. At that time, however, existential questions of "commitment" and the like were still in the ascendant, and in that cultural frame of mind, committing one's beliefs and values to metaphor seemed like crossing a deep gorge on a rope bridge: we may put all our trust in its ability to get us across, but there will be moments when we wish we hadn't. At the same time I was not happy with the merely let's pretend or let's assume attitude to literature. Nobody wants to eliminate the element of play from literature, but most poets clearly felt that what they were doing was more complex.

The complexities begin when we realize that metaphor, as a bridge between consciousness and nature, is in fact a microcosm of language itself. It is precisely the function of language to overcome what Blake calls the "cloven fiction" of a subject contemplating an object. In the nineteenth century the German philosopher von Humboldt had arrived at the principle that language was a third order of reality, coming between subject and object. Saussure, the founder of modern linguistics, also spoke of a world of "signification" in between the signifier and the signified. Language from this point of view becomes a single gigantic metaphor, the uniting of consciousness with what it is conscious of. This union is Ovid's metamorphosis in reverse, the transfiguring of consciousness as it merges with articulated meaning. In a more specifically religious area this third order would become Martin Buber's world of "Thou", which comes between the consciousness that is merely an "I" and a nature that is merely an "it".

III

To turn now to a slightly different aspect of the subject. We started with the conception of the god as a socially stabilized metaphor. The metaphor "Neptune is the sea" becomes a social datum if we build a temple to Neptune or address prayers to him when starting a voyage. The next step in this social stabilizing of a god is the story or narrative (*mythos* in Greek, whence "myth" in English) that is associated with a god and gives him a specific character and activities. We find such myths in the Homeric Hymns in an unusually concentrated form. Such myths, or stories about gods, are a normal part of every society's verbal culture: in structure they hardly differ from folktales, but the social use made of them is different. Folktales may be told for amusement, and tend to lead a nomadic existence, wandering over a wide area through all barriers of language. But myths, though they also travel widely, form in addition a central body of stories that it is particularly important for a specific society to hear, because they set out what are regarded as the essential facts about its gods, its history, and its social structure. Hence myths, in contrast to folktales, have a higher proportion of stories about recognized deities in them, and they also unify into a mythology and form the core of a body of shared imaginative allusion and shared experience for a society. They add the dimension of history and tradition to a society's verbal culture.

The myth, like the metaphor, conveys two contradictory messages. One is "this happened". The other is: "this almost certainly did not happen, at least in precisely the way described". The latter aspect has given us the common but vulgar sense of myth as simply a false statement. In Western culture the Biblical myths formed an inner core of sacrosanct legend, where, in contrast to Classical or other non-Biblical stories, the assertion "this happened precisely as described" was maintained for centuries by brute force. Thus at the end of the seventeenth century Bishop Burnet's *Sacred Theory of the Earth* explains how the world was originally smooth and uniform, without mountains or sea, until human sin provoked the Deity into causing the deluge, after which Nature appeared in its present preposterous and asymmetrical shape. The Last Judgment by fire will start with volcanic explosions in which Great Britain will burn faster than most of the world, because it has so much coal. However, in expounding these matters his orthodoxy was suspected and he lost an official job under William III, an example of the way in which people of that time, especially if they were clergymen, were effectively disqualified from trying to think seriously about such subjects as ancient history or the earth sciences. But as, later, people became freer to speak of creation, deluge, and even gospel myths, the positive as well as the negative side of myth became clearer.

A myth is a story, a word now distinguished from history, and of course many stories are "just" stories, making no claim to be anything else. But consider what happens when a great poet treats a historical subject. In studying Shakespeare's plays on Henry IV and V, for example, we can see that Shakespeare used the historical sources available to him, but made some deliberate changes, such as giving Hotspur and Prince Hal the same age when they were in fact twenty years apart. So we say that the myth, the story, of Shakespeare's plays follows history except for some deviations which are permitted only to poets, and are called poetic license, poets being assumed to be too weak-minded to handle documents accurately.

But let us look again at, say, *Henry V*. We see the victorious king winning Agincourt and becoming king of France; we also see something of the ghastly misery of France, the greatness of personality which still remains in the abandoned Falstaff, the fact that Henry is being merely pulled upward on an automatic wheel of fortune, that he died almost at once and that sixty years of unbroken disaster in England resulted. This growing "alienation", as Brecht would call it, means that the myth or story of the play is not "following" history at all. It incorporates a good deal of historical material, but it twists the events around so that they *confront* the audience. The audience is compelled to respond to a dimension of time that is no longer purely sequential. That is why the changes that poets make in their sources are so often in the direction of providing a greater symmetry in the narrative.

Similarly, the crucifixion of Christ was a historical event, or at least there is no discernible reason for its not being one. It is presented mythically in the Gospels, and that implies a certain amount of arrangement and contrivance, such as the way in which the sensibilities of Roman authorities are clearly being soothed down. But to concern ourselves only with the negative aspect of myth, its departure from history, would be to miss the whole point. As a historical event, the crucifixion of Christ is merely one more manifestation of that continuous psychosis which is the substance of human history, the activity of what Cummings calls "this busy monster, manunkind". It is only as myth that *this* crucifixion has the power to confront us with the vision of our own moral bankruptcy.

Poets, on the whole, prefer to work within their own history. That history tells us that the central event in the past was a ten-year-siege of Troy by the Greeks, that Rome was founded as an aftermath of that siege, that Britain was settled as a later aftermath, and that out of the British settlement there arose the titanic figure of King Arthur, with whom no other British sovereign can compare for an instant in majesty and power. Tennyson closes his account of that king's passing with the sombre lines:

> The darkness of that battle in the West,
> Where all of high and holy dies away.

It would be difficult to write with this kind of resonance about an actual event, where the chaotic untidiness and continuous anticlimaxes in human behaviour would be bound to get in the poet's way.

The value and importance of getting actual history as accurate as possible is not, of course, in question here. But our ordinary experience in time has to struggle with three unrealities: a past which is no longer, a future which is not yet, a present which is never quite. The myth is presented to us now, a present moment where, as Eliot would say, the past and future are gathered. Similarly, in metaphors of the type "A is B", the "is" is not really a predicate at all. The real function of the "is" in "Joseph is a fruitful bough" is to annihilate the space between the "Joseph" who is there, on our left as it were, and the "bough" which is there, on our right, and place them in a world where everything is "here". And as it becomes increasingly clear that the words "infinite" and "eternal" do not, except in certain aspects of mathematics, simply mean space and time going on without stopping, but the reality of the "here" and "now" that are at the centre of experience, we come to understand why all language directly concerned with the larger dimensions of infinite and eternal must be mythical and metaphorical language.

IV

My next step begins with what may sound like a digression. Several best-selling books lately have been telling us how the most advanced societies of our time, that is to say our own, are moving from an industry-based to an information-based form of social organization. This thesis doubtless appeals strongly to a middle management who would rather issue memoranda than produce goods at competitive prices. But what is really curious about such books is the conception of information involved. Surely everyone knows that information is not a placid river of self-explanatory facts: it comes to us pre-packaged in ideological containers, and many of these containers have been constructed by professional liars. There is such a thing, of course, as a genuine information explosion, but in even the most benevolent forms of acquiring information, such as research in the arts and sciences, most of the work involved consists in extricating oneself from a web of misinformation, after which the researcher hands over to posterity what he has put together, with *its* quota of mistakes and prejudices. The issue here has a direct bearing on the social function of writing.

A mythology is not a proto-science: it does not, except incidentally, make statements about the natural environment. It is a structure of human concern, and is built out of human hopes and fears and rumors and anxieties. When a mythology is looked at spatially, as a unified construct of metaphors, it turns into a cosmology, and in that form it may include or imply pseudo-scientific fallacies. The cosmologies of Dante and Milton are full of what is now pseudo-science, but that does not affect their worth in the literary structures they inform, because, as Paul Valéry remarks, cosmology is an aspect of literature. It still often does not matter to a contemporary poet whether his cosmology is in accord with the science of his day or not. Twentieth-century poets continue to talk about four elements and phases of the moon and other such features long excluded from the scientist's universe. In fact, as Valéry also says, the word "universe" itself, with its suggestion that all the millions of galaxies out there turn around one point, is mainly a word to be consumed on the licensed premises of poetry.

There is primary concern and there is secondary concern, and correspondingly there is primary mythology and secondary mythology. Primary concern is based on the simplest and baldest platitudes it is possible to formulate: that life is better than death, freedom better than slavery, happiness better than misery. Secondary concern is what we call ideology, the desire of a particular social group, or a class or priesthood or bureaucracy or other special interest within that group, to preserve its ascendancy, increase its prestige, or proclaim its beliefs. Every work of literature, as something produced for its own time, is in part an ideological document. The relation of a poet to the ideology he expounds or reflects is the genuine form of the "anxiety of influence", and it affects all writers without exception. The psychological and Freudian aspect of it celebrated by Harold Bloom seems to me mainly a by-product of the law of copyright.

What we call classics are works of literature that show an ability to communicate with other ages over the widest barriers of time, space and language. This ability depends on the inclusion of some element of insight into the human situation that escapes from the limits of ideology. Thus Shakespeare's *Henry V*, just referred to, contains the kind of ideology that his audience would want, and shows a heroic English king victorious over a swarm of foreigners. It was still exploiting that ideology in the Laurence Olivier film version in the Second World War, where the invasion of France became an allegory for a second front against Nazi Germany. At the same time the immense variety of events and moods in the play, which show us the context of such a war in the total human situation, constitutes a vision of life in terms of its primary concern with the struggle against death.

All through human history secondary concerns have kept an ascendancy over primary ones. We prefer to live, but we go to war; we prefer to be free, but we may accept authority to the point of losing our freedom; we prefer happiness, but may allow our lives to self-destruct. The century that has produced atom bombs and a pollution which threatens to cut off the supply of breathable air and drinkable water is the first period in history we know of when humanity has been compelled to face the conclusion: primary concerns must become primary, or else. Surely this suggests that it is becoming a central task of criticism, in literature or outside it, to try to distinguish the disinterested vision from the interested ideology. As the critic has his own ideology to become aware of, this is very difficult to do, and it is very natural for him to regard his own ideology as the Aaron's rod turned serpent that will eventually devour all its rivals. But as it becomes clearer that all the ideologies presented by political, economic and religious bodies fall short of a genuine mythology of primary concern, it becomes more and more urgent for critics to increase the awareness of their own and of others' mythological conditioning, and thus take up some of their real social functions.

And what good would it do if they did? I wish I had a glad confident answer to this. Previous decades in this century assumed that revolutionary action, self-determination on the part of third-world colonies, and the like, could revitalize our social consciousness, but that has led to one disillusionment after another. Today it is hard to dodge the fact that any form of intensified ideology is pernicious if it leads to another excuse for war or for exploiting either other men or nature. In the late sixties a state of mind developed that we might characterize as a feeling that the old subject-object consciousness, in which the individual is merely one of a social aggregate, had to give way to a new and heightened form of consciousness. Hence many forms of ecstatic metaphor reappeared. Certain drugs seemed to bring about something close to a sense of identity with one's surroundings; teachers of yoga and Zen forms of concentration became immensely popular; folk singers and rock music festivals seemed to symbolize a new conception of comradeship. It was a period of neo-primitivism, of renewed identity through ecstatic music or contemplation of a visual focus. McLuhan suggested that the physiological impact of television and other electronic media would create a new sensibility, forming bodies of social awareness in which nations and states as we know them would wither away and be replaced by a revitalized tribal culture. In the seventies he became less sanguine about this, but something of his earlier view survives as a vague hope that some technological gimmick will automatically take charge of the human situation.

At the same time it seems clear that metaphorical and mythical habits of mind are much more taken for granted today than they were thirty years or so ago. There seems little interest in reviving gods or nature-spirits: in contemporary academic journals references to Nietzsche and Heidegger are all over the place, but nobody seems to want to buy Nietzsche's Antichrist Dionysus or Heidegger's murky and maudlin polytheism. The feeling is rather a new awareness of a common identity of human consciousness engaged with a total nature. This conception of a total human consciousness is central to all the more serious religions: in Christianity it takes the form of the vision of Christ as total man, as the Word or total intelligibility, and consequently as the key to all metaphor as well as all myth, the identity of existing things. But it extends so far beyond Christianity as to strain our best "ecumenical" efforts. The notion of an antithesis between the religious and the secular-humanistic does not work any more, if it ever did. Everyone knows that all religious social phenomena have a secular aspect to them, and the same principle holds in reverse. The specific entity pointed to by the word "religious" seems to me to be closely connected with the principle of ecstatic metaphor that I have been expounding. What a man's religion is may be gathered from what he wants to identity himself with, and except perhaps for those who are devoted one hundred percent to pursuing their own interests, all activities have a religious aspect as well as a secular one.

In reading contemporary criticism, I have been interested to notice how the religious origin of many critical questions still peeps out of odd corners: in the tendency to capitalize "Word", in the theological subtleties of distinctions among *verbe, parole, langue* and *langage,* in the pervasive uncertainty about whether human consciousness is using language or is being used by it. Similarly with poets: Wallace Stevens speaks of a "central mind" or "major man", which or who includes all other minds without destroying their individuality. He also has a poem in which a fisherman, with his river and his fish and the doves cooing around him, consolidate into one form, though, again, the individual forms remain. One thing that is interesting about this poem is its title: "Thinking of a Relation between the Images of Metaphors". Scientists too: the physicist Erwin Schrödinger, the founder of quantum mechanics, informed an audience at Cambridge about thirty years ago that "consciousness is a singular of which the plural is unknown".

Well, of course, there are those who emphasize, quite rightly, the social and cultural conditioning that underlies every thought or experience we have, and they could just as readily say that consciousness is a plural of which the singular is unknown. But the real significance of such statements is in a different category from assertions that anyone can instantly refute. What is involved is rather the interchange of reality and illusion that language brings about. We start with the notion that the perceiving subject and the perceived object are the essential realities, brought together by the fictions of language. But in proportion as subject and object become illusory, the world of intelligibility connecting them becomes reality, though always the sort of reality that Wallace Stevens, again, calls a supreme fiction. To the extent that the subject-object relation is the sole reality and the metaphors and myths connecting them illusory, the poet will be a relatively unpopular leisure-class entertainer with a limited function and no authority. To the extent that the subject-object relation grows illusory and the fictions connecting them real, the poet begins to recover something of the social authority which, according to tradition, he orginally had. But we can never understand the poet's authority without Vico's principle of *verum factum*, that reality is in the world we make and not in the world we stare at.

I mentioned Bishop Burnet and his discussion of the deluge myth, the story of how human sin and folly caused the entire world to be destroyed. His treatment of the myth may seem to us naive, but the myth itself seems far less so now than it might have done not so long since. If the human race were to destroy both itself and the planet it lives on, that would be the final triumph of illusion. But we have other myths, myths telling us that time and space and life may have an end, but that the sense of identity which something other than these things will not, that there is a word which, whether flesh or not, is still dwelling with us. Also that our ability to respond to what it says is the only sensible reason yet proposed for our being here.

CONTEMPORARY THEOLOGIANS AND THE VISUAL ARTS

JOHN DILLENBERGER*

THE CONCERN WITH METHOD AND PLURALISM

For our time we need to think through the relations among theology, the arts generally, and the visual arts in particular. That involves nothing less than attention to theological method and the artistic mode, their differences and affinities. Attempting to do that in our time, however, immediately means having to come to terms with diverse theological approaches and methods, and their respective relations, if any, to the arts. That diverse reality is new, for a self-conscious preoccupation with method as a condition for doing theology has come to the fore only in recent decades. It is not unusual for contemporary theologians to write one or two volumes on method, with only occasional elaboration of the implications for specific theological concepts. In the past, when a community's beliefs were part and parcel of the fabric of that community's life, theological method was scarcely on the horizon of consciousness. Even in the theologians of the more recent past, Bultmann, Barth, Tillich, Rahner, Lonergan, theological method is integrally related to theological affirmation.

For Bultmann, demythologizing as existential interpretation places the gospel before us. Indeed, it is the Gospel itself that demands demythologizing even though Bultmann may have started his pilgrimage facing the question of the impossibility of accepting the Biblical world view in the modern world. In Barth, the prologomena is not a preliminary methodological analysis of the method to be employed, but a preliminary stating of the affirmations to be developed, a theblogical statement that sets forth his method. In Tillich's *Systematic Theology*, though the section on "Reason and

*Professor of Theology (Emeritus) at the Graduate Theological Union and Vice-President of the American Academy of Religion (1984–85), Dr. Dillenberger presented this paper as a Scholars Press Associates Lecture at the 1984 Annual Meeting of the American Academy of Religion.

Revelation" is placed first, that was primarily because of the expectation of his readers, particularly his American readers.

While Tillich and Rahner did not influence each other, there are similarities between the two in the way in which ontological and hence analogical thinking is dominant, and the extent to which a proper analysis of reason drives to its boundary, to horizons lying beyond but not in contradiction to reason. Hence our humanity drives us both to what we do know and to what we do not know, the inescapable mystery of our being. Theological method is already theological affirmation. The situation is not dissimilar in the instance of Lonergan, where in a modern scholastic style, various levels and modalities of theological work are spelled out.

Perusal of contemporary works as distinguished from the generation just passed discloses two main bases for a concern with method. First, we live in a secular world and if faith is to be credible in that context, it is argued, it must be convincing and intelligible when the procedures of a commonly acceptable discourse are utilized, whether that of philosophy or other public discourse. Among such interpretors, neo-orthodoxy was a short lived movement because its accent on revelation had no context in ordinary language or in a common universe of discourse. While neo-orthodox theologians believed precisely that it was the existing universe of discourse that needed to be broken in order for faith to be apprehended, many contemporary theologians believe that a proper analysis of human language, philosophically and critically developed, provides a credible context for faith through the removal of false stumbling blocks and in the creation of new human possibilities. The God we thought we knew, it is assumed, died because of the poor philosophical grounding of previous theology.

Pluralism within and among religious traditions is the second reason given for preoccupation with theological method. Now the search is for a method or mode of analysis which will make it possible to deal with variety while being true to the concreteness of historic traditions. That is why phenomenological analysis is a favored tool for coming to terms with pluralism.

But the question arises whether a world that is both secular and religiously pluralistic can be adequately dealt with by a single theological method, for the realities of these two worlds are distinct even as they inhabit the same terrain. In a secular world, the aim is to make credible; in a pluralistic world, it is to analyze existing and accepted facets and make the whole intelligible. In the secular, the goal is to explicate the possibilities of faith; in pluralism, to delineate the varieties of faith already present. It is thus not by accident that theologians mainly concerned with the secular question are interested in a philosophical grounding for issues of faith and truth, while those most impressed by pluralism are engaged more in phenomenological and structural analysis. Entering from the side of the secular question, one ponders the basis on which faith may be said to be firmly grounded; entering from the side of pluralism, one is concerned with how one can come to terms with existing faith expressions. Unbelief and belief, if not over-belief, are simultaneously present in our culture and it is not unusual for all facets to be present in the same group. Faith and the secular have come to inhabit the same world, with creative and ominous consequences.

Such is the context for the pervasive concern with theological method and, for the present, it may simply be noted that the result has not been a reigning method, but a plurality of methods and approaches to the theological task. In this variety, our concern will be, not with method as such, but with three types of method in relation to the arts, particularly the visual arts. The first is that in which no relation is seen between the arts and theological work; the second, in which a positive relation is articulated, sometimes successfully and sometimes not; the third, in which the arts provide paradigms and images that affect the nature of theological method.

THE DIVORCE BETWEEN ART AND THEOLOGY

In considering theologians who do not see the arts, particularly the visual arts, as having a role in theology, Bultmann, Barth, Ogden and Kaufman come to mind. Bultmann wrote poetry, indeed, used that medium in poignant reflective situations. Music and theatre delighted him. But the visual arts held little interest for him, personally or theologically. In the first edition of Jesus, the publisher insisted on plates of the Jesus figure, and Bultmann, according to Schubert Ogden, suggested Rembrandt's work as the only possible choice. For Bultmann, seeing belonged to the objectivizing of the world; hearing to its transformation. The Word of God was not identical with the verbal but no other area was articulated as a province in which the Word might be conveyed. Apparently, the Neo-Kantian heritage and personal predilections coincided.

The verbal imagination of Barth is indisputable. His delight in and his writings on Mozart are common knowledge, and Grünewald's *Crucifixion* meant much to him. But he opposed placing stained glass in the Basle minster and his theological comments on the visual arts of painting and sculpture in relation to the church were few and mainly negative in character. Images and symbols, he declared, "have *no place at all* in a building designed for Protestant worship" (Barth:93). His correspondence with the writer Carl Zuckmayer (1983) shows the human and cultural concerns so characteristic of Barth, but for him, theology as a discipline is different from all that. While Bultmann's negativity was mainly personal and philosophical, for his Lutheran heritage would not have made him opposed to the visual, Barth's negativity is theological, a part of his reformed heritage, for as a human being, he was interested in the arts.

Influenced by Whitehead and Hartshorne, Schubert Ogden has pursued an independent, rigorous metaphysical program, dedicated to providing a foundation on the basis of which one can speak appropriately and convincingly about the central theological concepts, such as the Reality of God and the Point of Christology, to use the titles of two of his major books. His logical, sharp mind turns old metaphysical affirmations into new metaphysical realities, a transcendental metaphysics of a neo-classical kind, to use the term which he uses to characterize his approach (143). Imaginative and clarifying definition is evident on every page of his writing, and within the confines of a thoroughgoing metaphysical analysis, one is astounded by what one sees and is given to see. The question remains, are there facets of faith which are left out in the rigor of this method? Ogden would agree that there are, that he is doing theology from a philosophical base, that this is what he knows and does, and one may add, does so superbly. The further question is, would what is left out in this single modality, when added, simply amplify or demand methodological change? If the latter is the case, as I think it would be, one could still opt for the version Ogden has chosen.

The word imagination is a key concept in the work of Gordon Kaufman, as, for example, in his volume, *The Theological Imagination: Constructing the Concept of God.* But the imagination is philosophical rather than aesthetic, that is, only what can be verbally designated belongs to theology. Hence, the various disciplines, including literature—but not the visual arts—play a role. For Kaufman, theology is a construction of concepts, centrally a concept of God.

While most theologians understand their discipline as one which involves second order discourse, Kaufman accents this point to such an extent that an undue chasm appears between the realities and the concepts. Theology is like a house that is built and one's clue to the character of its inhabitants comes only from what one knows about the nature of the building. Indeed, theology is an exercise in verbal, conceptual, philosophical construction, a series of regulative concepts that one hopes will be more satisfactory for our time than historic concepts now available. The visual arts have nothing to do with that enterprise.

AFFIRMATIONS OF A RELATION BETWEEN ART AND THEOLOGY

In the second category on method and the arts, the arts are seen in a positive role in relation to theology and theological method. In Edward Farley's *Ecclesial Reflection*, the visual arts play no role in his analysis, but he suggests that what he is doing has the character of theological portraiture. Portraiture, as distinct from ordinary pictures, is multi-layered, disclosing many levels simultaneously. It includes "contours, interrelationships, unity—in brief, . . . ecclesiality," as applied to theology (199). In this sense, the analogy of portrait painting is helpful. But Farley does not address the issue of the visual as a theological problem. His is a philosophical analysis, trying to be true to the life and shape of the community of faith.

Alone among the theologians considered in this survey, Langdon Gilkey gives little self-conscious attention to the problem of method. Probing the assumptions in our culture with a critical, sharp analytic eye, he proceeds to show the angles of vision that Christian faith brings to the orientations by which we live. That way of doing theology discloses a method, indeed one analogous to but not identical with Paul Tillich; it is a refreshing approach, for the substance of theology and method are simultaneously present.

Since Gilkey is concerned with total cultural configurations, the world of literature and the visual, as well as the political, social and psychological worlds, enter into the arena of theological discourse. From an address given at the Art Institute of Chicago, it is clear that he understands that the arts must contribute to theology, not by illustration of what we already know, but by what they themselves uniquely do. Talk about the arts must be appropriate to the arts. Art makes "us see in *new* and *different* ways, below the surface and beyond the obvious. Art opens up the truth hidden behind and within the ordinary; it provides a new entrance into reality and pushes us through that entrance. It leads us to what is really there and really going on. Far from subjective, it pierces the opaque subjectivity, the *not* seeing, of conventional life, of conventional viewing, and discloses reality" (189–90). However, there is no evidence that this insight about art in its prophetic and reality disclosing character has significantly influenced his theological work.

For the sake of both theology and the arts, George Lindbeck, in *The Nature of Doctrine: Religion and Theology in a Postliberal Age*, chooses to apply a cultural-linguistic approach to doctrines, a linguistic rule game, in which it is accepted that constancy of doctrine occurs in changing frameworks. This leads him to be more appreciative of traditional formulations than most contemporary theologians, for he sees them as expressions of central meanings in particular contexts. He finds that a language game approach makes it possible to take into account the diversity of past and current expressions, while contending that there is a constancy of doctrine throughout. Grünewald's *Crucifixion* and the Byzantine Pantocrator are united in their object, even if their experiences are historically different. Moreover, Lindbeck believes that in accenting how a tradition functions, it is possible to honor diverse modalities, for one does not have to choose one among others, as a philosophical or aesthetic orientation. It makes it possible to include "the aesthetic and nondiscursively symbolic dimensions of a religion—for example, its poetry, music, art and rituals," not as appealing decorations but as expressing basic patterns of religion itself (35–6). Finally, however, I could not avoid the conclusion that Lindbeck's radical agenda had produced conservative conclusions.

In this second category, three individuals–Paul Tillich, John Cobb, Jr., and Mark C. Taylor—have been most concrete in their use of the visual arts. But all three also show the problems inherent in a theological understanding of the arts that is not sufficiently grounded in the arts themselves.

For Tillich, the visual, as all aspects of humanity's modalities, belonged to the world with which theology is concerned. Hence, the visual arts too were interpreted theologically, just as were literature, politics, psychology. Biographically, Tillich's haunting and devastating experiences as a chaplain in World War I were confronted, illumined if not consoled, by paintings he saw in Berlin, particularly Botticelli's *The Virgin Child with Singing Angels*.

Indeed, the visual arts played a role throughout his life. More than any other theologians of his time, Tillich wrote and lectured on the subject at significant convocations, such as at the Museum of Modern Art in New York and the Art Institute in Chicago. Tillich made the visual vital for many of us, precisely because of his dazzling theological interpretations. But therein was also the major problem, for a theological interpretation which is grounded in theological seeing without faithfulness to the art works themselves is unconvincing to critics and art historians. The same criticism has been made of Tillich's interpretation and use of philosophers and psychologists, to name but two areas. But the problem is more acute in his comments on particular artists and painters. First, his preference for German Expressionism, allegedly for existential, theological reasons led him to view paintings in other traditions to be less significant. For Tillich, art found its height in delineating the human condition of estrangement. It is ironic therefore that while Tillich extolled the Renaissance in cultural and theological terms because of its creative, ordered form, renaissance art which expressed that modality was considered without religious significance, apparently because the form, for all its religious subject matter, did not exhibit the anxiety attendant to the human condition. Obversely, Picasso's *Guernica* is interpreted only in that context. Second, Tillich's interesting typological analysis does not fit a major part of the painting tradition. Its source, as Jane Dillenberger has suggested, was apparently the art Tillich knew so well, the museums in Berlin and the Museum of Modern Art. Limiting oneself to those magnificent collections, the typologies work remarkably well and they show how well he knew the collections. But that is not all of art. Third, one could argue with much that Tillich says of particular artists. Theological interpretations are not and need not be art historical ones. When they conflict with what is known of an artist and the context of that artist's work, problems of credibility do arise. For example, Tillich considered Giotto's paintings of St. Francis to be the best example of theonomy in the Middle Ages. But Giotto, as Michael F. Palmer has pointed out in his volume, *Paul Tillich's Philosophy of Art*, restored the natural and believed that the world must be observed before it is understood. Though nature appears minimally in Giotto's *Christ and the Magdalene*, the encounter clearly takes place in the world and not in the abstract golden zone of medieval art. The Magdalene's gesture is of infinite yearning and human tenderness, whereas in this medieval 13th century manuscript her posture has great decorative beauty but little human poignancy. The two views may not be contradictory, but the strength of Tillich's contention is surely compromised by a knowledge of what Giotto was about.

John Cobb's suggestive use of Whitehead's philosophy leads to clarity of statement on issues of faith in a pluralistic world. Facets of experience from every conceivable angle are brought into a unity of expression, with clarity of statement also evident where experiences diverge as well as converge. Cobb confesses that as the years have gone by, Whitehead has been even more suggestive on the issues of contemporary life than he had initially assumed. It is thus not surprising that in Cobb's writing the theological imagination is both enhanced and limited by Whiteheadian modalities. Whiteheadian or process categories have served as an antidote to the more static categories of traditional metaphysics, but they also, I think, become ways in which the hard and passionate realities of good and evil are both curtailed. However, who could not but be moved by the range and scope of central issues that Cobb has so directly addressed year after year. Indeed, that includes the arts. In *Christ in a Pluralistic Age*, Cobb has chosen to comment on the visual arts, utilizing Andre Malraux's works, mainly *The Voices of Silence* and *The Metamorpho-*

sis of the Gods. In this use of Malraux, Cobb has been joined by Mark C. Taylor in his books, *Deconstructing Theology* and *Erring—A Postmodern A/theology.* Malraux's fascinating and useful cultural judgments and schema corroborate for both Cobb and Taylor what they themselves see, namely, a secular development that can be positively rather than negatively understood. For Cobb, the explicitly Christian subjects may have disappeared but the logos is now hiddenly and immanently present, waiting to be named as Christ in a new form. For Taylor, Malraux and Foucault as well, show how in the history of art, the death of God, followed by the loss of the self, can be culturally documented. Specifically, both use Malraux's comments on Flemish painting to make their point. Taylor centers on the contrast Malraux makes between Byzantine art and the work of Van Eyck, while Cobb contrasts the Byzantine with Flemish art generally and its subsequent developments. Both accent that the reigning Christ of Byzantine art was a God removed from the human realm, and was characteristic of that theology. Aside from the fact that the reigning Christ does not need to be interpreted in negative form, both seem to forget that some of the most human and tender depictions of the Virgin and Christ Child also in Byzantine art. In the light of Malraux, both further interpret Flemish art as an indication of the new human, secular way in which religious subjects are now to be understood. Taylor calls attention to Van Eyck's *The Madonna of Chancellor Rolin,* in which the timeless Christ has been replaced by the babe on its mother's knee in the home of the patron, and the Chancellor's gaze, he states, is not on a figure that calls us to transcendence but on the incarnate human figure before him.

Barbara G. Lane in her book, *The Altar and the Altarpiece— Sacramental Themes in Early Netherlandish Painting* and Anne Hagopian van Buren in her article in *The Art Bulletin* on the canonical office and the Rolin Madonna (617–33) reconstruct the location of the painting in the chapel, and the Chancellor's gaze centers on the altar, just past the edge of the Child and Virgin, incorporating the two in a single vision. Lotte Brand Philip in *The Ghent Altarpiece and the Art of Jan van Eyck* provides us with an affirmation of the full religious significance of this painting. Given that the donor is the chancellor to Philip the Good, whose aspiration was to reconquer Jerusalem for its rightful King, Christ, the legitimate successor of David, the details of the painting now take on new significance. Writes Lotte Brand Philip: "The phantastic cityscape shown in this painting at the foot of the celestial castle, though certainly connoting the Heavenly City of the Apocalypse, points also to the earthly Jerusalem, which is and has always been the symbol par excellence of the celestial one. The glorious buildings to the right in

Van Eyck's background representation encircle the head of the Christ Child like a crown. While the Child is characterized as a ruler by the orb which he holds, the majestic circle of buildings signifies Him as the uncrowned King of Jerusalem. This idea explains the strange exaltation of the donor in Van Eyck's painting. Rolin, as the chancellor of a sovereign who was planning a crusade, is the very man to help the Holy Child and His mother resume possession of their rightful heritage, the Holy Land. The donor, to be more precise, is here portrayed as the chancellor to Christ" (191). Philip draws attention to Panofsky's suggestion that Van Eyck and the early Netherlandish painters did not distinguish between heaven and earth as we do, that they transformed "the vision of a distant beatitude into the experience of a world which mortals are permitted to share with the Deity" (193). In this painting, nature and architecture are interwoven with standard religious symbols to form a heavenly vision based on the Book of Revelation.

Granted that a change of perception is involved in the transition from Byzantine to Flemish, including all the stages in between, we are still left with the question whether that change is one from transcendence to immanence and a new secular viewing. The interpretation of the heavenly and earthly in Flemish art may make it possible for a more secular view to emerge; but in itself Flemish art belongs more to the medieval than to the modern secular world. One suspects that it would be better to deal with the works of art than with Malraux's interpretations of art, as his tantalizing perceptions are not grounded in any sense of historical structure. Nor is the situation improved by Taylor's use of Picasso and particularly Barnett Newman, in whom, according to Taylor quoting Altizer, we enter into non-art, into the totally anonymous (129).[1] That Newman himself believed that his paintings expressed the sublime in nothing less than absolute terms may not be instructive to structuralists and deconstructionists for whom the intention or even the existence of an author or artist is irrelevant. But surely deconstructionists in their wandering pilgrimage should also be open to the possibility that in our wanderings some of us also bump into ultimacies that need not be translated

---

[1] While I disagree with much in Taylor's theological agenda and with some of his comments on particular works of art, I am impressed by his knowledge of the visual arts, his deep interest in them, including his own involvement in painting. Thomas J. J. Altizer also has an impressive knowledge of the visual arts. In both Taylor and Altizer, Malraux's interpretations fit into their theological agendas. I do not believe that Malraux is right in his interpretations, though I can see his attractiveness for theologians.

into absolutisms. Thus our wandering may take us, not to a situation *between* belief and unbelief, as Taylor suggests, but to *both* belief and unbelief (10). The literary and the visual are also affirmative in their negations, indeed, negate in order to affirm.

THE ARTS AS MODELS FOR THEOLOGICAL WORK

The third category consists of those who use the arts, and the visual arts, as essential to proper theological understanding and method, who believe that nothing less than the style of theology is involved. Here we shall briefly consider Hans Urs von Balthasar, Karl Rahner, Ray L. Hart and David Tracy.

Quite different in approach and largely unknown except as a name because so little of his work has been translated into English, Balthasar was a theologian whose intention was to write an aesthetic theology, of which the first seven volumes of a three part system were oriented from the visual—and two volumes have been published in English—and the second part, from drama. Thomas O'Meara points out that while the visual arts are utilized at points in the exposition, the theology is not aesthetic in that sense but in that the modality in contemplating God is like the contemplation of art and because the New Testament confronts us with images (272–76). The execution of the work, however, seems less convincing than the thesis.

Whether or not the visual arts can be left out of theological work is sharply raised by Karl Rahner. In 1966, Rahner wrote a section on "Poetry and the Christian," and in 1967, on "Priest and Poet" in *Theological Investigations.* In the first he acknowledges that because Christianity is "the religion of the word proclaimed, of faith which hears and of a sacred scripture, [it] has a special intrinsic relationship to the *word* and hence cannot be without such a special relationship to the *poetic* word" (1966:357). In 1982, however, Rahner addressed himself to the wider scope and issue of the arts in his article "Theology and the Arts." What shall we do, he asks, about the non-verbal arts, architecture, sculpture, painting, and music? If they are "human self-expressions which embody in one way or another the process of human self-discovery," do they not "have the same value and significance as the verbal arts" (1982:24). If that is the case, and "if and insofar as theology is man's reflexive self-expression about himself in the light of divine revelation, we could propose the thesis that theology cannot be complete until it appropriates these arts as an integral moment of itself and its own life, until the arts become an intrinsic moment of theology itself. One could take the position that what comes to expression in a Rembrandt painting or a Bruckner symphony is so inspired and borne by divine revelation, by grace and by God's self-communication, that they communicate something about what the human really is in the eyes of God which cannot be completely translated into verbal theology. . . . If theology is simply and arbitrarily defined as being identical with verbal theology, then of course we cannot say that. But then we would have to ask whether such a reduction of theology to verbal theology does justice to the value and uniqueness of these arts, and whether it does not unjustifably limit the capacity of the arts to be used by God in his revelation" (24–5). Indeed, it is precisely in contending that the non-verbal provides what cannot be totally translated into verbal theology, that its necessary place seems assured. Rahner knows that there is art, even religious art, that does not have that revealing character, and that there are those whose artistic sensibility is not developed and who cannot see at all. Moreover, there are those whose philosophical gifts keep them confined to that modality, exhibiting on occasion why theology has lost so much of its poetry. Art and theology, different and related, both rest in humanity's transcendent nature. Hence they belong to each other. The theological question cannot exclude the non-verbal arts. Yet, how they are to be incorporated was not addressed by Rahner before his death.

Ray L. Hart, in *Unfinished Man and the Imagination: Toward an Ontology and a Rhetoric of Revelation,* as the title itself suggests, sees humanity's imaginative capacities as constitutive of what we may become in the process of living. We are always being completed and we are always unfinished. Living in that mode, we both manifest and continually create who we are. As a paradigm of the imagination which expresses that double aspect of our existence, Hart gives particular attention to the arts, literary and visual. Moreover, it is clear that the visual is considered to be constitutive of and informing to our humanity. The result is that the arts are taken as seriously as the metaphysical, that they are not an adjunct to the verbal, but provide, as do other modalities, fundamental clues to what we are and are becoming, facets which belong to the theological domain. Here theological method programatically includes the arts, indeed, the arts become a central imaginative paradigm. It is unfortunate that Hart's recondite style, necessary or not, has kept his views from receiving the attention they deserve.

In David Tracy's *The Analogical Imagination: Christian Theology and the Culture of Pluralism,* the title too suggests the particular theological method. Impressed by the plurality of interpretations within the Biblical materials, in theological history, in approaches to theology, in world history itself, Tracy believes that it is necessary to honor this diversity without theology becoming simply an array of unrelated perceptions. Building on an historical concept imaginatively refurbished, Tracy believes that analogy is the methodological key, provided its imaginative use takes due account of both the difference and likeness involved in all comparative work. Utilizing this concept, Tracy ranges widely, thoroughly and perceptively through historical and contemporary writers in theology, the social and psychological sciences, and the arts. Only the ephemeral, defined as that which excludes other alternatives, is not considered. That which affirms and stretches our sensibilities is worthy of consideration; indeed, it is that which has the earmarks of a classic. In a genuine work of art, that which defines a classic, we are " 'caught up' in its world, we are shocked, surprised, challenged by its startling beauty *and* its recognizable truth, its instinct for the essential. . . . we recognize the truth of the work's disclosure of a world of reality transforming, if only for a moment ourselves: our lives, our sense for possibilities and actuality, our destiny" (117). For Tracy, theological work now requires new conversations, the analogical tracing of diverse affirmations in their likeness and differences. Tracy may not intend to put it this way, but I learned from him the rich perceptions and affirmations that can emerge when one alternately looks at issues from a variety of angles and perspectives. Then a rich mosaic may emerge, one in which the pieces remain partly distinct yet related to a new whole. To execute such a theological task requires the keen knowledge and perceptive sensibilities so characteristic of David Tracy.

ALTERNATIVE THEOLOGICAL MODELS

These three foregoing categories include writings that have the characteristics of what we have historically recognized as theologies. Acknowledgement must be made, though time does not permit elaboration, of a group of writings and approaches to the theological task that do not fit the shape of traditional theological systems. They may serve as alternatives, or as correctives, or as additional angles of vision. Certainly liberation and feminist theologies accent a new agenda; artistic modalities, when present, are understandably not at the center of attention. The development of models as avenues of exploration, such as in Ian Barbour, opens the theological task toward the sciences; works such as those of Clifford Geertz, to social-cultural dimensions; and of Paul Ricoeur, to delineating symbols as the center of philosophical and theological work. Narrative or story, as represented by Stephen Crites or the essays edited by James Wiggins; metaphorical theology as developed by Sally McFague; and biography, as represented by James McClendon, confirm how the structure, style, and meaning of our lives form special unities. Then there are movements which, in spite of their contradictory nature, instruct us in the reading and understanding of texts, such as the mytho-poetic, in which as in Amos Wilder we learn how to see literal texts in non-literal ways; or structuralism, in which linguistic patterns and common meanings recur in history apart from historic conditioning; or deconstruction, in which meanings are not fixed, but multiple, suggestive, possibilities in total, historic flux. Many of the literary methodologies are creatively used in Biblical work by Robert W. Funk.

It is obvious that the concern with theological method has produced, not *a* method, but itself reflects the pluralism of our time. John Cobb and David Tracy particularly have given central attention to this issue in their writings, Cobb by learning from that which is different and interpreting it in his own expositions; Tracy, by incorporating new insights in such a way that an ever widening analogical interpretation is required.

There are many levels in our pluralistic situation. Today we accept that there are different theological accents in the New Testament. We know that cultural and religious orientations alike bind and divide Protestants and Catholics. We know that life-situations, oppression, e.g., helps us see the Gospel in ways we had not seen before, even when they also shrink other perceptions. We know the differences and affinities with non-western religions. All of these factors have transformed the theological enterprise in recent decades.

Largely absent from the writers we have considered is theology as true propositional statement. The concern with language has become more circumspect, even when the paradigm for theological work remains within the philosophical orbit. Nevertheless, the nature of the arts in relation to theological work still remains a critical question. Rahner has succinctly posed the issue in his recognition that the arts cannot be translated entirely into other modalities, and that what they uniquely disclose must nevertheless have implications for theological work.

THE LITERARY AND THE VISUAL ARTS

A central question needing attention is whether there is a fundamental difference between the literary and the visual arts. The literary arts have certainly found their way into theology, undoubtedly because of their verbal character. In their role in theological work, are they incorporated in order to make vivid what has and is being said, or are they used because they disclose facets and nuances of theological meaning analogous to but different from what ordinary or philosophical discourse might provide?

There is nothing wrong with the first, provided illustration is not considered the only or uniquely special character of literary art. Poetry and drama are unique both because they are a special genre and because their style discloses what another style cannot. Hence, poetry takes us into a world in which style conveys more than the subject which is present. David Daiches has put it well—"Great poetry carries beliefs into its language in such a way that it can achieve a communication transcending the bounds of those beliefs," and then he adds, "but we must learn to read it" (219). That is why talking about a poem dare only be an act of honoring that does not transgress the boundaries. A literary art may be said to have verbal facility and discipline in an imaginative suggestiveness that creates resonances in our being that would be violated by over-explication.

In this sense the literary and the visual arts are identical. Indeed, the literary arts can be said to stand closer to the visual arts than to the disciplines that share the verbal in ordinary and philosophical discourse as we usually encounter it. Just as in the case of the literary arts, so in the visual, the verbal has its place, its way of talking about, of suggesting, of pointing to, but in such a way that the painting or sculpture, if one may use the expression, speaks to us in its own way. Thus, seeing conveys more and in ways different from saying. Respecting the boundaries, avoiding transgression, is important to both literary and the visual arts.

This delineation of the literary and the visual implies that positive affirmations are as important to these arts as are the critical, allegedly prophetic nature of the arts. It may be true that the arts more quickly convey the seismographic shifts in a society than do other disciplines, perhaps because sensitivity is so central to the nature of the discipline, though one wonders why it should be less true in others. Nevertheless, the arts do not rest in either their pleasing or prophetic functions, but in that they, too, convey affirmations about life. Certainly the primary agenda of the Abstract Expressionists was to present the world anew to us, freed of forms that once had power but now had become banal. From their different orientations, they strove to present the grandeur of humanity, a mystery presented and represented to us. Mark Rothko evokes the mystical tradition; Robert Motherwell a humanistic stance in the grand classical sense; Jackson Pollock the visions of one who, though he descended into hell, saw new realities glimpsed from afar; Barnett Newman, the grand sublime in rigorous, demanding form.

The arts, as other disciplines, can be trivial, and with respect to religious issues, banal. But they can also convey facets of life and truth in either or both religious and non-religious subject matter. Significant art, as the classic, to use Tracy's phrase, purveys more than a time; from a particular time, it carries us into perceptions suggestive and illuminating to humanity in other times.

CONCLUSION

If this analysis is correct, it has implications for the theological task. It means that diversity, or pluralism, is not only a cultural matter; it is also indicative of our very humanity. There is a division in our very nature, an affinity with a difference among our sensibilities— sight, touch, taste, hearing, speaking. These modalities, understood from the standpoint of creation, define our full humanity in relation to God; understood from the standpoint of our actual state, the Fall if you will, the unity does not come naturally; understood from the standpoint of redemption, we need the discipline of each sensibility in order to express a full humanity eschatologically oriented to its fulfillment.

What does the pluralism in our culture and the pluralism in ourselves mean for the theological task? First, it validates a plurality of tasks. Second, it should make it possible for us to take on the tasks we think we can do well, without having to claim that the modalities in which we operate are most important or decisive. Theology can take different approaches. Third, it should make us aware that the disciplined cultivation of wider sensibilities is important for a full humanity and that it has implications even for selective areas in which we can and have decided to work. It makes collective scholarship important, the need to learn from each other, for we cannot be competent across the board.

There are those, of course, who think that theology has fallen on evil days, for the vast systems have disappeared. But the various and more limited approaches, if they do not claim to be the whole, can also enrich us and set the stage for untried and new forms for theological work. We have the possibility of a series of "as if" theologies, of approaches from differing angles of vision, of differing modalities, all for the explication of the variegated texture of what humanity may be in the light of God.

WORKS CONSULTED

Barth, Karl
  1965   "The Architectural Problem of Protestant Places of Wor-
                ship." In *Architecture in Worship: The Christian Place of
                Worship.* Ed. by Andre Bieler. Edinburgh and London:
                Oliver and Boyd.

Barth, Karl, and Zuckmayer, Carl
    1983   A Late Friendship: *The Letters of Carl Zuckmayer and Karl Barth.* Trans. by Geoffrey W. Bromiley. Grand Rapids: Eerdmans.

Daiches, David
    1984   *God and the Poets.* Oxford: Oxford University Press.

Farley, Edward
    1982   *Ecclesial Reflection: An Anatomy of Theological Method.* Philadelphia: Fortress Press.

Gilkey, Langdon
    1984   "Can Art Fill the Vacuum?" In *Art, Creativity and the Sacred.* Ed. by Diana Apostolos-Cappadona. New York: Crossroads Press.

Hart, Ray L.
    1968   *Unfinished Man and the Imagination: Toward an Ontology and a Rhetoric of Revelation.* New York: Herder and Herder.
    1985   Paperbound re-issue. Atlanta: Scholars Press.

Kaufman, Gordon D.
                    The Theological Imagination. Philadelphia: The Westminster Press.

Lindbeck, George A.
    1984   *The Nature of Doctrine: Religion and Theology in a Postliberal Age.* Philadelphia: The Westminster Press.

Ogden, Schubert M.
    1982   *The Point of Christology.* San Francisco: Harper and Row.

O'Meara, Thomas F.
    1981   "Of Art and Theology: Hans Urs von Balthasar's Systems," *Theological Studies* 42: 272–276.

Philip, Lotte Brand
    1971   *The Ghent Altarpiece and the Art of Jan van Eyck.* Princeton: Princeton University Press.

Rahner, Karl
    1966   "Poetry and the Christian." *Theological Investigations.*
                  Vol. IV. Baltimore: Helicon Press.
    1982   "Theology and the Arts." *Thought* 57.

Taylor, Mark C.
    1984   *Erring: A Postmodern A/theology.* Chicago: University of
                  Chicago Press.

Tracy, David
    1981   *The Analogical Imagination: Christian Theology and the*
                  Culture of Pluralism. New York: Crossroads Press.

van Buren, Anne Hagopian
    1978   "The Canonical Office in Renaissance Painting, More
                  About the Rolin *Madonna.*" *The Art Bulletin* LX No. 4.

THE LITERARY AND CULTURAL STUDY OF RELIGION: PROBLEMS AND PROSPECTS

GILES GUNN*

On this occasion I wish to discuss an anomaly, actually a double anomaly. It is an anomaly that is widely sensed but rarely mentioned in such settings as this, and yet it is dramatically in evidence all around us in this annual meeting of the two societies. The anomaly of which I speak concerns what in my title I refer to as the literary and cultural study of religion. By these two terms, *literary* and *cultural*, I intend to suggest, somewhat idiosyncratically, I admit, smaller and larger variants of the same thing—namely, what some would call the study of religion as a symbolic form; what I would prefer to describe as the study of religion as an imaginative or figurative formation.

This definition may very well strike some in my audience as potentially misleading, because the cultural study of religion is usually taken to include such disciplines as anthropology, iconography, history, philosophy, sociology, and folklore, while the literary study of religion traditionally encompasses no more than the disciplines of literary criticism, the theology of culture, and, perhaps, comparative mythography. There is abundant testimony, however, to the fact that such disciplinary genres as these, for all but those ideologically committed to them, have begun to grow more permeable, unstable, or just plain fluid. This phenomenon has resulted not only from the discovery that so many of these disciplines were accidentally created, not to say arbitrarily defined, to begin with, but also, and more importantly, from the realization that so much valuable intellectual work has been produced by crossing, confusing, or even collapsing the distinctions between them. Who can say, for example, where literary criticism ends and cultural theory begins, or where intellectual history terminates and the sociology of knowledge com-

*Professor of English and of Religious Studies at the University of California at Santa Barbara, Dr. Gunn presented this paper as a Scholars Press Associates Lecture at the 75th Anniversary meeting (1984) of the American Academy of Religion.

mences, or where oral history stops and popular ethnography starts? And who would wish to return to a time when, let us imagine, the theory of interpretation was of interest only to Biblical scholars, or the study of symbolic sign systems was of importance only to art historians and philosophical aestheticians? Just as we have grown to accept that the methodological differentiations which obtain between social anthropology and cultural sociology, or between the philosophy of religion and philosophical theology, are intellectually artificial even where they are historically defensible, so we are generally prepared to concede that the study of ideology is no more restricted to political science than it is to the history of ideas, or that structuralism as a theoretical predisposition is no less anthropological than it is literary or, to gauge from the claims of some of its practitioners, even metaphysical.

All of which brings me back to my topic. If the literary and cultural study of religion takes in everything from philology to ethnology, it nonetheless purports to view religion not merely as a material, or a social, or an institutional, or an intellectual phenomenon, but also as a metaphorical one; and the study of religion so conceived, at least as it is currently pursued in the United States, is almost everywhere characterized by a paradox, really by two interrelated paradoxes. On the one hand, the study of religion, in its literary and cultural expressions, is spreading rapidly and widely not only within the field of religious studies itself but also outside it, and particularly in those disciplinary quarters most open to exploring the symbolic and qualitative dimensions of experience.

On the other hand, within the field of religious studies itself, that specialty organized explicitly around the question of how religion makes itself meaningful not only in symbolic terms but in symbolic terms that are aesthetically resonant—that subfield, we may call it, variously named religion and culture, religion and art, or, more narrowly, religion and literature—is hard pressed to come up with an acceptable justification of itself and is therefore almost everywhere on the defensive within the field of religious studies. If this can now be discerned most obviously in the scarcity of job openings in this area, it can also be seen in the retrenchment, if not withering away, of graduate study in this subfield and felt in the general demoralization and often confusion that has sometimes overtaken many of its better students.

The reasons for this anomalous situation are no doubt numerous, but the sources from which they derive are basically two. One of them has to do with the general configuration and mindset of the field of religious studies as a whole, which in this instance, I would argue, is guilty of a certain disingenousness. That disingenuousness springs from the fact that, while there is no lack of interest in many of the methods and insights associated with this subfield, there remains, within the field as a whole, a general indisposition to take these methods and insights with full seriousness. Where, for example, within the field as a whole, do you find, except in selected instances, a determined and consistent attempt to interpret particular religious formations *as* a culture, that is, as a more or less systematically organized and experiencable way of life? For that matter, where within the field of religious studies, do you even find a general willingness to interpret religious phenomena, as Jonathan Z. Smith and before him Ray L. Hart recommended, with the help of models drawn from imaginative experience? Instead, such insights and methods as are appropriated from the study of literary and cultural forms are used to interpret religion in relation to models that are other than imaginative—models that are cognitive, psychological, or political—or to define religion as something other than a culture—a church, a text, or a system of beliefs.

A second source of this anomalous situation can be located within the subfield itself, where the principal energies of too many of its representatives seem to have been devoted to the apologetic task of establishing the religious and theological terms in which the study of literary and cultural materials might be made acceptable, rather than in undertaking the interpretive and evaluative or moral task of showing how, in their own figurative or aesthetic terms, literary and cultural forms provide an indispensable extension of, and corrective to, traditional religious formulations.

If this sounds like a minor distinction, it has nonetheless made a major difference in the way this subfield has attempted to represent itself. Instead of developing arguments for the way literary and cultural forms constitute some of our most compelling and often powerfully disturbing makers of religious sense, too many articles and monographs associated with this subfield have settled for performing the far less consequential task of defining the religiously intelligible sense literary and cultural forms sometimes make. As a result, comparatively little of the scholarship professionally associated with this subfield argues from—I don't say for—the perspective of its own selected sources of insight. In a word, the point should be to determine if Herman Melville was able to comprehend something about the relation between the natural and the supernatural that, let us say, Horace Bushnell did not, or to prove, or at the very least to hypothesize, that Raphael and Leonardo da Vinci and John Milton fathomed something about the nature of divine charity that Anders Nygren and Reinhold Niebuhr, not to say the Hebrew and Christian scriptures, just possibly missed.

The object in all this is not, of course, to replace the history of American religion in American culture, let us say, with the history of the culture of American religion any more than it is to replace the study of Reformation theology with the study of the theology of the Renaissance. The object is rather to realize that we can no longer produce satisfactory institutional or social histories of American religion without, at the same time, investigating the web of symbolic meanings through which that tradition was lived and the felt qualities of life (what Raymond Williams calls the "structures of feeling") by means of which that life was known; that we cannot presume to understand the theological controversies that divided Western Christendom at the end of the Middle Ages if we divorce the ideas which produced it from the experiences which those ideas formulated and the formulations which they made for the first time experiencable.

All of this, I would think, should now be perfectly obvious, but apparently it is not. While the literary and cultural study of religion remains, within religious studies today, one of the hotter subfields for what might be called "theoretical prospecting" or "conceptual mining," very few of the larger corporate enterprises within the discipline—theological studies, comparative religion, Biblical studies, religious sociology, the history of religious institutions, ethics, or even the psychology of religion—are willing to make any large capital investments. This reluctance, as I see it, is not so much a matter of hedging one's bets, perhaps in hopes that the market will improve; it is rather a matter of possessing investment goals quite alien to any associated with the materials or methods of this subfield itself.

If I were to hazard a guess as to what those goals are for the field of religious studies as a whole, I would suggest that they have something quite directly to do with the field's own perpetuation of itself, or, rather, with the perpetuation of a notion, an idea, with which the field identifies its own future prospects. In view of the numerous disciplinary and sectarian concerns that presently comprise the field of religious studies in the United States, it is impossible to link that idea to any specific definition of religion or to any specifiable conception of religious truth. Rather, the idea or notion which seems to hold the field together is associated with a more generalized but still firmly held, and widely supported, conviction as to the place of religion itself within the broader empire of human experience. That idea or notion could be expressed as follows: Among those who define themselves professionally in relation to the field of religious studies, there is a largely unspoken but still clearly operative, and sometimes coercive, belief not so much in the ubiquity or omnipresence of religion, nor in the primacy or even centrality of religion, but rather in its absolute indispensability to human life in its entirety.

I call this belief coercive as well as compelling because it tends all-too-often to foreclose the possibility of asking if people haven't found some perfectly acceptable alternatives or at least necessary substitutes for religion as we define it, and not only in modern life but also in ages past, and I also conceive this notion coercive because it sometimes acts as a deterrent to questions about whether religion, however integral to the structure of specific situations, has always proved an irremediable good. It seems to me that if religious studies was an interdisciplinary field like any other in the university curriculum, a field constituted by the family resemblance among its specific queries and methods rather than by the putative unity among its various discoveries, one would perceive considerably more puzzlement, if not disagreement, than one generally does over the merits of religion's historical effects and contemporary salience. This is not to suggest that there is any lack of dispute in religious studies over individual matters of interpretation; only that such disputes rarely, if ever, call into question the essential value of religion itself. By insisting, however tacitly, on the ultimate importance of religion, no matter how venal the corruptions to which it has been susceptible, students within the field have too frequently left the critical understanding of religious forms to the prophets within their own traditions, and religious studies as an intellectual enterprise has forfeited what I would have thought to be its most essential job of work: the comparative interpretation and assessment of religion in all its manifestations. And just coincidentally, by subordinating its critical responsibilities to its exegetical, analytic, and apologetic functions, religious studies has failed to comprehend the role that the study of literary and cultural materials might perform in fulfilling this heuristic function.

If the study of religion in the United States, perhaps more as it is professed in the classroom than practiced in research, is not in this sense always critical, then what is it? I would characterize it as being in the wrong sense theological. I say wrong sense to indicate that I also think that there is a perfectly appropriate sense in which religious studies, or at any rate an essential component thereof, should be theological. That is to say, the study of those traditions of systematic reflection in which particular institutions or movements of faith have sought critical self-clarification, and not only for its own sake but also for the sake of convincing others of the validity of their position— theology in this sense is a perfectly legitimate and often very necessary ingredient in the study of almost any religion. What is illegitimate, it seems to me, because it is not disinterested in the least and serves only the self-understanding of those involved in it, is that kind of study which pursues inquiries into some religion in particular for the sake of valorizing the importance of all religion in general.

Needless to say, this isn't the explicit form such arguments usually take. They tend to be shaped, instead, by an interest in what I would call the exigencies of ultimacy, and specifically by the desire to show that religion, however conceived, provides the clearest and most certain route of access to this dimension of things. However, in this "late, bad time," as W. H. Auden was fond of calling it, very few scholars outside the walls of confessionalism try to argue that the clue to the nature of ultimate reality lies in some form of supernaturalism, or revealed religion. Ever since the Enlightenment (and let us not forget that the study of religion derives from that period), it has been assumed that the key to ultimate reality no longer resides in the spiritual divinities that shape our ends but in the spiritual attributes that define our nature as human beings.

The assumption that the key to life's ultimate meaning lies in man's spiritual nature is a paraphrase of Maurice Mandelbaum's definition of metaphysical idealism, a system of ideas which the philosopher Richard Rorty has recently defined as but the first stage in the devolution of what he calls philosophical, and we might call metaphysical or religious, culture. In any case, the second stage in this devolution occurred when thinkers and artists associated with the nineteenth-century Romantic movement gave up the idealist assumption that reality possesses an ultimate nature whose essence is encompassable within a single vocabulary and proposed on the contrary that different vocabularies simply furnish us with different modes of access to the real and different images of what constitutes its ultimacy. Yet from here it was but a short step to the present or contemporary stage of things, where critical vocabularies can no longer claim the privilege of trafficking with ultimacy at all and are compelled to construct new definitions even of what might be meant by the real. This stage was reached, according to Rorty, when the Romantic notion that there are different modes of access to the ultimately real was displaced by the arguments of naturalists like Nietzsche, on the one hand, and pragmatists like William James, on the other, that different vocabularies are simply different ways of stating and sometimes getting what we want.

However one may assess the accuracy of Rorty's intellectual history, his main point, I think, is indisputable. The various critical discourses we now live with, from pragmatism and naturalism to hermeneutics and deconstruction, are the legacy of a tradition of critical questioning which has not only dethroned theology and philosophy as the queens of intellectual science but any other claimants to such privilege as well. Neither philosophy, nor theology, nor any other mode of intellectual inquiry, is any longer deemed capable of supplying us with an Archimedean point from which to survey the whole of cultural experience because all such Archimedean stand-points are now construed as but parts of cultural experience itself and the philosophical or intellectual search for them understood merely as ways of satisfying certain basic human needs.

Chief among such needs, as John Dewey long ago reminded us, is not the need to transcend experience but the need to clarify the nature and implications of our attachment to what we take to be its cultural constituents. Dewey realized that this could only be accomplished by a kind of "intellectual disrobing," as he put it. To understand such attachments critically—that is, in relation to the conditions from which they emerge and the consequences, whether actual or merely potential, to which they may give rise—Dewey realized that it is necessary to divest ourselves of our typical or habitual ways of viewing them. "We cannot permanently divest ourselves of the intellectual habits we take on and wear," Dewey wrote, "when we assimilate the culture of our own time and place. But intelligent furthering of culture demands that we take some of them off, that we inspect them critically to see what they are made of and what wearing them does to us" (Dewey:35). Yet the aim of this critical strategy of disrobing, Dewey held, with Dilthey before him and Ricoeur after him, is not the recovery of some "primitive naivete" of experience, but rather the creation of what he described as a kind of "cultivated naivete" or "artful innocence." Dewey realized that this secondary immediacy of experience, or recovered presence, was extraordinarily difficult to achieve for it entailed what we are now used to calling the overcoming of the effects of criticism by criticism itself. But Dewey had a better name for it: the achievement of this recovered immedi-acy, this reconstructed presencing of experience, required what he termed "the discipline of severe thought" (Dewey:35).

It is my contention that the materials and modes of reflection that the field of religious studies now wishes to expropriate—in some cases it would not be excessive to say cannibalize—from the literary and cultural study of religion, are instances of just such "severe thought," but the field as a whole, insofar as it remains in the thrall of a perspective that is essentially a variant of metaphysical idealism, has not undergone "the discipline" that such materials and modes of reflection exhibit and exact. As a consequence, the organized study of religion in the United States is becoming more and more dependent on concepts and techniques furnished by an investigation of the arts of symbolic inquiry and expression while, at the same time, reserving less and less space within its own organizational configurations for the disciplined examination of the relations between religion and cultural formations.

As for the amazing absorption of literary and cultural interests within religious studies itself, merely consider some of the highlights of the program at this annual meeting. Even if one allows for the fact that much of this program, or at least of the American Academy of Religion's portion of it, was arranged by Ray Hart, Paul Ricoeur's plenary address following this session on the nature is evil is bound to make heavy use of critical and aethetic models; Northrop Frye delivered a plenary address of his own two days ago on "The Expanding World of Metaphor"; Wayne Booth presented one on the 75th Anniversary lectures yesterday on "Systematic Wonder: The Rhetoric of Religion in 1984"; the other two Scholars Press lectures both concern themselves with issues bearing the strong imprint of this subfield, John Dillenberger's entitled "Theological Method and Artistic Mode," Martin Marty's called "Irony (figurative) and (literal) in Modern American Religion"; and we have even been feted to a panel in which such eminent theologians as Dillenberger himself, John Cobb, Langdon Gilkey, and David Tracy set about discussing the way the arts have informed their own procedures within theology.

These titles, and their respective subjects, constitute, it is true, no more than a minuscule portion of the topics addressed at this annual meeting; but when one remembers that every structuralist analysis of the Bible, every anthropological essay on American folk religion, every theological treatise on the theory of interpretation, every historical study of religious iconography, every sociological examination of religious ritual, every comparative study of religious myth and archtype, every psychological investigation of cultural theology, every form critical reading of a sacred text, every symbolic exploration of civil religion, every deconstruction of an ethical proposition either cuts across, or draws upon, or intersects with the interests of that subfield within religious studies devoted to the literary and cultural study of religion, then one begins to appreciate the centrality of its procedures and concerns within the present organization of the study of religion as a whole.

But what of the centrality of religious inquiry to the study of literature and culture generally? This question is simply too vast to address in its entirety, and beyond my competence anyway; but if I confine myself to what can be discerned from an inspection of contemporary literary study alone, I think it would be fair to state that "religion" or "the religious" remains one of the most frequently employed and intellectually crucial categories of analysis in literary and cultural criticism today. This assertion may come as something of a surprise. After all, it was the artist, we are used to hearing, who brought the news to the nineteenth century that the God of traditional Christianity was dead, a victim of his own most respected and respectable cultural defenders; but in the twentieth century, it was also the poet and not the preacher, we need to remind ourselves, who showed us how difficult it is to live with the palliatives that constantly offer themselves as contemporary replacements. Thus if we live in an age when imaginative literature has long since ceased to be regarded, except in certain sectarian circles, as a medium of revealed truth, much imaginative literature still functions, where it is seriously read at all, as a form of secular scripture, and the religious questions it raises are just as insistent and vexacious today as they ever were. They simply take a radically different form. The contemporary writer isn't asking what one must do to be saved, but how it is possible to live a life that is recognizably human in a public world all of whose structures and usages are specious or totalitarian or both. The modern intellectual doesn't wonder about how to restore the normative traditions of the past to their former glory, but how to go on thinking at all, as Hannah Arendt suggested, when the ground has been cut away from virtually every one of their foundations. In both instances, the questions have changed but the problem which elicits them remains relatively unchanged. Thus I would be prepared to claim that the only category that is more recurrent than religion in contemporary critical discussion may be the category of language itself. To confirm this, one need only consult such a survey of recent trends in critical theory as Frank Lentricchia's aptly named and ably argued *After the New Criticism*.

Lentricchia begins his overview of critical schools and approaches that have succeeded one another so rapidly in the postwar period with Northrop Frye and his magisterial attempt to overcome the subjectivism of the several variants of Anglo-American formalism by reorganizing the study of literature in terms of what Frye defends as the more scientific structure of myth and archetype. But when literature becomes defined, as it does in Frye's criticism, as displaced myth, myth can be reinterpreted essentially as displaced belief, and then all the imaginative postulates of faith and commitment will seem to acquire their origin, or to derive their justification, as they largely do for Frye, from the Christian Bible, a sacred and not a secular scripture for Frye which, despite its immense complexity and diversity, Frye sees as unified anagogically in the single archetypal image of the Jesus as the Christ.

From Frye and myth criticism Lentricchia then quickly moves to several versions of existentialism, where the category of religion reappears—for example, in the conservative fictionalism of Frank Kermode's *The Sense of an Ending*—as the imaginative quest for an idea of order, or Supreme Fiction, which can console us, at least for the time being, in the present poverty of our experience as inhabitants of a desacralized and openended world.

But almost before Kermode can flesh out the new lineaments of spirituality suggested by this Stevenseque religion of the imagination and its explorations of "the intricate evasions of as," Lentricchia sees it being supplanted by versions of phenomenology in which the category of the religious reappears in the guise of the unifying presence or consciousness of the artist, what we might call the creative cogito, that not only permeates all its expressive creations and makes of them a single act of sovereign intention, but simultaneously compels their interpreter to undertake in response a quasi-religious act of self-effacement.

This version of phenomenology is most often associated with the work of Georges Poulet and also with the earlier writing of J. Hillis Miller who brought Poulet's work, and that of the other Geneva critics, to the attention of many American readers. But it was Martin Heidegger and some of his followers who eventually pushed phenomenology much further. In Heidegger's work and that of his disciples, the category of religion is reintroduced into literary discussion in a way that very nearly swallows it: the work of art is reconceived as an act of revelation itself, an unveiling or *aletheia*, as it is called, which accomplishes, through the presencing of the artist's own consciousness in his forms, a disclosure of the ethos, even the pathos, of Being itself.

But long before phenomenology in any of its several expressions could obtain a secure foothold in America, Lentricchia points out that it was seriously challenged and largely overthrown by a theoretical orientation known as structuralism. Structuralism simply repudiated the phenomenological obsession with the divine or human knower in favor of coming to terms with the deeper structures of experience, primarily semantic and semiotic, underlying it. The structuralists therefore relocated the religious in those elemental linguistic grammars or codes which we use to stabilize our experience by inscribing it, that is to say, by textualizing it, and with the help of which we eventually make sense of such textually inscribed experience by, accordingly, learning how to read it, that is to say, to decipher it.

Yet the hegemony of structuralism could last only so long as critics and scholars didn't question the stability either of the cultural texts so inscribed or of the codes and grammars in which they were written. But once it became clear that all cultural texts are relatively unstable, that all textual codes and grammars are comparatively indeterminate, then structuralism gave way to a more deconstructive concern, as it is usually defined, with what does, or just possibly doesn't, exist not only beneath the structures of consciousness but also beneath the structures that underlie them. Deconstructionists and post-structuralists alike speak of what opens out below such constructs, undermining the epistemological privilege they presuppose, as an abyss of meaning or meaninglessness which can only be reached through critical acts of decentering, dismantling, demystification.

At this point, however, the category of "religion" or "the religious," albeit in negative form, slowly works its way back into criticism again and begins to subsume all others. It does so through the operations of deconstructive criticism itself as they conspire to show how all categories, like all meanings, seem to participate in a process of textual decreation and demolition within the text itself, a process that the critic merely joins rather than engenders, and which moves in the direction of a seemingly ultimate emptiness, an infinite nothingness, an absolute undecipherability. But it is precisely here, in the adjectival modifiers that must almost of necessity be employed to characterize this negative ontological space—"ultimate," "infinite," "absolute"—that this contemporary critical mode, by all appearances most antipathetic to religious concerns, begins to swerve in another direction, a direction not unlike the movement Northrop Frye first detected in advanced modernism itself, the movement from an extreme irony back toward religious myth, the chthonic source.

Taken by themselves, these critical shifts and alterations may attest to no more than the fickleness of modern critical fashion, or the uncertainty and nervousness that attends the practice of contemporary criticism, but in the context of this present discussion, they point to something additional. Whatever is meant by the term, and however it comes into play and affects the outcome of such discourse, the category of religion is no mere superfluity in current critical controversy but one of its principal elements and chief enablers. Even in those most radical and revisionist reconceptions of the critical enterprise, there is an obsession with the problem and possibility to which religion attests: the existence of modalities of experience that are unconditioned either by what is now called the privileges of perception or the predispositions of power. As but one example, let me cite Edward Said's moving and trenchant eulogy for Michel Foucault, the eminent French philosopher who died on June 25th of this year, ironically in the very hospital that had served as both the source and scene for his great study of the science of mental illness as one of the chief regulatory and repressive institutions of modern civilization:

> At the heart of Foucault's work [Said writes] is ... the variously embodied idea that always conveys the sentiment of otherness. For Foucault, otherness is both a force and a feeling *in itself*, something whose seemingly endless metamorphoses his work reflects and shapes. On a manifest level, ... Foucault wrote about deviation and deviants in conflict with society. More interesting, however, was his fascination with everything

> excessive, all those things that stand over and above ideas, description, imitation, or precedent . . . What he was interested in was, as he said in *The Archeology [of Knowledge]*, "the more" that can be discovered lurking in signs and discourses but which is irreducible to language and speech; "it is this 'more,' " he said, that we must reveal and describe (Said:5).

Thus Said concludes by remarking of Foucault's prose, and the same could be noted about the prose of other recent theorists, that the "Dislocations, . . . the dizzying and physically powerful prose, the uncanny ability to invent whole fields of investigation: these come from Foucault's everlasting effort to formulate otherness and heterodoxy without domesticating them or turning them into doctrine" (Said:5–6).

By quoting this long passage on Foucault, I do not wish to be misunderstood as building a covert case for a kind of critical reflection about which, as it happens, I possess some very strong reservations; nor do I wish to be interpreted as implying that the future prospects for the literary and cultural study of religion depend upon following the lines of intellectual inquiry laid down by post-structuralism. What I do mean to suggest is that all the recent forms of critical inquiry, from archetypal criticism to deconstruction, have shared in common a desire not simply to interpret otherness but, through such Midrashic exertions, to keep the sentiment or imagination of it alive. And they have done so, I would submit, because of a widely felt but deeply troubling apprehension, reflected alike in the most searching thought as well as disturbing art of our time, that the idea of the other, like the experience of otherness, may be the most serious casualty of modern life itself.

This is not the place to attempt to defend such an assertion; here I can only pause long enough to consider some of its implications for my present topic. At the most obvious level of things, I am saying that theories, in the case, of literature and criticism, participate in wider forums of experience, in deeper strata of feeling, of which they are sometimes only partially conscious but which they nonetheless work not only to refract but also to reinforce or to revise. On a less obvious level, I am suggesting that these wider forums of experience, these deeper strata of feeling, not only encompass much of what we usually mean by religion in its cultural expressions but actually comprise it. To argue this is not only to make the, by now, relatively innocuous observation that religion, however its priorities are defined, is but one cultural form among others; it is also to insist that from a cultural perspective religion is indistinguishable from the actual experience through which the forms of its priority are lived. Such a conception of the relation between religion and culture is far from novel, but the future prospects for the literary and cultural study of religion depend on its broader acceptance. More specifically, they depend on a considerable advance in our understanding of what cultures consist of and of how they change.

Social anthropologists like Clifford Geertz and social critics like Kenneth Burke have already made considerable headway in clarifying our notions about the nature of culture and its primary offices. Culture for Geertz consists of systems of symbolic meaning which serve an essentially functional or heuristic purpose. Designed as they are instrumentally, these systems help us survive our contacts with the environment, with the world around us, by interpreting them, that is, by translating them into construable signs so that we can not only better negotiate these relationships but also so that we can add the experience of others to our own.

One of the points that has been noted about such systems by Geertz, Hayden White, and many others is that they arrange their symbolic interpretations not only horizontally but also vertically, assigning to each a somewhat different value or quality in the general scheme of things. Thus to experience the world or life in terms of the signs or symbol systems of which cultures are composed is, essentially, to experience the hierarchies of significance in relation to which they organize the various components of life or reality. A second point to be noted about such systems is that they very often possess only a tangential relationship to the social patterns they are devised to comprehend and often to legitimate. Geertz explains this by saying that if culture and society are mutually interdependent, they nonetheless remain independently variable. By this he means that if the systems of meanings that comprise culture are in continuous interaction with the patterns of action that compose society, culture and society still operate according to distinctive principles of organization and therefore exhibit a tendency to move in different, sometimes even opposed or contrary directions. Cultures are integrated in terms of logico-meaningful relations, societies organized in terms of causal-functional relations, and this explains for Geertz the frequent incidence of discontinuity and disjunction between them.

But this formulation seems to leave unanswered the question so often raised in cultural study: namely, how culture and society can so consistently influence one another even when they are moving in different if not conflicting directions? In fact, it tends to remove cultural meanings from the sphere of social influence altogether, and just at a time when in the study of so many contemporary cultural forms we have come to realize how culture itself contributes to social processes, how, indeed, cultural meanings and values are often among the most important elements of social production itself.

Here is where the work of social theorists like Raymond Williams, Arnold Hauser, Marshall Sahlins, and Theodor Adorno has proved so helpful. What they have repudiated is the notion that cultural meanings can be studied in the abstract—either as belonging to a realm of absolute or universal values, or as related to a body of material in which human thought and experience have been specifically recorded, or in terms of the social patterns and institutional structures in which a particular way of life has been essentialized. Any adequate analysis of culture, they argue, requires detailed study not just of each one of these various elements but of the active relationships among them, will, in short, attempt to discover the nature of the organization "which is the complex of these relationships." But Williams has been particularly insistent that cultural study should not be restricted solely to the nature or principle of the organization as such, but to the nature or principle of the organization *as experienced*—"the particular living result of all the elements in the general organization." This "living result," according to Williams, will be expressed in what he calls "a structure of feeling," which is simply another term for "meanings and values as actually lived," the "affective elements of consciousness and their relationships"(1966:48).

For Williams and many other radical social and cultural theorists, from Antonio Gramsci to Frank Lentricchia, the singlemost important clue to the way these affective elements combine to furnish an experience of the interaction, even symbiosis, of culture and society is provided by the notion of hegemony. Hegemony simply refers to the lived system of meanings and values in any culture which become reciprocally confirming the more they are experienced as practices. Another way of putting this would be to say that hegemony projects a view of culture as the lived domination and subordination of particular concerns which are not always associated with, but are never wholly dissociated from, the hierarchies of significant values that not only differentiate one class or group from another but often serve the interests of some at the expense of the interests of others. To introduce the concept of hegemony into cultural study is not, as many of its detractors maintain, to reduce cultural study to another form of political science but rather to compel students of culture to raise new questions about what might be called its politics of organization. For what the introduction of the concept of hegemony does is to remind us that cultural meanings, however protected their status in enclaves of sacerdotal privilege, cannot be divorced from "the whole lived social process as practically organized by specific and dominant meanings and values" (Williams, 1977a:109).

But this, in turn, leads to my final point, and a point that I think needs most careful consideration for those interested in prospects for the future literary and cultural study of religion. Where do we find expressed the actual experience through which a culture's felt sense of hierarchical significance, of religious significance, is actually lived? If we are not ourselves among the carriers of that felt sense of life, carriers to the extent that our own capacities for communication, like that of all other members of this culture, are dependent upon the affective structures of signification that comprise it, then we must resort to the recorded culture of that time or place, a culture which is composed of everything from imaginative constructions to material facts. Unlike culture that is lived, cultures that are recorded are represented chiefly in the form of a selective tradition that has become dominant. The tradition is selective inasmuch as it remains a restriction and even truncation of the whole funded inheritance of experience. The tradition is dominant inasmuch as this selected form of the cultural inheritance constitutes that part of it which remains hegemonically meaningful, that part of the past culture which continues to live as a social process arranged in behalf of the promotion of specific meanings and values.

It is worth noting that we do not have to accept the Marxist view that the interests served by these meanings and values are necessarily economic to perceive that the maintenance of the selective tradition they compose still benefits some social collectivities at the expense of others. It is also worth observing that we do not need to accept the Nietzschean assumption that all action reduces to the will to power to appreciate the fact that the meaning of this selective tradition, at least for those who claim it as their own, can be described as the experience, through its instrumentalities, of the benefits associated with such processes of dominance and subordination.

But the selective traditions by which the recorded life of cultures is kept interpretively available for social use are always in the process of change. These changes come from other cultural formations which challenge their range of governance. One kind of formation, which we can call residual, refers to earlier or different phases of living which remain latent in the present but still active, and the more active when the currently dominant selective tradition fails to represent fully or adequately those meanings and values associated with residual traditions. The other kind of cultural formation which exerts pressures on the current selective tradition and lends complexity to the quality of its dominance can be designated the emergent and, in many cases, even pre-emergent, where, as Raymond Williams has written, "the recognition of new experience, new possible practices, new relations and possible relations, is apprehended but not yet articulated" (1977b:34). Thus to satisfactorily comprehend the dominant selective tradition that is operative in any culture and effective in any society at any given moment and place involves, necessarily, coming to terms with its felt relations both with formations that are residual and also with formations that are emergent. To understand the configuration of these elements in all the tensions of their relations may never suffice to provide us with an adequate understanding of any people and their traditions, ecclesiastical or otherwise, and it will certainly not put us in the same position occupied by those people whose cultural experience was essentially comprised of nothing but the felt sense of these particular tensions; but an understanding of the configuration of these elements in their contextual tensions can bring us as close as it is possible to get to fathoming something no less essential, something essential if not to the indispensability of religion, at least to our solidarity as human beings: it can help us to discover what creates any particular people out of a group of disparate and diverse individuals and enables them to share on the plane of experience what they have never necessarily undergone together in the realm of action or perceived together in the realm of ideas. This kind of knowledge is extremely hard to come by, and if it now seems indispensable to the study of religion, this is no doubt in part because it seems all the more indispensable to our survival as a species.

WORKS CONSULTED

Adorno, Theodor W
      1973   *Negative Dialectics*. Trans. by E. B. Ashton. New York: Seabury Press.

Dewey, John
      1929   *Experience and Nature*. 2d ed. La Salle, Illinois: The Open Court Publishing Company.

Geertz, Clifford
      1973   *The Interpretation of Cultures*. New York: Basic Books.

Hauser, Arnold
      1982   *The Sociology of Art*. Trans. by Kenneth J. Northcott. Chicago and London: The University of Chicago Press.

Rorty, Richard J.
      1982   *Consequences of Pragmatism*. Minneapolis: The University of Minnesota Press.

Sahlins, Marshall
   1976   *Culture and Practical Reason*. Chicago and London: The
                 University of Chicago Press.

Said, Edward W.
   1985   "Michel Foucault, 1927–1984," *Raritan Review*, 2/4
                 (Winter).

White, Hayden
   1978   *Tropics of Discourse*. Baltimore and London: The Johns
                 Hopkins University Press.

Williams, Raymond
   1966   *The Long Revolution*. New York: Harper Torchbooks.
   1977a   *Marxism and Literature*. London: Oxford University
                 Press.
   1977b   "Literature in Society." In *Contemporary Approaches to
                 English Studies*. Ed. by Hilda Schiff. New York: Barnes
                 and Noble Books.

EVIL, A CHALLENGE TO PHILOSOPHY AND THEOLOGY

PAUL RICOEUR*

That both philosophy and theology encounter evil as a *challenge* unlike any other, the greatest thinkers in both these disciplines are willing to admit. What is important is the way in which this challenge, or this failure, is received: do we find an invitation to think less about the problem or a provocation to think more, or to think differently about it?

What the problem of evil calls into question is a way of thinking submitted to the requirements of logical coherence, that is, one submitted to both the rule of non-contradiction and that of systematic totalization. It is this way of thinking that has prevailed in all attempts at a theodicy, in the strict sense of this term, and which however diverse they may be in their responses, all agree in defining the problem as follows. How can we affirm at the same time, without any contradiction, the following three propositions: God is all powerful; God is absolutely good; yet evil exists? Theodicies, in this sense, appear to be a battle for the sake of coherence, in response to the objection that only two of the three stated propositions are compatible, not all three at once. However, what is assumed by this way of posing the problem is never called into question, namely, the propositional form itself in which the terms of the problem are stated, along with the rule of coherence which any solution it is presupposed must satisfy.

In order to demonstrate the limited and relative character of this way of posing the problem, we need first of all to get some sense of the scope and the complexity of the problem with the help of a phenomenology of the experience of evil, secondly to traverse the levels of

*John Nuveen Professor (Emeritus) and Member of the Committee on Social Thought at the University of Chicago and Dean of the Faculty of Letters and Human Sciences and Professor of Philosophy (Emeritus) at the University of Paris X (Nanterre), Dr. Ricoeur presented this paper as a Plenary Address to the 75th Anniversary Annual Meeting of the American Academy of Religion (1984).

discourse taken by speculation on the origin and the *raison d'etre* of evil, so as to be able thirdly to reconnect the work of thinking, arising out of the enigma of evil, to other responses stemming from action and feeling.

I. Between Blame and Lament

The whole enigma of evil may be said to lie in the fact that, at least in the traditions of the West, we put under the same terms such different phenomena as sin, suffering, and death. However, evil as wrongdoing and evil as suffering belong to two heterogenous categories, that of blame and that of lament.

There is blame where a human action held to be a violation of the prevailing code of conduct is declared guilty and worthy of being punished. There is lament where some suffering is undergone. We do not make it happen, it befalls us. Being an effect, it may be related to a variety of causes—the adversity of physical nature, illness, the infirmities of body or mind, or affliction produced by the death of loved ones, the perspective of our own mortality, affronts to our dignity, and so on. Lament, therefore occurs as the opposite of blame; whereas blame make culprits of us, lament reveals us as victims.

What then invites philosophy and theology to think of evil as the common root of both sin and suffering, in spite of this undeniable polarity of blame and lament? The first motive lies in the extraordinary way in which these two phenomena are intertwined. On the one hand, punishment is a form of physical and psychical suffering, whether it involves corporal punishment, some deprivation of liberty, shame, or humiliation. This may be why we speak of guilt itself as *poena*, that is, as a "pain", a term that bridges the gap between evil committed and evil undergone. On the other hand, one principal cause of suffering is the violence human beings do to one another. In fact, to do evil is always, either directly or indirectly, to make someone else suffer. In its dialogical structure evil committed by someone finds its other half in the evil suffered by someone else. It is at this major point of intersection that the cry of lamentation is most sharp.

We are led a step further in the direction of a unique mystery of iniquity by the presentiment that sin, suffering, and death express in different ways the human condition in its deepest unity. Two indications in the experience of evil point toward this underlying unity of the human condition. On the side of moral evil, first, the experience of guilt entails, as its dark side, the feeling of having been seduced by overwhelming powers and, consequently, our feeling of belonging to a history of evil, which is always already there for everyone. This strange experience of passivity, at the very heart of evil doing, makes us feel ourselves to be victims in the very act that makes us guilty. This same blurring of the boundaries between guilt and being a victim can also be observed if we start from the other pole. Since punishment is a form of suffering allegedly deserved, who knows whether all suffering is not in one way or another the punishment for some personal or collective fault, either known or unknown? It is this dark background of both guilt and suffering that makes evil such a unique enigma.

II. Levels of Discourse in Speculation on Evil

We may not turn toward theodicies properly speaking, subject to the rules of non-contradiction and systematic totality, without having first passed through a number of levels of discourse in which we may discern an increasing order of rationality. I will consider three stages of discourse—myth, wisdom, and gnosis—as leading to the level of rational theodicies.

1. The Stage of Myth

Myth constitutes the first major transition from experience to language in several ways. In the first place, the ambivalence of the Sacred, as described by Rudolf Otto, confers on myth the power to assume both the dark and the luminous sides of the human condition. Next, myths incorporate our fragmentary experience of evil into those great narratives of origin, as Mircea Eliade has emphasized throughout his many works on this topic. By telling how the world began, a myth tells how the human condition came about as something generally wretched and miserable. But myth's function of providing order, thanks to its cosmological import, has as its corollary—and its corrective—the profusion of explanatory schemes it has produced over time. The realm of myth, as the literature of the Ancient Near East, India, and the Far East reveals, is a vast field of experimentation, or even of playing with hypotheses in the most varied and the most fantastic forms. Within this immense laboratory, it appears as though no conceivable solution to the order of the whole cosmos, and hence to the enigma of evil, has not been essayed at some point or another. These solutions oscillate between the level of legends and folklore, close to the demonic dimension of the experience of evil, and that of metaphysical speculation, exemplified by so many Hindu and Buddist documents. The counterpart of this tremendous contribution of mythical thought to speculation on evil is that one is ceaselessly brought back to the question of origin: *From whence comes evil?* Rational theodicies will get caught up in this search for an origin, which may finally be a blind alley.

2. The Stage of Wisdom

Can myth fully answer the expectations of acting and suffering human beings? Only partially, inasmuch as it does respond to a form of questioning that is inherent in the very form of the lamentation: "How long?" "Why?" To this interrogation, however, myth brings only the consolation of order, by situating the supplicant's complaint within a more encompassing framework. But it leaves unanswered one important part of the question, which is not just "Why?" but "Why me?" Here the lament turns into an actual complaint. It demands that divinity account for itself. In the biblical realm, for example, one of the important implications of the Covenant is that it adds to the dimension of partnership that of a lawsuit or legal process. If God brings a case against his people, the same may be said about their relation to God.

With this insight, myth has to change registers. It must not only narrate the origins, in order to explain how the original human condition reached its present state, it also has to explain why such is the case for each and every one of us. This shift leads us from myth to the stage of Wisdom. Myth narrates, Wisdom agrues.

The first and most tenacious of the explanations offered by Wisdom is, of course, that of retribution. All suffering is deserved because it is the punishment for some individual or collective sin, known or unknown. This is the stance taken, for example, by the deuteronomist school of historiography and superimposed onto the great traditions of the preexilic times. That the sages should argue against this dogma is easy to forecast. As soon as there are judiciary systems that attempt to apportion pain in terms of degrees of guilt, the very notion of retribution loses its spell. The actual apportioning of misfortune can only appear as arbitrary, indiscriminate, and dispro-portionate. Why did this person die of cancer and not that one? Why do children die? Why is there *so much* suffering, *far beyond* ordinary mortals' capacity for suffering?

If the book of Job holds the place it does in world literature, it is first of all because it provides us with a "classic" of this argumentative mode of wisdom. It is also because of the enigmatic and perhaps even deliberately ambiguous character of its conclusion. The final theophany brings no direct answer to Job's personal suffering, and speculation is left to pursue more than one direction. The vision of a creator whose designs are unfathomable may suggest either consola-tion that has to be deferred until the eschaton, or that Job's complaint is displaced, even set aside, in God's eyes, as the master of good and evil, following Isaiah 45:7 ("I form light and create darkness, I make weal and create woe, I am the Lord, who does all these things"), or that perhaps the complaint itself has to go through one of the purificatory tests I shall return to in concluding in order that Job should become able to love God "for nought" in response to Satan's wager at the beginning of the tale.

For the time being, let us leave open these questions and follow further the line of speculation begun by wisdom.

3. The Stage of Gnosis and of Anti-Gnostic Gnosis

Thinking would not have moved on from wisdom to theodicy if gnosticism had not elevated speculation to the level of a gigantomachy, where the forces of good are engaged in a merciless struggle with the armies of evil, in order to bring about a final deliverance of all the particles of light held captive by the shadows of evil. From this perspective, we may say that Western thought is in debt to gnosticism, broadly conceived, for having conceived the problem of evil in terms of one all-encompassing problematic: *Unde malum?* But even more important is the inclusion of philosophical categories in the speculation on evil set forth by Augustine in his fight against the tragic vision of this gnosis. From Neo-Platonist philosophers Augustine takes the idea that evil cannot be held to be a *substance*, because to think of being is to think of something one, intelligible, and good. Hence it is philosophical thought that excludes every phantasy of evil as substantial. In return, a new idea of *nothingness* comes to light, that of the *ex nihilo* contained in the idea of a total and complete creation, and associated with it, the idea of an ontic distance between the creator and the creature, therefore of the "deficiency" pertaining to creatures as such. In virtue of this deficiency, it becomes comprehensible that creatures endowed with a free will could "turn away" from God and "toward" what has less being, toward nothingness.

This first feature of the Augustinian doctrine should be acknowledged for what it is, namely, the conjunction of ontology and theology in a new type of discourse, that of *onto-theo-logy*.

The most important corollary of this negating of the substantiality of evil is that the confession of evil grounds an exclusively moral vision of evil. If the question *"unde malum?"* loses all ontological meaning, the question that replaces it—*unde malum faciamus?* (from whence comes wrongdoing?)—shifts the problem of evil into the sphere of action, of willing, of free will. Sin introduces a distinct case here, a *nihil privativum*, entirely brought about by the fall, whether this refers to human beings or to higher creatures such as the angels. For this form of nothingness, there is no need to search for a cause anywhere other than in a bad will. Augustine's *Contra Fortunatum* draws from this moral vision of evil the conclusion that most concerns us here, namely, that all evil is either *peccatum* or *poena*, either sin or pain considered as punishment. This purely moral vision of evil leads in turn to a penal vision of history. No soul is unjustly thrown into misfortune. Only divine grace may interrupt the curse of punishment.

The price to pay for the coherence of this doctrine is an enormous one, and its magnitude was to appear on the occasion of Augustine's anti-Pelagian quarrel. In order to make credible the idea that all suffering, however unjustly apportioned or however excessive it may be, is a retribution for sin, it was necessary to give the concept of sin a supra-individual, historical, and even generic dimension, which led to the doctrine of original sin or of a sinful nature. I shall not retrace here the stages of its constitution, which include a literal interpretation of Genesis 3 augmented by an emphasis on Romans 5:12–19, a justification for the baptism of infants, and so forth. Instead allow me to underscore the epistemological status of this dogmatic proposition about original sin. In one sense, it does take up one fundamental aspect of the experience of evil, namely, the both individual and communal sense of human impotence in the face of the demonic power of evil already there, long before any bad initiative may be assigned to some deliberate intention. However this enigma of the power of evil already there is set within the false clarity of an apparently rational explanation. By conjoining within the concept of a sinful nature the two heterogeneous notions of a biological transmission through generation and an individual imputation of guilt, the notion of original sin appears as a quasi-concept that we may assign to an anti-gnostic gnosis. The previous content of this gnosis is denied but the form of its discourse is reconstituted, that of a rationalized myth. As for suffering, which remains the leading thread in my presentation, the failure of this discourse on original sin is a double one. Besides the conceptual inconsistency just referred to, it leaves unanswered the protest of unjust suffering, by condemning it to silence in the name of a massive indictment of the whole of humanity.

4. The Stage of Theodicy

We only have the right to speak of theodicy as such (1) when the *statement* of the problem of evil rests upon propositions intended to be univocal, which is the case of the three assertions usually considered: God is all-powerful; God's goodness is infinite; evil exists. (2) When the *goal* of the argumentation is clearly apologetic: God is not responsible for evil. And (3) when the *means* used are supposed to satisfy the logic of non-contradiction and of systematic totalization. These conditions were only fulfilled within the framework of onto-theology, which joined terms borrowed from religious discourse, principally "God," and terms stemming from metaphysics, whether Platonic or Cartesian, to cite only two examples, such as being, nothingness, first cause, finality, infinite, finite, etc. Theodicy, in this strict sense, is the brightest jewel of onto-theology.

And in this regard, Leibniz's *Theodicy* remains the prime examples of the genre. On the one hand, all the forms of evil, not just moral evil, are taken into consideration and put under the title "metaphysical evil," which is the unavoidable defect of all created being, if it is true that God cannot create another God. On the other hand, classical logic receives an enrichment through the addition to the principle of non-contradiction of the principle of sufficient reason, which is presented as the principle of the best, as soon as we agree that creation stems from a competition in the divine understanding between a multiplicity of world models of which only one includes the maximum of perfections and the minimum of defects. This notion of the best of all possible worlds, so scoffed at by Voltaire in *Candide* following the disaster of the Lisbon earthquake, cannot be understood so long as we have not grasped its rationale, that is, the calculation of the maximum and minimum, of which *our* world is the result. It is in this way that the principle of sufficient reason can fill the gap between logical possibility—that is, what is not unthinkable—and contingency—that is, what could have happened differently.

The failure of the *Theodicy* results from the fact that a finite understanding will be unable to reach the evidence for this guaranteeing calculation, only being able to gather together the few signs for the excess of perfections over imperfections in the balance of good and evil. Therefore a robust human optimism is required in order to affirm that the final sum is unequivocally positive. But since we only ever have the small change of this principle of the best, we have to content ourselves with its aesthetic corollary, in virtue of which the contrast between the negative and the positive works for the harmony of the whole. It is just this claim to establish a positive total for the weighing of good and bad on the basis of a quasi-aesthetics that fails as soon as we are confronted with misfortunes whose excesses cannot be compensated for by any known perfection. Once again it is the lament, the complaint of the suffering righteous person or people that overthrows the notion of a compensation for evil by good, just as was the case with the idea of retribution.

The sharpest, although not fatal, blow to the idea of a theodicy, however, has to be the one Kant leveled against the very basis of the onto-theological discourse upon which all theodicies are constructed, from Augustine to Leibniz. Kant's implacable dismantling of rational theology in the Dialectic of his *Critique of Pure Reason* is well known. Once deprived of its ontological support, theodicy falls under the rubric of "transcendental illusion." This is not to say that the problem of evil disappears from the philosophical scene, however. Quite the contrary, in fact. But it now refers uniquely to the *practical* sphere, as that which ought not to be and which action must struggle against. This shift from the theoretical to the practical sphere of reason will provide us later with the needed transition to the last stage of my presentation, dealing with the connection between thought, action, and feeling.

Before reaching this last stage of our journey, however, I need to say at least a few words about a mode of thinking that claims to overcome both the shortcomings of the pre-Kantian theodicies and the Kantian critique of rational theology: the dialectical one. By a dialectical mode of thinking I mean an attempt to use negativity as the dynamic principle of a thought that would no longer be equated with knowledge, where knowledge is understood as a subject-object correlation.

I will use Hegel and Barth as two exemplary exponents of such dialectical thinking; Hegel being the paradigm of a conclusive dialectic, Barth the paradigm of an inconclusive, even a broken dialectic.

With Hegel we try to think more, with Barth to think differently.

For Hegel the dialectic is that of the Spirit that makes the difference between God and the human mind irrelevant, for Barth the dialectic deepens the gap between the wholly other and the world of creatures. For both of them, however, the "thought-work" leads to failure, yet to a productive failure, if I may dare put it this way. I mean, their thought leads to an aporia that calls for integration into a larger dialectic, that of thought, action, and feeling.

Thinking more with Hegel means following the painful but victorious "work of the negative" from the sphere of logic to that of Nature and of Spirit, and within the sphere of Spirit from the subjective, to the objective, and finally to the absolute Spirit. On every level, negativity is what constrains each figure of the Spirit to invert itself into its contrary and to engender a new figure that both surpasses and preserves the preceding one, in the twofold sense of the Hegelian concept of *Aufhebung*. This conclusive dialectic makes the tragic and the logical coincide at every stage. Something must die so that something greater may be born. In this sense, misfortune is everywhere, but everwhere it is surpassed, to the extent that reconciliation always wins out over what is torn apart.

The question is whether this triumphant dialectic does not reconstitute, with logical resources unavailable to Leibniz, another form of optimism issuing from the same audacity, with perhaps an even greater rational *hubris*. Indeed, what fate is reserved for the suffering of victims in a worldview where the pan-tragic is constantly covered over by a pan-logicism? We may say that the scandal of suffering is overlooked in two ways. First, it is diluted and defused by the very expansion of negativity beyond the human predicament. Second, it is silenced by the substitution of reconciliation (of contradictions) for consolation addressed to human beings as victims. The famous motto of the "cunning of reason" in the Introduction to the *Lectures on the Philosophy of History* is the well known stumbling block of this post-Kantian theodicy.

The irony of the Hegelian philosophy of history lies in the fact that, assuming that it does give a meaning to the great currents of history, an assumption that is not at issue here, it does so to the extent that it abolishes the question of happiness and unhappiness. History, it is said, is not "the soil in which happiness grows."[1] But if the great actors in history are frustrated as concerns happiness by history, which makes use of them, what are we to say about its anonymous victims? For we who read Hegel after the catastrophes and the sufferings beyond number of our century, the dissociation that his philosophy of history brings about between consolation and reconciliation has become, to say the least, a source of great perplexity. The more the system flourishes, the more its victims are marginalized. The success of the system is its failure. Suffering, as what is expressed by the voices of lamentation, is what the system excludes.

Will a broken dialectic—that of Karl Barth—do better justice to the phenomenon of victimization than the victorious dialectic of Hegel? Up to a certain point, yes. But beyond it, no. Up to what point? To the point when it acknowledges its broken condition as irretrievable.

The famous section of the *Church Dogmatics* entitled "God and Nothingness"—translating the strong German [*Gott und das Nichtige*] (E.T. vol. III, Part 3, #50, pp. 289–369)—may be assigned to a "broken" theology, to the extent that it sees in evil a reality that is not commensurate with the goodness of God and of creation, and furthermore a reality that is not reducible to the negative side of human experience, which was the only one taken into account by Leibniz and Hegel. Instead we are to think of a nothingness hostile to God, not just a nothingness of deficiency and privation, but one of corruption and destruction. In this way we do justice to the protest of suffering humanity that refuses to allow itself to be included within the cycle of moral evil in terms of the doctrine of retribution, or even to allow itself to be enrolled under the banner of providence, another name for the goodness of creation. Nevertheless we may say that we

---

[1] G. W. F. Hegel, *Lectures on the Philosophy of World History, Introductions: Reason in History.* Trans. by H. B. Nisbet. (Cambridge: Cambridge University Press, 1975), p. 79.

"know" the reality of evil, to the extent that we confess that nothingness is what Christ has vanquished by "nilhilating" himself on the Cross, and also that God met and struggled with this nothingness in Jesus the Christ. This "christological turn" given to the problem of evil is one of the paradigmatic ways of thinking more about evil by thinking differently. I would not say that the christological turn as such constitutes a breach of the pledge no longer to return to the conciliatory mood of pre-Kantian and post-Kantian theodicies, although I would feel more comfortable with the method of correlation applied to both Christian symbols *and* human experience by Paul Tillich, Langdon Gilkey, and David Tracy. The breach, to my mind occurs when Barth relates the reality of nothingness to the "left hand of God," the one which rejects when the right hand elects: "As God is Lord on the left hand as well, He is the basis and Lord of nothingness too" (p. 351).

Can this coordination without conciliation between God's left and right hands make sense? If it is not a covert concession to the failed theodicies of the past and accordingly a weak compromise substituted for a broken dialectic, does it not reopen the way to speculations such as those of Giordano Bruno and Schelling on the demonic aspect of the deity? Paul Tillich was not afraid to take up this issue that Barth both so encouraged and so refused. But how then does thinking guard itself against the drunken excesses that Kant denounced with the term *Schwärmerei*, which includes both the sense of enthusiasm and mystical madness?

Did not wisdom already encounter this *aporetic* aspect of thinking about evil, an aporetic aspect opened up by the very effort of thinking more and differently? With this open question my second part comes to an end.

III. Thinking, Acting, and Feeling With Regard to Evil

On the level of theoretical thinking the problem of evil remains a challenge that is never completely overcome. In this sense, we may speak of a failure of pure speculation. Yet this failure has never led to a sheer capitulation of thought, but rather to untiring refinement in speculative logic, under the prodding of the question "Why?"—"Why me?"—raised by the lament of victims. Hegel's triumphant dialectic and Barth's broken one are both instructive in this regard. The initial enigma is elevated to the rank of a terminal aporia by the very work of thinking that finally fails.

It is to this aporia that action and the catharsis of feelings and emotions are called upon not to give a solution but a response, a response able to render the aporia productive.

A turn from theory to practice was already initiated by Kant, as I have said. But this turn is not a turning away from thought. Instead it is the continuation on another plane of thought's interminable work. One symptom of this may be found in the meditation on radical evil with which Kant's *Religion Within the Bounds of Reason Alone* opens. This meditation by itself is sufficient to prove that practical reason has its own way of failing and of bordering on mystery when it comes to the question of evil. If we may think in conceptual terms of radical evil as the supreme maxim that grounds all the bad maxims of our free will the *raison d'etre* of this radical evil is inscrutable (*unerforschbar*): "there is then for us," Kant says, "no conceivable ground from which the moral evil in us could originally have come."[2] Along with Karl Jaspers, I admire this ultimate avowal on Kant's part. Like Augustine, and also perhaps like mythical thought, Kant caught sight of the demonic aspect of the ground of human freedom, yet he did so with the sobriety of a thinking always careful not to transgress the limits of knowledge.

Keeping in mind this transfer of the aporia from the sphere of theory to that of practice, we may nevertheless speak of the response of action to the challenge of evil.

For action, evil is above all what ought not to be, but what must be fought against. In this sense, action inverts the orientation of looking at the world. Myth tends to pull speculative thought back toward the origin of things. From whence comes evil, it asks. The response, not the solution, of action is to act against evil. Our vision is thus turned toward the future, by the idea of a *task* to be accomplished, which corresponds to that of an origin to be discovered.

But we should not assume that by placing the accent on the practical struggle against evil we have once again lost sight of suffering. To the contrary. All evil committed by one person, we have seen, is evil undergone by another person. To do evil is to make another person suffer. Violence, in this sense, constantly recreates the unity of moral evil and suffering. Hence, any action, whether ethical or political, that diminishes the quantity of violence exercised by some human beings over against other human beings diminishes the amount of suffering in the world. If we were to remove the suffering inflicted by people on other people, we would see what remained of suffering in the world, but to tell the truth, we have no idea of what this would be, to such an extent does human violence impregnate suffering.

But I readily concede that action alone is not enough. The

---

[2] Immanuel Kant, *Religion Within the Limits of Reason Alone*. Trans. by Theodore M. Greene and Hoyt H. Hudson. (New York: Harper Torchbooks, 1960), p. 38.

arbitrary and indiscriminate way in which suffering is apportioned whether by violence or by the ultimate part of suffering which cannot be ascribed to human interaction-illness, old age, or death-keeps rekindling the old questions: not just "Why?" but "Why me?" "Why my beloved child?"

The emotional response that the practical one calls forth as its necessary complement cannot be anything other than a catharsis of the emotions that nourish the lament and that transform it into complaint. I will take as my model for this transmutation of the lament the "work of mourning," as Freud describes it in his famous essay "Mourning and Melancolia." Mourning, Freud tells us, is a step by step letting go of all the attachments, cathexses, investments, that make us feel the loss of a loved object as a loss of our very own self. This detachment that Freud calls the work of mourning makes us free again for new affective attachments or investments.

What I should like to do is to consider Wisdom, with its philosophical and theological prolongations, as a spiritual help in this work of mourning, aimed at a qualitative change in the lament and the complaint. The itinerary I will briefly describe in no way claims to be exemplary in all regards. It only represents one of the possible paths by which thought, action, and feeling may venture forth together.

The first way of making the intellectual aporia productive is to integrate the ignorance it gives rise to, the *docta ignorantia*, into the work of mourning. To the tendency of survivors to feel guilty about the death of someone they loved, as well as to the tendency of victims to blame themselves and to enter into the cruel game of the expiatory victim, we must reply: "No, God did not want that, even less did God want to punish you. I don't know why things happened as they did, chance and accident are part of the world."[3] This would be the zero degree, so to speak, in the catharsis of the complaint.

A second stage in the catharsis of the lament is to allow it to develop into a complaint against God. This is the way taken by the work of Elie Wiesel. The very relationship of the Covenant, to the extent that it is a mutual action that God and human beings bring against one another, invites us to pursue this course, even to the point of articulating a "theology of protest," such as that suggested by John K. Roth in his *Encountering Evil.*[4] What one protests against is the idea of divine "permission," which remains the expedient of every theodicy and which Barth himself tried to rethink when he distinguished between the victory already won over evil and the full

---

[3] In this regard, the little book by Rabbi Harold S. Kusner, *When Bad Things Happen to Good People* (New York: Schocken Books, 1981), can be a useful pastoral aid in some cases.

[4] John K. Roth, *Encountering Evil* (Richmond: John Knox Press, 1981).

manifestation of this victory. Our accusation against God is here the impatience of hope. It has its origin in the cry of the psalmist, "How long O Lord?"

A third stage in the catharsis of the lament is to discover that the reasons for believing in God have nothing in common with the need to explain the origin of suffering. Suffering is only a scandal for the person who understands God to be the source of everything that is good in creation, including our indignation against evil, our courage to bear it, and our feeling of sympathy toward victims. In other words, we believe in God *in spite* of evil. To believe in God *in spite of . . .* is one of the ways in which we can integrate the speculative aporia into the work of mourning.

Beyond this threshold, a few sages advance along the path that leads to a complete renouncing of any and all complaint about evil. Some even reach the point of discerning in suffering some educative and purgative value. But we should immediately add that this meaning should not become the object of a specific teaching; it can only be found or rediscovered in each specific case. And there is a legitimate pastoral concern that this meaning taken up by a victim not lead him or her back along the route of self-accusation or self-destruction.

Some people, still more advanced as regards this path of renouncing complaining, find a consolation without any parallel in the idea that God too suffers and that the Covenant, beyond its conflictual aspects, for Christians, culminates in a partnership in the suffering of Christ. But the theology of the cross, that is, the theology that holds that God died in Christ, remains meaningless without a corresponding transformation of our lament. The horizon toward which this wisdom is directed seems to me to be a renouncement of those very desires the wounding of which engenders our complaint. This is a renouncement, first of all, of the desire to be spared of all suffering. Next it is a renouncement of the infantile component of the desire for immortality, one which allows us to accept our own death as one aspect of that part of the negative that Karl Barth so carefully distinguished from aggressive nothingness, *das Nichtige.* A similar wisdom is perhaps indicated at the end of the book of Job when it is said that Job came to love God for nought, thereby making Satan lose his bet. To love God for nought is to escape completely the cycle of retribution to which the lamentation still remains captive, so long as the victim bemoans the injustice of his or her fate.

Perhaps this horizon of wisdom, at least as it appears in the West under the influence of Judaism and Christianity, overlaps the horizon of Buddhist wisdom at a significant crossing point which only a long dialog between them could make more conspicuous. . . .

However, I do not want to separate these individual experiences of wisdom from the ethical and political struggle against evil that may bring together all people of good will. In relation to this struggle, these experiences are, like all acts of non-violent resistance, anticipations in the form of parables of a human condition where, such violence having been suppressed, the enigma of real violence will be revealed.

Translated by David Pellauer

TO BE *AND* NOT TO BE:
SIT AUTEM SERMO (LÓGOS) VESTER,
EST, EST; NON, NON . . .

RAY L. HART*

All the new thinking is about loss.
In this it resembles all the old thinking.
. . . There are moments when the body is as numinous
as words, days that are the good flesh continuing.[1]

What follows is a theme that has sought me, not I it. As human existence in large measure is a passion of the Not, so it is in even larger measure a passion for evading the Not.[2] But the Not can be as little evaded
as it can be sought, and to be found of it in its revealing is at once to be
distanced from it afresh in its re-veiling. The life of the spirit inhabits
the discrepancy between language and existence, and that spirit reaches
its deepest crisis when language is so stressed against its limits as to be
self-subverting, when one speaks, aspires to speak, the unspeakable. Said
Goethe, ". . . there are . . . cases . . . in which we are obliged . . . rather
to write nothing than not to write."[3] The Not is such a case, is perhaps
its cardinal instance. I am sooner obliged to a speech that risks saying
nothing about the Not than not to speak.

In such an enterprise one prays to be defended against the delusions
of an inherited clarity, the blessing and the curse of tradition. One
would hope for *analysis* in Hegel's sense, to rid an idea of the form in
which it had become familiar. That would take the clarity of light not
just into its "other," the obscurity of the night, but into its doubling, into
the "other night." That would of course impress language into such
extra-vagance as to make it mourn a lost good (and make it for once at

---

*Dedicated to Thomas J. J. Altizer

1 Robert Hass, "Meditation at Lagunitas," *Praise* (New York: The Ecco Press, 1979),
pp. 4–5.

2 ". . . What you have sought now seeks you; what once you pursued, now pursues you;
what once you fled, now flees you." Meister Eckhart, *The Talks of Instruction*, in *Meister
Eckhart*, trans. Raymond B. Blakney (New York: Harper & Row, 1941), p. 7.

3 Johann Wolfgang von Goethe, *Elective Affinities* (New York: Frederick Ungar Publishing Co., 1977), p. 8.

one with nature), make of language a gesture in directions beyond the confines of syntax and lexicography, make of language (*mirabile dictu*) a coincidence of signifiers and signified, a linguistic being that makes yonder be no longer beyond.[4] It is all quite impossible. Impossible, because language aspires to Being and, like Being, language aspires to an unmediated presence which it cannot attain or sustain. Yet what language has as a base from which to aspire, has by way of direct presentiment and absentiment, is not Being but specific existence, the compound of Being and the Not. Thus, Maurice Blanchot says, profoundly to my mind, the formulary of language is "Lazarus, come forth from the grave," resurrection from beyond existence.[5]

However foolish and impossible the resolve, then, I will not not speak of the Not, will speak of No, Not, Nothing; of No, Not Nothing. Being found of and claimed by this theme, I respond to the injunction of Henry David Thoreau: "Suffer yourself to be attracted . . . Obey . . . Report."[6] What follows is a token of my obedience and constitutes my preliminary report. And I begin in the language of avowal with a specific existence; without apology, my own.[7] Discourse, as Jabès has taught us, takes root in a wound.

THE DARK NIGHT OF THE BODY
AND THE FAR COUNTRY OF NOT

A florilegium of quotations from some who have mangaged to interest words in the dark night of the body and the journey to the Far Country. Nietzsche: "What does your body proclaim of your soul?"[8] " . . . It

---

[4] "I fear chiefly lest my expression may not be extravagant enough . . . to be adequate to the truth of which I have been convinced. *Extra vagance!* it depends on how you are yarded . . . I desire to speak somewhere without bounds . . . for I am convinced that I cannot exaggerate enough even to lay the foundation of a true expression . . . The volatile truth of our words should continually betray the inadequacy of the residual statement." Henry David Thoreau, *Walden and other writings*, ed. Brooks Atkinson (New York: The Modern Library, 1950), p. 289.

[5] Maurice Blanchot, *The Gaze of Orpheus*, trans. Lydia David (Barrytown, NY: Station Hill Press, 1981), p. 181.

[6] Henry David Thoreau, *A Writer's Notebook*, ed. Laurence Stapleton (New York: Dover Publications, 1960), pp. 83–84.

[7] Mediating the classical Greek religious experience of "the miracle of being in its only knowable mode, the miracle of individual existence" through its parallel with that of American poetry (notably Walt Whitman and Wallace Stevens), Curtis Bennett has shown that and how the miracle of being is known only in knowing the miracle of being *not*. "Never, not even in birth or sex, is that sense of the given form and its given expressiveness more poignant than in death: that he or she should never see or speak again is the most moving definition of how marvelous it is that someone would speak and see." Curtis Bennett, *God as Form* (Albany: State University of New York Press, 1976), p. 240.

[8] Friedrich Nietzsche, *Thus Spoke Zarathustra*, in *The Portable Nietzsche*, trans. Walter Kaufman (New York: The Viking Press, 1970), p. 125.

was the body that . . . heard the belly of being speak to it."[9] ". . . At last my abyss stirred and my thought bit me."[10] ". . . Your nothing too is a spider web and a spider, which lives on the blood of the future."[11] Ishmael, speaking of Ahab: ". . . Then it was, that his torn body and gashed soul bled into one another; and so interfusing made him mad. . . . If such a furious trope may stand, his special lunacy stormed his general sanity, and . . . Ahab . . . did now possess a thousand fold more potency than ever he had sanely brought to bear upon any one reasonable object."[12] "The intense concentration of self in the middle of such a heartless immensity, my God! who can tell it?"[13] Edmond Jabès: "What I am is only what I will be without me."[14] "Any coercion is a ferment of freedom."[15] "My exile is anticipated in the exile of God."[16] "You can never be absolutely sure of your age . . . . We grow old through the word. We die of translation."[17]

It was a day like any day in specific existence, a day filled with the hecceities of academic life, that 30th of May 1980. The last class of the spring quarter was met in the morning and the take-home final handed out; farewells and best wishes for the summer were exchanged with students. The three reasons for being a professor, June, July and August, were at hand, estopped temporarily only by the inevitable chairing of a faculty committee that took three hours of the afternoon to conclude a review of a graduate program in another department. That concluded, I piled into the previously packed station wagon, a copy of Goethe's *Conversations with Eckermann* on the empty seat beside me (to mark the beginning of a sabbatical year to be devoted to Goethe's theology of nature), and headed out for the sacred northcountry of Polebridge. The car was stacked to the gunnels with garden plants, for it had been my practice since coming to Montana to join Demeter in greeting Persephone on the banks of the North Fork of the Flathead River by planting my garden on Memorial Day. Perhaps the pomegranate seed Hades gave Persephone had a double whammy on it that year; in any case, I joined her in the underworld, the other world, which is to say in the *this* world of which we are nescient. My last sure recollection is olfactory, a passion

[9] Ibid., p. 143.
[10] Ibid., p. 274.
[11] Ibid., p. 283.
[12] Herman Melville, *Moby Dick* (New York: Modern Library, n.d.), pp. 182–83.
[13] Ibid., p. 412.
[14] Edmond Jabès, *The Book of Yukel*, trans. Rosemarie Waldrop (Middletown: Wesleyan University Press, 1977), p. 57.
[15] Edmond Jabès, *The Book of Questions*, trans. Rosemarie Waldrop (Middletown: Wesleyan University Press, 1976), p. 115.
[16] Jabès, *The Book of Yukel*, p. 86.
[17] Jabès, *The Return to the Book*, trans. Rosemarie Waldrop (Middletown: Wesleyan University Press, 1977), p. 196.

of the old or former body: the pungent smell of cabbage, broccoli, cauli-
flower, Brussels sprout plants in spindly youth. No doubt in the future
some University of Montana botanist will get a million dollars from NSF
to determine how Evaro Pass came to be covered by New Zealand Brussels sprouts.

For scattered they were, the Brussels sprouts, as was I, though I in
time to weeks of comatoseness and three years of intermittent hospital-
ization, and in space to latitudes and longitudes there is no sextant extant
to shoot. Certain words fall fumblingly from the lips now, flutteringly
upon the ear: the word "accident," for example. Deconstructed forever is
the arcane, recondite discussion among Aristotelians and Thomists about
the relation between "substance" and "accidents." For an "accident" of
this sort radicalizes the matter of "substance" in its every modality, finite
to infinite—as we shall have occasion to expand, beyond the language of
avowal, when we take up with Hegel's reflection on the same or like
phenomenon. Suffice to say that it is *unheimlich*, uncanny, to return to
home; to return from substantial continuity broken, from initiative stolen
away, to continuity putatively in habituated course. That it should
require *unheimlich* "accident" to bring the not of substance home itself
seems strange. Were not the "religious" always at home in homelessness,
homeless at home?

I had of course been decently fetched up. In early technical philosophical studies I had joined the battle between the Gods and the Giants,
between Parmenides and Plato, over whether nonbeing can in any sense
be, and had followed the aftermath of that contest in the exoteric traditions
of the west. It was for the most part a triumphalist campaign in which the
telos of existence was the conquest of nonbeing in the march toward plenary Being, of which God was the absolute lode and center. In technical
religion studies, insofar as one remained ligated to religious practice, it was
less easy to be siphoned off into the plenum. Religion that has not sedi-
mented as a mere substantive, religion activated by the very verb in it,
religion that *religates*, such religion comprises two kinds of rites in ceaseless alternation. There are Rites of Kenosis, of emptying, of mortification,
of negation; there are Rites of Plerosis, of filling, of enlivening, of
affirmation.[18] If one is to bound to the sacred one must be unbound and
rebound; no filling is without pollution; it must be poured out, emptied,
negated, religated. This company will not need telling that religious studies
can be and often is prosecuted in high abstraction from specific existence,
as much so as philosophy is, but the more culpably since religious studies,
unlike philosophy, has communal constituencies of specific existence

---

[18] The terms "Rites of Plerosis" and "Rites of Kenosis" are from Theodor Gaster, *Thes-
pis: Ritual, Myth and Drama in the Ancient Near East*, new and rev. ed. (Garden City,
NY: Anchor Books, 1961), p. 23.

outside the groves of academe. Because one can extrapolate from a litle to more, there is an inherent bias in the philosopher of religion toward the plenum. Consider the annual meeting of the American Academy of Religion: are not the climactic events called "Plenary Lectures"? Would it occur to us to call them "Kenary Lectures"? (You may call this one that.)

These confessions of an erstwhile ontotheologian duly noted, a residuum of religious sensibility kept watch over self-education in the texts of the tradition's underside, the theologies and chapbooks of the apophatic, of kenosis, of the nought-y; notably, the "mysticisms" of Neo-Platonic Christianity, and of that oxymoron, the gnostic Judaism of the *Kabbalah*. So the language of the Far Country, at least *about* it, was minimally at hand, wanting the surprise of defamiliarization. Edmond Jabès: "You dream of writing a book. The book is already written."[19] One writes in the surprise of reading the found and founded book, in Bachelard's words, of repeating its creation and continuing its exaggeration.

Surprise, in the etymological sense: overtaken, taken over. Trespassing the verges of the Far Country, accidentally desubstantialized and restantiated, it was my surprise to be engulfed not by the almighty forlornness and destitution of widely circulated report and ontological gossip but by the benign well-being of being not. How could one have been schooled in creation, fall and fault, captivity, exile, crucifixion, diaspora, and Holocaust and still require to be surprised that there is being that appears only with the loss of being, that some "somethings" appear only in, out, from No, Not, Nothing? It is a matter not of the "presence" or "absence" of Being in this our life of specific existence, but of absence *as* presence, absence *as* the presence not of Being *simpliciter* but of its redress, the genius of negation lurking in all surprise.

I return from the Far Country, like everyone else on the excursion of specific existence, without any information, not even a weather report, save that it is a darkness in which one sees but cannot say.[20] I return, verted, reverted, adverted, if not subverted or converted, with a charge and a conviction. That Far Country of the Not, the yonder being of *dabar* and *lógos*, of the *mysterium tremendum et fascinans* where the lips are sealed, where there is water, water everywhere and not a drop to drink, that country lays on one the charge to make of one's lips and pen, in Blanchot's words, "the echo of what cannot stop talking."[21] This is the

---

19 Jabès, *The Book of Yukel*, p. 39.
20 My point is the same as Maurice Blanchot's even if my language inverts his. See the third essay, "Parler, ce n'est pas voir," in *L'Entretien infini*; cited in Maurice Blanchot, *The Gaze of Orpheus and other literary essays*, ed. P. Adams Sitney (Barrytown: Station Hill Press, 1981), p. 193.
21 Blanchot, op. cit., p. 69.
Strained through specific existence, the echo sounding through speaking and writing is not a mere duplication or repetition of "original" sound. Thoreau again: "The echo is, to some

sole rationale of one's speaking and writing. And it deposits this conviction: who does not come to terms with the Not can only make of his/her life not a "scrutiny of signs" but a filing of grievances against specific existence. To Nietzsche's list of revenges, those against transience and the body, must be added a third as their source and instrumentality, the *ressentiment* against the Not. Nietzsche's own revenge against the Not, notwithstanding his approbation of nay-saying and his fun-poking at the yea-uhs of jackasses, especially at theological assininites, this revenge against the Not was Nietzsche's own unthought thought, and brought him to the brink of nihilism. Truly has Jabès said, "Nothing vowed to nothing, that is evil."[22]

Setting out for and in the Far Country of the Not is not like coming in with the ebb tide, not like washing out of the almighty tempest first into the lees of things, then upon the shore of Being, safe and secure from all alarm, not like a return to a harbor of nativity in an infinitesimal, primordial past, no hint of an eternal recurrence. No, it is the experience of tide change from ebb to flood, whether one be near or far from shore. The journey to the Far Country of the Not is a flooding toward the coincidence of the modes of time, rich in potency for being what we are not, rich in failing. It is a journey which invites us to throw overboard the bags of accumulated revenge (*ressentiment*) against the "it was" and the "not yet," to travel light and feel the howling infinite in our finite members. No one has known this better than the two great epic theopoets of water in the western tradition, Homer and Herman Melville.

Norman Maclean, in *A River Runs Through It*, asks the most searching of all questions, which came first, water or the word?[23] Most searching because it asks, in metaphor, the order of Not and Being. The authority of the priority of word in western orthodoxies, whether of *dabar* in Judaism, of *lógos* in Christianity, or the coincidence of *nous*, *lógos*, and *phōs*[24] in Hellenism, none suffices to stay the perturbing power of the watery not. One recalls that before God broke silence forever with word he brooded over the face of the waters, that his word was with, to, and over them. And one recalls on these shores that American literature has long situated itself in this *mysterium fascinans*. Robert Frost, man of words about water, is heard to say in "West-Running Brook":

---

extent, an original sound, and therein is the magic and charm of it. It is not merely a repetition of what was worth repeating in the bell, but partly the voice of the wood. . . ." Op. cit., p. 112.

[22] Jabès, *The Return to the Book*, p. 182.

[23] Norman Maclean, *A River Runs Through It* (Chicago: The University of Chicago Press, 1976), pp. 95–96.

[24] Greek thought was as much *philophosia* as it was *philosophia*.

(The black stream, catching on a sunken rock,
Flung backward on itself in one white wave,
And the white water rode the black forever . . .)
Speaking of contraries, see how the brook
In that white wave runs counter to itself.
It is from that in water we were from
Long, long before we were from any creature.
Here we, in our impatience of the steps,
Get back to the beginning of beginnings,
The stream of everything that runs away . . .

But it flows over us. It flows between us
To separate us from a panic moment.
It flows between us, over us, and *with* us.
And it is time, strength, tone, light, life, and love—
And even substance lapsing unsubstantial;
The universal cataract of death
That spends to nothingness—and unresisted,
Save by some strange resistance in itself,
Not just a swerving, but a throwing back,
As if regret were in it and were sacred.
It has this throwing backward on itself
So that the fall of most of it is always
Raising a little, sending up a little.[25]

In quiet moments when thinking is on the leeward side of the rocks, one puzzles why one thinks what one thinks *when* one thinks it. One were tempted to say there is a schedule of bodily energy that fixes the range of the ontological eye, such that in youth for example one is taken, overtaken, and taken over by all things generative, with their power to appear, be present, to be and perdure. But we know that the ecstasies of puberty are accompanied by those of thanatos verging on thanatomania, and that it is mostly the young among us today who are overtaken by the Not on cosmic scale, by the threat of genocide, nay omnicide, through nuclear Holocaust. Whatever bodily bias there is generically in reflection, it is qualified by *Zeitgeist*, and above all by the idiosyncratic variation of the specific existence from which one's language is discrepant. However much, as Kierkegaard says, "the question is asked in ignorance by one who does not even know what can have prompted him to ask it,"[26] one can find at least retrospectively the reflexive occasion in specific existence for reflection.

To find just that occasion which sources a text, which normally is the great unsaid in the text, and to find that that occasion coincides with one's own, is to be made ready for the passion of a text. Petrarch said on

---

[25] Robert Frost, *The Poems of Robert Frost* (New York: The Modern Library, 1946), pp. 286–87.

[26] Søren Kierkegaard, *Philosophical Fragments*, trans. David Swenson, rev. Howard V. Hong (Princeton: Princeton University Press, 1974), p. 9.

finishing Augustine's *Confessions* that he accounted himself to have read not the narrative of another man's life but of his own. Or as Meister Eckhart was wont to say, "readiness [read as well: *read*-iness] and the giving of form occur simultaneously."[27] Perhaps we value oral discourse because the speaker by voice can immediately realize occasion and thus make us ready, *read*-y, for and of the imposition of form. In any case, I neither sat down on a fine day and asked what it would be nice to talk about on this occasion, nor did I assume you would or should find some special fascination in the interiorities of my specific existence (the reigning presumption of TV talk-show participants and supermarket magazine authors). You have had or will have in the specificity of your own existence something analogous to my own experience of the Not. Nothing is more reliable than . . . nothing. No, Not, Nothing. No, not nothing. Attend to your own specific existence, and to the simultaneity of readiness (*read*-iness) and discourse. Let your communication be yea, yea; nay, nay. Let your *lógos*, your *sermo* be: be, be; not, not.[28]

THINKING NOT

"All there is to thinking . . . is seeing something noticeable which makes you see something you weren't noticing which makes you see something that isn't even visible."[29]

"Destiny grants us our wishes, but in its own way, in order to give us something beyond our wishes."[30]

Thinking not, or thinking the Not, is not, of course, not thinking. Parmenides had claimed as evidence that nonbeing cannot in any sense be the alleged fact that nonbeing cannot be *thought*. Plato disagreed ontologically while agreeing epistemologically; he held out for becoming as being something on pain of being nothing at all, while holding that becoming is "known" only by sensation and imagination, thus by "opining."[31] The correlation of thinking with being and of sensation with becoming and/or nonbeing has remained the regnant perennial tradition in the west from classical to modern times.

As the crowning thinker of modernity and the shaper of the agenda of postmodernity, Hegel aspired to a logic of thinking that would topple the antecedent correlations, that would make of thinking the realization in consciousness of (to use Goethe's term) the *Steigerung* of being and

---

[27] Meister Eckhart, "Eternal Birth," in *Meister Eckhart*, trans. Raymond B. Blakney (New York: Harper & Row, 1941), p. 121.

[28] Matthew 5:37.

[29] Norman Maclean, op. cit., p. 92.

[30] Goethe, op. cit., p. 205.

[31] These matters are elaborated in Ray L. Hart, "The Imagination in Plato," *International Philosophical Quarterly* V (September, 1965): 436–61.

nonbeing that constitutes the life of spirit. In the Preface to *The Phenomenology of Spirit* he stands the old correlations on their heads. It is to sensation in its "impotent abstract immediacy" and its attachment to "mere being as such" that all fixity and familiarity of knowledge owe. Wherever thinking is captive to "being-familiar" or the "well-known," that owes to the priority of a glazed sensation that abstractly departs from and returns to a perduring, self-enclosed circularity of fixity—and that extends not just to sticks, stones, and bones but to subject, object, nature, God. "What is 'familiarly known' is not properly known . . . it is the commonest form of self-deception."[32]

Thinking that proceeds in concert with lived spirit really gets underway with *analysis*, which is a process of defamiliarization. It is this part of the Hegelian project that the French deconstructionists have taken up in latter days with such passion. For his part, Hegel was aware of the necessity of this move by the Understanding, "the most astonishing and greatest of all powers," for by defamiliarization or deconstruction thinking breaks an idea into its original elements and attains access to them in a form that is disjunctive with present immediacy. But, unlike at least some of the contemporary deconstructionists, Hegel was aware of and insisted upon the limited usefulness of a thinking that exhausts itself in the defamiliarization of its own history. As necessary as the breaking of the power of abstract immediacy is, that office of thinking is insufficient. For what such thinking attains is still an idea or thing that is self-divided, self-moving, self-active, self-enclosed, and hence arousing "no sense of wonderment" that is characteristic of concrete spirit.

That wonderment, that incursion of the circle of self-enclosure, is potentiated for thinking that reaches its spirited term only by radical negation. The pertinent passage may be quoted at length:

> The circle that remains self-enclosed . . . has nothing astonishing about it. But that an *accident* as such, detached from what circumscribes it [cut loose from its containing circumference] . . . should attain an existence of its own and a separate freedom—this is the tremendous power of the negative; it is the energy of thought, of the pure "I." Death, if that is what we want to call this non-actuality [unreality, *Unwirklichkeit*], is of all things the most dreadful, and to hold fast what is dead requires the greatest strength. Beauty hates the Understanding for asking of her what it cannot do. But the life of Spirit is not the life that shrinks from death and keeps itself untouched by devastation, but rather the life that endures it and maintains itself in it. It is this power, not as something positive, which closes its eyes to the negative, as when we say of something that it is nothing or is false, and then, having done with it, turn away and pass on to something else; on the contrary, *Spirit is this*

[32] G. W. F. Hegel, *The Phenomenology of Mind*, trans. J. B. Baillie (London: George Allen & Unwin Ltd., 1949), p. 92.

power only by looking the negative in the face, and tarrying with it. This tarrying with the negative is the magical power that converts it into being.[33]

We may allow these powerful words to stand, for the nonce. They inscribe the essence of thinking, of thinking not, as astonishingly "accidental," as looking the negative in the face and tarrying with it. Whether the *telos* of that tarrying is to convert the Not into being, that is something we shall return to and tarry on. Hegel seems to have had an antecedent conviction that there is no nonbeing being cannot mediate, nothing outside the circle that cannot be brought in or the circle expanded to include. That rests on a theology we shall have occasion to tarry with and over.

Now in thinking something, especially when the "something" is No, Not, Nothing, it is useful to determine ways of thinking *about* that something. In doing so one remembers Spinoza's truism that "all determination is negation," i.e., *this* something is *not that* something, this way of thinking is not that way of thinking. Are there determinably different kinds of negation, of No or Not, and what kinds of thinking and language would be commensurate with them? Following Henri Bergson and Kenneth Burke, I believe there are different kinds of negation and that the theologian has her/his attention riveted to *two* orders of them and the problematic of their relation.

Burke discriminates two kinds or orders of negation, the "active" and the "scenic."[34] Negations of act are claimed by him to be the more primordial of the two. He locates the origin and development of human language, as he does the moral identity of the person, in the use of "no": the child is differentiated by learning to say "no" and having "no" said to him/her. The active negative, the no pertaining to action, is imperative in mood, admonitory or hortatory in tone, is directed to audience, the ear, and finds its paradigm in the "thou shalt nots" of the Hebrew Decalogue

---

[33] Wilhelm Hegel, *Phenomenology of Spirit*, trans. A. V. Miller, (Oxford: Oxford University Press, 1977), p. 19. Material in brackets is alternative translation by Baillie, op. cit., p. 93. Emphasis is mine.

The German text will be found in G. W. F. Hegel, *Gesammelte Werke*, vol. 9, *Phänomenologie des Geistes* (Hamburg: Felix Meiner Verlag, 1980), p. 27.

Hegel's reference to Beauty despising Understanding for the latter's asking the former to do what it cannot do is taken by J. B. Baillie in an editorial gloss to be a slap at the Romantic "cult of beauty" generally and Novalis in particular. But it seems to me more fundamentally an assault upon a Platonic understanding of Beauty as the goal of contemplative understanding. In the *Symposium* (209e–212c), Plato has Diotima instruct Socrates on "beauty in itself" as that which transcends every instance, that "is eternal and neither comes into being nor decays . . . does not increase or decrease . . . becomes neither less nor more nor suffers change."

[34] Kenneth Burke, *Language as Symbolic Action* (Berkeley: University of California Press, 1966), see especially part II, chap. 7, "A Dramatistic View of the Origins of Language and Postscripts on the Negative," pp. 419–79.

(Ten Commandments). The scenic negative by contrast is indicative in mood; its intention is to describe not what is admonished or commanded but what is already there. Its appeal is to the visual sense; the scene is the seen, what appears, is present; and it finds its paradigms in the western ontological systems shaped by the Greek metaphysics of light.

Now lest this distinction between act-negatives and scene-negatives appear too clean, and lest we overlook the problematic of their relation to each other, let us consider the character of "scenic" judgments, both affirmative and negative. Going at least initially with Bergson's move[35] we may say that an affirmative judgment bears directly on a thing or things. A thing in nature (or reality) is just what it is, and an affirmative judgment says what that is. An affirmative judgment indicates, describes it as it is: thus, "This lectern is brown." And when I say "this" ostensively, an implicit affirmative existential judgment is made as well: thus, "This (existing) lectern is brown." A negative scenic judgment on the other hand does not hold a thing or things *directly* in view. A negative judgment is more a judgment of an implicit affirmative judgment, less a judgment of a thing or things. If I say "This lectern is not white," I am denying the implicit affirmative judgment that it *is* white; so an explicit negative judgment negates an implicit affirmative judgment. Moreover, in a negative judgment I implicitly announce that some implicit affirmative judgment, whose content is not explicitly announced, will have to be *substituted* for. At the same time I imply my *interest* in that affirmative to the extent that I consider it worthwhile to negate it in the interest of an an expected or hoped for substitute. The negative judgment is therefore a covert passion for the affirmative which cannot be envisaged through the negative *qua* negative, but which can emerge only through negation. As has been pointed out by many, the affirmative can yield only itself whereas the negative can yield itself and the affirmative, the negation of negation being affirmative (if I negate all the colors this lectern is not, I affirm the color it is).

These judgments about negative judgments conduce to indicate that act-negations and scene-negations do not differ *qua* judgments as sharply as their discrimination earlier may have suggested. We have just seen that a negative judgment about what putatively is, is teleologically admonitory or horatory, however implicitly. The unspoken supplement to a negative "scenic" judgment is: you shall or should substitute for the (unspecified) affirmative judgment. . . . Thus the feeling-tone of negative judgment is expectation (that the hearer or reader will substitute) or regret (that he/she has not substituted, or will not). Herein lies the indeterminate character or

---

[35] Henri Bergson, *Creative Evolution*, trans. Arthur Mitchell (New York: Henry Holt and Company, 1913); see especially the section in chap. IV on "The relation of metaphysical problems to the idea of 'Nothing,'" pp. 272-98.

open-endedness of negation *qua* negation, that in its implicit admonition of a substitution it takes account only of the need for replacement and does not, *qua* negative, concern itself with what replaces or substitutes. The negative *qua* simple and single negative does not go on to the affirmative which replaces the negated implicit affirmative. ("The lectern is not white" will not of itself get you to "The lectern is brown.")

Turning abruptly to the interest theology takes in the relation between act-negatives and scene-negatives, we may find that the preceding judgments about judgments help us understand better the Hebrew prophetic, indeed the whole Yahwist tradition, the tradition of what Herbert Schneidau has called "sacred discontent that dismantles the schema."[36] That Hebrew tradition is rife with negative imperatives rather than ontological or meontological indicatives, with act-words rather then scene-words. In the Hebrew scriptures there are few if any existential or attributive judgments about what is and what is not, but a plethora of admonitory negative act judgments. The canvas on which narrative is painted is that of the decalogic "thou shalt not" and that of the prophetic (in which tradition Jesus also stands) "ye have heard it said, but I say . . ."

Rarely do we find explicitated affirmative, attributive judgments in scriptural writ, either Hebrew or Christian; that is, rarely do we have equally evident the affirmative judgments, presumably humanly made, that are clearly negated by sacred voice. Largely unsaid in scripture is the implicit affirmative judgment that is explicitly negated by divine speech, for that is precisely what is to be sought in the aura of the divine negation *qua* negation. The divine negative *qua* negative as little precisely identifies the affirmative it negates as it specifies the affirmative that will substitute with divine approbation. Formally, "thou shalt not" says: change, be other, do other, do not do *this*. For Jesus, the form of the prophetic *not* was *parable*: through the parabolic working of parable, the hearer has identified for her/him, in the concreteness of specific existence, the implicit affirmative that is negated and the emergence of the divinely sanctioned affirmative in the specific existence of the hearer that substitutes for it.[37]

---

36 Herbert N. Schneidau, *Sacred Discontent: The Bible and Western Tradition* (Berkeley: University of California Press, 1977). The phrase recurs throughout Schneidau's book but is developed most fully in chap. V, "The Bible and Literature: Against Positivism," pp. 248–306.

37 Important distinctions between Hebrew and Christian "act-negatives," and in early Christianity between the synoptic Jesus and other traditions within the New Testament canon, require to be made. Such distinctions are beyond the scope of the present effort. Suffice to say that the Jesus of the Matthean sermon on the mountain is far less interdictive than the decalogic and prophetic admonitory negatives of the Hebrew tradition. Perhaps we should say, Jesus is *differently* interdictive or negative. Chapter 5 of Matthew

Missing from, or at least rare in, Hebrew scripture is language about the *scene* of divinely issued negative imperatives, language about *what is* and *what is not* "behind" them. The negative commands of holy voice are shot through with the feeling-tone of all negation directed to act, that of dissatisfaction, lack, absence. The hearer of divine negative command is put in quandary not only by the lack of the implicit affirmative negated (though its range of possibles will have been limited by the negative *qua* negative) and the absence of its replacing affirmative. As if that were not enough there is more, which is to say less: the quandary of the hearer is compounded by the fact that even the divine speaker of dissatisfaction, regret, expectation, even that one is absent.[38] (Man's exile, we heard Jabès say earlier, is anticipated by the exile of God.) What we have is language (entrusted to prophetic amanuensis) that fixes the parameters of privation. The single primordial affirmative is governed by two admonitory negatives: I am the Lord thy God, ye shall have no other. Thou shalt not . . .

The quandary of the individual hearer has its counterpart in the quandary of Christian thinking (to call it that, for want of a better term) about the Not, as the long and varied history of the latter attests. The quandary of Christian thinking about the Not centers in the relation of "thou shalt Not" to "it is not," of the act-negative to the scene-negative, of deontological ethics to ontological/meontological theology, one may even say of Hebrew voice to Christian eye, and of the qualifying power of the one over the other. For the most part, perennial exoteric Christian theology has taken the scenic route.

---

opens with the beatitudes which are uniformly free of negatives. They are not so much admonitory as *scenic* affirmatives: "Blessed *are* . . ." The first "not" in the sermon (5:17) is "Think not that I come to destroy the law, or the prophets . . ." The balance of chapter 5 is a litany of "Ye have heard . . . thou shalt not . . . but I say . . ." followed by an explicitation of the affirmative(s) that is to substitute (while leaving the *range* of substituting affirmatives parabolically open). Chapters 6 and 7 are much more negational in tone than chapter 5, for in them the "nots" accelerate and proliferate; they comprise a "new" list of admonitory negatives that at once follow upon the explicated substituting affirmatives and suggest a "new" range of implicit affirmations negated. (I count nineteen "nots" in the sermon as a whole.)

In a different religious tradition, that of the ancient Greeks, yet one into which primitive Christianity moved and from which it absorbed much, the admonitory negative was largely absent in favor of scene. On a column in front of the temple at Delphi were inscribed *fifty-three* precepts of the seven sages. Of these, only *three* are "do nots." The precepts are in G. Dittenberger, *Sylloge Inscriptionum Graecarum*, 3d ed. (Leipzig, 1915–1924), 1268; in English, in David G. Rice and John E. Stambaugh, *Sources for the Study of Greek Religion* (Missoula: Scholars Press, 1979), pp. 96–97.

38 The encounter of Elijah and YHWH in I Kings (19:11–12): "And, behold, YHWH passed by, and a great and strong wind rent the mountains, and brake in pieces the rocks before YHWH; but YHWH was not in the wind: and after the wind an earthquake; but YWHW was not in the earthquake: And after the earthquake a fire, but YHWH was not in the fire: and after the fire a still small voice."

That has led western Christian theology, in intention if not in fact, not so much to the loss of the admonitory active Not in favor of scenic Nothing as, allied with a Greek metaphysic of light and presence, to a perduring gnostic reverie of the pleroma, to a final no to Not. That reverie in intention coincided with transtemporal participation of the interiority of godhead that devalued creaturely existence; it was estopped intermittently only by "reformation" that centered religiously in the admonitory nots of sin, erring, and failing, and theologically in the vivification of the scenic Not as Hell.[39] Again and again doctrinal closures on God and creation have had to be cracked and the canon itself effectively reopened. If God created the world out of nothing and not out of Himself, called mankind freely to be not nothing and not Himself and pronounced it good, promising to give Himself to humankind until the end and exacting of humankind advertence to limiting nots while leaving a broad range of negations and affirmations to human responsibility and freedom: if this is the theopoetic reality of the person *coram Deo*, the doctrines of creation and God *in principle* cannot atttain the kind of closure they have in Christendom.

CREATOR AND CREATURE: GOD AS NOT GODHEAD, MAN AS NOT GOD AND NOT NOTHING

Once one has self-consciously opened the trunks of doctrinal closure one has the scholarly responsibility to look as well in the boxes of rags and partial bolts discarded in the fashioning of the tradition's *haute couture*. What is *not* in the trunks is as important, for thinking the opening of closure, as what is. Like nature in the genetic structure of every cell, history has its trunks and rag bags packed with variation. Like children, we scholars ought to go often to the attic and try on the old clothes and play new people. But the project is unlikely, for, if joined by our students, that would amount to *education*: to be led out and away.

You will have discerned that this scholarly playful responsibility is one I do not shoulder in these remarks; it is part of the larger project of

---

[39] One is tempted to generalize, both historically and systematically: no hell (or its hermeneutical equivalents), no reformation. Hell and its hermeneutical equivalents (including modern and postmodern grieving over specific existence and what is not) is the Scenic Not that awaits all ignoring of the admonitory nots of the moral life, is the scenic counterpart of the hortatory negative extended beyond or as the base of the temporal frame of specific existence. Hell is as little indispensable as Heaven, for the former has its own modality in perfection of negation as has the latter in perfection of plenitude. The fascination which the great Christian epics hold for the modern mind (notably those of Milton and Blake) lies in the perfection of their Hells, and this notwithstanding the fact that for the most part hortatory nots are present to modern men without voice, are present only as written traces and thus without claiming admonitory power. Hell for modern man is thus *mere* Scene and not active Epic.

which these remarks are an earnest. Here I place myself at the margins of closures attained through long discursive inquiry. In doing so I would not flaunt feathers not my own. They are drawn from the boxes of those who also stood at the margins in order to surprise the centers of their own convictions; they assist in being overtaken by my own. Those who recognize fragments from Eckhart, Cusanus, and Boehme, and Neo-Platonic Christian mysticism generally, with even a tad of Zoharic and Lurianic Kabbalah, will also recognize that my vestment is as little theirs as is the mannequin.

From those margins four substantive areas of closure require to be breached and broached. Prescinding from the large question of signifiers, I speak of them as signifieds. In no special order, (1) there is the classical signified of man in his/her ontic/meontic instability. Does this ontic-meontic instability owe, as in the classical closure on "Fall," to human negation of a primal state or condition of being from which we have declined or that we have evaded; or to vertigo before a proleptic negation, a consequent state or condition that we have not attained and to which we have not acceded? There is (2) the signified in respect of Being. What is the transcendental ontological ground of the aforementioned human ontic/meontic instabilty? Can God as Being-Itself exhaustively and without remainder account both for itself *and* this instability without the effective loss of either? If it cannot, how is Being cradled in nonbeing, how does Being come to fruition through the Not? There is (3) the signified in respect of godhead and God/gods. If the divine Simplicity cannot account for the negational identity of the human creature, can it account for its own? Does not negational identity point to the *derivative* reality of God, however ultimate He is for us and our salvation; to a primordial identity of God in Godhead comparable to the unnegated identity of man before negation, i.e., before the onset of history, but more importantly to God *qua* God of creation whose negational identity is derivative proleptically as well, whose being is covenanted through the negations of apocalyptic history? Finally, there is (4) the signified of creation as the Labor and the Ecstasy of the Not, the signified of salvation. Do we aspire to God as God aspires to Godhead, each "returning" to the primal other through a burning up of all Not (as in Eckhart, and in many mysticisms west and east)? Or do we aspire to an intensification, a *Steigerung*, of the Not, a consequent or apocalyptic Not; for man, a not being God, and for God a not being Godhead, united in the Kingdom in which each differs from and defers to the other, the apocalyptic kingdom that comprises the redemption of *both* creature and God?

You will have sensed that the questions about these putative signifieds are weighted in a certain direction. Let me now point that direction with the requisite brevity.

Lurianic Kabbalism had an instinct for this trajectory: creation originates in the rupture of Godhead, is itself the divine rapture of that rupture. But there I stop, or pause. For the "Notting" that coincides with the
rupture of Godhead is not a contraction (*Zim Zum*) to form a space for
sefirotic creation within Godhead, and simultaneously the withdrawal of
Godhead into an In-Itself or En Sof. This Jewish-gnostic passion for the
Majestic One for whom creation, however much a rupture, is still an
internal affair of Godhead, is not shared in the theopoetic reality by
which Christian thinking is claimed. For the substratum of that reality,
the self-benotting of Godhead is radical. If Godhead is not to realize its
identity solely through the disconsolate impiety of the Alone with the
Alone, it must realize its identity through difference, through its inmost
outer other, reconciliation with whom or which would constitute eternally enriched Godhead, the eschatological piety of peace among the
One and the Many. The rupture of Godhead is simultaneously the rapture of God and the ecstasy of creation. In this rupture of Godhead, this
difference of God from Godhead, in this benotting of God in the primordial negation, lies both the freedom of God and the freedom of man: it
permits God to interrogate Himself as he interrogates us, to place us and
Himself in question. The question is opened first in God, this Not of the
Exile, before it is put to us, and ruptures forever the Simplicity of Godhead. Henceforth, with the sonority of holy voice, pure Being is as silent
as is pure Nothing; the former because of God, the latter because of man
authorized as free. The self-negation of Godhead is the liberation of
historicity and the authorization of both sacred and human speech.

Exoteric ontotheological closures on creation have construed creation
as the Labor of Being in contest with the Nothing in which the creature,
notably man, is the counter of all moves. The Creator as Being-Itself or
the Power of Being sources every resistance to non-being; out of his inex-
haustible *plenum* the Creator rescues man and things from their nisus
toward nothingness. Man only passes through the Not to reach the source
of sponsorship in Being, aspiring to be coincident with Being-Itself and
its power and thus conquering all not being. (Note well here that Hegel
was a strictly orthodox Christian theologian in his claim that "tarrying
with the negative is the magical power that converts it into being"!)
Creation as the Labor of Being in contest with Nothing was the labor of
making beings unto Not to be, of ontically finishing things that would
otherwise be finished off; it was a kind of victory of the Creator over his
own creation.

We have thought of creation as becoming something, have largely
left unthought creation as benotting something, forgetting that God
became not Himself in order that man might become not himself, i.e.,
that man might be saved from the double terror and risk of creation, on
the one hand the dread of all-devouring nothingness, on the other the

dread of constricting singularity, the solitude of mere identity (the human counterpart of the anxiety of Godhead).

Creator and creature in covenant, creation as the Labor and Ecstasty of the Not, signify that *both* God and man pass through the not in order to realize the covenantal intention. Each stands out of a primordial Not beyond initiative, man out of the abyss of nothingness, itself outside the interiority of Godhead; God out of the abyss of Trinity. Each is possessed as well of a primordial being, but a primordiality of being that is an untested, ahistorical contest of being and its abyss, a primordiality of unexercised freedom. Biblical covenant obtains not between a Godhead of pleromatic innocence and a man who is an automaton of the nought: both come into covenant having exercised freedom, that exercise being the moment of creation. History begins with the human benotting of the first sacred interdict. Creation as covenant and history as salvation are geared not to the promordial but to the consequent, apocalyptic Not, and thus is unfinished. Creation as covenant is God teaching himself not to be Godhead in concert with time, man teaching himself not to be God and not Nothing in the same theater, eternally. It is the pathos and pain of God, in the cacophany of the symphony of history, that he has had also to teach himself to get along without man; the pathos and pain of man to get along without God, without the succors of transcendent plenary presence.

From the Genesis myths one remembers that, cosmogonically, creation coincided with the separation of light from darkness, with the *fiat lux* that was the first sacred word. Themselves out of the dark and the dry, Adam and Eve benot the first interdict and through that negation first exercise the *imago*. They knowingly realize the separation and situate themselves in its parts: the moisture of the Dark Not in the knowledge of light. There east of Eden, the terrain of history, where the sweat of the human brow is the Labor of the Not, the ecstasy of the likening of unlikes continues through the exacerbation of difference begun *in illo tempore* of Eden.

I have argued elsewhere that "essence" for humankind is not some transcendental being laid up in the Great Ontological Somewhere, to which existence is to adjust and which it is to embody. No, essence is potency; the *potentia obedientalis* for man is historically potentiated *coram Deo* through the complicit passage of specific existence through the Not, east of Eden.[40] Merely to exist (i.e., an existence unordered by essential potency) is as little admirable in man as it is in God, and nothing hangs on the mere existence of either. Existence *qua* existence for man is only a temporal/temporary conquest of the Nothing (an eternity of such existence is what Adam and Eve gave up in benotting the first

---

[40] For an expanded discussion of *potentia obedientalis* see Ray L. Hart, *Unfinished Man and the Imagination* (New York: Herder & Herder, 1968), pp. 170–79. That discussion, however, neglects the role of negation in obedience.

interdict), is not a vocation but the condition of a vocation, is at best the theater of evocations that may be inverted as invocations.

From the nothing through the not to being *and* being not *coram Deo*: this is the career, the saga, of refunding potency. Without the power of the historically accidental Not, the power of being degenerates into mere existence. Merely infinitely existing God and merely finitely existing man can only rage against each other, the one in wrath, the other in *ressentiment*, across an abyss of infinitely unequal ontological/meontological power. What fuels the substitution for that abyss that salvation is—the mystery that mesmerized the mind of Kierkegaard—is the grace of the holy kenosis of the plenum and the human plerosis of the void, the career of salvation through the Not. Kierkegaard understood that the likening of unlikes proceeds through *each* becoming not merely itself, through communion in the kingdom of difference. In his parable of the love between the King and the humble maiden, Kierkegaard sets the pathos of salvific love against the dread of Nothing—and opts for the divine pathos. "The minds of men so yearn for might and power . . . they do not even dream that there is sorrow in heaven . . . The deep grief of having to deny the learner what he yearns for . . . precisely because he is the beloved."[41]

And here it is worth remembering that the Greek word for English *truth*, *aletheia*, is an a-privative, is indeed an a-privative metaphor.[42] Lethe was the river in Hades to cross which was to be deprived of life and memory. *A-letheia* is the privation of privation, the negation of negation, an undeadening, an unforgetting, a shaking off of the lethargy and lethality of an identity that had come merely to its "other." *A-letheia*, the wound in which is rooted the discourse of *a-theology*, is the other other, knowledge in its privy parts.

o o o

This book is always unfinished, never so much as at the end, and as one affixes one's signature to it in a gesture toward the anonymity of one's life that exceeds and authorizes the failure of the book. In the time allotted I have, like Thoreau, spoken conformably to the rumors I have heard. Like Wallace Stevens's "Snow Man," I would behold "Nothing that is not there and the nothing that is." If something was heard, as William Faulkner said, "Something worth saying knew better than I did how it needed to be said."

Let your communication, your *sermo*, be: yes, yes; no, no. Let your *lógos* be: be,be; not, not.[43]

[41] Kierkegaard, op. cit., p. 37.
[42] Burke, op. cit., p. 476.
[43] Matthew 5:37.

IRONY (FIG.) AND (LIT.)
IN MODERN AMERICAN RELIGION*

MARTIN E. MARTY

LITERARY AND HISTORICAL IRONY

The dictionary names "an ironical speaker or writer" an ironist. D. C. Muecke (3–13) has named those who study irony "ironologists." Paul Russell (68) calls "irony hounds" those who pursue ironic outcomes in human affairs. While ironists keep on providing texts for the other two, it is ironologists in literary criticism and irony hounds in historical inquiry who coexist in religious studies today. Given the preoccupation with textuality in such studies, literary irony has received much attention. The writings of Muecke himself, along with those of Wayne C. Booth, J. A. K. Thompson, and the many scores of critics referred to in their bibliographies, are book-length elaborations of this literary trope.[1] Most modern literary critics in England and America, among them Cleanth Brooks, Erich Heller, and Kenneth Burke, have included such irony in their analyses, and it is common in works on religion and literature. Booth admits that he has been tempted to propose "a requiem for the *terms* 'irony,' 'ironic,' and 'ironically,'" because of their overuse and misuse" (1983).

Meanwhile, the irony hounds have less frequently been busy at book-length work, and they have been less central in religious studies. Three books come to mind. Hayden White has been chiefly attentive to European historians in *Metahistory: The Historical Imagination in Nineteenth-Century Europe.* Richard Reinitz has written an American counterpart, *Irony and Consciousness.* The subtitle of that work includes

Martin E. Marty. is Fairfax M. Cone Distinguished Service Professor at The Divinity School of the University of Chicago.

*This article is based on a Scholars Press Associates Lecture at the American Academy of Religion, December 9, 1984, in Chicago. I wish to thank Conrad Cherry of Scholars Press for the invitation, encouragement, and contribution to the theme, as well as William R. Hutchison for arranging a seminar at Harvard University on the subject in November, 1984. Wayne C. Booth and David Tracy provided valuable counsel in respect to literary and theological themes, while students in my seminar on Irony in Modern American Religion in Autumn, 1984, made the greatest contributions of all.

[1] See the references to Booth, Thompson, Brooks, Heller, and Burke in the attached bibliography.

the name of the religious figure who made irony a focus, Reinhold Niebuhr, in his *The Irony of American History*.[2] Such works are less interested in tropes than perceptions of situations. The distinctions between
the two sorts impel one to visit the *Oxford English Dictionary* (Oxford,
1933: s.v. "irony") for definitions.

The irony of ironists, observed and dissected by ironologists, literary
irony is "a figure of speech," defined as one "in which the intended
meaning is the opposite of that expressed by the words used; usually
taking the form of sarcasm or ridicule in which laudatory expressions are
used to imply condemnation or contempt."

On the other hand, the irony of situations, observed and dissected by
irony hounds, is *not* a figure of speech though the dictionary marks it
"(*fig.*)"; instead, it is "a condition of affairs or events of a character opposite to what was, or might naturally be expected; a contradictory outcome of events as if in mockery of the promise and fitness of things."

One additional element appears in almost all such ironic perception,
an element that separates it from, among other things, "the irony of
fate." This is the responsibility of the human actor or agent. Gene Wise
(1973:300) typically accents this ingredient: "An ironic situation occurs
when the consequences of an act are diametrically opposed to the original intention, and the fundamental cause of the disparity lies in the
actor himself, and his original purpose." Observation of such actors by
people gifted with nothing more than the hindsight that comes with
later birth can lead to what Kenneth Burke (514) calls "romantic irony,"
an aesthetic stance that would represent a standing *outside of* or in a
posture *superior to* the roles of others. For reasons that will soon become
clear, Richard Reinitz (19) has chosen to name the actor-centered version
that is not bound to fate or given to detachment and superciliousness,
"humane irony." This version most deserves attention in religious studies
when they focus on the human subject.

AN APOLOGY FOR IRONIC INTERPRETATION

When identification with or sympathy for the actor is neglected, and
when the observer of irony therefore stands outside of or in a posture
superior to the agent, cynicism about others' actions and passivity about
one's own can result. It was because of this possibility, indeed, tendency,
that Hayden White concluded the introduction to his 448-page master-
work on irony with his own requiem for irony:

> It may not go unnoticed that this book is itself cast in an Ironic
> mode. But the Irony which informs it is a conscious one, and it
> therefore represents a turning of the Ironic consciousness against

---

[2] See the references to White, Reinitz, and Niebuhr in the bibliography that follows.

> Irony itself. If it succeeds in establishing that the skepticism and pessimism of so much of contemporary historical thinking have their origins in an Ironic frame of mind, and that this frame of mind in turn is merely one of a number of possible postures that one may assume before the historical record, it will have provided some of the grounds for a rejection of Irony itself. (xii)

His claim that an ironic frame of mind informs much historical writing in modern times corrects an impression possibly left several paragraphs ago in the reference to but three sustained books on the subject. The list of historians cited by White and Reinitz serves as a reminder that anyone who comes on the scene isolating and advocating ironic perception and writing cannot do so with breathless announcements about fresh discoveries. Such makers of announcements would be quickly dismissed by ironologists and those in White's camp, for their great leaps forward in cultural lag, their obsolete *au courant*ism. I am especially sensitive to this situation because I am publishing the first of a four-volume work on the twentieth century in the United States, *Modern American Religion: The Irony of It All*. Such a choice demands a rationale, of the sort that follows.

First, if a condition, situation, or outcome best admits of an ironic interpretation—over against, say, a tragic or comic or pathetic one—the conscientious historian will favor it, no matter what the fashion. Second, historians, of all people, should not resent but should welcome the observation that what they are doing is in a long tradition, that it has numbers of precedents. Tradition and precedent are their stock in trade. One does not, for example, stop writing about the sacred or the family or the frontier or tragedy because "it's been done." Third, the recovery of figurative irony is part of the return to narrative in historical writing (Stone: 74–96). Thus fashion, old-fashion turned newest-fashion, also has its place. Figurative irony has to deal with the diachronic, with passages through time, since it concentrates on outcomes. Fourth, narrative needs a thread if it is dependent upon nothing more than a series of "and thens," and ironic observation provides a plausible connector in certain circumstances.

To all this, I would add a fifth, one which acknowledges the influence of and participates in the recovery of an important element in the thought of Reinhold Niebuhr. This element provides a response to White. It belongs to the hermeneutical preunderstanding of numbers of us and, in my case, in respect to *Modern American Religion*, the understanding, the *Verständnis* itself. *The Irony of It All* proposes this perception of outcomes as the most important thing I would like to say about the turn of the century—in this case, a period from 1893–1920—the time that more than any other is the matrix of modern conceptions of reality in America.

I would have no interest in seeing all interpreters of twentieth-century American religion give themselves over to irony hounding.[3] If not all observers are to be preoccupied by ironic perception, one would hope that their outlook would be partly informed by it.

By now it should be obvious that both the ironic trope in literature and ironic perception in history appear to a large extent as choice. Samuel Hynes (41–42) correctly notices that irony represents "a view of life which recognizes that experience is open to multiple interpretations, of which no *one* is simply right, and that the co-existence of incongruities is part of the structure of existence." That assumption poses two sets of issues: why the ironic outlook for a particular historian, and what does the choice of it say about his or her work; and why the ironic perception in respect to specific stories?

First, the historian. Once more, because White is the irony hound who would banish irony, he provides the best critical voice:

> The late R. G. Collingwood was fond of saying that the kind of history one wrote, or the way one thought about history, was ultimately a function of the kind of man one was. But the reverse is also the case. Placed before the alternative visions that history's interpreters offer for our consideration, and without any apodictically provided theoretical grounds for preferring one over another, we are driven back to *moral* and *aesthetic* reasons for the choice of one vision over another as the more 'realistic.' (433–34)

On such terms White promoted, as alternatives, "the great poetic, scientific, and philosophical concerns" of the nineteenth century that were being eclipsed by the ironic in the twentieth century.

THE ISSUE OF BIAS IN RELIGIOUS STUDIES

"Irony, like beauty," writes D. C. Muecke, "is in the eye of the beholder and is not a quality inherent in any remark, event, or situation" (14). In the case of American religious concerns, the moral and the aesthetic are uncommonly interconnected, but here is it fair to accent the former: what is the moral concept of the ironic beholder and, by indirection, what is the moral vision of the beheld, the actors in this kind of historical narrative?

Such questions are urgent in religious studies because behind the quiet words "ironic perception" or "ironic outlook" looms the more portentous

---

[3] I shall be treating these *ironic* outcomes in respect to the *modern* as a projection into later times, while turning to the *conflictual* in respect to *religion* and then to the *pluralistic* in respect to *America* in later volumes covering 1920–52 and 1952–1973/74; that leaves who-knows-what for 1974–. But those are topics for other days and other articles five and ten and fifteen years from now.

notion that a philosophy of history is somehow at stake. Especially when one cites Reinhold Niebuhr, such a philosophy is redolent of theological concerns, which, covertly or overtly, might introduce the value-laden into such studies. Overtly, it might be said in the Niebuhrian case, since that theologian argued that "the Christian faith tends to make the ironic view of human evil in history the normative one." On these terms, he irony-hounded American culture to engage in critiques, to notice that "everything that is related in terms of a simple rational coherence with the ideals of a culture or a nation will prove in the end to be a simple justification of its most cherished values" (150, 155).

This is not the place to settle the issue of value-freeness in religious studies or historical inquiry; suffice it to say that in the latter area the notion of utterly value-free history has few defenders today. More positively, one might allow for the possibility that the hint of a biblical or specifically Christian outlook on history might help bring into bold profile the fact that positivist, progressivist, Marxist, or other outlooks also transcend "simple rational coherence" and are also philosophies of history that belong to the hermeneutical *Vorverständnis* of scholars who hold them. And, more neutrally, it is to be noticed that already in Niebuhr's prime, agnostics like Arthur M. Schlesinger, Jr. and Hans Morgenthau helped form an informal club of "atheists for Niebuhr" (Bingham: 360), who did not share his theological normativity in order to acquire his ironic stance. Nor, for that matter, did Reinitz (90–104), who emphatically did not share Niebuhr's religious faith or theology, yet who advocated his insight into irony.

HUMANE IRONY: ILLUSION AND ASPIRATION

What led Reinitz to name the Niebuhrian form "humane irony," and what leads me to see in it a corrective to the "skepticism and pessimism" that led White to want to dismiss the ironic mode, was condensed in a sentence that clearly set forth the Niebuhrian dialectic. It is well known that his favorite biblical verse referring to divine transcendence as a background to irony was Psalm 2:4, referring to the illusions of pride among the earth's agents: "He that sitteth in the heavens shall laugh: the Lord shall have them in derision." What kept Niebuhr from using such a reminder to induce skepticism and pessimism, not to say detachment from and superciliousness toward the human agents, was the corollary to this claim, in the important urging that this God was "a divine judge who laughs at human pretensions *without being hostile to human aspirations*" (155; emphasis mine). The secular advocates of humane irony are humanists of the sort who honor human aspiration and endeavor.

The eye of the ironic beholder focuses first and always on the illusions, especially those of innocence, virtue, wisdom, and power, that help lead to the "contradictory outcome of events" (Reinitz: 178).

Humane irony does not degenerate into a sneer whose only message is, "What fools these mortals be!" Humane irony, whether theologically motivated or not, always has to be marked by empathy on the part of the scholar for the people who are victims of powerful historical actors and agents as well as for those actors and agents themselves. The Niebuhrian passage on this is classic:

> The knowledge of [irony] depends upon an observer who is not so hostile to the victim of irony as to deny the element of virtue which must constitute a part of the ironic situation; nor yet so sympathetic as to discount the weakness, the vanity and pretension which constitutes another element. (153)

Niebuhr elsewhere sees situations to admit of ironic interpretation if "virtue becomes vice through some hidden defect in the virtue" (viii), but this would not permit overlooking the virtue. Similarly, this is the case "if wisdom becomes folly because it does not know its limits," but the wisdom is also to be observed. To the extent that historians or other interpreters retain some sympathy for people who act, who must act, in history, they are likely to be more faithful to the human subject, less prone to identify with a quasi-divine viewpoint that would make them victims of illusions that would lead to ironic outcomes on a grand scale. Should someone feel that employment of this perspective must lead to the passivity, apathy, even anti-activism that White and others have feared as a corollary to ironic interpretation, the hyperactive, energetic, pro-activist career of Reinhold Niebuhr in the human *polis* must be an impressive contradictory example.

THE ISSUE OF EXCEPTIONALISM

When humane irony is to be employed in specific cases, the parallel issue remains: why *these* cases? Just as too expansive definitions of "religion" dissipate the value of that word—if everything is religious, nothing is religious, it is said—then too expansive uses of "irony" dissipate the value of that outlook: if everything is ironic, then nothing is irony, in any useful sense. From transcendent and common sense angles alike, of course, all human history is ironic. Outcomes usually contradict "the promise and fitness of things." One uses restraint, then, in applying it to cases. The issue of what historians call "exceptionalism" comes to the fore.

Normally, one would be restrained in the turning of an ironist's eye on the poor or oppressed of the world, even or especially in the rare cases when good things happen ·to contradict what might have been expected to happen, as in the case of their victory in a revolution when the odds were in favor of their defeat. Of course, the poor and oppressed are capable of living with illusions, but these are not of the sort that usually evoke ironic interpretation. On those terms, the vast majority of pages devoted to social history would have little reason to display irony. One would not readily apply it to victims of the Irish potato famines or of religious persecutions in Europe. The generous natural, human, and political resources of America, on the other hand, have been more rich in developing illusion thanks to "the promise and fitness of things" that seem to be inherent in its situations.

Religion, the present subject, intensifies the potential for illusions. Religion in America, of course, admits ironic interpretation before any elements of "the modern" are plausibly to be discerned. Reinitz singles out and successfully makes the case for irony in Francis Parkman, Richard Hildreth, Henry Adams, down to Carl Becker in respect to those longer American pasts, and especially shows how Richard Hofstadter's ironist eye informed his writing on earlier periods (III, 2, 3; V, 2). Thus the American Puritans, as Perry Miller constantly observed (Wise, 1968), in respect to their aspirations and illusions relating to their covenant and their chosenness have been ripe subjects. Similarly, in the national period, as the concept of the covenant and chosenness were enlarged into the notion of the *Redeemer Nation* (Tuveson), many occasions credibly call forth and even demand the ironic vision. Both South and North in the Civil War lived with illusions of innocence, virtue, wisdom, and power. There are, most scholars admit, more reasons to discern tragedy than irony in the South, though C. Vann Woodward (209–10) also employs and observes irony there, and irony marks much of the North's contradictory outcomes. Given this background, it would be vain to speak of the unique validity of irony in the modern unfolding. But the exceptionalist is content with distinctives as opposed to uniqueness, and distinctive reasons abound. The age almost universally spoken of as liberal, progressive, and modern provided a stage full of actors for whom religion was the intensifier of illusions, and the way they lived with those illusions and the outcomes of their ventures set the matrix for later twentieth-century events. Thus whenever "modernisms" in theology are reasserted, as they were in the mid-twenties and mid-sixties, one sees in the denial of "the promise and fitness of things," as perceived by the agents who propound modernisms, something that extends an element first discernible around the turn of the century. Similarly, whenever "fundamentalisms" in reaction to the modern find aggressive restatement, as they did in the mid-twenties and mid-eighties, one is prepared to see the beginnings of new ironic outcomes to match their illusions. Yet there is no reason to dismiss out of hand the plausibility and human aspiration in many endeavors of both camps.

THE EYES OF THE BEHOLDERS

Four sets of eyes are involved with the exceptional stories of modern American religion. The first two belong to people with the advantages of longer hindsight, who have the better perspective on outcomes and the distance that makes sympathy for intentions more difficult: the historians and their readers who come on the scene long after. The other two sets of eyes belong to people who have had less time and, because of their own involvement with illusions, less motivation to gain perspective on outcomes: the actors themselves. Yet even in their brief years, enough of them gave evidence of ironic awareness to legitimate a chronicling of these. To take a vivid example from modernist camps, the Social Gospel progressives, it is well known, had to deal with the trauma of World War I and the frustration of Wilsonian idealism as almost instant contradictions to the promise and fitness of things—and they as actors, and their original purposes, had been part of "the fundamental cause of the disparity" between intention and outcome. Their antagonists, who became the parties of Fundamentalism, in their intention to come up with a single, verifiable, authoritative orthodoxy, ironically observed themselves fighting with each other over a wild pluralism of anti-modernist options, many of them self-contradictory even if all based on a Bible now called inerrant, interpreted by Common Sense Realist rationalists.

RHETORICAL CRITICISM AND HISTORY

In order to track the interpretations of the actors who saw ironic outcomes on their own, or the other possessors of eyes among their contemporaries, their enemies, one develops particular genres of historical writing. For example, the illusions of the American poor and oppressed, the followership in religion, are less the subject than are those who give voice to and sustain the illusions and are agents of acts based upon them. This means that one must hear the voice and read the evidences. What results is what I would call "rhetorical history," or history of rhetoric, which lies between more pure intellectual history on the one hand and deliciously impure social history on the other.

Paul Crawford provides some guidelines for such rhetorical history, history written by the critics who first "must so absorb the realities of conflict and the climate of opinion and audience attitudes of the time under consideration" that they can mentally place themselves in the past under study, yet must not pretend to divorce themselves "from the advantages that recent scholarship has given to hindsight" (102–3). The actors in this story did not wake up one morning in 1893 and decide to be subjects of ironic interpretation. Historians must remember that as much as they are alert to outcomes.

Second, critics must try to identify and distinguish ideas and attitudes of rank-and-file members of a movement and the views of its leaders, "particularly as embodied in their private expressions or in remarks to relatively sophisticated hearers who may not be typical of ordinary members" (ibid.). In these transactions, the occasions rich in ironic potential are given nuanced expression. The accent is likely to remain on the rhetoric of the leader and one must deduce from it something of what the followers heard or read. Thus if a Milwaukee priest and journalist can, over a period of years, fill halls and parks with Polish Catholics who agitate for Polish bishops for Polish people, one need not follow home all members of the audience to search for their probably never-existing diaries or likely lost letters in order to learn something of these peoples' expectations.

In respect to method, third, there must be attentiveness to the written or oral discourse *and* other forms of symbolic behavior, since many of the actors' intentions and expectations come in a complex of communicative modes. Finally, especially when studying the subject of religion, which can be epiphenomenal in a pluralist culture, the rank and file members and leaders may have only been identified with one or two phases or aspects of a movement for brief periods of time. These four observations are not a complete methodological prescript, but they do remind that rhetorical history, like rhetorical criticism in the literary world, follows some broad sets of rules.

MODERNIST AND ANTI-MODERNIST EXTREMES AS CASES

This is not the place to detail as a case study the five sets of actors who crowd my stage at the turn of the century, the matrix of Modern American Religion. Suffice it to say, by way of illustration, that the world view of the theological modernists, who saw themselves as cosmopolitan or universalizing propounders of a progressive religion on the lines of a single rational and scientific model, turn out today to sound more dated and less accessible to most readers than do or would agents of Hassidic Judaism, Asokan-era Buddhism, or primitive or medieval Christianity. The British social philosopher Ernest Gellner spoke to this ironic situation: "As the Christians have found, the modernism of one generation is doubly dated in the next" (123).

Yet these modernists, as people of conscience and responsibility, had to act, and their intention to make the faith come out with what they saw to be a humane and in any case inevitably progressive unfolding of history, was marked by a spirit that can easily evoke admiration. Similarly, their enemies, who came to be called fundamentalists, who formed their party not as simple old conservatism but in reaction to modernism, can be seen to have had responsible intentions before the outcomes of

their agency contradicted the promise and fitness of things. The fundamentalists were able to show that modernists were failing with their
apologies, most notably among the secular intellectuals at whom they
were aimed; and the modernists could quote fundamentalists not finding
the unitive orthodoxy that seemed so obvious to them, but instead engag-
ing in internecine warfare and sectarian battles. Thus one kind of pre-
millennialist said of another that it was bannered as inclusive primitive
Christianity, yet it "had nothing new in it that is true and nothing true
in it that is new."[4] And while each camp made the claim that its orthodoxy of fundamentals was manifestly the right interpretation of the
Bible, one reactionary could ask another, in lines that suggest an awareness of irony, "Do you think it wise to exalt into a 'test of fellowship' a
doctrine so recently enunciated, that does not have a single passage of
Scripture beyond the question of a doubt upon which to rest its feet?"

THREE OTHER CASE STUDIES ANTICIPATED

The three other sets of actors include the literary and philosophical
"moderns," leaders of religiously bonded ethnic groups and denominations, and discerners of the negative effects of modernity who invented
modern therapies (the ecumenical movement, the Social Gospel, and
imperial civil or public religion). Ironically, the first of these, who ordinarily saw themselves, and were seen as, secular, turned out to devise
religious or quasi-religious alternatives to the religion they would displace. Ironically, the leaders of the groups devised means to distance
their members from confusing and beguiling elements in the surrounding pluralist culture, only to see that participants in the groups came in
any case to find conflict between parties within them to be more urgent
and satisfying than with parties around them. Ironically, discerners of
differentiation, in their interest in promoting "wholeness," the organic,
the *restitutio ad integrum* of which William James spoke, succeeded
chiefly in being dismissed as adding to the competition of claimants to
loyalty, and for being modernists who did not find their way back to the
integrum at all. One should also add a grand "ironically" in respect to
the already-referred-to reactionaries: ironically, it was precisely in the
period that historians almost universally mark as modern, liberal, and
progressive that all the enduring twentieth-century intransigencies and
conservatisms were born. Here we might cite Conservative Judaism and
organized Orthodox Judaism, unyielding Eastern Orthodox Christian tra-
ditionalisms, anti-modernist Roman Catholicism that would dominate
until Vatican II (1962–65), many forms of black Protestant conservatism,

---

[4] The several allusions and quotations in the brief illustrative portion of this case study
are not germane to the theoretical material here; references to these will be provided in
the long narrative chapters in Marty, 1986.

and the panoply of Protestant options including fundamentalism, reactionary evangelism, pentecostalism, premillennialism, and the like.

These five sets of actors, here so cryptically referred to, become the subjects of a narrative hundreds of pages long. The narrative is the place to test the case study, but the framework of the narrative, the hermeneutical preunderstanding, has, I believe, broader promise for religious studies in general. The ironic interpretation of religion may have a quiet contribution to make to modern politics, when religion is so often the bonding agent in aggressive, national, ethnic, and cultural aggressive movements.

HUMANITIES AND HUMANE IRONY

I cannot resist the suggestion as well that while not all humanities studies must be humanistic—some structuralisms and formalisms, it is often suggested, are not, even in intention—so they need and will not always be humane, as in the sense and case of "humane irony." Yet, since historians remain in the humanities, and ply their trade in the company of scholars in religious studies, and since they will, in this reading, willy nilly bring presuppositions and assumptions to their narratives, it is valid to project some consequences of the particular ones they bring.

Insofar as their inquiries, teaching, and writing have a bearing on the outlooks of colleagues, students, and readers, it is valid to ask whether the weariness of ironologists about the concept of irony itself, or the wariness of irony hounds like Hayden White, should preempt the space that might be given to the Niebuhrian irony that Reinitz calls "humane." One need not bias religious studies by working out of the background of a belief in a God who is perceived as "not hostile to human aspirations." On purely humanistic grounds, one can promote sympathy for such aspirations; indeed, many humanists would keep religion at a distance precisely because it does not always promote such sympathies through its accent on the transcendent.

As a consequence, Hayden White's contention that "irony tends to dissolve all belief in the possibility of positive political actions" because it tends to a view of "the essential folly or absurdity of the human condition" (434) can be countered. The folly and absurdity may be essential *to* that condition, but they are not, at least not for all irony hounds, *the* essentials *of* that condition.

REFERENCES

Bingham, June
    1960   *Courage to Change: An Introduction to the Life and Thought of Reinhold Niebuhr*. New York: Scribner's.

Booth, Wayne C.
1974   *The Rhetoric of Irony*. Chicago: University of Chicago.
1983   "The   Empire   of   Irony."   *The   Georgia   Review*
            XXXVII/4:719ff.

Brooks, Cleanth
1947   *The Well Wrought Urn: Studies in the Structure of
            Poetry. New York: Reynal and Hitchcok.*

Burke, Kenneth
1945   *A Grammar of Motives.* Englewood Cliffs, NJ: Prentice-
            Hall.

Crawford, Paul
1980   "The Farmer Assesses His Role in Society," in Paul H.
            Boase, ed., *The Rhetoric of Protestant and Reform,
            1978–1898.* Athens, OH: Ohio University Press.

Fussell, Paul
1970   "The New Irony and Augustans." *Encounter* XXXIV. June,
            1970.

Gellner, Ernest
1964   *Thought and Change.* Chicago: University of Chicago.

Heller, Eric
1958   *The Ironic German: A Study of Thomas Mann.* London:
            Secker and Warburg.

Hynes, Samuel
1969   *The Pattern of Hardy's Poetry.* Chapel Hill, NC: Univer-
            sity of North Carolina.

Marty, Martin E.
1986   *Modern American Religion: The Irony of It All.* Chicago:
            University of Chicago (in process).

Muecke, D. C.
1969   *The Compass of Irony.* London: Methuen and Co.

Niebuhr, Reinhold
1952   *The Irony of American History.* New York: Scribner's.

Oxford
1933   *Oxford English Dictionary.* Oxford: Clarendon.

Reinitz, Richard
1980   *Irony and Consciousness: American Historiography and
            Reinhold Niebuhr's Vision.*

Stone, Lawrence
1981   *The Past and the Present.* Boston: Routledge and Kegan
            Paul.

Thomson, J. A. K.
1927   *Irony: An Historical Introduction.* Cambridge, MA:
            Harvard.

Tuveson, Ernest Lee
1968 *Redeemer Nation: The Idea of America's Millennial Role.* Chicago: University of Chicago.

White, Hayden
1973 *Metahistory: The Historical Imagination in Nineteenth-Century Europe.* Baltimore: Johns Hopkins.

Wise, Gene
1968 "Implicit Irony in Perry Miller's *New England Mind.*" *Journal of the History of Ideas* VII/.
1973 *American Historical Explanation.* Homewood, IL: Dorsey Press.

Woodward, C. Vann
1968 *The Burden of Southern History.* Baton Rouge, LA: Louisiana State University Press.

AMERICAN PHILOSOPHY OF RELIGION FROM A EUROPEAN PERSPECTIVE: THE PROBLEM OF MEANING AND BEING IN THE THEOLOGIES OF IMAGINATION AND PROCESS

FRITZ BURI*

The presumptuous task of presenting to this honorable convention a European perspective on American philosophy of religion contains two difficulties. One consists in the fulness of material, too much to be treated in an hour. The second consists in the question: how does "European" differ in meaning from "American"? The first difficulty forces me to make a selection from the varieties of American philosophies of religion, to which—also in my mind—theology belongs as a principal part. From the fulness of American philosophy of religion as represented by outstanding theological and philosophical thinkers of this country, I shall choose two types: the so-called theology of imagination and process theology. In dealing with these two manifestations we obtain at the same time a certain characterization of European theology and philosophy. In contrast to the American situation we have in Europe no real equivalent to either the theology of imagination or process theology and until now neither has found a great echo there, although both of them have important roots in Europe, too. So you may take it as a sign of repentance for my brethren when I direct my European perspective on American philosophy of religion to the theologies of imagination and process.

There is, however, a further reason for this choice. From its origin in New Testament eschatology and in view of the non-arrival of the Parousia, Christianity has been occupied in different formulations

*Professor of Systematic Theology (Emeritus) at Basel University, Dr. Buri has lectured and taught in the United States and Japan and is widely acknowledged as the leading European interpreter of North American theology and philosophy of religion. Professor Dr. Buri's essay was presented as a 75th Anniversary Lecture at the 1984 annual meeting of the American Academy of Religion. For the Academy, the Editor expresses gratitude to Professor Harold H. Oliver (Boston University School of Theology) for the present English translation of Professor Buri's German text.

with the problem of meaning and being throughout its whole history, searching for ever new solutions to it. In contrast to other kinds of theology and philosophy of religion the theology of imagination and process philosophy and theology are basically struggling with this problem, even when they are not always sure of its historical roots, or when they transform its mythological form into a more or less secular philosophical-speculative one. Their truth lies not so much in their pretended solutions to the meaning-being problem as in their striving with it, as is the case in the biblical understanding of history—and throughout the whole history of Christianity.

That is the point I should like to make in my following confrontation with the theologies of imagination and process which is presented as a contribution not only to the American but to the European philosophical-theological situation as well, and possibly also as a basis for a real encounter with Far Eastern thinking. For this purpose I have chosen two pairs of representatives of theologies of imagination and process, and a third pair who combine them. For the first I have chosen Ray L. Hart and Gordon Kaufman; for the second, John Cobb and Schubert Ogden; and, for the last, David Tracy and Robert Neville. I think that the outstanding position of these thinkers justifies my restricted choice, and I hope that those who represent other kinds of thought will profit from the critique, also, and that those whom I critique will have some understanding for my bold undertaking to try to understand them better than they understand themselves.

I

We shall begin our series with Ray Hart who, with his book, *Unfinished Man and the Imagination* (1968), was to my knowledge the first to introduce the concept of imagination to the American theological scene, although not initially with great success because of the difficulty of reading his book. In one remark he mentions Horace Bushnell's book, *Our Gospel a Gift to the Imagination* (303). Otherwise he comes to terms mainly with philosophers, with Aristotle and with Kant's concept of the transcendental imagination, appeals to historians of literature and philosophers of language, such as Dilthey and Gadamer, and also makes use of Husserl's phenomenology. In an appendix he deals with "pre-modern" cognates of his concept of imagination in catholic and protestant scholasticism.

This concept gained special significance for Hart when he endeavored to use the kind of knowledge inherent in it to render intelligible the concept of language- or word-event taken over by him from the Bultmannian school. While Bultmann still spoke of the Word of God as an "eschatological event" whose mythological form is to be interpreted existentially, that is, as an expression of a self-understanding which finds its fulfillment of meaning in an alignment with it, several disciples of Bultmann abandoned the questionable concept "eschatalogical" because it appeared to them still too mythological for speaking of the proclaimed Christ event as a language-event which—mediated by language—is said to occur in faith. Without entering into a discussion of the ontological significance which arose with this existential-ontological concept, that is, to what extent it occurs in the divine and to what extent in the human realm, Hart believes he can resolve the difficulty of the beingness of meaning which arose in connection with the understanding of the Christ event as language-event, and can make it more intelligible, by more accurately describing "the mystery of the Word of God" for believers in terms of imagination.

That he is concerned primarily with the question of meaning is evident at the beginning of his book where he deplores the fact that for modern man the Christian faith is no longer what it had been for so long, namely, a "house of meaning". But he is convinced that it can become so again if only the "Given" of theology—the event of the Word of God—can again be made valid. For this purpose it is necessary to distinguish between two kinds of language: a "first order language" which—as he characterizes it—"preserves that body-heat intimacy which obtains between apprehension and the reconfiguration of linguistic debris which expresses it" and "as such is eventful", and a "second order language" which "withdraws from the language-event in order to place it in a larger frame, to connect it with apprehensions embedded in the language of common currency, and so to enhance its communicability in and to the public domain" (28). In contrast with what is "immediately given" for theology, namely, the "Word of God" as the "event of the Word of God in human audition" and to the "paradigmatic events" which have "left the stamp of their immediacy upon language" (44), theology belongs to second order language; and the decisive question for theology may be "whether its own linguistic debris can be used to erect a new house of first order language; i.e. can be used to bring the subject-matter of theology to language-event" (28). Otherwise than in a mere philosophy of culture or even in a neo-orthodox "senkrecht von oben" (118) this can only happen in the imagination as an "event-inverbalizing language" (49).

It is understandable that Hart in this connection also mentions Kant's use of the concept of imagination in his *Critique of Pure Reason* (186, 236, 338f.). For just as Kant in his transcendental imagination deals with the ontological character of perception, representation and comprehension which are bound together in it into a

unity, so also Hart vindicates the ontological character of his imagination not only—in contrast to Kant—in the sphere of phenomenality,
but for salvation facts of faith knowable as such. Hart reproaches Kant
not only for the lack of such an ontological knowledge, but also for
omitting the role of feeling and for failing to take into account the
historicity of the understanding. With his combination of imagination
and will—"Imagination is the intellectual organ of the will" (196)—he
already stands nearer to Fichte when in his own "anthropological
analysis" he replaces the Fichtean self-positing by an indefinable
"being situated and self-situating" (156n71) and sees in it the basis for
an "ontology of revelation" (109ff.).

There are experiences of meaning—the hindrances which resist
the will to meaning and the creative realization of meaning which
arises out it in the imagination—on the basis of which Hart believes
he can accede to pronouncements about being. When the consciousness of reality is shaken because of its meaning and points beyond
itself, man can become ready to accept the gospel of God's salvation in
Christ as valid for himself and is thus able to understand his existence
in the world *coram Deo*.

Hart describes in detail this eventful becoming of salvation in self-
and world-understanding by recourse to a "hermeneutical spiral"
(61f.) and to Gadamer's "horizon-fusion" (58) by means of Husserlian
phenomenology and by analogy to the nature of the work of art.
Instead of a demonstration of the problematic of this existential-
ontological meaning-being-construction—which would not be very
fruitful—I should like to call attention to a passage in Hart's explication in which he speaks of a possibility—though not for himself—of
overcoming this problematic. This takes place in connection with a
discussion of the concept of *potentia obedientalis*, that is, the predisposition of man for divine grace (177f.).

Hart correctly rejects the use of this concept for a intra-divine
occurrence, as in Ebeling, in favor of an event in human self-
understanding, in which the awareness of incompleteness forms the
point of contact of true human existence. He speaks here in the words
of Merleau-Ponty of an "antinomy of grace" as the "turning" point
"where the real self '. . . as the trembling of a unity exposed to
contingency and tirelessly recreating itself' accedes to being constituted out of community with being—care-fully refunded for its good
.out of its ownmost potency" (178). This corresponds to the formulation of Martin Buber which he also mentions: "It depends on me" and
"I am given over for disposal" (177). One could here also recall
Jasper's "reception of one's self as a gift" (Sich-selber-geschenkt-
Bekommen).

Hart, however, mentions Jaspers only in a remark referring to a secondary source, for he regards this philosophical self-understanding as insufficient, because "the Christ-event", "the subject-matter of theology" which—in Hart's view—"is what [theology] and it alone can say" does not get stated. Since for all his stress on the necessity for imagination Hart is and remains a theologian of the word, he misses the chance to see in the forms of a not-specifically Christian, more universally human self-understanding which experiences itself in its enactment as graced, the substance of the Christ-event and thus as a symbol for the meaning-possibility of human existence attested and experienced in these forms, and thus remains stuck with his imagination in the "word-prison" of an ambiguous "language-event".

What about the other representative of the theology of imagination, Gordon Kaufman? Did he take the opportunity to be liberated from the "word-prison" in which Hart, no less than Bultmann, though in different ways, is confined? Does Kaufmann take the chance indicated of understanding Christian existence as symbolic of human self-understanding, or with his concept of imagination does he become entangled ever deeper in its snares?

Initially it could seem that the former is the case. In his first book of essays, *God the Problem* (1972), there is a chapter that carries the title, "God as Symbol", to which he assigns an important role in the development of his thinking. While in his *Systematic Theology* (1968) he reckoned with the objectivity of salvation-facts in a manner more massive than does Hart, here he begins to understand these as products of the symbolizing knowledge of faith, which is quite different from Hart's persistent ontological talk about a "language-event".

For this turn in the development of his theology Kaufman has provided a comprehensive justification in his *Essay on Theological Method* (1979). In the collected essays on essential topics of Christian theology in his second book of essays, entitled, *The Theological Imagination* (1981), he makes use of this method, as the subtitle shows: "Constructing the Concept of God". While with Hart imagination, since it occurs as an "intellectual organ of the will", represents the sphere in which the revelation of God occurs as "language-event", with Kaufman it is man who in imagination constructs the concepts of the religious tradition, so that they form for him "constructs of imagination". Language-events are apparently quite different from imaginative constructs, in that the former occur in imagination, while the latter occur through imagination. In comparison with Hart's Husserlian foundational theory, Kaufman's epistemological conceptualizing is less demanding, as is evident in the fact that he speaks in an undifferentiated way of "image/concepts" (1981: 14).

When considering imagination Kaufman also differs from Hart in taking account not only of Christian theology and especially its Christ-event; for he sees imagination as a longing for meaning and orientation to meaning in all human culture and in the veneration of meaning-giving powers in all religions (1981: 172ff.). This human estimation makes possible for him a positive evaluation of the world of religions, as is not the case in Hart's restriction of the imagination to the Word of God given only for theology.

This enlarged way of regarding the history of culture and religion becomes effective in Kaufman's understanding of revelation in two ways: on the one hand, in a negative-critical manner, insofar as it liberates him from the exclusivity claim of Christian mythology, and on the other hand, in a positive manner insofar as this cultural and historical view in whose context he discusses the biblical-Christian history of salvation offers him an alternative for what is put into question with this kind of consideration, in that for him the histori- cally conditioned biblical-Christian view is now replaced by the religious and cultural evolution of mankind. As he appeals for this to a salvation-historical conception of creation, Kaufman does not hesi- tate to include nature in this universal conception of world and history (1981: 209f.), and to attribute to man, whose completion he sees in the image of Jesus Christ (1981: 114ff.), a special significance as the center of the possible realization of salvation and meaning in the whole of being.

Kaufman sees a difference between the two universal worldviews only insofar as the mythological one is cultically more effective than the more abstract-scientific and metaphysical one, but which for the sake of its effectiveness has to be corrected by the latter. For all their differences what is common to both formulations, according to Kauf- man, is that they are constructions of the human longing for comple- tion of meaning and that according to their mutual testimony this completion of meaning consists in the humanization of man in active love.

In the measure of their humanizing effect as in the truthfulness of the religious or metaphysical grounding of this historical effectiveness Kaufman believes to have found the criterion by which the truth of the two constructions can be judged in their similarities and differences. Under this perspective he submits these different patterns of an unending critical examination and demands correspondingly also their continuing reconstruction.

Since Kaufman is a theologian of the Church it is quite obvious that in this concern he is especially occupied with the God whom Christians in "worship and service" trust as the meaning-ground of human existence, while for him the corresponding abstract-metaphys- ical worldviews form only its negative background insofar as he, with

Kant, considers an empirical-rationalistic or speculative proof of God as impossible. With Kaufman it is imagination which takes over the role which Kant in this connection assigns to the practical reason for which God is a postulate of morality. For the humanizing significance of the idea of God Kaufman appeals not only to the history of culture and religion in general, but in particular to his development in the history of the biblical faith in God which peaks in the figure of Jesus as the "model of true humanity". In the humanizing force of faith in God which actualizes human nature he believes he can detect the proof that it deals "with actuality, not merely fantasy", and that God as meaning-ground of reality is simultaneously its ground of being. "Faith", declares Kaufman, "lives from a belief in, a confidence that, there is indeed a cosmic and vital movement . . . toward humaneness, that our being conscious and purposive and thirsting for love and freedom is no mere accident, but is undergirded somehow in the very nature of things". For such a faith "God is the personifying symbol of that cosmic activity which has created our humanity and continues to press for its full realization" (1981: 49f.).

For this kind of thought in which Kaufman comes to this connection between the ground of being and meaning in God, it is significant that he interrupts the critical discussion of the mythically transparent picture of God just at the point where it comes into conflict with the modern image of man and history (1981: 38f.) and that he takes it up anew after having exhibited the meaning-giving moments in reality contained therein, in order to conclude from them the existence of God, and thus to establish the reality of God in its function as the fulfilment of the human longing for meaning.

The imagination in which this occurs consists therefore not only in the fact that this theologian—like the famous man from Muenchhausen—thinks he can draw out of his own head—that is, from his longing for meaning—the problematic of human meaning, but that the place at which he could connect with it—in contrast to Muenchhausen—he takes as a product of his imagination. Or, to illustrate his situation with a less malicious, but by him seldom used image: On a map he designates individual points of meaning by means of which he thinks he is able to reach the goal of complete realization of meaning (1972: 100; 1979: 28). But not only does this destination lie outside the map, but with the intelligibility of these milestones he runs the risk that the map which he inscribes renders only an imaginative landscape of longing and does not provide access "to the things as they really are". If, despite this, he appeals to Feuerbach's judgment that the transcendence of his concept of God excludes the illusion of a mere satisfaction of needs (1981: 43), it cannot achieve this purpose for him, because it too represents such a construct of the imagination arising out of the human need for meaning.

II

Obviously it is not sufficient—with Kaufman—to enlarge the half-mythological Christ-event, to which Hart refers the imagination, into a history of culture which peaks in Christianity. This the process theologians seem to have known when they have attempted to understand being as such as an occurrence of meaning and to include Christology in it. Two of the most representative contemporary process theologians have made this attempt, each in his own way: John Cobb, in his most extensive publication, *Christ in a Pluralistic Age* (1975) and in his systematic sketch, *Process Theology*, published a year later with his pupil, David Griffin (1976); and Schubert Ogden, in his *The Point of Christology* (1982) which appeared sixteen years after his collection of essays, *The Reality of God* (1966). For Cobb, as for Ogden, Christ represents the center of meaning of Whiteheadian-Hartshornean process philosophy, with whose help they believe they can solve the problems of traditional Christian salvation history, and with their philosophical mentors they base their de-substantialized metaphysics of meaning on experience. Both also confess that they have passed through significant changes in their theological development, in that for their originally rationalistic thinking the imaginal or symbolic has gained decisive significance. But in contrast to the theologians of imagination with whom they share the need for meaning in experience, they do not orient it merely to history, or to a single event; rather as they see it, the cosmic process as a whole constitutes the event of meaning in which the man of faith participates, for it culminates in Christ and is pervaded by him.

John Cobb begins his Christology by taking on André Malraux's art-historical thesis that in Western art the supra-earthly figure of the redeemer is increasingly replaced by an earthly figure who finally totally disappears in the plurality of profane styles. While Malraux sees in this course of the history of art which he analyzes a proof for the irresistible weakening of Christianity, Cobb believes he can draw just the opposite conclusion from Malraux's view, insofar as he believes he can see in the transformation of the divine figure of the Christ into a human one and the subsequent richness of new creative styles a typical example of that with which Christian faith deals, viz. the incarnation of God in Christ and the "creative transformation" which originated in this divine occurrence of salvation and became effective not only in the history of humanity, but even in the entire cosmos. This takes place in forms which are not limited to Christianity, but appear in other religions as well. Cobb summarizes his positive interpretation of Malraux's thesis as follows: "The process that relativized the Christ figure and then omitted it altogether was itself the power represented by the Christ figure, namely, the Christ himself" (1975: 54).

As this sentence indicates, Cobb distinguishes between the "Christ figure" and "Christ himself" as the "power" represented in the figure. From the art-historical discussion it is obvious that Cobb also employs for the Christ-figure the concept of "image" as is also customary in theology. But it is out of theology that there arises the concept of "Logos" which he employs for "Christ himself" and his "creative power". While the image is a way of depicting what is meant imaginally or even in abstract conceptuality, with "Christ himself" or the "Logos" we are dealing not with its depiction, but with its "power"; i.e., as Cobb says, with an "ontological status" and—as we can now say on the basis of the theologians of imagination previously treated—not merely with an affair of the imagination. To be sure, the latter emphasize that they deal not merely with products of the imagination; rather, to such products are to be ascribed veridical value provable in reality. It is in this sense that Cobb makes use of the imagination (1975: 75), insofar as the significance of the "world of images" has been disclosed to him, as he notes in the Foreword (1975: 14). But he regards an ontological foundation as indispensable for his Logos metaphysics and is convinced that with the help of Process Philosophy it is also possible.

In this sense he appeals to Whitehead, as he has done in all of his publications, so now in all three parts of this book in which he represents "Christ as the Logos", "Christ as Jesus" and "Christ as Hope". While in this book this takes place only in the form of individual characteristics and their application in aspects of Christology previously discussed, in the book, *Process Theology* (1976), which he published with David Griffin, the epistemological and metaphysical foundation of his Christology and of his entire theology is set forth in a systematic way. David Griffin, to whom was entrusted the first four chapters, argues in a very apodictic way, in that he simply presupposes the validity of Whiteheadian Process Philosophy. Rather than hindering us, this fact gives us reason to register critical objections against some of the individual expositions of this thinking and its application in theology.

Right at the beginning Griffin gives us reason for such a critique when, with reference to Whitehead's identification of "actual occasions" and "occasions of experience", he declares that Process Philosophy understands human experience "as a high-level exemplification of reality in general". For this "high-level" he refers to the reflexive experience characteristic of man—an experience which however is grounded in a "pre-reflexive" universal processual event independent of the former, but with which it is "merging" and therein experiences its "metaphysical depth" (Cobb & Griffin, 13).

This mutual dependence of human experience and cosmic event does not prevent him from speaking of this state of affairs by conceptually distinguishing between two kinds of process: a temporal process consisting of a transition from one real occasion to another in such a manner that the individual entities "perish immediately upon coming into being"; and a process which occurs within these individual occasions as they become concrete or "grown together" as they originate, but which now—in contrast to the former—are "timeless" (Cobb & Griffin, 13f.).

Aside from the fact that this doctrine of process is an "hypothesis" which cannot be proved scientifically but represents a speculative extension of a process interpretation of human experience into something universal and cosmic, this speculation is burdened with difficulties: What about the timelessness of this moment of process within its temporality? Griffin explains that "concrescence" does not entail "things which endure through a tiny bit of time unchanged", but with things which need just "that bit of time to become" (Cobb & Griffin, 15) If, on the one hand, they need time in order to become, then they are not timeless indeed. On the other hand, the "experience of the 'eternal Now' " is incompatible with the basic principle of thinking "that all reality is fundamentally process". If "to be real" means to be in process, then becoming concrete would not exactly be "reality".

That here a basic problem of Process Philosophy is at stake becomes evident in Cobb's debate with the Buddhist doctrine of "dependent co-origination" (Pratitya-samutpada) which dissolves all occurrences into a flux which cancels every temporal thingness, but loses on that account the personality of man, as Cobb rebukingly speaks of it (1982).

This problematic character of Process Thought becomes even more apparent in the characterization of "concrescence" as "enjoyment" (Cobb & Griffin, 16ff.). "To be, to actualize oneself, to act upon others, to share in a wider community, is to enjoy being an experiencing subject". For Whitehead this enjoyment occurs universally. "Every unit of process, whether at the level of human or of electronic events, has enjoyment". The distinction consists only in its becoming conscious, and this depends on the selective choice by which each unit of process determines in a creative way what it accepts from the past and transmits as an impetus to new experience, with the result "that each occasion is a selective incarnation of the whole past universe" and "that our activities will make a difference throughout the future" (Cobb & Griffin, 23).

What really takes place here: the single occasion or the universe? Not one without the other, but rather only one with the other in a selection and a particularity which belongs to the nature of the process as an event that is simultaneously temporal and timeless. Or with reference to what is human: human experience serves as a model of the cosmic process which in turn actualizes itself most completely in man's becoming aware of its universal character as a model. Because this speculation deals with a level of self-consciousness in which there is a loss of the subject according to Pratitya-samutpada and in a way which threatens process thinking, it occurs to us that process thought is nothing but a construction by which human beings in the world provide a meaning that is anchored in being as becoming. Griffin confirms this wishful character of process thought when—in view of our experience of the world as "a place of process, of change, of becoming, of growth and decay"—he speaks of "our basic religious drive" as "to be in harmony with the fully real" and of its fulfillment not in a flight from the world, but in an "immersion in the process" (Cobb & Griffin, 14).

While there are process philosophers who do not consider the religious striving for harmony and understand it purely in an immanent way, process theologians take it into account by including in the universal process the idea of God as its origin and effect. In contradistinction both to classical substance metaphysics and the thought of a "becoming God" they do that in the form of a "dipolar theism" in that they distinguish between God's "primordial and consequent" nature in a way dependent upon Whitehead and Hartshorne's partial correction of the former's terminology (Cobb & Griffin, 43). The two poles of the "creative-responding love" of God which as the "initial aim" toward creative transformation and also its "eros" actively permeate the processual event in each of its single acts and allows this absolute activity to complete itself in a passivity which respects human behavior—these two poles have as their metaphysical transcendental equivalents the becoming and perishing which characterize the processual event. Both of these poles are incarnate in the Logos, i.e. in its incarnation in Christ.

That is the point where Cobb in both of the books mentioned introduces his Logos Christology and from which he interprets the person of the historical Jesus as well as trinitarian-Christological dogma and from which there unfold eschatology and the doctrine of the Church—and from which finally he speaks of special problems like ecology, relations with other religions, especially Buddhism, feminist theology, etc.

As a whole, this process theology, which is carried through with great skill, although fraught with questionable vagueness, represents an interesting counterpart to the theology of imagination. Both are concerned with establishing the meaning of human existence. Their difference lies in the fact that the latter seeks with the help of the imagination to find it in the Christ event, or in its expansion into the history of culture or religious imagination; whereas process theology thinks it can anchor both moments in a speculative-cosmic metaphysical understanding of being as becoming. The problematic character of both of these undertakings consists precisely in their attempt to establish meaning in terms of an optimism about the meaningfulness of being which is not fully sensitive to the problematic of meaning.

In a way matched by few other process theologians, Schubert Ogden has been engaged in an extension and validation of the metaphysics of the dipolar God which is characteristic of this kind of theology. But in this circle he is the one who—as he confesses in his book on Christology—has become "increasingly sceptical" about this undertaking (1982: 135). However promising this may sound, the consequences which he has drawn out of this change of attitude about metaphysics which sounds much like a conversion are even less convincing. For the "boundless love of God", for which he has been concerned from the beginning, he no longer wishes to refer to its embodiment in the historical Jesus and its metaphysical exemplification in dipolar process metaphysics, but primarily to the apostolic witness of the experience of God's love associated in the tradition with this figure and which—as he claims—gives us the victory (1982: 126ff.).

In connection with our question about the possibility of founding the meaning of human existence we have to deal neither with the methodology which Ogden uses in the interpretation of the eschatological witness of faith nor with its results; rather we note that in both respects he overcomes neither the problem of faith and history unsolved in the theology of Ritschl and his school nor Martin Kaehler's theology of needs. What interests us here is the treatment he devotes to the problem of metaphysics. To that we must say that, contrary to his own assumptions (1982: 46f.), he does not arrive at a convincing solution of the problem of meaning and being. What he finds objectionable in classical Thomism as well as in the "neo-classical metaphysics" of process theology is the "categorial" character of their speculation about analogy which he would like to replace with a "literally symbolic one" which can be confirmed in praxis (1982: 133f.).

For this purpose he retains as before Hartshorne's dipolar conception of God and is not able to make clear the difference between the "categorial" analogy-speculation which he rejects and the non-analogical "symbolic", "transcendental" metaphysics which he postulates in its place (1982: 143). For even he engages in analogy-speculation when he seeks to reinstate his old fundamental sentence that the quest for the final meaning of our human existence presupposes a "basic faith in the worth of life" (1982: 30).

The difference between his position and that of classical metaphysics, which actually is not capable of giving an account of the Christ-event, consists in the fact that he thinks he can explain Hartshorne's dipolar view of God through this distinction between—as he says—the "symbolic rather than literal metaphysical assertion" that God "in himself" "as ultimate reality is boundless love" (1982: 144), and the fact that his love "for us" which has the effect of enabling us to deal in love with all our fellow-creatures, is "expressible only in non-cognitive religious language". For the former assertion he refers to the apostolic testimony about experience in Christ. In the latter he expands this view of experience by a reference to the nature of our own experience of love, which "implies not only acting on the other, but also, and just as surely, being acted on by the other" (1982: 145).

In view of this distinction we have to ask: How can Ogden say of the former assertion that it is "not literally metaphysical" although it speaks of what God is "in himself", and how is it possible that such a differentiated experience as he has in mind can be a "non-cognitivist" one? It is not doubted that the representatives of the apostolic witness are not interested in metaphysics, and certainly the praxis of love is something other than a theory of love. But this state of affairs does not become clear in the terminology used by Ogden, but is rather deposed from the intention he has in mind. According to their true intention symbols are the unavoidable as well as necessary "literal" objectifications of an existential self-understanding which experiences itself as related to Transcendence in community (Cf. Buri, 1984).

When Ogden quotes the Parable of the Last Judgment as the conclusion of his Christology and remarks that therein "in no way a christological, or even theological criterion" is brought out (1982: 167), and that we are obliged "not only to talk about the point of Christology but also to make it" (1982: 168), we are justified in seeing this as a self-problematization of his theology as well as a hint as to how one can understand him better than he understands himself, namely, that for existence no abolition of risk is possible, but that we can experience ourselves as blessed only in risking ourselves—in theory and in practice.

III

Now that we have demonstrated the nature and problematic of the theologies of imagination and process by means of two very different pairs of theologians, we still have to take into account two other theologians who attempt—apparently on the basis of their insight into the insufficiency of both of these kinds of theology—through combining them to overcome their shortcomings and to validate their elements of truth. As already indicated, they are David Tracy and Robert Neville.

Now that Ogden has so sharply criticized the use of analogy in the classical metaphysics of the churchly tradition (1982), David Tracy would not evaluate the theology of Ogden in as positive a manner as he did in an extended treatment of Process Theology in his book, *Blessed Rage for Order* (1975) and in a longer remark in *The Analogical Imagination* (1981) where he declares with more reserve:

> My own option is basically for the process theology tradition but not, I hope, without a more adequate treatment of some of the subtleties and the complexities of the Thomist (especially transcendental Thomist) position than the latter was accorded in BRO. I continue to believe (as in *BRO*) that process theologies need to develop and be corrected by the symbolic (and, therefore, radical mystery) side of the tradition and need, as well, a profounder sense of the negative in their developments of analogical language. I remain convinced, however, of the greater basic adequacy of the process tradition for interpreting the central Christian understanding that 'God is Love' and for resonating to a contemporary sense of change, process and internal relationships (see *BRO*, pp. 187–204). Still, the symbolic, the negative and the sense of radical mystery (incomprehensibility, hidden and revealed God, etc.) need more dialectical incorporation into a process systematic theological understanding of God (1981: 439–40).

Despite his denial of analogy, it may be that Ogden who has more recently (1982) advocated a "literal symbolic" conception of metaphysical assertions now complies at least intentionally to some degree with the demand Tracy brings forward vis-à-vis Ogden's earlier position. A closer juxtaposition between them is evident also in the fact that Ogden now advocates the establishing of faith in Jesus Christ on the authority of the apostolic witness (1982: 245)—a point positively stressed by Tracy with respect to Ogden's former position—in a more extensive and emphatic manner.

Despite Tracy's sympathy for Process Philosophy and Ogden's recourse to the "apostolic witness" as a source and norm of faith alongside one's own experience, there remain as before significant differences between the two theologians. Not only does Ogden avoid the concept of imagination which has won thematic significance for Tracy in his second book, but the difference between them noted by Tracy that he continues to ascribe "truth value" to "poetic language" over against Ogden's predilection for "non-poetic," "abstract" language (1981: 86) still persists, insofar as Ogden remains, as before, in the service of abstract metaphysical language and shows no interest in the use of literature and art which play a major role in Tracy's thought. It is true, as Tracy indicated, that Whitehead's "subjective principle", in consequence of which man serves as a model of process cosmology, corresponds to the transcendentalism of Rahner's metaphysics—as represented by Tracy—according to which the sought-for metaphysical point of relation is already contained in the question, insofar as in both methods an individual moment of meaning is confidently extended to the meaningfulness of the whole of being (1981: 412ff.). But even in this special kind of "natural theology" we must not overlook the important difference that with Ogden, as is generally the case in Process Philosophy, this metaphysics is represented in a rational way and on the basis of a directly established evolution, while Tracy, following the classical catholic pattern, appeals to analogy as a relation of "similarity in dissimilarity". Strange to say, he does not mention the dogmatized formula of *analogia entis* as a greater dissimilarity in similarity, but rather prefers to speak of a "soft" metaphysics which he advocates, with Rahner, as opposed to the "hard" classical one (1981: 161).

Wherein then consists the "analogical imagination" from whose formulation as the title of Tracy's second major work we learned the two points by which the latter distinguished himself from Ogden's Process Philosophy? We have already begun to speak of the nature of analogy in the comparison between the Whiteheadian "subjective principle" and the transcendental metaphysics of recent catholic theology, insofar as it determines the relation of immanence and transcendence, or of transcendence in immanence, epistemologically and ontologically. Between these two spheres a being-ful analogy exists, insofar as being is so ordered that from the perspective of human immanence a logical conclusion is possible, not only for being as a whole but also for its transcendent ground. According to the transcendental conception this immanence of transcendence is already present in the epistemological act of transcending and, as such, forms the natural presupposition for supernatural revelation, which on its side functions as the basis of the order of being and so makes possible that epistemological transcending, as Tracy characterized it in the title of his first book (1975).

In his book on analogy-speculation he introduces as his methodology of knowledge the concept of imagination which had been occasionally mentioned in his first book (1975:78), and explains it in detail. Referring to the "famous word" of Aristotle, "to spot the similar in the dissimilar is the mark of poetic genius" (1981:410), Tracy combines analogy with imagination as "a reflection upon the self's primordial experience of its similarity-in-difference to the event" (1981: 410). Between both of them exists a dialectical relationship insofar that "the same power—at once participatory in the originating sense of wonder, trust, disclosure and concealment by the whole, and positively distancing itself from that event by its own self-constituting demands of critical reflection—releases the analogical imagination of the systematic theologians to note the profound similarities-in-difference in all reality" (1981: 410).

As is evident from this quotation and its context, the event that is here at stake is a "religious event", or more precisely, the "Christ-event" and its efficacy as "all pervasive grace". But Tracy's intention is to see in this analogical imagination not merely an affair of theology; rather he wants to exemplify its theological application to the spheres of literature and art in their classical formulations, which for their understanding require the same methods as the Bible and the Christian tradition and teaching on the reality of God in general and salvation in Christ in particular. While earlier (1975) he viewed the revelation of transcendence in a dialectic of the limit of thinking as a self-manfestation of that which limits ("limit to" = "limit of"), later (1981) he unfolded the same dialectic in relation to the christological salvation-event and its "not yet and already"—in one case as the shattering of conceptual-objective knowing which has to be taken into account in the use of a symbol, and in the other case—in view of the problematic of the fundamental presupposition of the Christian faith—as the claim that the promised salvation in Christ has already occurred, but—in view of the non-arrival of the Parousia—has always to occur anew (1981: 252ff.).

In view of this irritating state of affairs Tracy speaks repeatedly of the "dangerous, provocative, subversive" memory of Jesus of Nazareth (1981: 424, *passim*). On the one hand he sees therein a warning against every false desire for harmony as it belongs to religiosity (1981: 154ff.). On the other hand he points to the whole of the Christian tradition and its classic formulations preserved in the Church as an indispensable help (1981: 164, 235ff.). Trust in these instances is for him included in trust in God's love revealed—albeit in a dialectical manner—in Christ, which—in accord with the nature of this faith—is to be extended through the analogical imagination to the whole of "God, man and world" in a way which justifies in an unending dialectic a pluralism of interpretations and religious bodies (1981: 447).

That is the manner in which Tracy would correct the Process Theology of his friend Ogden through analogical imagination. In accord with this intention he restricts the attempt by process theology to ground cosmologically the meaning of human existence in the meaning of being as a whole to an interpretation of meaning in the realm of social history effected on the basis of the Christian faith. If Ogden would see the relation between his experience of God's love witnessed in the apostolic faith and his own personal love-faith experience in a less rationalistic and metaphysical and more poetic, imaginative way, he could probably follow Tracy on his way to Rome, although this way would still need some analogical imagination even for Tracy. But I fear, or hope, that for both theologians the "dangerous memory of Jesus" would be a blessed obstacle on the way, since—as Tracy once concedes and Ogden takes quite seriously—to it belongs the fact of the non-arrival of the Parousia (1981: 265f.) as the great paradigm of the foundering of all universal constructions of meaning—a shattering that could become the symbol of true realization of meaning, if it is not eliminated, historically by Tracy, psychologically by Ogden, to their detriment.

Robert Neville has chosen another path on which he did not stop in the Christian West, but on which his Daimon guided him to the Tao of the Far East.

That and how we conclude the series of our selected representatives of American theology and philosophy of religion with Robert Neville results from the fact that he is, on the one hand, a keen-sighted critic of the theologies of imagination and process, and on the other, that as an equally great systematic thinker, he tries in one system to bring together the concerns and results of the two kinds of theology corrected by him, trusting that he is able to do justice to Christian faith in creation and redemption as well as to the Tao of Far Eastern thinking in a completion that unites the two.

In contrast to the ontological problematic of Hart's concept of event and Kaufman's use of imagination as pragmatic satisfaction of need, Neville univocally defines the nature of imagination as valuation bound up with norms in the context of the experience of thinking. Against their claim to overcome the subject-object split of consciousness, he reproaches the representatives of Process Philosophy and Theology for still treating process as an object and only in such a way that the subject of thinking as well as the subjectivity of God become problematic, insofar as one does not know who is doing the thinking, the process-event or the thinking subject, and insofar as the identity or non-identity of God with this process, or with its thinker, does not become clear (Cf. especially:1980). In his major, unfinished work (1981a), he contends—against the aprioristic-rationalistic character of

Kant's transcendental imagination—that it does not in his judgment take valuing feeling into account and is not able to explain the source of the forms of representation and the concepts of reason (1981a: 149ff.). He will hold fast to the "Naturalism" of Process Thought, insofar as he understands it to be far more differentiated than do its other representatives (1981a: 68ff.).

Neville's reconstruction of thinking represents an extremely differentiated network of several interrelated kinds of thinking which—each in its own way—appear in the special realms of the spirit and of culture and in which they validate their criteria. Imagination forms for Neville the starting-point and final basis of thinking. It consists in a valuing selection of individual components out of the manifoldness of experience, and the norm consists in their adaptibility into the totality of a harmony of "beauty". Religion is the pre-eminent field of appearance of this imagination. But thinking does not exhaust itself in imagination, for it involves a further structural element—interpretation—in which the contents of thought are tested for their "truth"—a criterion which is important in the field of "politics", but which plays no role in imagination itself. Furthermore, thinking demands theory which intends "formal unity" and results in "knowledge". This series concludes with the responsibility of the valuing one for his valuation in the "philosophical life" as "obligation to goodness" (1981a: 27ff.). Despite their differences these four aspects are not to be separated, but in fact entail each other, in that on the one side the valuing imagination continues in the succeeding ones as they presuppose it, and on the other side because responsibility is actualized in those which precede it.

Of this complex system of an "Axiology of Thinking" Neville has so far produced only the first part, viz. the imagination, and only indicated the pertinent parts which are to follow, so that it is not possible for us to make a conclusive judgment about his pretentious undertaking. Nevertheless, systematic difficulties are evident in what has appeared already, in that in the preview of the whole work "beauty" as a criterion is ascribed to the synthetic function of the imagination (1981a: 18), whereas in the exposition of the imagination in the present volume, in which interpretation forms an aspect of imagination, it is assigned to the sphere of "perception" in the "interpretation" (1981a: 177f.).

Another more important difficulty with which Neville is obviously struggling, is evident in the different location of imagination in the series of the different structures of thinking. While in his main work he places imagination at the beginning and allows thinking to begin with imagination (1981a: 135), in the recent sequel to it (1982: 236), it stands only in the third place, after interpretation and theory. Of course he does not fail to emphasize immediately that this "third dimension"—the imagination—is "in fact the one on which the others rest". But why doesn't he admit at the beginning, as he does in his basic theses, that thinking is grounded in "valuation", which first appears in imagination (1981a: x, 146f.), since this corresponds to the detailed analysis in this work and also agrees with what he set forth briefly in his later work (1982)? These final concluding remarks in the latter work are so instructive that a long citation is here in order:

> I use the word *imagination* here roughly as Kant did—to mean the basic activities of synthesis by which various causal impingements of the environment are transformed into the stuff of experience. The goal of the imagination is engagement. Images, the basic forms of imagination, are the terms in which experience is taken up; they constitute the basic orders of the world. In fact, they constitute the world in a crucial sense. Experience orders what otherwise would be merely mechanical pushes into a world with spatial and temporal dimensions, values and interests, vectors of forces and possibilities with various degrees of attractiveness. The function of imagination is to supply this order so that the other dimensions of thinking have structure and horizons in which to exist. This is not to say that the world is a solipsistic, subjective construct or that there is no external world; rather it is to say that the way human beings experience external elements is to "worldize" them. Any consideration of the truth of a particular assertion about what is real is based on, and therefore relative to, its own imagery, its own fundamental structure (1982: 236f.).

Anyone who is at least to some extent familiar with "the transcendental deduction of the pure concepts of understanding", which as is well known belongs to the most difficult and problematic sections of Kant's *Critique of Pure Reason,* will doubtless recognize the differences between Neville's and Kant's understanding of imagination which the former—in a way different from this summary—demonstrates in various places in (1981a: Cf. index, p. 342). Neville replaces Kant's apriori forms of intuition and understanding with the pictorial world of imagination. Although he also adds to these both "interpretation" and "theory", he exempts himself from the difficulties associated with the apriority of these forms, but at the same time through this connection of interpretation and theory with the imagination he ascribes to the latter the capacity for knowing "external reality" which Kant's restriction to its phenomenality does not permit.

Whereas proper theologians of imagination, with their images, do not escape the suspicion of an illusory wishful thinking, Neville can refer for his imaginal world to Process Philosophy in which these form a constituent part of reality conceived as process, but only so at the expense of the "unity of self-consciousness" which, according to Kant, accompanies all acts of thinking and which finally grounds their character as reality. The loss of the self in exchange for a "self-less", universal occurrence which is ultimately identical with some kind of impersonal deity is the price Neville has to pay for his overcoming of Kant through his processual theology of imagination, in which God becomes for him the "creativity" of the Holy Spirit (1981b). This problematic becomes most apparent in Neville's positive advance into the Far Eastern idea of the Tao, in which the dualism represented by Hart and Kaufman, and inherent in Kant as well, is replaced by a monism of being, and through a radically understood Pratitya-samutpada even the last vestige of objectivity in Whitehead's "concrescence" is overcome. He believes he can succeed in his attempt to secure the Daimon of theory might emerge. This could happen, however, not in a universal speculation about imagination or process, but only in a Christological theology of a self-understanding which experiences itself as related to its special Transcendence and which forms the basis of a community with a corresponding structure.

IV

To present such a theology here, even in its bare essentials, would exceed the framework of what could be expected of me as my task and far exceed the time we have at our disposal. As an indication of the epistemological and metaphysical structures of such a theology, I shall be content to close with some concise principles for appropriately treating the problem of meaning and being which could help a bit to clarify and correct the six types of contemporary American theology already discussed, so that they not only remain typically American, but may become even a bit more Christian.

For this aim we sum up the critical viewpoints used in the preceding in the following manner.

The two terms of the problem of meaning and being, namely, meaning and being, can and must be conceived at the same time as different as well as inseparable:

Meaning, first, as an (as much as possible) univocal *designation* of something meant in logical conceptuality, which in view of what is meant—constitutes an abstraction and always remains relative. This relativity becomes even stronger when what is at stake is not an (as much as possible) objective explaining, but an *interpreting* of what is meant in its subsequent enactment in a subjective valuing which, together with explaining, belongs to *understanding.*

This leads us, in the second place, to meaning as *value* which is characterized by the fact that its being is preferred to its non-being. This concept of value is only possible where the concept of meaning is understood as a striving for logical univocity and gives to the formality of the latter its being-ful content. Over against what is unknown even what is only relatively known represents a value, even though it is not possible on the basis of the first mentioned concept of meaning to establish an absolute order of value.

The connection between these two concepts of meaning—meaning as designation and meaning as value—leads necessarily to a corresponding differentiation in the concept of *being*:

First, we are dealing in the first instance in this meaning-thinking with a being rather than with the being which must for conceptual thinking remain a void.

Second, we can conceive *being* neither as the sum of all beings in the sense of the first concept of meaning—because in it we are always dealing only with a part of the totality of being—nor can we "mean" it as the foundation of beings without making it into a being.

While the being that is available to us only in this particularity remains a *riddle* both in itself and in relation to those of us who interrogate the meaning of our existence, in our *self-understanding*—which represents a void for our conceptualizing as well as for being, but nevertheless remains the root of our consciousness of being—we experience the *mystery of being* in a special way, namely, as the origin of what is for us the problematic of meaning and being. For man, because of the problem of meaning, being becomes a crisis and therein exhibits itself in its transcendence which can only be spoken of in *symbols* as indispensable objectifications of what is not objectifiable.

Philosophical and religious worldviews are expressions of this crisis as well as questionable attempts to overcome it. In theology, corresponding to these different philosophical connections or antitheses of meaning as designations of what is meant and meaning as value is the distinction or relationship between reason and faith. The problematic of the concept of being in the ontological difference is reflected in the distinction between God as Creator and the creatureliness of his creation, on the one hand, and on the other, between God as Redeemer and his salvation history in the salvific work of his Son—both united in the open mystery of the Trinity.

The problem of *language* is evident in philosophy as well as theology in the possibilities of mystical silence and the existential interpretation of objectifying mythology and speculation as the basis of a dialogue with other religions, and of a positive, critical attitude toward their redeemer figures. While the silence grows out of the awareness of the mystery of being and its riddle of meaning, the existential interpretation has the function of endowing that awareness with speech as a special revelation of the mystery of being by making possible particular realizations of meaning as a grace of being. It is the destiny of religions to inform one another in theory and practice of such real possibilities of individually restricted experiences of solutions of the problem of meaning and being and thereby to understand themselves and one another more deeply.

In *Christianity* the *problem of meaning and being* takes a special form, because in its historical origin it arose out of the non-fulfillment of the eschatological, being-ful expectation of meaning, or out of its transformation in the different churches based on this hope and their means of salvation. Christianity will have to do with the truth in respect to itself as well as in contrast to other conceptions of salvation only to the extent that it absolutizes none of the alleged solutions to the problematic of its origin which have arisen in the course of history, but rather sees in them only housings which have repeatedly to be dismantled in order to see itself constantly confronted anew with the problem of meaning and being, as we have experienced it in a partial way in our debate with six American theologians. Even in their self-conscious failures I know myself to be with them on the way to a future Christian theology, and I hope that you will in your own manner accompany us.

WORKS CONSULTED

Buri, Fritz
1956/1962/1978   *Dogmatik als Selbstverständnis des christlichen Glaubens.* 3 Volumes. Bern: Paul Haupt Verlag.
1970/1973   *Gott in Amerika.* 2 Volumes. Bern: Paul Haupt Verlag.
1982   *Der Buddha-Christus als der Herr des wahren Selbst.* Bern: Paul Haupt Verlag.
1984   "Bedeutung und Problematik der Christologie Schubert Ogdens." *Theologische Zeitschrift* 40, 223–28.

Cobb, John B., Jr.
1975   *Christ in a Pluralistic Age.* Philadelphia: Westminster.
1982   *Beyond Dialogue: Toward a Mutual Transformation of Christianity and Buddhism.* Philadelphia: Fortress.

Cobb, John B., Jr. and Griffin, David Ray
1976   *Process Theology: An Introductory Exposition.* Philadelphia: Westminster.

Hart, Ray L.
1968   *Unfinished Man and the Imagination: Toward an Ontology and a Rhetoric of Revelation.* New York: Herder and Herder.

Kaufman, Gordon D.
1968   *Systematic Theology: A Historicist Perspective*. New
               York: Charles Scribner's Sons.
1972   *God the Problem*. Cambridge: Harvard University Press.
1979   *An Essay on Theological Method*. Revised Edition. Mis-
               soula, MT: Scholars Press. Orig. publ., 1975.
1981   *The Theological Imagination: Constructing the Concept
               of God*. Philadelphia: Westminster.

Neville, Robert C.
1980   *Creativity and God: A Challenge to Process Theology*.
               New York: Seabury.
1981a   *Reconstruction of Thinking*. Vol. 1, Axiology of Thinking.
               Albany: State University of New York Press.
1981b   "The Holy Spirit of God." In *Is God GOD?*, 233–64. Ed.
               by Axel D. Steuer and James Wm. McClendon, Jr. Nash-
               ville: Abingdon.
1982   *The Tao and the Daimon: Segments of a Religious In-
               quiry*. Albany: State University of New York Press.

Ogden, Schubert M.
1966   *The Reality of God and Other Essays*. New York: Harper
               & Row.
1982   *The Point of Christology*. San Francisco: Harper & Row.

Tracy, David
1975   *Blessed Rage for Order: The New Pluralism in Theology*.
               New York: Seabury.
1981   *The Analogical Imagination: Christian Theology and the
               Culture of Pluralism*. New York: Crossroad.

SYSTEMATIC WONDER: THE RHETORIC OF SECULAR RELIGIONS

WAYNE C. BOOTH*

"Whatever the truth about these deep conceptual issues, the universe must have come into existence somehow, and quantum physics offers the only branch of science in which the concept of an event without a cause makes sense.... For millenia mankind has believed that nothing can come out of nothing. Today we can argue that everything has come out of nothing. Nobody needs to pay for the universe. It is the ultimate free lunch."——Paul Davies, *Superforce: The Search for a Grand Unified Theory of Nature* (pp. 203, 205).

"The third way [to prove God's existence] is taken from possibility and necessity, and runs thus. We find in nature things that are possible to be and not to be, since they are found to be generated, and to be corrupted, and consequently, it is possible for them to be and not to be. But it is impossible for these always to exist, for that which can not-be at some time is not. Therefore, if everything can not-be, then at one time there was nothing in existence. Now if this were true, even now there would be nothing in existence, because that which does not exist begins to exist only through something already existing. Therefore, if at one time nothing was in existence, it would have been impossible for anything to have begun to exist; and thus even now nothing would be in existence—which is absurd."——Thomas Aquinas, *Summa Theologica*, Question II, Article Three.

Last spring I spoke to a bunch of experts in religion, on a topic related to mine today—and I was scared. A rank amateur, I was trying to argue that the movement called deconstruction—by its opponents deconstruction*ism*—is best viewed as a religious revival, an essentially religious response to certain naive and dogmatic modernisms that outlawed "God-talk." I was scared because I knew that in

*George M. Pullman Distinguished Service Professor and Member of the Committee on Ideas and Methods at the University of Chicago, Dr. Booth presented this paper as a 75th Anniversary Lecture at the 1984 Annual Meeting of the American Academy of Religion.

addressing that learned body, I was threatened by boobytraps at every turn in my argument. So I felt obliged to cover my tracks in advance with elaborate professions of humility and pleas for indulgence. Today, tackling what I fear will seem an even more dubitable thesis, I see no point in wasting your time with that kind of rhetorical softening up. So I simply ask you to incorporate here the best exordium you have ever heard, the one that seemed, when you heard it, to establish the speaker as the most humble, sincere, energetic, open-minded, generous-spirited, critical yet devout inquirer you have ever encountered. Then please add whatever you can think of that will establish you now as the most forgiving audience in the history of religious thought, and we'll be ready to go.

It's hardly surprising that rhetoric and religion have always had troubled relations, no doubt for the same reasons that rhetoric and philosophy have been suspicious of each other. For thinkers who claim to have *the truth,* or at least claim to be seeking it, rhetoric often seems like a corruption of thought. If rhetoric is defined in the all-too-popular way as the art of winning arguments, regardless of truth—the art of making the worse seem the better cause—then it will often be considered the enemy of truth, and the rhetorician will appear as the very opposite of the religious or philosophical inquirer. You will remember how Augustine, after his conversion, wrestles with his former career as a rhetorician. He finally decides not to repudiate rhetoric, but only on the ground that since the devil is master of every rhetorical device, men of God cannot afford to surrender this dangerous tool (*De Doctrina Christiana,* Bk. 4)—a line of argument, by the way, that has proved useful to members of the National Rifle Association.

If rhetoric were nothing more than the art of persuasion, a way to give one's truths a fair chance in public debate, if it were only the art of adorning a truth that is discovered by other arts, then it would at best be a handmaiden to religion, at worst an enemy. As a handmaiden it might help the already converted to make more converts, and the study of rhetoric might help a modern scholar to understand the power of traditional texts. But rhetoric could not be seen as an indispensable ally in any specifically religious inquiry. It might reasonably be considered an irrelevancy or distraction, on the ground that the truly religious spirit wants to find more certain, more direct sources of faith and inspiration than any artificial study can provide.

On the other hand, if we think of rhetoric in a less familiar way, it might take over the whole show. If rhetoric is not the art of persuasion but the art of discovering together, in discourse, what we can or should believe, when we should or should not change our minds, when we have or lack good reasons for our faiths and commitments, then surely all religious inquiry, except perhaps for pure divination or mystical trance, is rhetorical. Whenever any theologian or preacher hopes to be understood, whenever any listener appraises the validity of what is spoken or written, the art of rhetoric will be employed, skillfully or clumsily. All religious discourse is by its nature disputable, dubitable to all who are committed to dubitation. All key religious terms refer to what W. B. Gallie calls "essentially contested concepts"—concepts that by their nature can never be finally fixed in a form acceptable to all inquirers (1964, chapter 8). In the language of some theologians: if the notions of religion had been made absolutely demonstrable, there would be no merit in faith. All religious discourse is therefore rhetorical—that is, it is *not* what we often think of as the opposite of rhetorical, namely scientific or apodictic demonstration.

Though I sometimes use this second definition of rhetoric, I think that it's not very helpful when we turn to specific subject matters. Since it turns almost everything into rhetoric, it doesn't say much about religious discourse that it doesn't say about other subjects we care about. So today I must turn to a third definition of rhetoric— rhetoric as the art of inter-translation among alternative rhetorics. If, according to the second definition, everyone has been "talking rhetoric" all the while without knowing it, according to this third definition the rhetorician will study how various rhetorics inter-translate, or resist inter-translation. We might want a new term for this third kind of rhetoric: meta-rhetoric, or perhaps meta-hermeneutics, but in practice it is almost impossible to draw a sharp distinction between it and the more everyday notions.

Used in this way, as intermediator, rhetorical study will always be useful to ecumenical movements and to pluralisms of various kinds. The reason is obvious. When we make a serious effort to look behind surface languages to the commitments and grounds that motivate them, we often find that people who think they are opposed to each other are actually saying the same thing. The ultimate in this direction has always been the search for some perennial philosophy or world religion that by its generality would discover and teach the essence of all actual philosophies or religions. At its extremes, this ècumenical drive in rhetorical study can turn into a wishy-washy sentimentalism—we're all brothers and sisters under the semantic skin; just ignore our seeming differences and we'll all enter heaven together.

But the effort to discover inter-translations need not assume that differences will disappear. It need only assume the importance of erasing differences that are not in fact there.

Among these seeming differences, I find the most interesting ones when I look at various modern secular languages and discover that they are grappling with what traditionally were thought of as religious problems. For some time now I've been trying to think about the various ways in which explicitly secular talk fills niches that were formerly filled by conventional religious language. (One might almost say, "feeds hunger," rather than "fills niches." But I don't want to suggest a reduction to psychological categories.) My claim is not quite that everybody talks religion without knowing it. But I do think that a lot of people do—that almost everyone uses language in a way that can be called religious, once we get our definitions straight. Indeed it is my general thesis that many ardent secularists, otherwise well-educated, are so badly informed about serious religious discourse that they unknowingly rehearse its problems and solutions clumsily, in languages that on the surface do not appear religious at all.

I

Everyone here knows just how deep is the seeming chasm between what we talk about at this convention and what is talked about in America's daily life and in our academic journals. Religion is one thing; hard practical affairs and genuine, objective, intellectual inquiry are in another domain entirely. A professor of religion told me last week of the difficulties he has encountered working within the American Academy of Arts and Sciences. He simply cannot convince the academics he works with, mostly from the natural sciences, that his subject, Christian Ethics, has any academic substance. We all know that the business of most of our colleagues is conducted with no reference whatever to explicitly religious language; indeed for public institutions to use religious language might well mean the cutting of federal grants. Nobody in faculty meetings in my lifetime has ever suggested—not even at the two Quaker institutions where I have taught—that we should adopt a given policy because it is God's will, or because a given scripture commands it, or because Christian or Jewish traditions require it. (I do remember one assistant professor who in 1969 tried to persuade me, as Dean, to embrace a position because it was dictated by the Tao—but that was in another epoch, and besides, the movement is dead.)

On the other side of this chasm, we see that those who use God-talk find no easy way to address secular affairs. When the Bishops speak, they do so as across the chasm, as if to say "we rare birds who have religion are now going to tell you, who don't, just what religion says about all that stuff over on your side." Those who consider themselves saved show little awareness of how much of the language of the damned rehearses issues of salvation.

Consider for a moment the program of this Annual Meeting. I see little in it (though titles are no doubt misleading) about how this or that academic discipline might be viewed *as* a religious movement—about how American sociology, say, is doing a job that was once done by this or that Church, or about how the study of texts in English departments echoes or fulfills needs once fulfilled by Talmudic or patristic studies. (The two exceptions are philosophy and political action. For perhaps obvious reasons these two extremes on the theory/praxis line are not neglected.) I note that even in the Rhetorical Criticism session, there is nothing about contemporary religious rhetoric. It's all confined to analysis of traditional religious texts. One would assume that nothing in the work of the great modern secularists—Wittgenstein, Marx, Hegel, Dewey, Derrida, the cultural anthropologists—could be relevant *as* religious discourse. Where are the sessions about their disguised or truncated theologies, theodicies eschatologies?

In short, my subject is not the pertinence to secular subjects of explicitly religious talk; nor the usefulness of secular subjects to religious study; but rather the ways in which secular languages *are* religious: not—to choose just one discipline that I shall *not* talk about today—not the religious study of biology nor the biological origins of religion, say, but biological science—this or that form of modern inquiry—*as* religion.

I am of course aware that to talk of secular religions is not exactly to break new ground. We all know the history of Cox's secular city (Cox, 1965, 1984), and some of us have followed Langdon Gilkey in his pursuit of religious themes through the whirlwinds of our thoroughly secularized lives—in our ultimate encounters with births, disease and health, old age and death, with life insurance ads, with appeals to philanthropy, with family counselors (1969, pp. 247–365). Perhaps the most concerted efforts approaching what I have in mind have been our various "religion and literature" programs. Nathan Scott, Giles Gunn, Amos Wilder, Anthony Yu and many younger scholars have taken seriously the sense in which our great secular fictions resemble or serve us as surrogates for explicitly religious narratives. If their programs were called "literature *as* religion," they would be working entirely in my garden—or rather (let's keep things straight) I would be working in theirs. Of course I hope that rhetorical study might plant some new seeds in that by now much-tilled ground.

II

According to some notions of religion, the chasm between God-talk and secular-talk is indeed unbridgeable. If religion is what people choose to call religion, then we would be foolish to consider various secular movements as in fact disguised efforts to fill niches left empty when God died. But any definition of religion that is sufficiently general to fit all explicit religions is almost certain to fit many secular movements.

Conflicting definitions of religion abound, and every definition must be taken as provisional, conflicting, and misleading. I should like here to incorporate, tacitly, the several pages of apology and demurrer that William James offers, in *The Varieties of Religious Experience* [Lecture II], before offering his definition. James insists that there can be no final, fixed definition; definitions will differ according to the purposes of the inquirer. But this does not mean that we can get along without them. His pursuit of religious *experience* leads him to an experiential definition: "Religion . . . shall mean for us *the feelings, acts, and experiences of individual men in their solitude, so far as they apprehend themselves to stand in relation to whatever they may consider the divine.*" My pursuit of varieties of religious/ secular *language* will lead to a definition that, while not conflicting with his, offers a clearer invitation to rhetorical analysis.

My definition for today is developed from one that I first encountered more than forty years ago. Working as a missionary for the Mormon church, I began to read widely and a bit desperately in non-Mormon thought, hoping to find some sort of common ground between what I was doing as a missionary and what the rest of the world thought about religion. Most of what I read made me increasingly miserable—Bertrand Russell, say, or George Bernard Shaw. But then a professor at Brigham Young University wrote me to recommend a book by William Ernest Hocking, *Living Religions and a World Faith*. I bought it, and in chapter 2, "The Nature of Religion," came to a definition that I've never forgotten.

"If, to agree on a name, we were to characterize the deepest impulse in us as a 'will to live,' religion also could be called a will to live, but with an accent on solicitude—an ambition to do one's living well. Or, more adequately, *religion is a passion for righteousness, and for the spread of righteousness, conceived as a cosmic demand* (p. 26)."

For my purposes now, that formula requires a bit of translation, as indeed it did for Hocking himself. As he says, "the term 'righteousness' is not [here] used in the conventional sense of compliance with a known law. It is a search for a law: there is a right way of living, it must be found. There is a primitive assurance . . . that living is intended to be good; and an equally primitive denial that living as it offers itself *is* good" (p. 27).

We could thus translate the definition—perhaps a bit awkwardly— as follows: Religion is the passion, or the desire, both to live right— not just to live but to live *right*—and to *spread* right living, both desires *conceived as responses* to some sort of cosmic demand—that is, to a demand made to us by the *way things are*, by the way the world is, by the nature of Nature (as some would say) or by God himself (as explicitly religious people put it). Life as we meet it and live it is not all that it *should be*; the world does not work as it should. Something is radically wrong. Everybody agrees to *that*. Religion enters when I add *"and I ought* to help put it right, first by righting myself." If the "should" or "ought" in that notion is thought to be my private invention, I am still not, for our purposes today, religious. But if it is thought somehow to come from some legitimating or legislating cosmos that made or makes me, however I conceive it, then I *am* religious. The "should," the "ought," somehow derive from my sense that the world, the universe, whatever really is "the case," whatever precedes, underlies, and outlasts my private experience, whatever invisible but intelligible order somehow explains or speaks to the visible world—*that cosmos* makes demands on me to acknowledge its nature and to try to order my actions according to *its* workings, not according to my accidental desires.

While I'm at this task of amateur definition, I may as well go further and say that in this highly general conception of religion, God becomes similarly—and I think productively—generalized. God—for those who still find a use for the term—is whatever *works for* working *well,* or if you prefer, God is what demands and makes possible every instance of working well; or, in the linguistic language of our time, God is whatever enables us to use the phrase "works well" and mean it. Whatever works *well* does so in the service of, or in imitation of, the supreme Wellworker (in older language, Prime Act); and our passion for righteousness, our passion for living better, is in the service of, in imitation of, the Prime Source of Betterness.

Any such definition of religion, and of the mysterious God who is the fountainhead of religion, will have consequences for what we will take to be religious language. While it draws into our ken every secular inquiry that connects an *order* with an *ethics*, it leaves out many of the marks that have often been considered essential to religious discourse. We can expect that each "secular religion" that we investigate under this broad definition will exhibit only a selection from the broad range of spiritual functions that the great religions of the past served. Secular religions, in short, are almost certain to be *truncated* religions; if their language for dealing with cosmic demands were not much reduced in range, their religious character would not be disguised.

It will be important, therefore, before we look at how such secular religions work, to have a rough notion of what would be missing from any life from which *all* religious discourse were banned.

I see at least eight niches in our basic architecture that traditional religious confessions have purported to fill. They have offered us *understanding* of an order or wholeness not visible in secular experience. They have offered a sense of the *sacredness* or inviolability of that order—to deny it or offend it is not just a mistake but a blasphemy. They have offered us mythic embodiment of the order in a form of a *sacred story*, a Supreme Fiction about how our lives relate to ultimate Order. They have offered, in these myths, explicit acknowledgement of *mystery*, since the wholeness of the invisible is beyond rational demonstration. The order is always some kind of numinous *mysterium tremendum* (Otto 1923, pp 1–30). They have thus offered an occasion for the exercise of *faith*—for a surrender to something more reliable than but less demonstrable than experience of the senses. They have offered, in consequence, good reasons for *humility*—a critique of hybris: we are puny as compared with Supreme Reliability. Yet they have offered ground for *hope*, some reason to believe that pain and despair are redeemed (usually this has come to us in the form of a hope for future reward, but that is not the form that hope has taken in all religions). And finally, they have offered, as derived from all this, unanswerable reasons for exercising *charity* toward fellow worshippers, who were potentially all humankind. (That many religions also offered, in some versions, legitimation of hatred and killing is irrelevant here today, though that fact has always provided rich material for mockery by non-believers. As Kenneth Burke quipped, "Yeah, I know you're a Christian, but who are you a Christian AGAINST?")

We could easily add to these eight if we looked at the practices—the rituals, prayers, taboos—that all religions make use of.

It's an impressive list, when you come to think of it. We are not likely to find, as we turn now to look at how these niches are filled or ignored by some secular languages, that any one of those languages will prove to be as comprehensive as traditional religions have aspired to be. We cannot hope for anything more than truncated religion in the secular religions we're turning to, if only because their founders have explicitly rejected the need to fill one or another of the eight traditional niches. Indeed most secular religions have their beginning in some "enlightened" attack on some "superstition" or "error" of the past; new faiths, new hopes, and new understandings are offered if only we will give up our primitive notions. In short, it is unlikely that we will find secular religions that provide understanding of a SACRED ORDER, with FAITH in a MYSTERY, embodied in narrative MYTH, justifying our HUMILITY in worship but offering grounds for HOPE and CHARITY.

My claim is only that wherever we find any secular language that offers the first three of these, understanding of and faith in an order that is somehow not to be blasphemed, and then relates that order to some demand upon our lives in any one of the other ways, we have something that deserves to be thought of in religious terms. We may want later on to categorize it as this or that heresy, but we should avoid that kind of dismissal at the beginning.

As everyone knows, the natural sciences have always provided the chief threat to traditional notions of a God-centered cosmos. It is fairly common to see histories of philosophy or theology tracing the reluctant accommodations of religious views to what science has learned about the universe. The converse history has not, I think, been written: a history of science that traces the struggle of scientists to make their science fill those empty niches I am talking about. It is true that the struggle is often carried on by popularizers, while front-line scientists at least pretend to be above that kind of thing. But a close reading of any statement by scientists *about* their science and its import—not just explaining the details but arguing for why the details are important—will uncover lines of argument closely akin to those followed by this or that theology.

All debates among theorists of biological evolution, for example, reveal elements, or fragments, of theological controversy about the way God's love relates to God's impassivity. But I find even more interesting the way in which astrophysics and particle physics have led to passionate cosmological speculation the like of which we have not known since the 17th century, perhaps even since the pre-Socratics. Theses about the genesis and structure of the universe, speculations both popular and recondite, flood our presses. Books with titles like *The Moment of Creation* (Trefil), *Cosmology: The Science of the Universe* (Harrison), *The First Three Minutes* (Weinberg), books that ask, nervously, what preceded those minutes, articles suggesting that human life was implicit in the "choices" made by the universe in the first nanoseconds, conferences on cosmology—these all testify to our immense hunger to discover how it all works, and usually how we fit into the working.

I think that with a little dredging, one could find in the works of the cosmologists versions of most traditional arguments about the existence or nature of God. But what is clearest to me—though far from really clear—is the way in which the current pursuit of cosmological clarity echoes versions of the traditional ontological argument.

No physical scientist I know of has referred explicitly to the ontological proof, and I doubt that many scientists have ever heard of it, let alone considered how it might work in thinking about the physical universe. If you look in their indexes under G-o-d you find Gödel but not God. But versions of the proof can be discovered underlying every investigation that confidently pursues further scientific knowledge in the conviction that the pursuit will finally lead not only to more knowledge but to an ordered picture of harmonies rather than irresolvable contradictions. It is true that many current theorists profess some doubt that science will finally yield a coherent body of knowledge. But every investigator must assume that such a body is inherently the object of study (Toulmin 1982, p. 235; Davies 1984, p. 237).

The popular version of the debate about such matters is too often reduced to the quarrel between Einstein and the quantum physicists, with Einstein's position reduced further to his expressed doubt that God dices with the universe. When the debate is conducted in those terms it looks as if Einstein were defending religion, while the quantum physicists were all a bunch of atheists preaching disorder. But I would argue that both sides in that dispute are in fact pursuing traditional religious questions—debating the nature of the God of order, not whether he/she (or it) exists.

The god that the ontological proof yields in this modern surrogate version is not, of course, the Lord of Hosts, the loving Father, nor his Son, the Prince of Peace. But It, with a capital I, *is* Supreme Being and Act. And the existence of supreme order is so self-evident, after one has considered the proof, that one can say, as Anselm and Augustine were fond of saying of those who denied the ontological proof, that those who deny the proof simply have not understood it. "Only the fool" could deny the god arrived at in the proof, and even the fool, in his or her heart, knew that the proof was sound. We also find the cosmologists uttering versions of the Augustinian claim that we must believe first, in order to understand. What's more, it is clear that the cosmos they discover in the proof dictates their "righteousness" in the pursuit of their sciences. As Bronowski and others have shown, an entire ethic follows rigorously from the belief in an ordered universe that will yield its truths only to those who follow that ethic (Bronowski 1965, ch. 3).

In contrast to what we find the popularizing cosmologists actually saying about their subject, their remarks about religion are often ludicrously perfunctory and uniformed. Unfortunately typical of those I have looked at is William Bonnor, professor of mathematical physics at the University of London. He is as aggressive in rejecting God-talk as any early positivist could have been:

> Unfortunately, some cosmologists have been sympathetic to this attitude [the notion that God started things off at the beginning, billions of years ago]. This seems to me quite reprehensible for the following reason. It is the business of science to offer rational explanations for all the events in the real world, and any scientist who calls on God to explain

something is falling down on his job. This applies as much to
the start of the expansion as to any other event (1964, p. 119).

We see already here that Bonnor is just as sure that rational explanations are forthcoming as he is that God-language cannot provide them.
And note how he goes on.

> If the explanation is not forthcoming at once, the scientist must
> suspend judgment: but if he is worth his salt he will always
> maintain that a rational explanation will eventually be found.
> This is the one piece of dogmatism that a scientist can allow
> himself—and without it science would be in danger of giving
> way to superstition every time that a problem defied solution
> for a few years (p. 119).

Having thus unwittingly expressed his faith in one God while
denouncing those who express faith in another, Bonnor naturally must
find substitute languages for the mysteries and difficulties that his
science encounters. But instead of mystery his science encounters
"irony" (p. 52); instead of providence he must talk of "luck."

> Whether or not the universe is cycloidal, cosmologists will be
> *very relieved* when *the correct* type of world model is known.
> At present we feel *a certain indignity* [not humility but indig-
> nity] that we do not know for certain even the broad outlines of
> our subject, such as whether the expansion [of the universe] is
> slowing down, and whether space is curved. It is rather like
> being a geographer and not knowing whether the Earth is
> round or flat. *With luck* we shall not have to wait many more
> years now (my italics, p. 205).

No traditional Christian could have ended his statement of faith in
God's providence in a more cheerful and trusting vein. The truth is
somehow out there, waiting for us; it is single, it will prove to be clear,
coherent, and finally—here is where the grand difference enters—it
will be mastered. We shall not belong to it, it will belong to us. The
prophets of this God do not feel humility in their ignorance but rather
"a certain indignity," a sense of temporary frustration.

But the popularizing cosmologists are not the only current believers in supreme order. Perhaps the most aggressive version of what we
might call the religion of physicalism can be found these days in the
speculations of computer enthusiasts. In them we find not only a naive
faith in the God-of-simple-coherence expressed by Bonner but a kind
of hope for the future that makes his seem tentative by comparison.
For sheer eschatological bliss, do not these days go to the Bible belt
for talk about how nice it will be to find oneself lifted, on the Great
Day, out of this world. Nay, go rather, to the computer magazines, go
to the now defunct *MT* (for *Machine Translation,* founded in the
glorious days when computerites thought that even poetry would be

machine-translatable within ten years); go to the A-I people, where indeed all who enter seem to hope for all things. In these domains, there *is* a God, the same God, essentially, as the God of the cosmologists—a God who guarantees that everything will finally fit together.

Three years ago Herbert Simon, the Nobel Prize-winning economist who has become a fanatical devotee of computerism, made once again the popular claim that computers not only can think, but often out-think us, in every dimension. He defines us all implicitly as deficient computers.

> Now maybe some of us think that the human mind already represents perfection and therefore there is nothing we ought to do about it. But there are universities and their task is to improve the human mind, and it's a pretty tedious process, isn't it? Most of us have spent twenty-six years or so at the task. When we look back on the process we wonder how it could have been so inefficient.
>
> It's been inefficient because we are operating with an exceedingly primitive technology. . . . We know a few brute facts. We know that if you take a group of people and keep them captive for a while and spray them with words, some of those words will turn out to be infectious, and that really is the central design proposition on which educational processes are founded in our society today.
>
> Now suppose we really knew what was going on in the human head when a human head was learning. We are beginning to find that out (1981, 20).

Simon then elaborates, in astonishingly simplistic terms, just how that is.

> [With the invention of computers that can duplicate the thought of mankind], there exists in the world another species—a man-made species to be sure—computers, which by any intelligence or task test we would give, also are capable of thinking. So man isn't unique in that respect either (p. 21).

He then concludes with what really is our interest today, a brief statement of his probably unconscious substitute for God-talk.

> . . . I guess I have a lot of confidence that as human beings are exposed to the idea that thinking also is not a uniquely human quality, . . . that we also will find a way of describing our *place in the world* without resting on that particular kind of uniqueness. . . . Perhaps the idea that we should base our notions of meaningfulness in life . . . on the idea that we are somehow or other unique was rather a poor idea to start with. It raised a kind of species prejudice. . . . We need to construct some kind of system of values that is not centered on human uniqueness but is centered on the fact that we are very much a part of nature,

*not apart from nature, but part of a scheme of things to which
we are going to have to adapt, and with which we are going to
have to live in peace and harmony* (my italics) p. 21.

There's a lot of faith here, faith in the existence of ultimate order, and
there's a lot of blind hope. There is also a clear "passion for righteousness," a notion of how we should behave, "conceived as a cosmic
demand." But the mystery is gone, and the humility is that kind of
arrogance that recommends humility to other people. The preacher
has no weaknesses that will not, "*in principle,*" be removed by time.
The world is his oyster, and it will teach all those people who have
doubted the march of science just how humble *they* should be.

When I encounter the Bonnors and Simons of our world—and
they seem to multiply like computer-generations—I often have a
fantasy that Anselm or Augustine might return, educate himself in
modern science, and then conduct a dialogue—not with Simon or
Bonnor, because it is hard to imagine them pausing for true exchanges—but with some open-minded young scientist who is eagerly
engaged in research. The dialogue would go something like this:

> *Master*: I see that you are applying for a National Science Grant
> to study how the protein encoded by src Oncogene, a protein
> kinase composed of 526 amino acid subunits . . . is anchored at
> the amino NH2 end of a cell's plasma membrane and thus may
> . . . [I skip a bit here. We could fill in any detail of any field of
> knowledge now under study. The most dramatic would be
> current efforts to figure out how to unify the four basic forces,
> including gravity and the weak force. But any bit of research,
> however trivial, would do almost as well.]
> *Disciple*: Yes, Master, I am, and I am quite excited about the
> prospects for favorable results.
> *Master*: By favorable results you mean, I presume, that you will
> discover some piece of scientific knowledge about Oncogene
> that has not been known before?
> *Disciple*: Of course. What would be the point of my investiga-
> tion if I did not expect to learn something unknown?
> *Master*: May I ask, where *is* this piece of knowledge *now*, as
> you work?
> *Disciple*: Master, I do not understand your question.
> *Master*: Let me try again. Is this piece of knowledge that you
> expect to find now already in existence anywhere?
> *Disciple*: Of course not. That's why my discovery of it will be
> original and perhaps win me a Nobel prize.
> *Master*: Yet you are confident that you will find it, or if not
> exactly it, something else that can be called knowledge?
> *Disciple*: Of course. We all know that there's a lot more to be
> learned.
> *Master*: But I must ask again, *where is* that knowledge that is
> not yet learned?
> *Disciple*: Well, I suppose it's sort of in the stuff I'm studying,

sort of in the way those carcinogenic genes work. It's sort of there waiting for me to discover it.

Master: But where, then, is *there*? Is it in some one cell or gene?

Disciple: (reluctantly) Well, no, I suppose I must say it's in the *nature* of the stuff I'm studying.

Master: So you do believe that even the knowledge that you have not yet discovered has some kind of existence, though not the kind of existence that it will have when you have discovered it and written your paper?

Disciple: I guess so, though that's not the way I like to talk about it.

The master now moves aggressively into his second phase:

May I ask now whether you expect this as yet undiscovered knowledge to relate to other knowledge in your field or to be rather an isolated or contradictory bit?

Disciple: Well, I hope it will be sufficiently new to startle people and make a stir.

Master: Yes, of course, but that's not exactly what I mean. Do you expect that it will sooner or later be shown to harmonize with all other genuine knowledge in your field? Or will it be just an isolated conclusion, unconnected with what we know now or will learn in the future?

Disciple: Of course I expect it to fit everything we really know or will ultimately learn. Any knowledge that *really* clashed with other *genuine* knowledge is either not knowledge or must be modified by further study.[1]

Master: And will it harmonize with what the chemists and physicists really know?

Disciple: Of course.

Master: Why?

Disciple: Why what?

Master: Why do you believe that these as yet undiscovered bits of knowledge will relate to each other at all?

Disciple: It's obvious. That's what scientific knowledge is— what fits other knowledge.

Master: But surely the question should be: *How* does it fit? Is there simply an infinite amount of amorphous knowledge, joined together bit by bit like nails in a keg, or is there some kind of ordering, some hierarchy, that both simplifies the system as we move toward the "top" and joins the parts like cells in an organism?

Disciple: Oh, I see where you're going, but you're going too fast. Everybody knows that scientific knowledge doubles every ten years.

---

[1] "No physicist would seriously believe that his subject matter was in fact a disorderly and meaningless mess, and that the laws of physics represented no real advance of our understanding. It would be ludicrous to suppose that all science is merely an artificial invention of the mind bearing no more relation to reality than the constellation of Pisces bears to real fish." Davies 1984, p. 237.

Master: Do you really believe that? And even if you do, can you conceive of that process continuing forever?
Disciple: I'm not quite sure why not, if there's an infinite amount to be learned.
Master: Let's try it another way. What do you make of the current research trying to unify the four basic forces? Are those forces more basic than other kinds of knowledge?
Disciple: Of course. That's what basic means.
Master: When they finally get them unified, will there be others left over still?
Disciple: Maybe. How could we know?
Master: But if there are, will the new general unification theory combining *those* forces be more basic than what is now being sought?
Disciple: I suppose so. I kind of see what you mean now. There *is* some kind of hierarchy; there must be. I guess I do assume that somehow it all works *together*.
Disciple: "It" is, then, quite unlike the total disorganization, or entropy, that the second law of thermodynamics claims will mark the end of the *material* universe—the opposite of it, in fact?
Disciple: If you say so. Oh, all right, I guess that's correct.

The master now moves, with increasing (though still delicate) confidence, into his third phase.

We seem to have agreed, then, that the parts of our knowledge somehow work together in an ordered way, even when the parts of the physical universe seem to be steadily falling apart. I now must ask whether you assume that you and your colleagues are manufacturing that "working together," or does the "working together-ness" somehow determine what you will discover about *it*?
Disciple: Well, a lot of people are talking as if we simply invent our discoveries. But most of us, I guess, still think that when we put Nature to the rack she refuses to answer in any but her own way, complicated as that is.
Master: So your mind, in its conclusions about your current research, will be controlled by what *is*, and not the other way round. And if you simply invent conclusions you will be no true scientist?
Disciple: Yes.
Master: So you believe that to "cook" your evidence and invent conclusions would be a *wrong* thing to do?
Disciple: Oh, yes. Every true scientist believes that.
Master: Why?
Disciple: Why what?
Master: Why would just inventing conclusions be wrong?
Disciple: Because the results wouldn't be knowledge. They would have no relation to *the way things work*.
Master: So, then, the "way things work" determines what you do and what you find, and your mind assumes that they work in

some kind of coherence or harmony not yet discovered, perhaps not even discoverable?

Disciple: (fighting back) Yes, but let me remind you again that some philosophers of science don't agree with that assumption.

Master: Yes, I know. But you do. And in rhetorical inquiry—that's the sort of thing we're doing here, I should warn you—we are more interested in *what we really believe* than we are in what someone else, bent on doubting everything that can theoretically be doubted, might have to say. Now then, having faced your assumption about the coherent body of knowledge somehow "out there," waiting to be discovered, would it make any sense to you if I suggested that though you have *thought* it and work daily on the belief that it is somehow *there* to be discovered, it does not exist?

Disciple: Could you repeat that? That doesn't sound scientific to me.

Master: (repeats, and both remain silent for a time).

Disciple: Well, I can conceive of somebody saying that it does not exist. Some theorists have done that.

Master: But can you conceive of anybody seriously doubting its existence, once they got the idea of it clear in their heads? I don't mean just saying that in principle it can be doubted, because it cannot be proved, but really doubting its operation in physical processes?

Disciple: No, of course not. Because the very idea includes its existence, its operation. That's what it is, the unique pattern of all working scientific law. If it didn't *work*, it wouldn't *be*. But it's impossible for me to think of it *not* working. Only a fool would go on doing serious science if he or she thought that the results finally wouldn't make some kind of sense.

* * *

Something like that dialogue, I submit, is implicit in every scientific investigation.

We see, then, that every scientist who takes science seriously as an enterprise reveals a "passion for right action—scientific honesty and industry—and for the spread of right action—the instruction of others in the right methods—conceived as a cosmic demand"—the demand of a cosmos that *must* exist, once we have really thought it.

Yet when we read the rare speculations about religion conducted by cosmologists and other scientists we find surprisingly often that religious issues are reduced to the question of whether a providential, intervening God exists. In an earlier book, *God and the New Physics*, Paul Davies often talks as if the whole question of God were reducible to the question of whether what he calls the "universe" was created by a separate power, called God, at a single moment in time. Though he claims to be seeking energetically to find God somewhere, he seems puzzled by his failures, sounding at times almost as naive as those Soviet astronauts who reported triumphantly after the first space flights that they found no God out there.

"Does it require any greater suspension of disbelief," he asks, "to suppose that the universe causes itself than to suppose that God causes himself?" (p. 38). And again, reducing the question of religion to the question of a miracle-working God, he says, "However astonishing and inexplicable a particular occurrence may be, we can never be absolutely sure that at some distant time in the future a natural phenomenon will not be discovered to explain it," (p. 31). And the implication is clear: If a natural explanation *is* found, God is wiped out. Yet his book is full, like all such books, of fine illustrations of what I would call a religious faith, what we might call "cosmologism," a faith that always persists in spite of any setback. Any signs he discovers that suggest a chaos of competing and incompatible goods are never more than momentary frustrations.

III

Well, where do these examples, chosen from many possible secular religions, take us?

It is easy to "prophesy after the event," as Burke puts it, that as traditional God-talk died, everyone seeking a legitimating cosmos would turn to some unifying conception of human nature and of its possibilities. A really shrewd student of rhetoric in, say, 1350, could have predicted that humanism was the next big move for what I am calling religious rhetoric. Religions dethroning God and placing *our* virtues and potentialities increasingly toward the center proliferated over the centuries, and were often proclaimed with an optimism that now strikes most of us as astonishingly naive. But in its later decades, humanism's prophets spoke in increasingly melancholy tones. One of the greatest prophets of humanism was also one of the most successful evangelists of all time, Bertrand Russell. His most famous sermon, written before World War I had made faith in us and our works a bit more difficult, ends with religious language like this:

> United with his fellow-men by the strongest of all ties, the tie of a common doom, the free man finds that a new vision is with him always, shedding over every daily task the light of love. The life of Man is a long march through the night, surrounded by invisible foes, tortured by weariness and pain, towards a goal that few can hope to reach, and where none may tarry long. One by one, as they march, our comrades vanish from our sight, seized by the silent orders of omnipotent Death. Very brief is the time in which we can help them, in which their happiness or misery is decided. Be it ours to shed sunshine on their path, to lighten their sorrows by the balm of sympathy, to give them

the pure joy of a never-tiring affection, to strengthen failing
courage, to instil faith in hours of despair. "[For Man it remains
only] to sustain alone, a weary but unyielding Atlas, the world
that his own ideals have fashioned despite the trampling march
of unconscious power. . ." (1903, 1917, pp. 53–4).

Now *there* is a religion that promises almost everything that
traditional religion promised, everything except a heavenly reward
and a sense of sacred mystery. An order, dictating faith and charity,
promising intellectual respectability and hope for future improvement, though not quite the future happiness for all humankind that
some humanists promised—all are preserved in a passion for righteousness, conceived as the demand not of a *divine* cosmos but of a
cosmos nevertheless: the total order of human beings, united in a
common fate and endowed, by physical nature, with a common
human nature.

I don't have to tell you that most people don't talk like that any
more. Humanism of that kind is as dead as Russell says our hopes for
divine comfort are. Though it originally seemed to be supported by
the inexorable march of natural science, the "sciences of man" no
longer offer us the hope that we can find, in our noble human nature,
a source of salvation. Contemporary science is more likely to talk like
Herbert Simon, when he attacks our "species prejudice." But when it
does so it still exhibits another kind of hubristic bias: belief in the
supremacy of "scientific method" over all of our thought. Contemporary scientists, in their theory though often not in their practice, are for
the most part as convinced as were scientists in Russell's time that the
one true way to discover who and where we are and what we should
do about it is to think "scientifically"—which generally means to
doubt and discard everything that can even in theory be doubted.

Again exercising our privilege of "prophecying after the event,"
we could predict that the triumph of various humanisms would
produce a reaction of aggressive forms of anti-humanism. In that other
lecture I mentioned at the beginning, discussing the new "decontruc-
tionism" as a sign of a religious revival, I tried to show how the
movement attempts, point for point, to fill some of the religious niches
that humanisms and religions of physicalism had left empty: particularly mystery, faith, and hope based on a human myth. Explicitly
anti-humanist, aggressively repudiating all notions of the centrality of
human beings and their language, openly celebrating the ambiguities
and mysteries that science attempts to defeat, these new manifestations of *Geisteswissenschaft* look on their surface considerably more
like traditional religions than do the cosmologism and computerism I
have described today. But they share one striking feature: they are, as
religions, mutilated versions of the grand religions of the past; each of

them can aspire to fill only a small number of the niches. Though the
new anti-humanisms, whether based on *Naturwissenschaft* or
Geisteswissenschaft, do a fine job of restoring our humility, they are
all truncated religions. Cosmologism offers order and faith in ultimate
grandeur, but only the feeblest guide to conduct in a very narrow part
of our lives, and little hope (Carl Sagan's almost desperate passion for
"life in outer space" is the fullest flowering of this dessicated hope).
Computerism offers a total order and a passionate hope for the
future—but an order that is trivial and an almost empty notion of
"righteousness"; if I believe everything the computer enthusiast says,
what follows for my conduct? Deconstruction*ism* restores mystery and
passion, but sacrifices order—and again offers no real hope, despite
the "apocalyptic tone" of many of its offerings (Derrida 1982). And
none of these offer any grounds for charity that I can discern; for
instruction in how to behave *today*, with my brothers and sisters, I
must fall back on whatever I may inherit from traditional religions.

From the perspective of a rhetorician, these truncated religions
are also truncated rhetorics. Modern students of classical rhetoric
have described the enlightenment project, still powerful today, as in
effect a purging of most of the riches of rhetoric, most of the
complexities and shaded dubieties of a fully human thought. Through
three centuries, an increasingly narrowed reason arrogated to itself
greater and greater certainties while banning from its house more and
more of what it had formerly welcomed: human emotions and commitments; all ethical appeals, including testimony, authority, and
tradition; all eloquence, all grace, all beauty—all these came to be
viewed as non-rational or even anti-rational, while a newly powerful
but truncated reason claimed, in the name of truncated religions, to be
able to explain everything—ultimately, or, as all physicalists still like
to say, "in principle."[2]

Any history that attempted to trace the many counter-efforts to
recover a fully human world would cover the same topics as the many
histories we have seen of the so-called "warfare of science and
religion." But it would look rather different from those histories,
because the warring sides could not be polarized as science vs.
religion. It would look rather more like a history of *many* warring
religions, some of them versions of what we call science. We would
find innumerable factions defending contrasting Gods with contrasting rhetorics, under labels and slogans that would be more confusing
than helpful. We would find that many of those who would most
nearly resemble traditional theologians would call themselves athe-

---

[2] From many recent discussions of the dessication of rhetorical study in modern times,
I mention only four: Genette 1982; Perelman 1969; Booth 1974; and Grassi 1980.

ists, and many of those who claimed to defend religion would not look very religious, in our terms, because their language, unlike that of cosmologites, would have no way of relating *their* cosmos, in meaningful discourse, to the demands they attribute to that cosmos. Some who seem most committed to total rationality would, like Bonnor and Simon and Davies, turn out to look like blind believers, and some who professed to embrace irrationalities would be in fact most fully committed to following the Logos wherever it chooses to lead. The picture would become even more complicated if we added, as we would have to, the religions that underlie and make possible our various popular arts. What is the cosmos implied by "Kojak" or "The Hill Street Blues"? Most TV dramas make strong implicit ethical demands on their viewers—one ought to be more like Kojak and Furillo than like the hoods and killers and deadbeats and crass politicos against whom these saints must operate. But if you ask such programs *why* anyone should, in such worlds, behave more like Kojak and Furillo than the others, why the world is so dependent on one or two saints, saints who offer no hint of a reference to a cosmos supporting, demanding, or rewarding their sainthood, you get very puzzling but very important answers—which I happily do not have time to offer here.

IV

What then is the use of this kind of effort at intertranslation? What good does it do "secularists" to learn that the God-talk they joyfully kicked off the back stoop has snuck back through the front door? What good does it do "religious" folk to know that they have all these unconscious allies?

After I had argued, last spring, that deconstruction is best viewed as a religious revival, perhaps the fullest, most effective secular rival to religions like cosmologism and computerism, a colleague jumped me with the question, "What does it matter? Why are you so eager to turn enemies into allies? What have you done for me if you convince me that something I have said, in the languages of science or deconstruction, was formerly said in God-talk? Don't I get as much good, even judging from your religious perspective, from my secular languages as I could possibly earn by turning back to languages of the past?"

A full answer, even if I had one, would obviously require far more than my remaining time. A couple of hints only, then:

The point is not simply to turn enemies into allies, though if any such turning occurred we all ought to rejoice. The real point of this kind of rhetorical analysis, for *secularists*, surely would be the discovery of just how perfunctory and unsatisfactory their treatment of complex religious issues has been. It is not that they do not have faith in a supreme cosmos; it is that they have not thought through what such a faith entails, and they are thus left with impoverished worlds, worlds in which a good share of their actual values are torn loose from all rational connections and left to wander in a vast desert of private, accidental, unconnected preferences. The cosmologite, by thinking as hard about assumptions as about scientific elements, could discover revived forms of God-talk that would be entirely in harmony with all that science can learn and yet would more adequately fill the niches that science had seemed to vacate.

A second service for the secularist would be the revelation of just how large a brotherhood or sisterhood he or she joins when doing scientific inquiry. When Simon states that we must get rid of our species-centured views and see ourselves as part of a "scheme of things," he joins, perhaps unwittingly, the vast community of religious inquirers throughout history, all those who have recognized God's absolute command to transcend the self and its visible surroundings and embrace the author of all selves. Of course it is always possible that to discover that community would remove some of the fun, for both cosmologites and computerites; but would it not also remove some of the gloom and bitterness from the various disillusioned humanisms that have bought various half-understood scientific views and then tried to invent affirmations and negations out of whole cloth?

For those who already profess religion, one use of rhetoric, or meta-rhetoric, is implicit in what I have just said: it is the only possible tool of evangelism, if we wish to evangelize in the educated part of our world. That world will rightly refuse to reject whatever science can genuinely establish, and unless we want to have only ignorant converts, we will want to find ways to translate from the languages of secular truth, whatever it is, to the languages of religious belief. And if we are serious, we will not be able to resist proselytizing. If we have some notion, however dim, of a cosmos that demands that we try to live right and *spread our notions of right living*, we have a duty to proselytize, embarrassing as all proselyting is for all who have been educated in modernism. The devotees of various fundamentalist religions—religions that are often as truncated as anything I have described today—feel no such embarrassment about broadcasting their views; they are out to save the world, often using some of the shoddiest kinds of rhetoric ever known. We can choose either to let them dominate the field or to enter the lists with them. If we choose to engage, as I think we must, no matter what our religion is, no matter how fully it may be couched in secular language, then we cannot choose not to employ rhetoric. We can only choose between doing it poorly or well. And if we perform it well we will in fact be discovering our true gods, in contrast to those that our surface language suggests.

Few among us will ever do original or valuable theology; most of us are going to prove clumsy as evangelists. But rhetorical analysis of a careful, informed kind is within the range of everybody. Indeed, we've all done it all our lives, without calling it that; we're all to some degree natural exegetes and hermeneuts, and as soon as we think about how authors and listeners get together *through* texts, we discover that we are also natural rhetors—or meta-rhetors. What we all can do, then, is to probe our secular lives to discover the various disguised religions that partially fill the eight empty niches with which we began.

Some of the truncated religions we discover we may still want to call heresies; they are almost sure to look like fragments, salvaged from the wreck of former systematic encounters with wonder. But we all know that heresies can surprise us. They have a way of surviving into new syntheses that become new orthodoxies. Some of the prophets of deconstruction are fond of saying that nobody knows what new decenterings lie over the horizon. As Derrida says, "for that future world and for that within it which will have put into question the values of sign, word, and writing, for that which guides our future anterior, there is as yet no exergue" (1976, 1967, p. 5). I would put it just a *bit* differently. "For that future world, and for that within it which will have provided new visions of order and new commands for righting our lives within that order, for that which guides our eternal present, the rhetorician cannot serve as exergue." The rhetorician is always in large part a secularist, inhabiting the here and now, Christmas time, 1984, not the future—even when the subject is eternal things. It is in the here and now that we can perform the intertranslations among our always inadequate statements about the eternal, thus serving our kind of "heteroglossic" cosmos—the shifting order of human understanding.

The first task, then, in any rhetoric of religion, in any time, is to discover just how our various pictures of cosmic demands harmonize or conflict with each other. The second task is to appraise the reasons offered for believing in any one cosmos, and to discover just what passions for what notions of righteousness really deserve to be promulgated. And the ultimate task, served best only when these first two are also performed, is to be about the business of propagation of the faith. Or rather the faiths, because I do not have any faith that, in life as we live it, life that is always in a sense secular, always in a sense rhetorical—I have no faith that we will ever discover one final ultimate invulnerable language for the mysterious ways of the Lord.

WORKS CITED AND CONSULTED

Alfvén, Hannes
1966   *Worlds-Antiworlds: Antimatter in Cosmology.* San Francisco: W. H. Freeman and Co.
1969   *Atom, Man, and the Universe: The Long Chain of Complications.* San Francisco: W. H. Freeman and Co.

Anselm
1948   *Proslogion.* Trans. by S. N. Deane: *St. Anselm* (La Salle, Ill.: Open Court.) There have been many recent efforts to rehabilitate the ontological proof (see, e.g., Malcolm, below). It first made sense to me in the brief summary offered by McKeon, pp. 146–47.

Augustine   *On the Free Will (De Libero Arbitrio),* Book II, as selected and translated by McKeon, pp. 3–64.
1958   *On Christian Doctrine (De Doctrina Christiana)* Book IV. Trans. by D. W. Robertson, Jr. New York: Liberal Arts Press.

Bonnor, William
1964   *The Mystery of the Expanding Universe.* New York: MacMillan.

Booth, Wayne C.
1974   *Modern Dogma and the Rhetoric of Assent.* Chicago: The University of Chicago Press.

Brownowski, Jacob
1965   *Science and Human Values.* New York: Harper and Row.

Burke, Kenneth
1961   *The Rhetoric of Religion.* Boston: Beacon Press.

Callahan, Daniel
1966   *The Secular City Debate.* New York: MacMillan.

Capra, Fritjof
1975   *The Tao of Physics.* New York: Random House.

Cox, Harvey
1965   *The Secular City: Secularization and Urbanization in Theological Perspective.* New York: MacMillan Rev. ed. 1966.
1984   *Religion in the Secular City: Toward a Post-modern Theology.* New York: Simon and Schuster.

Davies, Paul
1983   *God and the New Physics.* New York: Simon and Shuster.
1984   *Superforce: The Search for a Grand Unified Theory of Nature.* New York: Simon and Schuster.

Derrida, Jacques
1983   *D'un ton apocalyptique adopté naguère en philosophie.* Paris: Editions galilée.
1976 (1967)   *Of Grammatology.* Baltimore: The Johns Hopkins University Press. (*De la Grammatologie,* Paris).

Feinberg, Gerald
1977   *What is the World Made Of? Atoms, Leptons, Quarks, and Other Tantalizing Particles.* Garden City, N.Y.: Anchor Press/Doubleday.

Gallie, W. B.
1968   *Philosophy and the Historical Understanding.* New York: Schocken Books. First edition, 1964.

Genette, Gérard
1982   "Rhetoric Restrained." *Figures of Literary Discourse.* Trans. by Alan Sheridan. New York: Columbia University Press. Originally in *Figures III,* Paris, 1972.

Gilkey, Langdon
1969   *Naming the Whirlwind: The Renewal of God-Language.* New York: The Bobbs-Merrill Co.

Gingerich, Owen, ed.
1977   *Cosmology + 1.* Readings from *Scientific American.* San Francisco: W. H. Freeman and Co.

Grassi, Ernesto
1980   *Rhetoric as Philosophy: The Humanist Tradition.* University Park, Pa.: The Pennsylvania State University Press.

Gunn, Giles
    1979   *The Interpretation of Otherness: Literature, Religion,
                    and the American Imagination.* New York: Oxford Uni-
                    versity Press.

Hartshorne, Charles, and William L. Reese
    1953   *Philosophers Speak of God.* Chicago: The University of
                    Chicago Press.

Harrison, Edward R.
    1981   *Cosmology: the Science of the Universe.* Cambridge:
                    Cambridge University Press.

Hocking, William E.
    1940   *Living Religions and a World Faith.* New York: MacMil-
                    lan.

James, William
    1902   *The Varieties of Religious Experience.* New York:
                    Longmans, Green and Co.

Kolakowski, Leszek
    1983   *Religion.* New York: Oxford University Press.

McKeon, Richard
    1930   *Selections from Medieval Philosophers.* Vol. I: From
                    Augustine to the Great. New York: Charles Scribner's
                    Sons.

Malcolm, Norman
    1963   "Anselm's Ontological Arguments." In *Knowledge and
                    Certainty: Essays and Lectures.* Englewood Cliffs, N.J.:
                    Prentice-Hall.

Otto, Rudolf
    1923   *The Idea of the Holy.* Trans. by John W. Harvey. London:
                    Oxford University Press.

Perelman, Chaim, and L. Olbrechts-Tyteca
    1969   *The New Rhetoric: A Treatise on Argumentation.* Notre
                    Dame: The University of Notre Dame Press.

Russell, Bertrand
    1957   "A Free Man's Worship." In *Mysticism and Logic.* Lon-
                    don, 1917. New York: Doubleday Anchorbooks.

Scientific American. See Gingerich.

Scott, Nathan
    1958   *Modern Literature and the Religious Frontier.* New York: Hay.
    1971   *The Wild Prayer of Longing.* New Haven: Yale University Press.

Simon, Herbert
    1981   "Is Thinking Uniquely Human," *The University of Chicago Magazine.* Fall:12–21.

Toulmin, Stephen
    1982   *The Return of Cosmology.* Berkeley: The University of California Press.

Trefil, James S.
    1983   *The Moment of Creation: Big Bang Physics from Before the First Millisecond to the Present Universe.* New York: Charles Scribner's Sons.

Weinberg, Steven
    1976   *The First Three Minutes: A Modern View of the Origin of the Universe.* New York: Basic Books.

Weizenbaum, Joseph
    1976   *Computer Power and Human Reason: From Judgment to Calculation.* San Franciso: W. H. Freeman and Co.

Wilder, Amos
    1952   *Modern Poetry and the Christian Tradition: A Study in the Relation of Christianity and Culture.* New York: Charles Scribner's Sons.

Yu, Anthony
    1969   *The Fall: The Poetical and Theological Realism of Aeschylus, Milton, and Camus.* Ph.D. Dissertation. The University of Chicago.

THE FUTURE OF FEMINIST THEOLOGY IN THE ACADEMY

ROSEMARY RADFORD RUETHER*

The title given this talk, "Theology and Feminism, A Future Together," is somewhat misleading. It seems to suppose that there is one fixed thought-world called "theology" and another called "feminism" and one can then ask whether they have a future together. Theology is seen as something which can be defined without reference to feminism and *vice versa*. But any theology which can be defined without reference to feminism is a particular kind of theology, namely, patriarchal theology. Patriarchal theology is the kind of theology we have had in the past, a theology defined not only without the participation of women, but to exclude the participation of women. What is emerging today is a feminist critique of patriarchal theology, or feminist theology.

To ask whether patriarchal and feminist theology have a future together is, to say the least, grotesque; a bit like asking whether Judaism and anti-semitism have a future together or whether racist and Black theology have a future together. The question is not whether they have a future together, but which will prevail. Will feminist theology succeed in sufficiently transforming the definition of theology, as taught in the seminaries and preached in the churches; will we no longer have patriarchal theology, but an inclusive theology, a theology that affirms the full humanity of women and men and their mutuality with each other? Or will patriarchal theology succeed in confining feminist theology to the margins of the theological enterprise, ridiculing, vilifying, and finally silencing it so that the next generation of theological students will no longer even be able to raise the questions because they will be told that these questions are non-questions, questions already ruled out-of-bounds by the guardians of theological "orthodoxy"?

*Georgia Harkness Professor of Applied Theology at Garrett-Evangelical Seminary, and Co-Chair of the AAR Women's Caucus 1982–1985, Dr. Ruether presented this paper as a 75th Anniversary Lecture at the 1984 Annual Meeting of the American Academy of Religion.

Before entering further discussion of the problematic of feminist *versus* patriarchal theology, I wish to state at the outset that I speak from a white Western Christian context. Theology should overcome patterns of thought within it that vilify or exclude persons by gender, race, or religion. But this does not mean that one seeks to arrive at a theology that is neutrally universalistic, in the sense of encompassing all cultures and religions. Such universalism is, in fact, cultural imperialism, an attempt by one religious culture to monopolize not only theology, but salvation; to claim that it alone has authentic access to the divine. Christian patriarchal theology has typically been imperialistic in this way, claiming that white male Christian experience was equivalent to universal humanity.

Feminist theology, by contrast, must be consciously pluralistic. Although there are similarities of patriarchal patterns, nevertheless a feminism done in a Christian context will be different from a Jewish feminism or a feminism which takes Islam or Buddhism for its cultural orbit. Moreover, an Asian Christian feminist or an African Christian feminist or an American Black Christian feminist will also have distinct and different problems and will come up with different syntheses. Pagan feminists, who seek to break with all patriarchal religious contexts, to rediscover an ancient female-centered religion or create one today, pose yet a different problematic. There are issues that need to be clarified here, but what is not at issue, in my view, is the legitimacy of encountering the divine as goddess.

Feminist theology needs to be seen as a network of solidarity between many feminist communities engaged in the critique of patriarchalism in distinct cultural and religious milieux, rather than one dominant form of feminism that claims to speak for the whole of womenkind. So I state that it is from a Western Christian context that I speak of patriarchal and feminist theologies.

Feminist theology is engaged in a critique of the androcentrism and misogyny of patriarchal theology. What does this mean? First of all it means that, in patriarchal theology, the male is taken to be the normative and dominant representative of the human species. The male is the norm for imaging God, for defining anthropology, sin, redemption, and ministry. The female is seen as subordinate and auxiliary to the male. Therefore women never appear in patriarchal theology as representatives of humanity as such. Their normative position is that of absence and silence. When patriarchal theology mentions women, it does so to reinforce its definition of their "place" in its system. When women challenge this definition, patriarchal theology becomes not only androcentric, that is, unconsciously male-centered, but overtly misogynist. Overt misogyny arises when women break the silence and assert their presence as subjects in their own right, rather than simply objects of male definition. Misogyny is male-dominance engaged in self-defense of its right to define and control women and all other reality.

These characteristics of androcentrism and misogyny are characteristic of Christian patriarchal theology. The attempt to exclude women as subjects of theology begins within the New Testament:

> I permit no woman to teach or to have authority over men; she is to keep silent. (I Timothy 2:12)

This ban against women as teachers or preachers, that is to say as creators and exponents of theology, is continued in the early Church orders, such as the *Didascalia* (early third century) and the *Apostolic Constitutions* (late fourth century). The *Constitutions* declare that Jesus chose to commission men and not women, and that the male is the head of the woman, and it concludes that, for these reasons, a woman may not teach. This silencing of women as teacher continues in the Middle Ages and is renewed in the mainline Protestant traditions of the Reformation. It continues to be echoed in nineteenth- and twentieth-century arguments against women's right to preach. Although a few theological schools, such as Oberlin College, were open to women in the nineteenth century, theological schools have been slower to open to women than other professional schools, such as law and medicine, whose record is bad enough.

Some of the first theological schools to open to women at first still required that women be silent, even forbidding them from asking questions in class. The first woman theological graduate and first woman to be ordained to a Christian denomination, Antoinette Brown, was valedictorian of her class, but had to have a male read her speech for her, since she was not allowed to speak. Major theological schools, such as Harvard Divinity School, were open to women only in the 1950's and the right of women to attend some Catholic theological seminaries is still in dispute. Women have only begun to attend theological schools in significant numbers in the last ten to fifteen years in the United States.

Thus the question of feminist theology is very recent. While patriarchal theology reaches back more than three thousand years, into the roots of the Hebrew Bible, women have only very recently gained enough of a foothold in theological education even to begin to ask the questions about the androcentric and misogynist bias of this three-millennia tradition. It is not surprising, therefore, that women do not yet have all the answers, and indeed are only beginning to formulate the questions. What is surprising is the enormous amount of solid work in all fields from biblical studies to history to theology to ethics, pastoral psychology and ministry that has been accomplished in these last fifteen years. It is no longer possible in any field of religious studies today to claim that there are not good materials that can be incorporated into the curriculum. The problem lies rather in the refusal of most theological teachers to read these materials and to redefine their teaching to incorporate them. As a result, they in turn reproduce another generation of students socialized to identify theology with patriarchal theology and to pass on the patriarchal tradition as normative Christianity.

One can speak of three moments or stages in the development of feminist theology, although these stages do not simply succeed each other in mechanical fashion, but are constantly developing in interaction with each other. The first moment of feminist theology is the critique of the masculine bias of theology. One begins to criticize the overt misogyny of the tradition and thereby to throw its authority into question. Only gradually does it become apparent that overt misogyny is only the tip of the iceberg and indeed probably occurs in the tradition precisely at those moments when some women are challenging the male dominance of the tradition.

Underneath this overt misogyny is the buried continent of unconscious androcentrism which has shaped all stages of the theological enterprise, from revelatory experience and its earliest statements to all its redactions and commentaries, with the pervasive assumption that the male is the normative human subject. This androcentrism is more difficult to unmask and make visible precisely because it is so unconscious and taken-for-granted, as the endless debates about sexist language have shown. The invisibility of women can never be seen by those for whom the generic "man" is simply assumed to include "women."

This work of unmasking the androcentric bias of the tradition grows in sophistication, starting with surveys of the more blatant types of discrimination and misogyny and developing to more specialized discussions of particular thinkers or schools of theology and to more subtle analyses of methodologies of discernment. Gradually one begins to see and to define the full impact of androcentrism on theology, not only as it runs through all periods and schools of theology that we have received, but also as it has biased every theological symbol. Starting with the basic assumption that the male is the normative human person and therefore also the normative image of God, all symbols, from God-language and christology to church and ministry, are shaped by the pervasive pattern of the male as center, the female as subordinate and auxiliary. This is true also where female symbols appear, such as feminine imagery for the immanence of the divine or for the church or for the human soul, which on careful examination turn out to be further expressions of this androcentric assumption. Androcentrism defines not only the male as the generic human, but also defines the "feminine" as that which is auxiliary and mediating between male subjects, whether the two male subjects be father and son or God and "man."

Most importantly, androcentrism biases the definition of sin, or the naming of evil, in the Christian tradition. By adopting the Hebrew folk story of the expulsion from paradise as its key paradigm for the origin and nature of evil, Christianity reinforced theologically a victim-blaming ideology of patriarchalism. The myth of female primacy in the origin of evil reinforces the patriarchal definition of woman as subordinate and auxiliary, by claiming that woman caused evil to come into the world by speaking and acting autonomously. The subordination of women as "nature" is redoubled as punishment for sin.

Redemption for women is defined as voluntary submission to her gender roles, defined as childbearing, sexual repression, and social subordination. Women are thus asked to accept the guilt for their own victimization by patriarchy. This extends in patriarchal culture even to acts of violence of men against women. If a man rapes her, it is presumed that she "asked" for it. If her husband beats her, it is because she has provoked it by her complaints. That she must have "deserved it" defines the basic stance of patriarchy toward assaults on woman. Victim-blaming ideologies of sin prevent a culture from rightly naming evil and function to justify evil by describing it as nature, just punishment, and divine will. The essential core of feminist theology lies in the unmasking of this victim-blaming ideology of sin. Patriarchalism is named as evil, as a system that both produced and justifies aggressive power and domination of women and all subjugated people. The quest for an authentic humanity, for humanizing relationships, begins at the point where its claims to name the world are de-legitimized.

The second moment in feminist theology is one which seeks alternative traditions which support the autonomous personhood of women. This quest takes many forms at the present time. It takes the form of feminist studies of Hebrew Scripture and the New Testament to discern alternative traditions that affirm women's personhood, her equality in the image of God, her equal redeemability, her participation in prophecy, teaching, and leadership. This does not mean a denial or cover-up of patriarchal bias, but rather a demonstration that, even amidst this bias, there are glimpses of alternative realities. Patriarchal ideology did not succeed in defining what women actually were or did in past times. Woman is there in the biblical drama, not merely as object, but as subject, as an actor in her own right, as seeker and questioner of God, and as agent of the divine Spirit.

The quest for alternative tradition also goes on in the various periods of Christian history, in the early Church, the Middle Ages, the Reformation, as well as the more recent centuries, discovering and chronicling the church mothers who were there, but whose stories have been covered up or silenced. Yet this historical quest also makes all the more clear the power of patriarchal control over the tradition. Those women who have been lifted up for us as models by the tradition have been selected by men and have functioned, by and large, to reinforce male ideologies about female roles. This means that their lives were censored by patriarchy, both within their lifetimes and after their deaths, so we should know about them only those things which patriarchy wishes us to know. This meager procession of masochistic women is what patriarchy called the female "saints." Sometimes by digging deeper, we can glimpse an alternative, more autonomous personality in these women, but such information has survived censorship by accident.

Occasionally a woman in the tradition stands out as so powerful and so central that she can neither be silenced or sanitized. Here the patriarchal censure introduces what might be called a "mud-slinging job" to displace them from authority and dignity. Thus Miriam, named as co-equal leader of the exodus with Moses and Aaron, is besmirched in the book of Numbers by being turned by God into a leper in punishment for her criticism of Moses. She becomes like one whose father has spit in her face; that is, has totally repudiated her as daughter. God is said to be the father who has spit in her face.

Likewise, the Christian tradition marginalized Mary Magdalene by turning her into a repentant prostitute, thus marginalizing her from her position as leading female apostle and first witness of the resurrection, commissioned to bring the good news back to the male disciples who had fled the scene and were trembling in the upper room. The controversy stories between Peter and Mary Magdalene in the gnostic gospels have made it clear to us to what extent the controversy over the status of Mary Magdalene was indeed understood in early Christianity to be a controversy over women's apostolic authority.

Many other women's stories have been pushed to the margins of the tradition. They have been defined as heretics, witches, or lunatics, their writings have been destroyed and their memory survives only in the negative judgments made against them. Woman Studies seeks to read between the lines of these judgments and to gather the fragments of writings which have survived. Occasionally a lucky find, such as the Nag Hammadi library, buried by fourth-century Christian dissidents to prevent its destruction by the Orthodox and disinterred in modern times, allows us to read the writings of banished traditions in their own voice. Only in more recent centuries has a new Christian pluralism allowed dissident writings to survive, such as Margaret Fell's defense of women's right to preach, written in the seventeenth century. Orthodox patriarchalism has marginalized these traditions by simply not incorporating them in that which is read by students in the dominant theological traditions. But the documents are, at least, there to be discovered.

As this work of making women who have been marginalized and silenced visible and audible progresses, it becomes apparent that ours is not the first feminist critique of patriarchal theology. Again and again such a critique has begun, sometimes in what appears to be an isolated voice. But that isolated voice itself points to a forgotten movement. Whether it is Christian de Pisan in the fourteenth century, Margaret Fell and other feminist writers of seventeenth-century English radical puritanism, or Elizabeth Cady Stanton in the nine-teenth century, we discover again and again the same arguments against patriarchal ideology, the same refutations of its claims to define God, humanity, and reality.

Feminist theology has been endlessly reinventing the wheel and endlessly losing its own inventions, precisely because it does not control the definition of the tradition. It has not been able to deter-mine that which will be read and remembered by the next generation of theological students. So it ever loses its own history and has to begin again as though its questions had never been asked and answered before. This raises the question for the future of feminist theology today. Will we, too, despite all the impressive work of recovery and development of the last fifteen years, lose our history again, because this work that has been done will not be recorporated into the main curriculum and taught as part of what must now define our heritage and our identity?

The third moment of feminist theology then takes the form of tentative efforts to restate the norms and methods of theology itself in the light of this critique and alternative tradition. One needs to re-envision the basic categories of theology itself as a new center and norm. It is not enough merely to show that the myth of Eve is a victim-blaming ideology that mislabels evil. One needs to ask what then is *our* understanding of good and evil that can rightly name our authentic potential and that which corrupts it, which can lead us to a more mature and responsible humanity for women as well as men, and not simply to a reversal of patriarchal distortions.

It is here that the feminist theologian must operate, not simply as a critic of the past or as a historian seeking to recover something of our lost story, but as a constructive theologian for a contemporary com-munity of faith, for a contemporary understanding of church which seeks to live its faith as repentance of sexism, exodus from patriarchy, and entrance into a new humanity. Such an understanding of the gospel and the mission of the church will place such a community in tension with the self-understanding of existing historical churches for whom patriarchy remains normative. As it becomes evident that feminist theology is not just a minor tinkering with the externals of dress, language, and personnel, but a major recentering of the meaning of the story itself, hostility will grow. To know this and to be prepared for it is not paranoia, but realism. But this means that, as reactionary negativity begins its counter-assault to feminist theology, the maturity of feminist spirituality becomes all the more urgent. One needs to learn both to "love one another," and also to "love one's enemies" as well, in the sense of refusing to dehumanize them, without denying that their enmity is real, serious, and dehumanizing. One must be prepared to suffer, but also to grow in solidarity and self-knowledge, if one is serious about gaining a new whole.

The feminist theologian stands, not as an isolated academic, but as an "organic intellectual" within a feminist community of faith that is engaged in exodus from patriarchy. It is the task of feminist theology to clarify the vision and make clear the criteria for testing what is authentic and what is inauthentic. The community of the good news against patriarchy needs the courage of its convictions, the confident trust that they are indeed in communion with the true foundations of reality, the true divine ground of Being, when they struggle against patriarchy, despite all claims of its authority. This faith lies first of all not in the Church, its tradition, or its Scripture. The patriarchal distortion of all tradition, including Scripture, throws feminist theology back upon the primary intuitions of religious experience itself, namely, the belief in a divine foundation of reality which is ultimately good, which does not wish evil nor create evil, but affirms and upholds our autonomous personhood as women, in whose image we are made.

This means that feminist theology cannot just rely on exegesis of past tradition, however ingeniously redefined to appear inclusive. It is engaged in a primal re-encounter with divine reality and, in this re-encounter, new stories will grow and be told as new foundations of our identity. Such a new encounter with the divine, generating new stories, is expressed in a recent account in my class on violence against women. One woman in the class recounted her experience of being raped in a woods. During the rape she became convinced that she would be killed and resigned herself to her impending death. When the rapist finally fled and she found herself still alive, she experienced a vision of Christ as a crucified woman. This vision filled her with relief and healing, because she knew that "I would not have to explain to a male God that I had been raped. God knew what it was like to be a woman who had been raped."

Thus feminist theology does not just rework past language and tradition. It allows the divine to be experienced in places where it has not been allowed to be experienced before, and in ways that it has not been allowed to be imagined before. It must and will generate new stories, new primal data of religious experience, which will become the symbols of a new tradition. This may not be experienced as total discontinuity with the past; in the case of the story I have just recounted, the new story builds upon and re-envisions the old one of the Christian tradition, just as the Christian story built upon and re-envisioned the stories of the Hebrew tradition and Hebrew stories, in turn, built upon and re-envisioned Canaanite and Babylonian stories. One does not have to totally lose or repudiate one's past to also claim the right to build a new future, in which the divine is experienced from women's perspective in a way not previously allowed, or, at least, not remembered by a religious tradition biased by patriarchy.

Feminist theology, then, is not just engaged in a reformation to some original good moment in the past, some unblemished period of origins, because no such period can be discovered for women, either in the Judaeo-Christian tradition or before it. Even for those who claim some continuity with the Jewish or Christian traditions, feminist theology must stand as a new midrash or a third covenant, that does not merely repristinate a past revelation, but makes a new beginning, in which the personhood of woman is no longer at the margins but at the center, where woman is not defined as object, but defines herself as subject.

This then raises the final question in this discussion of the future of feminist theology, namely, the institutional and historical base for such a future. Feminist theology must take seriously this question of an institutional base for its survival, because without an institutional base it has no future at all. Feminist theology will be once more pushed to the margins and forgotten. Its story will not be told to our daughters and sons; its writings will not be read by the next generation of teachers and preachers of theology. Its memory will have to be resurrected and its questions rediscovered by a future generation of women who have lost their history.

The question that feminist theology and the feminist community of faith need to ask is whether we can rely on existing churches, seminaries, and theological schools, on existing "fraternities" like the American Academy of Religion, to be such an institutional base for our survival. My answer is that we cannot *rely* on these institutions, but we must claim them nonetheless. We have no choice. Women are not a separate community or a separate class. We have few resources of our own. Women are men's daughters, mothers, and sisters. For better or worse, we are one family. These institutions belong to women as much as to men. We have a right to contend for their ownership and definition, and we will do so. The library budget needs to be used to buy feminist books; the curriculum to teach feminist courses; the church bureaucracy to organize feminist conferences; the vehicles of communication to communicate feminist messages.

Feminism is not a special interest group or passing fad, of concern only to a minority of women and a few "odd" men. Feminist theology, along with other forms of liberation theology, Black theology, Asian theology, Latin American theology, are engaged in redefining the agenda and constituency of theology itself. We are contending, not simply for a part of the pie, but for a new way of baking the pie itself, even to rewriting the basic recipe.

In addition to claiming and making use of the main institutions of the church, and its vehicles of education and communication, feminist theology must also build its own autonomous institutions. This is not as an alternative to claiming and using existing institutions, but a complement to it. We must do this because patriarchy is not benign and ultimately does not wish us well. It tolerates us only when it thinks it can make use of us and fit us into its agenda. But, if it becomes increasingly clear, as it must, that we do not fit into its agenda, but intend to change the agenda, its powers of repression, vilification and expulsion are formidable. This is not simply a question of women against men, but rather of the system of male dominance itself, both as ideology and as organized power, to which both males and females are asked to capitulate if they are to be acceptable. In Paul's language, we "do not struggle against flesh and blood, but against powers and principalities."

Thus if feminist theology survives within institutions which are still basically committed to patriarchy as normative tradition, it will do so through profound and continuous struggle. One needs to have other spaces, autonomous spaces, where feminist theology is normative, rather than marginal, where the immediate struggle against patriarchy does not define the context of the discussion, where the agenda of feminist theology can be more fully and freely developed. Such autonomous spaces for feminist theology have already begun. The Grailville summer quarter in feminist theology was an important arena for such development for many of us in the 1970's, and the Boston Feminist Theological Center is such a project today.

Such autonomous spaces will probably not have the resources to rival existing theological schools and so will have to be built by piggy-backing on existing institutions to some extent. Such projects are essential to the maintenance of our sanity. But they are not alternatives to what must remain our main agenda, which is the redefinition of the central tradition itself, as it is taught to the next generation of theological students, and as it shapes the next generation of the religious community. Feminist theology is not engaged in creating a sect, but in rebuilding the definition of the center by which the whole is perceived; how we define good and evil, our fears, our hopes, true and false relationships to each other, to nature and to divine Wisdom.

The future of feminist theology is hopeful, but it is not assured in our generation. What is assured is that its questions cannot be finally repressed, because the humanity of women cannot finally be repressed. Thus the questions of feminist theology may be marginalized and silenced for a season, only to be recalled and remembered again, until the tradition itself submits to being questioned and transformed into a new creation, no longer patriarchal, but truly a human and humanizing theology.

EVENTS, MEANINGS AND THE CURRENT TASKS OF THEOLOGY

LANGDON GILKEY*

HISTORY AND INTERPRETATION

Amid all the ups and downs of twentieth-century theology, two certainties have dominated its entire scope: Revelation or illumination—whatever its content—is *historical* and comes to us through historical events, and (secondly) all events and their meanings are *interpreted*. Yet strangely most (though not all) of the long line of theologians—from 1918 almost to the present—who have said this have frequently denied the relevance of the interpretation of historical events to theology in principle and have rarely practiced it explicitly as a part of their own theological tasks. On the contrary, having said this about history, they often turn from events outside their windows to concentrate their powerful attention only on texts piled high on their desks. Theology, to live, must combine a hermeneutic of texts, even classical texts, with a hermeneutic of events; a hermeneutic of the confusion of tradition, with a hermeneutic of the even greater confusion of events, of the chaotic concantenation of forces and of meanings that make up any present and in which texts are both embedded and interpreted—as we not too long ago found that words and experience must be brought together if religious language is again to live.

This address will, then, essay a modest hermeneutic of events in our time; a small enough weight on the scale, to be sure, but one seeking to balance the massive contributions of the hermeneutic of texts that dominate the theology of our day. Our question is: What does a hermeneutic of events in our time bode for theology and the tasks of theology? Not surprisingly, since the two forms of hermeneutic are deeply interconnected, the message to theology from events is not, I feel, dissimilar to that from contemporary literary and

*Shailer Matthews Professor of Theology at the University of Chicago Divinity School, Dr. Gilkey presented this paper as a 75th Anniversary Lecture at the 1984 Annual Meeting of the American Academy of Religion.

philosophical texts, from deconstruction, neohistorticism and theological hermenutics. To me, however, it contains some new and more radically unsettling elements yet unrecorded in contemporary texts, and thus is its message more dialectical, even more contradictory.

Ours has been a tumultuous century, a deepening time of troubles. Such times are at once generative of contradictions, of discordant messages, and of spiritual and theological ups and downs—of the appearance and disappearance again of centers of meaning, a time of lostness and of being found again—and of being found wanting! Such times of upheaval produce crises for theology, one after the other; we have in our professional lifetime experienced a remarkable series of apparent dead ends. And they suggest or call for ways out, new beginnings, renewed certainties and commitments—again one after the other. One could see all this coming and going on the surface as merely the age of evanescent fads, as many have done who have not felt the cauldron underneath. But once one feels those seething depths, such a series seems natural, even intelligible in the kind of tumultuous epoch that is ours—and we in theology are by no means the only discipline to illustrate this rocky passage.

ANXIETY, TRANSCENDENCE AND IDOLATRY

We begin with the characteristic of theology that dominates, I think, the first two-thirds of the 20th century: *the quest for transcendence.* This search was for a ground, an absolute point, beyond the threat of meaninglessness, doubt and endless suffering; for a trustworthy basis for criticism beyond false and dangerous claims; for a stable point of renewal and hope in a directionless flux. I was spiritually weaned, most of you were spiritually born, and the rest were conceived in the age of anxiety; we all take for granted the loss of ground and of center. In fact it is so familiar a theme in the great texts of recent generations as to have become by now almost boring to us all. Those texts told us of the dangerous consequences of this sort of spiritual situation, but probably most of us saw only their theological fruitfulness, and so have we fed ourselves and our students on them for decades. But these predicted consequences have now appeared, small but powerful and menacing, in the events we ourselves witness, and that appearance makes the whole familiar story very different. As hermeneutic tells us, previous traditions reappear differently when seen in the light of new sorts of contemporary events, a new historical situation. Thus we might well look briefly once again at the career of this age of anxiety and of its multi-faceted search for transcendence in order to understand the new situation of events, arising out of this familiar context, that faces us today.

What was it, then, that constituted the age of anxiety and that instituted the search for transcendence so characteristic of theology in the first half of our century? (1) First of all, of course, was the encounter with the flood of violence and death—the ultimate, so to speak, of disruption—that occurred with the First World War, heralding as it surely did the imminent collapse of European hegemony over the world and so the end of the Western golden age. This revelation of negativity, of the evacuation of power, order and meaning from the European West, evoked, or better, set the stage for, the appearance of revelation as transcendent and God as Other in the European theology that followed. (2) Following on this apocalyptic beginning, and it was only a beginning, in subsequent decades were the new evidences of the continuing ambiguity of modern culture, its possibilities for destructive as well as for creative consequence; the economic disorder and suffering of the Depression; the inhumanity and efficiency of fascism and the new totalitarian state; the dehumanization of a growing technological and industrial culture—and in recent decades the multiple threats of an expanding industrial society to our ecological environment. I have not added the Second World War to the list because in the last two decades it has, I think, become for us what Studs Terkel called "the good war" and thus now tends to appear in another more positive ledger than this one. In any case, external contradictions in our social life and a sense of arbitrariness or fatedness in our historical existence have multiplied in our century, instigating a continuing search for transcendence.

(3) Corresponding to this developing outer ambiguity, has occurred an almost visible emptying of inner life, what we might call the dissolution of the soul, the loss for many of the sense of inner reality and personal meaning, the loss of an authentic or real self. Documented in a vast amount of twentieth-century art, literature and drama, this has been manifested positively in the search for an *experience* of transcendence (not the same as the earlier search for a revelation of transcendence) on which our personal being, individually and communally, might be re-established. This search for personal identity, an identity grounded on some experienced transcendent reality, has, I feel, been the genuine ground for the recent proliferation and continuing growth among us of new and old religious movements, movements largely centered about spiritual techniques that make such experiences available. These groups have not been founded on new theological certainties nor even on new ethical requirements or insights; they live and continue to live on the experience of the renewal of personal and communal reality, a renewal based on experienced identity with the divine. The appearance and spread of new religious movements represent a parallel, if

somewhat later, response to the age of anxiety than does the theological renewal.

(4) Finally, permeating these other sources of anxiety and shaping each, has been the experience of the *Unthinkable* in history: what was thought to be impossible for civilized modernity, and what was in itself unspeakable in the ordinary categories of worldly experience. I refer of course to the Holocaust on the one hand and the threat of a Nuclear Ending on the other. A new terror is here stalking our time: it permeates all our consciousness; and yet, like the *Mysterium Tremendum* itself, we feel helpless before it, unable either to run or to ward it off—for apparently we must, as Jonathan Schell says, remake history in order to defuse this fate. It seems at once absolutely terrible and yet hardly avoidable. No wonder we refuse to think about it, to plan policies in its light, even to let ourselves feel the full weight of its meaning for our future.

In any case, let us note that in relation to this whole series, but especially to this last, we have for some time been surrounded by historical events such that they can be fully interpreted only if we also apply to them *religious* categories, and in fact apocalyptic religious categories: categories of ultimate violence, of the disintegration of meaning, of loss of soul, and of apocalyptic ending. This reappearance objectively of the religious dimension in and through our historical events, while a boon to theologians of culture, also provides an objective ground, an explanation, for the surprising fact that literalistic and fundamentalist religious discourse seems to make such good sense to other ranges of our American population than the professional, and thus does popular religious apocalyptic return in force. In our century a "hierophany" of an apparently transcendant evil has appeared—ironically at our own hands, as the child of even our highest human intelligence. Once again a transcendant principle of renewal and hope seems all that we have left.

All of this tale of anxiety and disruption is familiar to us, a little bit "old hat." What has been neither familiar nor old hat to us is, however, one of its consequences—a consequence that manifests itself in political events though neither usually in the literary nor philosophical reactions to those events. I refer to the consequence which we in religion label *idolatry*, what John Dillenberger called "overbelief." For idolatry—and here is the rub—also stalks the terrain that anxiety has inhabited. Thus is it also partner, though an unwanted one, to the search for transcendence we have just associated with anxiety. We could, therefore, say with some validity that not only is our age one of anxiety and of the search for transcendence—even more it can be characterized: politically, economically, socially, as well as religiously, as the age of idolatries, or, in more secular language, of pervasive and lethal *ideologies*. The travail of Europe in 1914 and its aftermath produced not only Barth but Hitler; and subsequent to that, wherever a culture was dismembered or threatened as had been that of Germany, a similarly virulent idolatry has appeared: in Shinto Japan, with Stalin's Russia, in the excesses of Maoist China, and in Islam with the Ayotollah. All this we too have seen, recognized and proclaimed, not least because our greatest theological texts pointed it out to us.

What is really new, then, is the appearance, or the beginning of the appearance, of this same spectre in our own midst, an idolatry of the first order, a lethal ideology. What we had contemplated with *Schadenfreude* in others, and what our texts had predicted in print, the threat of a powerful heteronomy, has now appeared as a small seedling, perhaps one with no staying power but still quite visible to us all last summer in Dallas. Like the poor they scorn, the Religious Right have been with us always. What is different, therefore, is their sudden appearance center stage and their new acquisition of impressive power: the power of vastly increased following; the power of effectiveness and universality of communication; and above all the possibility of real political leverage. This political power, incredible a few years ago, is at least now credible; both at the top (these religious leaders have access to the White House), and it appears they are becoming dominant politically at the grassroots level in many areas west of us here. Their aim to infiltrate and eventually to dominate the Republican party would be humorous as an ironic reversal, a reversal of the similar effort in the thirties of the Far Left to infiltrate liberal politics, were it not so plausible. I was never really worried about the creationist movement until I stared in horror at the events taking place in the Dallas Convention and contemplated the effects in law relevant to church and state of a radically changed Supreme Court. Here a new "Christian America" is projected, a *theocracy* where Christians, as Falwell puts it, can finally run "their own country," where an incredibly heteronomous science, history and social theory snuff out legitimate scientific and humanistic education, and where a virulent and dangerous idolatry centered on the nation and on capitalism seeks to determine all private commitment, all public theory, and all political action. This, mind you, is not yet here; it has a long, long way to go. But it has appeared, and appeared center-stage. And its possible implications, like those of the first appearances of the Nazis in the München Bierhallen of the early twenties, are worth pondering for a learned society devoted to the study of religion and the bizarre career of religion in history.

This is more than something for those of us who do theology of culture to write about. It also raises issues for systematic theologians and implications for philosophers. As does every idolatry or ideology, such an appearance—and it is not all *that* strange in history—raises first of all issues of *method* and of *authority*, as the Barmen confession rightly and powerfully noted. To combat what one takes to be a virulent false truth, some approximation to and possession of a healthier truth—for Barmen the truth of the gospel—is necessary as a basis for disengagement, for protest, and for dissident political action—that is for the renewal of the public sphere. The total loss of center, the eradication of a stable perspective and a firm criterion—of an absolute in *any* form—merely encourages the ravages of the disease and in fact prevents any possibility of a cure. Heteronomy, fortunately, need not be fought with an alternative heteronomy. But it must be fought; and a grasp of a firm structure is necessary to make one's way against it. Correspondingly, idolatrous faith—the commitment to an unconditional nationalism fueled by deep anxiety about unconditional loss—must be countered by an equal commitment, an equally unswerving faith, whether the situation demands protest, political counteraction, at the end revolution—or possibly martyrdom. In short, a transcendent point of criticism, of judgment and certainty, of hope of renewal is necessary in political action and in political theorizing as well as in theological reflection on events, whenever idolatry is abroad in the land.

Now my point in mentioning the appearance in power on our political scene of the Religious Right is not so much to sound the alarm of an imminent take-over—though enough anxieties in the future can do strange things to our republic. Despite the many constitutional and customary guards against it, we are in the end no more immune to this disease than are other human communities, and plenty of them have succumbed in our century. My point is to remind us, via this still tiny reality, of a real and ever-present historical possibility, namely that at certain historical junctures definite political action becomes utterly necessary, a *demand*, as Tillich put it. Such a demand for action is experienced continually by groups who suffer, who are oppressed and so who seek liberation. We all know this. But we will only *feel* it as a demand on ourselves when we see ourselves as also those threatened by oppression—and this is the role of the possible heteronomy of the Religious Right.

Further—and this is the real point—such liberating action requires as its condition some very definite, stable and particular standpoint: a commitment to some understanding of the human, of persons and of society, that does not waver and that defines our understanding of injustice and so our search for justice and liberation, in short, an affirmed anthropology of individual and community. At the least this condition of liberating politics is humanistic: ultimately this is also theological, that is inclusive of a view of all of history and even of the whole. All liberating political theologies rest on such a centered vision, a *relative absolute*. This was clear in the Barmen challenge to Hitler; it is clear in current liberation theologies—but it is also true of creative political action anywhere, at anytime. This is important to recall in an age not only of persistently present unjust structures but also of ever novel oppressive heteronomies.

Anxiety, ideology, idolatry, and the search for transcendence are all of one historical piece; as are oppression, injustice, resistance and the search for a liberating structure. Resistance to idolatry and to oppression alike call for some fixed world and much stable commitment. In such an age some relation, however tenuous, to an absolute point is necessary, whether it be humanistic, theological or mystical, if the ravages of an oppressive ideology are not to rule unchecked. The historical possibility and the historical facts of idolatry and of oppression call even more urgently for some center, some structure and for transcendence than does the dank sea of anxiety. A quite centerless world heralds the end of creative and liberating praxis as it does of reflective theory, and thus does it represent a historical and communal disaster, a disaster in which cooperative society, humane relations and healthy piety are alike impossible—however strongly the intellectual currents of our time may flow in that direction.

PLURALITY AND RELATIVITY

A center, then, must be found, but how can we in our time find it? That, I suggest, is the theological as well as the political question—a kind of maddening historical Koan—which our age tosses in our direction. For, as is plain, ours is an unusually contradictory age. It is an age of idolatry, as well as oppression, of a sequence of absolute and yet demonic centers. Yet it is also the age of an almost equally unyielding relativity, of no center at all. In fact, in a kind of cumulative progression since 1918, we have experienced the steadily mounting onset of relativity, the supremacy of plurality, the multiplicity of evanescent centers, the disappearance of any guiding thread—even of any author! Some of us twenty years ago characterized our secularistic age as one of radical contingency and relativity, and noted the difficulty this mood posed for metaphysics, rational ethics and theology. The secularity of that period continued, however, to be sure of its scientific method and its democratic values, and above all to assume the universality and finality of the Western civilization founded on these two bases. Apparently—and we shall soon note the causes—we have moved far beyond this into a much more uncentered world, the post-modern world, in which no final point of reference in cognition or in value is easily available or long tenable.

Our cultural space seems, therefore, at once filled with absolute visions, meanings and laws, and the threat of more. Yet in the next instant the same space appears as utterly void of any continuous perspective at all, groundless, empty of order and of transcendence alike. Politically we are menaced by radical absolutism, intellectually by radical relativism. Here a history replete with one absolute after another, and texts saturated with relativity, seem quite at odds with one another.

The literary and philosophical expressions of this radical pluralism are familiar to you all: in deconstruction, as Mark Taylor's, Tom Altizer's and Charles Winquist's books remind us; and in neohistoricist political theory and philosophy, as Bill Dean's studies inform us. I will not, because I could not, seek to illumine further these important textual witnesses to this, our present spiritual situation. What my essay into a hermeneutic of historical events may provide is a view of what are to me the two major historical processes or sequences of events that have been *causative* of this onset of radical relativity in post-modern experience, of the loss of center and/or of all moorings. If we ask—as we should—*why* our age's reflections are so full of the experience of the dissolution of encompassing charts, the historical answer, I believe, lies not only in that impressive series of what Tillich termed "shocks of non-being" cited earlier, but also, and perhaps especially, in these two further more recent processes I will now describe. To grapple with them is at least as important as grappling with the current intellectual movements that reflect and parallel them.

The first is the issue that fascinates and lures each one of us, alike in the study of religion and of theology, the moment we come within range of its orbit. I refer to the new awareness of the *plurality of religions*. This awareness of plurality has, however, a new sharpness today, or put another way, it is *more* than mere plurality. After all, from the beginning it was realized that religions were numerically plural! Thus for us has been added the qualifier: namely that there is a *rough parity* between these diverse and multiple religious ways. Consequently, on the one hand, it is felt—if not yet made intelligible theologically—that there is truth and grace, enlightenment and saving power in all faiths, or at least certainly not exclusively in one. Each is, therefore, in a sense a relative and no longer a final means of true understanding and of true fulfillment, only an approximation of some level of truth and of grace that lies beyond each of them. The radical, not to say devastating, effects of this apprehension on most traditional theological views of revelation, incarnation, atonement, law and justification, not to mention eschatology, are obvious. It is by no means easy—though it is surely interesting—to try to do constructive theology in this atmosphere. How can we interpret human existence, its meaning and obligations to God or to one another—how can we interpret God—if there is no fixed and final perspective, be it Biblical, metaphysical, or merely anthropological, from which to view all of this? Yet few can avoid this relativistic atmosphere and stay in touch with the historical destiny of our moment.

On the other hand, and even more radical, it is—as Wilfred Smith has rightly reminded us—also impossible in this new epoch to interpret other religions from the perspective of our own. The interpretation and assessment of other faiths from the stable viewpoint of one's own was a mode of interpretation long practiced in the more tolerant (than we) circles of Hindu, Buddhist and Sikh reflection; and liberal Christian theologians assumed it to be legitimate right up to yesterday. Even those great figures who granted the saving work of God outside their own tradition, Schleiermacher, Ritschl, Barth and most of the neo-orthodox, and most open of all, Rahner, Tillich and Pannenberg, took it for granted that their own Christian perspective represented a universally valid principle capable of interpreting other faiths. No such fixed and universally valid center of interpretation of our human existence, of the divine, or of other perspectives seems available to us; for we are well aware that each such perspective reduces any other religious stance to the status of an object understood from an alien standpoint, and thus both compromises its truth and appropriates its grace. And yet how can we proceed, either in the business of existing humanly in time or in dialogue humanely with one another, without a principle of interpretation, a fixed point of reference?

In any case, it seems clear that one of the historical roots of the current immobilization of the constructive theological mind, and in part also of the loss of center in the common reflective life of the wider culture, has been the vivid experience of religious plurality and of religious parity wherein no universal point of view or principle of interpretation, religious or humanistic, seems possible. It also appears evident, and by no means irrelevant, that a deep, if quite unarticulated, subliminal awareness of this religious relativism in our age is one powerful factor in the rise of reactive fundamentalism. As anyone who has toured the college scene knows, the touchiest issue with the new fundamentalist associations does not concern such doctrinal questions as creation, virgin birth, infallibility, and so on, but precisely the sole and so the exclusive efficacy of Jesus Christ for salvation. One effect of religious pluralism is the rise of a fundamentalist reaction, as another effect is our fascination with dialogue. In sum, religious pluralism and parity have together made it even more difficult than did secularity to apprehend theologically any principle of universal structure or of transcendence, while perversely the same relativity continually breeds and fosters the unwelcome weeds of heteronomy.

Important as it is to theology, church and even to the future interaction of world cultures, the newly apparent plurality of religions has not been, I think, the major "hierophany" of pluralism in our recent historical situation. Back of it is beginning to appear a much more fundamental plurality—at least more fundamental to our secular culture and to us as participants (willingly or unwillingly) in that secular culture. I refer to the awareness of the *plurality of cultures*—in particular, since the West is the only one in our epoch to have made claims to absoluteness—the *relativity of Western culture*. It is an ironic characteristic of Western culture that it has been the tradition to have introduced into the human consciousness a systematic awareness and understanding of relativity. To the developed Western consciousness nothing anywhere is absolute: no document, perspective, moral law or dogma, not even its own "truths." And via that consciousness it has successfully relativized most of its own tradition as well as the traditional elements of other cultures. (Except, of course, where the idolatries referred to have appeared and sought to eliminate, as if it were a curse, this relativizing consciousness.) One important element of the Western consciousness, however, has consistently escaped this relativizing process, namely the Western consciousness itself. Accordingly, this consciousness has been taken, and still is by most of academia, to be universal, a consciousness that can, and ultimately will, include and transform the plurality of viewpoints of the world's other cultures, and transmute them into itself. If this consciousness is not universal yet, soon it will be—and that is precisely what is meant by Civilization and by Progress. Thus as nations become "developed," they become Western: scientific, technological, industrial, democratic and secular, illustrations of our universal modern consciousness.

This strange, arrogant assumption of our modern secular culture was almost totally dominant through the Second World War. Steadily since then, however, questions about its credibility have grown in force; and now the claims of the Western scientific and humanistic consciousness to represent the apogee of human and cultural consciousness seem as bizaare as do the earlier claims of the universality and exclusivity of Christianity. With the loss of the political and military dominance and supremacy of the West after 1945, the historical basis for the dominance and clear superiority of its consciousness has vanished; in time a new and much more radical cultural plurality will join the already present religious plurality. In that case there will be no obvious and available universalizable center, religious or secular, transcendent or humanistic, anywhere—except (again) where appear partial and enforced centers on the basis of some idolatry or ideology. For example, even such apparently presuppositionless and universal viewpoints as positivism, instrumentalism, philosophical naturalism and language philosophy now reveal themselves as expressions of the Western scientific and humanistic consciousness and thus as immensely partial, dependent upon *one* cultural vision of things, and one now under criticism. Awareness of this imminent deconstruction of the centrality, universality and permanence of the Western consciousness and so of the universal validity of its varied forms, is, I think, the main historical root of the sense of the loss of center, and of the loss of the possibility of mono-theorism in any form, in our current reflective life.

Again it is by no means irrelevant to point out the effect this even deeper vision of relativity has had on the recent rise of fundamentalist religion. Whether the Religious Right puts more trust in the Bible or the American Way of Life, in God's law or "Our Traditional Values," in the power of God or of the Pentagon, is, I gather, an open question, and arguments can be made on both sides. Again flags and crosses seem to have linked arms; the essence of the Religious Right, as evidenced both in Washington and at the Dallas convention, is the intricate interweaving of these two false but potent absolutes: a heteronomous and exclusivist Christianity and a rampant nationalistic and capitalistic ideology. Thus to this vision the pluralism of cultures, relativizing Western capitalistic and social values, and the pluralism of religions, relativizing Christian doctrines and certainties, are equally unacceptable and in combination devastating. And so, appropriately, there appear in reaction the new goal and the new requirement—unheard of before with this explicitness and quite contrary to their own religious tradition—of a "Christian America," that is, of the rule of the political and the cultural spheres by those who are Christians. This combines or unites the religious and the social spheres; it represents a theocratic demand intelligible as a defense against their double fear, first of political and cultural relativism and secondly of religious relativism.

The currents of relativism in our time run very, very deep. Apparently there is neither a secular nor a religious standpoint or center from which either reflective interpretation or constructive political action may proceed. And since the same relativizing forces that impel some intellectuals to numbed reflective silence also evoke in reaction among others oppressive and destructive idolatries, our situation seems contradictory and vulnerable in the extreme. Neither theological reflection nor religious praxis will by themselves resolve these dilemmas on every level of our existence; but without the possibility of such positive reflection and of a praxis implied therein, nothing at all by us can be done to stem the tide.

PRAXIS, DIALECTIC AND PARADOX

We were left facing a stark contradiction, the painful debris of a stormy age. On the one hand we reviewed the forces of anxiety that drive towards transcendence, towards idolatry and ideology, and towards the requirement of some sort of absolute standpoint against both of the latter. And on the other we surveyed the even more awesome forces dissolving and repudiating any absolute center and thus seemingly any center to all. As a result, coherent reflection, meaningful commitment and creative action alike—much less any reference to transcendence—appear impossible.

One way out, so we are told, is through the category of "play," the reflective deconstruction and practical non-attachment of those who have accepted centerless relativism and made it the new key to their existence. Play does have, to be sure, its enriching place in personal and group existence—though Kierkegaard gives us storm warnings even there. But in the public realm play as the clue to existence becomes helpless and cringing whenever a new demonic absolute appears, for such an absolute sweeps aside the varied assortment of pluralisms perennially dear to any leisure class. Needless to say, it is also toothless if one faces oppression. Play as a category, therefore, assumes unjustifiably the stability and even the justice of a public order outside of and yet supportive of itself; and on the basis of that assumption of the stability of social structure (an error historically and contradictory to its own deconstructing implications), play abjures responsibility for the order on which it is itself dependent. No, in our day of renewed idols the contradiction cannot be resolved that easily.

Faced with this reflective impasse, I suggest we refer to the venerable, practical American tradition. The puzzle which to reflection may represent a hopeless contradiction, said John Dewey, can through *intelligent practice* be fruitfully entered and successfully resolved. And in fact praxis is another of the key words descriptive of reflection in our century. Along with history, interpretation, anxiety, transcendence, idolatry and pluralism, praxis as liberation represents a category to which we must pay attention if we would understand ourselves, our recent cultural past and our historical present. As James reminds us, moreover, praxis brings with it a *forced* option, one that cannot be avoided. When praxis is called for, the puzzled immobility before a contradiction or the playful acceptance of a plurality of options must both cease—for to be humanly existing we must wager, and must enact our wager. So is it with the dilemma forced on us by an oppressive ideology: faced with that menace, we *must* act, that is, we *will* act whether we wish to or not; more specifically, we will *either* cease to play and conform, *or* we will cease to play and resist; and both are actions, choices that transform much about ourselves that went before, not least our relation to our social environment. Praxis and its demands do not leave us alone. Thus does praxis push as well as lure us into the heart of our puzzle.

That puzzle has revealed itself as the apparent contradiction between the requirement within political action for some fixed or absolute center and an equally unavoidable relativism. Let us look first at this requirement of a center for praxis, and then see how it relativizes itself if it is to remain healthy. If we would *be* as personal and social beings, and even more if we must take a role in liberating action, we must stand somewhere and act from somewhere. We need a ground for the apprehension and understanding of reality which undergirds our choices, our critiques of the status quo, our policies; we need a ground for the values and eros which fuel our drive towards justice; and for our confidence and hopes necessary for consistent action. We need criteria for the judgments essential alike for reflective construction and for liberating doing; and we need priorities in value if we would creatively and actively move into the future. All this is as true of the pragmatic humanist as of the theologian, and for the reflection and the action of both. Experienced as an unconditional requirement in an age of anxiety and relativity, this need instigated in the first part of the century the search for a stable structure and for transcendence. And it has crescendoed with us into an unavoidable requirement insofar as we too feel the necessity of political participation or resistance to the threat of heteronomy.

Not surprisingly, what is here unconditionally required in action is what had been—in our classic theological texts—intellectually seen, as a requirement of authentic human being: namely a relation on the one hand to some stable and assumed, and in that sense, absolute standpoint, a participation in it, and commitment to it. But, and here is where the other side of the dialectic appears, in order to avoid repeating in ourselves the same oppressive idolatry which we confront, there must at the same time be a deep apprehension and recognition of the relativity of our standpoint. [Such a fixed center, in method and in steady aim, characterized Dewey's instrumentalism as it does, in the forms of transcendence, the best dialectical theologies; and both understood the parallel need of a thorough relativity. Against total systems, of metaphysics or of theology, pragmatism seems thoroughly relativistic. But compared to radical and centerless plurality, it reveals its own need for and use of some absolute principle or standpoint, epistemological, ethical and so at the last anthropological.] A dialectic or paradox combining and interweaving both one part of absoluteness and two parts relativity, *a relative absoluteness*, represents a posture essential to public and political praxis, again whether humanistic or theological.

With regard to praxis in the other large area of our common life as students of religion, the same dialectic or paradox, this interweaving and mutual dependence of apparent opposites, appears. I refer to the issue of the new religious plurality or parity characteristic of our epoch. In the face of this plurality it is almost impossible at the moment to formulate a theological resolution of the doctrinal dilemmas and contradictions involved: for the interplay of absolute and relative—of being, and affirming being, a Christian, Jew or Buddhist and yet at the same time relativizing that mode of existence—both stuns and silences the mind, at least mine. But again praxis, now in the form of dialogue, pushes and lures us into the middle of a maze we still can hardly enter intellectually. As we do in creative political action, so now in "doing" dialogue we embody and enact this paradox; and we do so most fruitfully step by step. That is, on the one hand we do not relinquish our own standpoint or starting-point: what is the dialogue if our Buddhist partner ceases to be Buddhist? Nor on the other hand do we absolutize our own standpoint—lest no interchange take place at all. On the contrary, we relativize it radically: truth and grace are *also* with the other, so that now ours is only *one* way. And yet we remain *there*: embodying stubbornly but relatively our unconditional affirmation; or, in reverse, qualifying our acknowledged relativism by participating in one quite particular but still stoutly affirmed perspective. Again in praxis we uncover a relative absoluteness.

What to reflection is a contradiction is to praxis a workable dialectic, a momentary but creative paradox. Absolute and relative, unified vision and plurality, a centered principle of interpretation and mere difference—contradictions that structure our age of deconstruction—represent polarities apparently embodiable in crucial practice despite the fact that they seem numbing in reflective theory. Moreover—and this is the basic principle of theory based on praxis—what is necessary to praxis is also necessary for reflection and theory—though the reverse is *not* true.

In any case, reflection is important and must be begun. Let us, therefore, start our reflections with this dialectic or paradox uncovered as the heart of praxis, of political liberation and dialogue, and let us then push it reflectively outward toward theory, toward theology. I suggest we use this paradigm within praxis—the dialectic of infinity and the finite, of the absolute as *relatively* present in the relative—as now the clue to the center of theological understanding: to the interpretation of our relation to the sacred on the one hand, and on the other as the key to reflection on that to which we are related, to the absolute as it manifests itself relatively in the relative. Recall: the structure of praxis is our most helpful clue to the structure of being as we now seek to reflect on it.

This weird mystery of paradox of absoluteness within relativity, or infinity and its relative manifestions, of the unconditional and its conditioned embodiments, represents, I am suggesting, *the* theological problem for our century. As we have seen, theology in this century tended towards the absolute in its first half, towards the relative in its second—and now it seems forced back towards the absolute when faced with injustice and with heteronomy. The problem or dilemma of the dialectic of infinity and finitude, of absolute and relative, appears and reappears: in our experience of events and the liberating praxis they demand of us, in reflective issues of method and interpretation in hermeneutics, and in the theoretical construction of symbols—in theology. Wherever we turn, it will not go away—it is *our* problem.

The infinite manifests itself in the particular, the absolute in the relative—and the aroma of *each* pervades all we do and think. Is this principle or insight new? Is it not the heart of Hegel, even of Kierkegaard; is it not what Whitehead meant when he speaks of an infinite mystery hovering over and relativizing any system of rational coherence; what Dewey pointed to when amid perpetual flux and relativity he lifted up a method that was not relative and did not change; what Tillich pointed to with his concept of the *true* symbol that relativizes and sacrifices itself in pointing beyond itself; or Niebuhr who orchestrated the theme of a mystery deeper than any revealed or reflected scheme? What is different, what is more radical, in our situation than in these classical texts? Each of these saw clearly the dialectic of infinity and manifestation, of absolute and relative, of unconditioned mystery and conditioned meaning. The difference is that each, true to their cultural and religious epoch, saw their own particularity, their concrete scheme of meaning, be it theological or philosophical, as somehow privileged, as final, as less relative than the others, as *the* clue to the mystery that transcended it—whether it was Hegel's or Whitehead's logos, Dewey's expanded scientific method, or Tillich's and Niebuhr's revelation. But an objective and universal rational order turns out to be a *Western* logos, and this defies for us the awareness of the plurality and relativity of cultures and so of all logoi. And the claim to a final and definitive revelation defies the plurality and relativity of religions. No cultural logos is final and so universal (even one based on science), no one revelation is or can be the universal criterion for all the others (even, so we are now seeing,

one based on Christian revelation). Mystery is here more encompassing because the particular center, the concrete principle of meaning,
now is *itself* relative, one among many centers. This is the new
situation, and again it seems to stifle any philosophy grounded on a
universal logos or any theology on a universally valid revelation.

So we shall return to our dialectic incarnate in unavoidable praxis:
the infinite manifests itself in *relative* relativities, the unconditioned
in *conditioned* concretions. Liberating theologies and dialogue are
based on this; but can we *think* as well as act on this new basis? Let
us turn this over: these manifestations are particular and relative,
agreed. But despite this, they also participate in and manifest the
absolute or the infinite. The infinite *is* in the concrete, the absolute is
unavoidably in the particular; that is, it cannot be approached except
through the particular and the relative. But also the particular and the
relative are not completely relative, for neither praxis nor reflection
can be without this absolute ground and meaning. A symbol or a
criterion points beyond itself and criticizes itself if it would not be
demonic: but it also points *to* itself and *through* itself if it would not
be empty, and if we would not be left centerless. The dialectic works
both ways; relativizing the manifestation on the one hand and so all
incarnations of the absolute, and yet manifesting as well *through* the
relative an absoluteness that transcends it—else again there be no
liberating praxis and no creative reflection possible. I suspect our
wider culture, and so academia, will soon—but by no means yet—
have to deal with the same dilemma: the relativity, and yet the
continued affirmation, of the Western forms of scientific, historical and
social consciousness—as the AMA is having to deal with acupuncture
and Detroit with Toyota! We are now in the very middle of this in
theology: how are we to understand Christian revelation and promise
as our affirmed ground of life, of political praxis and reflection, but *as
relative*, as one among other manifestations and grounds?

We must, then not be ashamed to start with our particularity, our
relativity—for no universal standpoint, cultural or religious is readily
available to us. But we must incorporate into the theological elaboration of these particular symbols a new and pervasive realization and
expression of their relativity, a new and deeper speaking and not
speaking at once. Thus I will attempt to give this dialectic—or
paradox—of infinity and manifestation, of absolute and relative, one of
its *Christian* or particular forms as at the moment the best I can do—
for as any vision of plurality is itself qualified by the affirmation of a
relative center (as the proposition that all propositions are relative
itself shows) so each apprehension of infinite meaning is qualified by
and expressed through particular symbols.

In Christian symbols—as in the historical events that were their occasion and inspiration—there is a *relative* manifestation of *absolute* meaning. They are true and yet relatively true; they represent a particularization of the absolute, and yet are relative and so only one manifestation. The relative here participates in and manifests the absolute; and thus, as relative, it negates and transcends itself. It is final and yet not the only one; it is definitive and yet so are other ways. These are paradoxical assertions. Are these paradoxes impossible, that is contradictory and so cancel each other out? Or are they strange windows to an even stranger mystery, and so keys or clues to renewed theology? If the latter, then they represent challenges to what are in that case conventional but false dichotomies: (1) The absolute is lost if its relative expression becomes relative—in answer, possibly relativity and absoluteness could in reflection, as they do in praxis, coexist. (2) The relative loses all participation in and communication of the absolute if it is relative to others, if there *are* others. In answer again, possibly a series of manifestations can co-exist on the same level and with genuine validity. At least it is this that seems to me now existentially and theologically possible, as it is in any sane, liberating and humane praxis.

Thus, to mention briefly a further theological elaboration of this fundamental dialectic: (1) The infinite can be seen as God—and yet that symbol recognized as transcended by an infinite mystery, a mystery consequently pervaded by nonbeing as well as being (as the Cross might remind us), and so a mystery truly but relatively manifest as God but also made particular and concrete in other ways and through other symbols. (2) Correspondingly, the infinite is revealed as absolute love, as agape, that is Christologically. Here is a truth, yet a truth whose vehicle of manifestation, that whereby it is known and apprehended, is relative—and yet true. What is here truly apprehended, acknowledged and witnessed to, may be also expressed through other media and by means of other symbols (for example, the Bodhisattva). (3) The infinite mystery is, finally, understood as redemptive power and promise, and truly so understood—and yet the grace there known far transcends the bounds of its own manifestation to us and is creatively present in the symbols derived from other manifestations. To understand God in relation both to a mystery that transcends God and to the non-being that seems to contradict God; to understand revelation in relation to other revelations that relativize our revelation; to view Christology and gospel in relation to other manifestations of grace; anthropology in relation to annatta and identity—this is the heart of our present baffling but very exciting theological task.

Perhaps the secret here is like the secret of existing itself, that is existing with inner strength and outer liberating power: to hold on with infinite passion to both ends of the dialectic of relativity and absoluteness. Perhaps, if one keeps these poles together in a synthesis, such a posture for theological reflection may seem possible, as it is already acknowledged to be possible in political action and in dialogue. If such a relativized theology seems, as it certainly will to its cultural critics, a foolish and illogical impossibility, then let them remember that they will face tomorrow the same baffling dialectic as the Western consciousness appropriates to itself its own destined travail of relativity. Meanwhile, let us not forget that the present flood of relativity is balanced by the stern demands for liberating praxis and for creative theory.

THEOLOGICAL PLURALISM: AN ASIAN
RESPONSE TO DAVID TRACY

PHILIP SHEN*

I

The topic originally given to me was very broad and I have taken the liberty to narrow it down drastically to the present one. Although I have not managed to keep up much with American theology since I completed my graduate theological studies at Chicago and left for Hong Kong over twenty years ago, I have not forgotten the impression of richness and vitality of American theology, a characteristic of its pluralism. Now David Tracy, himself a product of this pluralism, seeks to address it directly with a revisionist model of theology.[1]

In *Blessed Rage for Order* (1975) and *The Analogical Imagination* (1981)[2] Tracy has presented to the American public not only an analysis of the pluralistic situation of contemporary American theology but also a reconstructed model of how theology should be done in just that situation. A third volume, when it appears, should complete his great work, which will likely become a milestone in the development of American religious thought.

I am much impressed by Tracy's work and have learned much from him, not only for his encyclopedic learning but also, more important, for his liberal and irenic spirit. I wish to thank Professor Ray L. Hart for suggesting Tracy to me for this occasion and am grateful to the Academy for allowing me the honor to make an address on American theology as Tracy has envisioned it.

There is much in Tracy's works to which I resonate. As I read him, I often found that he seemed to be addressing me, describing what I in my own situation was trying to do in theology or philosophy of religion. There are many things in his works that are exciting to

*Senior Lecturer in Religion at The Chinese University of Hong Kong, Dr. Shen presented this paper as a 75th Anniversary Lecture at the 1984 Annual Meeting of the American Academy of Religion.

[1] In this paper "theology" is short for "Christian theology."

[2] Citations of works by Tracy will be by title abbreviations (see Works Consulted).

anyone in the field, for example his exposition of the new hermeneutics and its application to New Testament materials, the analogy between religious classics and literary or artistic products, the Christ of faith *vis-à-vis* the Jesus of history, and so forth. But all these I must forego on this occasion. With the limited time I have, I shall confine myself rather to the problem of the nature and task of theology itself, given its pluralistic situation. I believe I can respond to this aspect of Tracy's work from a definitely *Asian* perspective.

The question of pluralism is particularly important for us in Asia. In this vast continent the diversity of cultural and religious traditions is much more extensive and profound than anyone in the west could ever imagine. Just to take for example the comparatively tiny phenomenon of Protestant Christianity itself. It was transplanted from Europe and America only less than two hundred years ago but has grown in various spots in Asia—separately, and in almost complete mutual ignorance or disregard. When Protestant theologians started to meet about thirty years ago to consult one another on matters concerning theological education and scholarship, the fact of pluralism has always been the first to reveal itself and be clearly recognized, before any effort could be made to explore common grounds of understanding and cooperation. We have come a long way since, yet the fact of pluralism remains. But instead of being a cause of division it has slowly become a source of enrichment.[3]

It seems appropriate therefore for me to address this question in response to Tracy from an Asian point of view, but I must hasten to emphasize that it is only *one* Asian response. I cannot speak for other Asians, speaking as I do from my limited perspective as a Chinese Christian who lives and works in Hong Kong, which is itself quite a unique place undergoing at this historic moment a unique crisis of destiny.

---

[3] *The Southeast Asian Journal of Theology* was published by the Association of Theological Schools in Southeast Asia, founded in 1956; it merged in 1983 with its sister organ *The Northeast Asian Journal of Theology* to become *The East Asian Journal of Theology*. For recent theological developments see also the *CTC Bulletin* (or *Bulletin of the Commission on Theological Concerns, Christian Conference of Asia*), which started in 1979. There are at least four anthologies which attempt to give a broad coverage of contemporary Asian theologies: Anderson (1976), Elwood (1980), England (1981), and Nácpil and Elwood (1978). All except the last have bibliographies (of writings in English). The most recent survey is found in England (1984). There is some contribution from individual Roman Catholic theologians in these journals and books, but little from the more strictly Conservative-Evangelical side. The lines separating them and the "ecumenicals", however, are getting less marked in recent years than before.

II

Let me start with a few observations on Tracy's work as a whole. First, the work seems to fall short of being a systematic theology in the usual sense, since it does not deal with the full range of Christian doctrines.[4] The doctrine of the Trinity, for example, is touched upon only in two notes at the end of *AI* (443 n.30; 444 n.41). Tracy explains that he is attempting an analysis of the basic structure of systematics, not to provide one on the full range of doctrines and symbols.[5] Christology, on the other hand, receives a rather full treatment, which appears already in *BRO*. The whole revisionist model, from fundamental theology to systematic theology, and not excepting practical theology either, one suspects, is Christocentric through and through. The idea seems to be, if it is Christian theology, it has to be Christocentric. As I will suggest later, if it is Christocentric, it has to be Christian.[6]

Secondly, the work intends to be, I believe, ecumenical in scope.[7] Tracy discusses the contributions of different schools of contemporary theology, both Roman Catholic and Protestant. The copious notes are themselves masterful guides to recent Euro-American, including Latin-American, theological scholarship and debates. There are, however, no references to non-Western works. Neither is any mention made, within American Christianity itself, of the conservative evangelical tradition as distinct from fundamentalism.[8]

Thirdly, there are some references to other world religions,[9] or Eastern religions such as Hinduism or Buddhism.[10] Toward the end of *AI*, Tracy states clearly that "the attention of Christian theology cannot be confined to Christianity alone," suggesting a method of conversation with "all the other religions and their classics" in the extended use of the analogical imagination (*AI*:449). This, however,

---

[4] "Systematics" should "promote an understanding of the great doctrines of Christianity," according to Lonergan, so read by Lambino (1980:93).

[5] A summary of the classic symbols and doctrines in *AI* (373) does include, at the head of the list, "God, Christ, Grace," which looks trinitarian.

[6] See discussion below, p. 29.

[7] See *BRO* (4), where the author states his approaches to the contemporary situation in "global terms," starting with the "Western, indeed global, crisis of meaning as the initial context for contemporary theology."

[8] Fundamentalism is included in the orthodoxy model of contemporary theology (*BRO*:24). Tracy identifies it with Biblical literalism and supernaturalism and generally dismisses it as such (*BRO*:126; 145 n. 93).

[9] Two references are made to Islam in *AI* (248; 287 n. 6). Judaism, however, is much discussed in *AI*.

[10] E.g., *BRO*:138 n. 24; 234 n. 94.

remains the sort of work to be done in the future or by others having the interest and the competence.

III

One of the most interesting aspects of Tracy's revisionist model is the systematic correlation of the three traditional disciplinary divisions of theology (fundamental, systematic, and practical) with the three social realities or *publics* for theological discourse (academy, church, and society respectively).[11] This correlation has the important effect of specifying the demand for accountability to the public for each of the three theological disciplines (in terms of reason, faith, and action, respectively).[12] More important, it also displays the *public* character of theological discourse, which requires the theologian to render explicit, or to develop, public criteria for the claims to meaning and truth in each discipline.[13]

The task of theology, in this regard, is essentially one of *interpretation*. There are three things to be interpreted: (1) the fundamental, religious questions of human existence, or the religious dimension of the contemporary situation (in fundamental theology); (2) the religious tradition in its classical expressions (in systematic theology); and (3) the models of human transformation (in practical theology).[14]

These interpretations, however, must not be done in isolation from one another. There must be, rather, *mutually critical correlation*[15] between them, i.e., between their respective meanings and truths, of the common human experience or the contemporary situation on the one hand and the religious tradition or the Christian fact on

[11] Sociologically considered, society comes before academy and church, as they are discussed in this order in *AI* (Ch. 1). Logically, fundamental theology comes before systematic theology which is followed by practical theology, in a progression, according to Tracy, from the relatively abstract to the more concrete. The order follows the Aristotelian arrangement of the disciplines of metaphysic-dialectic, poetics-rhetoric, and ethics-politics, which in turn are correlated with the true, the beautiful (as true), and the good (as true), in their respective relations to the holy or the religious (*AI*:97 n. 114). The connections of systematic theology with poetics and rhetoric is particularly significant in Tracy's understanding of what theology *as* hermenentics is, i.e., for systematic as distinct from fundamental theology.

[12] Or, respectively, rational, critical inquiry; fidelity to the religious tradition; and commitment to praxis in a social movement.

[13] "Those criteria also range from the necessary and abstract (transcendental or metaphysical criteria in fundamental theology through the hermeneutical criteria of truth as disclosure and concealment in systematic theologies) to the concrete praxis criteria of truth as personal, social, political, historical and natural transformation and ethical reflection in practical theology." (*FPT*:62–63).

[14] Or, alternatively, "the goal of the good and virtuous life," or "ideals of the future of the self, society, history, and nature" (*FPT*:75–76).

[15] Tracy cites Schillebeeckx as the source of this important idea (*CT*:88).

the other.[16] And this would involve not just the questions from one side and the answers from the other side, but *both* the questions *and* the responses of both sides. One sees here an internal relation between fundamental theology and systematic theology, which cannot be separated. (I shall return to this important point later.) Practical theology, following as the third discipline, attempts in its turn "mutually critical correlation of the interpreted theory and praxis of the Christian fact and the interpreted theory and praxis of the contemporary situation" (*FPT*:76).

Theological *pluralism* is inherent in this model. It is located first in the social and intellectual environment in which the theologian is immediately confronted with different publics with different expectations or demands, which he learns to internalize. The differences are shown not only in the criteria of meaning and truth and the modes of argument he uses but also in the ethical and religious stances he takes. In other words, like St. Paul, the theologian must "become all things to all men" (I Cor. 9:22), depending on which public he participates in.

Secondly, pluralism refers to the diversity of interpretations of both the contemporary situation and the Christian fact or tradition. The fundamental questions of human existence may be the same,[17] but every interpretation presents a different situation analysis.[18] The theologian should be open to the "fuller pluralistic realities in the entire global situation and . . . the full range of fundamental questions disclosed in that situation" (*FPT*:65; cf. *AI*:258). Interpretations of Christianity, on the other hand, are also as diverse as the Christian tradition. "The New Testament itself," says Tracy, "is internally pluralistic" (*AI*:372). The theologian must then select the "central clue" or "focal meaning" for the whole, but the choice must be open to "correctives from the full range of symbols, texts, images, events, and so forth. Only then is the full range of the Christian fact allowed to play its proper hermeneutical role" (*FPT*:64; cf. *AI*:257–258).

Pluralism, in the third place, refers to the "full logical spectrum of possibilities" open to the theologian in his work of mutually critical correlation. The contemporary situation and the Christian fact, or their

---

[16] The Christian fact or tradition includes the whole range of classic texts, events, images, persons, symbols, rituals, and practices "from the New Testament forward" and retrospectively the Old Testament (*FPT*:64). (Cf. *AI*:100; 108; 126.)

[17] Human existence is characterized by the "limit-situation" of "finitude, mortality, anxiety, fundamental trust, guilt, alienation, or oppression" (*FPT*:65), in the "negative mode." The "positive mode" includes "intense joy, love, reassurance, creations" (*BRO*: 105).

[18] Such as "alienation, privatizations, and oppressions, . . . massive human suffering, . . . demand for a truly global culture, etc." (*FPT*:65). See also *AI*:342–345.

respective meanings and truths, may be identical or mutually exclusive,[19] or there may be similarities-in-difference or complementarities between them (*FPT*:63). Tracy prefers the middle way himself, which allows the contraries to confront and correct each other, in mutual illumination or possible reconciliation in a fuller vision of the whole (*BRO*:32). Here as elsewhere the analogical imagination attempts to create an enriched order out of pluralism which otherwise might lead straight into chaos.

IV

It is necessary to see that the Tracian model, as briefly outlined above, is one that is forged in the American context. The context helps shape the model. Tracy's basic problematic arises out of the ambiguous relationship between Christianity and the modern or post-modern mind, or between the religious tradition and the "culture of pluralism" (as the subtitle of *AI* puts it).[20] More particularly, it is the "crisis of cognitive claims for Christianity" that is central to Tracy's concern (*FPT*:65). The crisis nevertheless presupposes that Christianity still remains the major *religious* tradition in American culture, however powerful secular or anti-Christian influences might have become in the contemporary situation.[21] Four other theological models are considered and found wanting mainly because either they take their received Christian tradition for granted with little or no historical or critical sense; or they do not take the contemporary post-Christian or post-modern mind seriously enough; or both. The theologian, insists Tracy, has a "dual commitment" to both authentic secularity and authentic Christianity (*BRO*:33). The task for him is to interpret or re-interpret both of them rightly for authentic faith and existence today, by searching for their truths and meanings in mutually critical correlation.

Pluralism in Tracy's works is thus actually limited to the pluralism (a) within the cultural tradition in which Christianity has played a very significant role, and (b) within the Christian tradition itself. Even if he speaks of different church traditions and different societies

---

[19] Tracy's actual expression here is "pure confrontation," not "mutual exclusion" (*FPT*:63).

[20] As *AI* (84 n. 18) makes clear, the contrast between "tradition" and "situation" is analogous to that between "church" and "world."

[21] The story of Jesus Christ is likely found in the memories of ancestors or in memories of childhood and therefore it is possible, according to Tracy, to hear it or "over-hear" it anew. We also need to learn "with fresh mind those other stories—of the Buddha, of Mohammed, of Krishna—which we have too long and too ignorantly kept at a psychic distance" (*BRO*:240).

regarding the role of the theologian (*AI*:27),[22] he might still be thinking primarily of the conditions of Western culture.[23]

The situation in Asia is quite different. Except in the Philippines, Christianity is a religion of a small though in some places not uninfluential minority. The gospel of Jesus Christ is to be sure not totally strange to many but to most it is at best one among many stories, perhaps heard at times but not listened to. Except in a few spots, Christianity is not the source of the basic values and symbols that inform the dominant cultural tradition, although certain Christian ideas and sentiments may be found here and there, sometimes in surprising places.[24] Even if Christianity succeeds in being indigenized—which has a long way to go in most Asian nations—it would still remain one religion among others, with no likely claim to preeminence. In some places where a traditional religion or a modern ideology is being actively promoted as an official or exclusive faith for the nation, Christianity may be discriminated against or even suppressed. Where religious freedom is guaranteed by law and made effective, as in a modernized, secular but not totalitarian state, Christianity may coexist with other faiths. This is where pluralism of religions[25] and ideologies may become an ideal, more or less realizable with a corresponding degree of pluralism of cultural traditions. This is to many thinkers a possible and desirable by-product of the process of modernization in Asian societies today. Pluralism in the Asian context, in short, seems a much more complicated matter than what is found in the American context.

The main concerns of Christianity, under such circumstances as described above, are understandably different. They have first of all to do with mission and service which define the primary purpose of the church in the world. Secondly, there is the urgent need for Christians to participate in the ongoing struggle of the people for modernization, for freedom, justice, and equality, for human rights and democracy, and so on—what Tracy calls "praxis movements" in his works.

[22] No attention, however, is paid to the sectarian and other religious movements or ethnic minorities in the American situation. Black theology is mentioned as a liberation movement (*BRO*:20 n. 51). Much reference is made to Judaism in relation to Christianity, while Islam is mentioned in a couple of places, together with Judaism and Christianity (see Note 9 above).

[23] The passage in question refers to the Third World, specifically Latin America, which is still part of Western culture, however different it may be from Euro-America.

[24] As for example in certain post-Cultural Revolution stories in mainland China. This suggests a need to look into the actual "presence" of Christianity, in whatever aspects, in modern Chinese literature. A recent effort has been made by L. S. Robinson in articles published in *Ching Feng* (English edition), 26/2–3 (August 1983), 26/4 (December 1983), 27/2–3 (July 1984).

[25] See Lai (1984) for the historic situation in China.

Thirdly, there is the long and complex process of indigenization, to develop a Christianity that takes roots in the ongoing life and continuous culture of the people, in appropriate and lively expressions of faith and spirituality.

Theology in service to the faithful[26] has a vital role to play in all three areas, particularly (1) in critical reflection upon the mission and service of the church; (2) in formulating a basis of common understanding and action, concerning, e.g., the suffering of the people, the destiny of the nation, etc., in which all may share, whether Christian or not, whether, indeed, religious or not; and (3) in continuous engagement with the basic ideas and values of culture in its traditional or persistent forms and in its modern transformations. This may in the long run include dialogue with other religious traditions, toward mutual understanding and cooperation and maybe even bring about "mutual transformation".[27]

V

For such a context as described above, I would propose a somewhat different view of theology from the Tracian model, a revision upon his revision, so to speak. Christian theology, in my definition, is primarily reflection on Christian life in relation to the Christian gospel which is its source or ground, and to the world which is its context or environment.

This definition stresses first both the contextual reality of the Christian life as lived here and now and its ultimate grounding in the gospel of the presence of God in Jesus Christ. The person and event of Christ, originating about two thousand years ago in Palestine, is mediated through the tradition of the church.[28] This is a point well expounded by Tracy. And if theology is a mutually critical correlation as he says between the tradition of the church and the contemporary situation, it must be clearly located in the concrete living of the Christian life by the Christian believer or the believing community and must be engaged in critical reflection on its believing and living. Theological reflection is a second order activity arising out of

---

[26] Cf. Lambino (1980: 90).

[27] As Cobb (1982) proposes.

[28] In Tracy's words, the Church is "the living reality of the originating religious event . . . [which] remains the primary concrete, social and theological locus of all systematic theologies" (*AI*:422). In saying that the church is both "sacrament of the Christ *and* eschatological sacrament of the world," Tracy is in effect making the church the locus of the meeting of the gospel and the world, which is similar to what I have in mind.

this concrete experience.[29] Without this experiential grounding we fall into the "fallacy of misplaced concreteness". This point I believe is implicit in Tracy but needs to be stated more explicitly.

The definition, secondly, stresses the personal identity of the theologian in his self-understanding, which incorporates a dual commitment to both his religious and cultural heritages. This is important in our Asian context.

I am, for example, a Christian and a Chinese who lives and works in a mixed and fast-changing environment. I do not wish to be alienated from my Christian faith because of my cultural heritage, or from my cultural birthright because of my religious belief. I therefore live with the tension between being Christian and being Chinese. The tension may be so great that I cannot hold both together without breaking apart myself. Or the tension may be so creative that it leads to a new and enriched sense of personal identity and integrity. This is, if you will, a "mode of being in the world" for me which I must risk and explore in my own "journey of intensification",[29] in my self-understanding and self-affirmation. My theological reflection should be able to help me in this personal project or it is not worth much.

To relate what I have in mind more closely to the Tracian model, several comments are in order. First, the dual commitment and tension I have described my illustrate the kind of mutually critical correlation which precisely is the central task of theology. Tracy insists that the correlation must be *mutually* critical. "I must allow the text to interpret me, my questions and answers, by its own questions and answers" (AI:255). The theologian operates with a "dual focus of our real situational religious fundamental questions and the text's own disclosure . . ." (AI:259). My point is simply that the question of the Christian's personal and communal identities is very much a part of our fundamental question in our Asian situation.

Secondly, as mentioned above, there are various logical possibilities in the mutually critical correlation of the contemporary situation and the Christian fact. H. Richard Niebuhr's typology of *Christ and Culture* is useful and one may agree with Tracy that the last ideal type, Christ as the transformer of culture, is to be preferred (AI:374). The encounter of the Christian fact with Asian cultures, however, may be more complicated than could be accounted for by Niebuhr's

---

[29] Tracy also characterizes theological discourse as "second order, reflective discourse" but it is reflection "upon the originating Christian religious discourse" (TAG:2).

[29] These two expressions are borrowed from Tracy (see BRO:102; 115 n. 54; AI:122–123), and are used here in a somewhat different context from his, but I hope not entirely different.

typology, as some recent studies have shown.[30] Other modes of relationship have to be recognized with broader sampling.

Thirdly, Tracy points out the profound ambiguity inherent in both world, which includes culture, and church—even as it mediates the reality of the Christ event (AI:47–51). This point is well taken but it does not relieve the tension and perhaps only increases it. The Christian, says Tracy following St. Augustine, must be aware of the "radical contingency and ambiguity of all culture, all civilization, all institutions, even nature itself (in sum, the 'world') . . . and their constant temptation to self-aggrandizement and self-delusion" (AI:48). The same of course can be said of the church as a sociological or historical phenomenon. A "hermeneutic of suspicion" is called for.[32]

Nevertheless, the church is "fundamentally to be trusted," Tracy declares, "yet ever in need of self-reform, self-correction, self-clarification" (AI:236). This Protestant principle suggests the relevance of the Catholic idea of "indefectibility" of the church "in spite of errors" (AI:244 n.15, citing Hans Küng). As for the world, instead of following the adage that Christians are in the world but not of it (John 17:11, 14), Tracy proposes the principle that Christians are "released from the world for the world . . . *as it really is* (AI:48, italics original), indicating an even more positive attitude.

The conclusion, then, is that "existentially, the theologian accords loyalty and trust in both church and world, [yet] only God is an ultimate object of loyalty and trust." To live with the ambiguous reality of both and, I would add, the unrelieved tension between them, is "incumbent upon every Christian" (AI:51).

VI

It was stated earlier that the basic problematic for the Tracian model is determined by the crisis of meaning of Christianity in the modern and post-modern world.[33] The crisis concerns particularly the criteria of meaning and truth brought about by the historical and hermeneutical consciousness (TAG:2), which has been primarily developed and nurtured in the academic disciplines in the modern university setting.

---

[30] E.g., by Kiyoko Takeda Cho, which were introduced in an article by Rev. C. S. Lee in *Ching Feng* (Chinese ed.) 46 (1975). See also Yoshinobu Kumazawa, "Where Theology Seeks to Integrate Text and Context" (Anderson: 1976, 179–208) for a historical review of the development of Protestant theology in Japan, with comments on the issues of indigenization, and reference to Prof. Cho's works among others.

[32] Particularly that of Freud, Marx, and Nietzsche. See the contrasting notes in AI:137 n. 16; 190 n. 71; 220 n. 17; and the fuller discussion of these figures in AI:346–50.

[33] Though Tracy would insist that the crisis is of the "Enlightenment model of modernity" as well for the post-modern secular mind (TAG:2; BRO:10–14).

For theology to be a discipline today, therefore, it must meet "the highest standards of the contemporary academy" (*AI*:21). This is a responsibility most contemporary theologians recognize. It is required by the nature of theology as *public* discourse (*AI*:20–21). The academic public is thus the first of the three publics to which theology must address itself.[34] The concern for public criteria of meaning and truth is determinative for all theological reconstruction.[35]

It was suggested before that in the Tracian model, fundamental theology is concerned with the interpretation of the fundamental questions of human existence or the religious dimension of the contemporary situation while systematic theology is concerned with the interpretation of a particular religious tradition as expressed in its classics. The situation is not that simple, however, since in theological discourse as a whole *both* interpretations are "constants" in continuously mutually critical correlation. The subject matter of theology must therefore be the same although the orders of discourse upon it should be distinguished.

In Tracy's own effort, for example, fundamental theology (as presented in *BRO*) deals logically with the questions of religion, God, and Christ, providing in that order a religious interpretation of human experience, a theistic interpretation of religion, and a Christian or Christocentric interpretation of theism (*BRO*:237; 250 n.3; cf. *FPT*:66). Systematic theology (as presented in *AI*), on the other hand, reverses the order. It starts with the Christ event and proceeds to interpret in the light of that event God and the human, church and world, and so on (*AI*:241–242 n.1), ending in fact with the interpretation of the contemporary situation, coming thus to a full circle.[36] Both fundamental and systematic theologies are thus integral parts of the same system and cannot in practice be separated, although for purposes of analysis they can be distinguished.

The distinction between them has to do rather with the approach to the subject matter. Fundamental theology interprets both "constants" in philosophical terms while systematic theology does so in terms of a hermeneutics, developed in contemporary literary criticism and aesthetic theory, in contrast to the use of a transcendental metaphysics and a phenomenological analysis for fundamental or

[34] The three publics are arranged, as noted before, in sociological order of society, academy, and church in *AI*, ch. 1. In ch. 2 it is logically academy, church, and society. In Asia, the order of importance is likely to be church, society and academy.

[35] In the university, religious studies "may but need not render the question of the truth of religion explicit," concerned as they are with meaning primarily. Theology, however, is concerned with both meaning and truth (*AI*:29).

[36] In chs. 8 and 9. Pt. I of *AI*, Tracy points out in a very important note, is "in fact an exercise in fundamental theology" (*AI*:85 n. 31).

philosophical theology. As such, systematic theology is specifically directed to the classics of the religious tradition. This application of contemporary hermeneutical method is perhaps the most creative part of Tracy's work.

Systematic theology, explains Tracy, is "fundamentally a hermeneutical enterprise, the issue of both the meaning and truth of religion is related to the analogical issue of the meaning and truth of art. The central claim advanced is a claim to both meaning and truth in our common experience of any classic" (*AI*:x, Preface). Indeed, Tracy goes so far to say, "the systematic theologian is nothing more or less than an interpreter of the religious classics of a culture" (*AI*:155). This, of course, makes sense in the context of Western culture in which the religious classics of Christianity are its cultural classics (cf. *AI*:68), given the predominant position of the Christian religion. Presumably not every cultural classic is a religious (Christian) classic (e.g., the Homerian epics)[37] for the systematic theologian, if it is not part of the Christian religious tradition. If so, for a Christian theologian in China, the Confucian, Taoist, and Buddhist classics would similarly be excluded, no matter how classical they have become in that culture. But I am not sure of Tracy's position here.

Fundamental Theology, on the other hand, according to Tracy, has the primary task of determining "criteria for theological argument" which will also be applicable in systematic theology (*BRO*:250 n.1).[38] It uses "the approach and methods of some established academic discipline to explicate and adjudicate the truth claims of the interpreted religious tradition and the contemporary situation" (*TAG*:8). Fundamental theology is "fully public" in that "any attentive, intelligent, reasonable, and responsible person can understand and judge [it] in keeping with truly public criteria for discourse" (*TAG*:9). In comparison, systematic theology is "less concerned with such obviously public modes of argument" (*AI*:57), since it is explicitly linked with a particular religious tradition (*BRO*:25 n.1). Still, the criteria of meaning and truth in the interpretation of the tradition, particularly its classics, are fully open to the public as the classics themselves are as a matter of fact in the "public realm of culture" (*AI*:68).

This makes sense, I think, in the academic and cultural context of the West and, as Tracy would say, especially in its contemporary post-modern situation. The great metaphysical and theological ideas are still part of the cultural tradition and continue to excite discussion

[37] In *TC*, other classics of Western culture besides the Bible are mentioned, including Homer.

[38] Tracy's statement is: "the criteria advanced in fundamental theology should find a place in dogmatics [or systematic theology] as well."

in parts of the academy at least. They only need to be retrieved and reinterpreted for the post-modern mind. This is so with the ideas or reality of "self, world, and God".[39] It is so, too, with the reality of Christ. Theology, whether fundamental or systematic, assumes this important fact, namely, the deeply embedded existence and basic meaningfulness of these classical ideas in the cultural and religious tradition and therefore their retrievability for theological reinterpretation today. Is this true with our Asian situation, where varieties of theistic, polytheistic, humanistic, naturalistic, and atheistic traditions in religion and philosophy abound?

In such a pluralistic context, one could argue for or explain the idea of God as the "one necessary existent" or the "sole strictly necessary reality" (AI:160–161), or interpret it as the necessary "referent" of the "religious dimension of our *common* human experience" (AI:183 n.25; italics original).[40] But one must do so on philosophical or metaphysical grounds. To do so *theologically,* I believe, one would have to presuppose some *common* faith commitment, which must be explicitly acknowledged for the argument to have any force. In other words, I would see what Tracy has proposed to do in fundamental theology as more properly belonging to the field of philosophy of religion than theology, however philosophical or fundamental that theology may be.

The idea or reality of Christ, on the other hand, is central to Christian theology, even more so than God in certain regards, as the works of Tracy amply demonstrate. Given the Christocentric character of both fundamental theology and systematic theology, one might distinguish the former from the latter, but one could not, it seems to me, abstract it completely "from all religious 'faith commitment' " (AI:57) without doing violence to its internal connections to the latter. If it is Christocentric in any sense, it has to be somehow related to a particular Christian tradition. It must confess itself to be a *Christian* theology, no matter how philosophical or fundamental it aspires to be, or how universally meaningful the reality of Christ might be by any metaphysical analysis of phenomenological interpretation.

---

[39] These are the "three basic realities" for metaphysical analysis in the West (*BRO*:154). In saying this Tracy may imply that non-Western metaphysics, e.g., Buddhism, might be different.

[40] In *AI* (183 n. 25) Tracy says he is open to conversation between theistic and non-theistic religions (presumably Buddhism in particular) on this understanding of the reality of God from a metaphysical analysis of the religious dimension of human experience. He cites the "largely, but not exclusively, Western" philosophical conversation anthologized in Charles Hartshorne and William Reese, eds., *Philosophers Speak of God* (Chicago: University of Chicago Press, 1953).

VII

In Asian universities, with few exceptions, theology is not a university subject.[41] It is still mostly done in church seminaries or denominational or interdenominational theological colleges. This, however, does not necessarily mean that theology in such a condition cannot aspire to the "highest academic standards", though doing it within or at least in relation to a university setting would help. One sometimes suspects that there is still a strong anti-intellectual attitude in the churches, especially those of a pietistic or evangelical tradition, which is always uneasy about the academic character of modern theological studies, pursued as they are under the influence of modern historical consciousness and critical methods. Modern Theology, like it or not, tends to have the disturbing effect of mediating the modern mind to the church.

Nevertheless, a theologian doing theology in Asia today must strive for academic standards or intellectual excellence among other things which are required, such as loyalty to his religious tradition. He does this not primarily because of the public or publics to which he is called to address but because of the inherent requirement of theology itself as a critical, reflective discipline. As such theological discourse is open to public participation and examination, to people's acceptance, modification, or rejection, whether that public is church, academy, or society. To make that kind of openness possible the theologian, as Tracy insists, must articulate or develop criteria of meaning and truth, but it may be just as important to make clear his faith commitment as well as his basic ideas, principles, and methods. And to do so in a consciously ecumenical vision, for example both Protestant and Catholic, both "ecumenical" and "evangelical", too, may at this point of Asian theological development be as important as to follow the best scholarly standards as defined by the contemporary academy.

At present Asian theologians are perhaps preoccupied with the more concrete and urgent issues of Christian life and practice than with the more abstract ones as discussed in Tracy's fundamental theology. Situational analysis seems more useful than metaphysical analysis or the fundamental questions of human existence common to all humanity.[42] It is more urgent particularly to explore and develop

---

[41] The Theology Division at The Chinese University of Hong Kong is one of those exceptions, which is significant in the present Chinese context.

[42] The two latest examples I know (in English) from our Chinese situation are Wang (1984) and Lee (1984). Both attempt to confront the Biblical text—Old Testament in both cases rather than New Testament, significantly enough—with our contemporary political situation.

theologies of mission, culture, and politics.[43] Such efforts, I suppose, would be suitably classified under practical theology on the Tracian model.

But there is less inclination with us to divide theology up into distinct, even if not separate, disciplines. For the purpose of theology is one. It is to serve the faithful in their faith and life, by achieving for them at least some measure of understanding of what and why it is to become Christian in the world, and by providing some measure of guidance as to how to do so properly and effectively, in ways not only relevant to its context—the world or contemporary situation—but also true to its source—the gospel of the presence of God in Jesus Christ. This is a comparatively modest task but to us sufficient for the day.

WORKS CONSULTED

Anderson, Gerald H., ed.
1976   *Asian Voices in Christian Theology*. Maryknoll: Orbis.

Chan, Alan
1984   "Mission Theology: A Hong Kong Chinese Understand-
                ing." (Paper read at Pan-Anglican Symposium
                1984.9.1–10 at Hartford, Conn., USA, to be published.)

Cobb, John B., Jr.
1982   *Beyond Dialogue: Toward a Mutual Transformation of
                Christianity and Buddhism*. Philadelphia: Fortress.

Elwood, Douglas J., ed.
1980   *Asia Christian Theology: Emerging Themes*. Philadel-
                phia: Westminister. (2nd edition of *What Asia Christians
                Are Thinking*, Manila: New Day, 1976).

England, John C., ed.
1981   *Living Theology in Asia*. London: SCM.
1984   "Sources for Asian Theology: A Working Paper." *East
                Asian Journal of Theology* 2:205–221.

[43] See Chan (1984) and Song (1984a) for two more recent examples. S. C. Song has been perhaps the most articulate Chinese theologian writing (in English) outside mainland China. See his works (1975; 1979; 1982; 1984a; and 1984b). I have also expressed, much more briefly, similar concerns with culture and politics in my works (1978; 1982; and 1983), the last article in not explicitly theological language, since it was originally addressed to a broader and not necessarily religious audience.

Lai, Whalen
        1984   "Religious Pluralism in China: The History and the
                       Dynamics." *Ching Feng* XXVII/1 (March 1984):1–18.

Lambino, Antonio B.
        1980   "A Critique of Some Asian Efforts at Contextualization
                       with Reference to Theological Method." *South East Asia
                       Journal of Theology* 21/2 (1980)–22/1 (1981):88–96.

Lee, Archie C. C.
        1984   "Doing Theology in Chinese Context: The David-
                       Bathsheba Story and the Parable of Nathan." (To be
                       published in *East Asian Journal of Theology*.)

Nacpil, Emerito & Douglas J. Elwood, eds.
        1978   *The Human & the Holy: Asian Perspectives in Christian
                       Theology*. Manila: New Day.

Shen, Philip
        1978   "Our Theological Tasks in Relation to our Theological
                       and Cultural Heritages." *Ching Feng* XXI/4
                       (1978)–XXII/1 (1979):183–196.
        1982   "Concerns with Politics and Culture in Contextual The-
                       ology: A Hong Kong Chinese Perspective." *Ching Feng*
                       XXV/3 (1982):129–138.
        1983   "Modernization and the Autocratic Tradition in China."
                       *Modernization and Traditional Values: New Challenges
                       in Asian Education* (50th Anniversary Lectures of the
                       United Board for Christian Higher Education in Asia).
                       New York: UBCHEA. (To be published with an added
                       Chinese bibliography in *Ching Feng*, 1984.)

Song, C. S.
        1975   *Christian Mission in Reconstruction: An Asian Attempt.*
                       Madras: Christian Literature Society.
        1979   *Third-Eye Theology.* Maryknoll: Orbis.
        1982   *The Compassionate God.* Maryknoll: Orbis.
        1984a   "The Kingdom of God & the People" (Chinese version).
                       Theological Division News (Chung Chi College, Chinese
                       University of Hong Kong), 25 (1984.11):1–7.
        1984b   *Tell Us Our Names: Story Theology from an Asian
                       Perspective.* Maryknoll: Orbis.

Tracy, David
        1975   *BRO: Blessed Rage for Order: The New Pluralism in
                       Theology.* New York: Seabury.
        1981   *AI: The Analogical Imagination: Christian Theology and
                       the Culture of Pluralism.* New York: Crossroad.

1983a   *TAG: Talking About God* (with John B. Cobb, Jr.). New York: Seabury.

1983b   *TC*: "On Thinking with the Classics." Criterion 22/3 (Autumn 1983):9–10.

1983c   *CT: Cosmology and Theology (Concilium* 166). Co-ed. Nicholas Lash. New York: Seabury. vii-vii, 87–92.

1984   *FPT*: "The Foundations of Practical Theology." *Practical Theology: The Emerging Field in Theology, Church, and World.* Ed. by Don S. Browning. New York: Harper and Row. 22–82.

Wang, Hsien-chih
1984   "Some Perspectives in Theological Education in the Light of Homeland Theology in the Taiwanese Context". *Educational Mission in the Mature Church.* Seoul: The Presbyterian Church of Korea Department of Education.

BLACK THEOLOGY IN AMERICAN RELIGION

JAMES H. CONE*

More than eighty years ago W. E. B. DuBois wrote in *The Souls of Black Folk* his classic statement of the paradox of black life in America.

> It is a peculiar sensation, this double-consciousness, this sense of always looking at one's self through the eyes of others, of measuring one's soul by the tape of a world that looks on in amused contempt and pity. One ever feels his twoness,—an American, a Negro; two souls, two thoughts, two unreconciled strivings; two warring ideals in one dark body, whose dogged strength alone keeps it from being torn asunder.[1]

The "two warring ideals" that DuBois described in 1903 have been at the center of black religious thought from its origin to the present day. They are found in the heated debates about "integration" and "nationalism" and in the attempt to name the community—beginning with the word "African" and using at different times such terms as "Colored," "Negro," "Afro-American," and "Black."

In considering black religious thought in this essay, let us give clearer names to the "two warring ideals"—clearer, that is, from the point of view of religion. I shall call them "African" and "Christian." Black religious thought is not identical with the Christian theology of white Americans. Nor is it identical with traditional African beliefs, past or present. It is both—but reinterpreted for and adapted to the life-situation of black people's struggle for justice in a nation whose social, political, and economic structures are dominated by a white racist ideology. It was the "African" side of black religion that helped African-Americans to see beyond the white distortions of the gospel and to discover its true meaning as God's liberation of the oppressed

*Charles A. Briggs Professor of Systematic Theology at Union Theological Seminary in New York, Dr. Cone presented this paper as a 75th Anniversary Lecture at the 1984 Annual Meeting of the American Academy of Religion.

[1] W. E. B. DuBois, *The Souls of Black Folk* (Greenwich, Conn.: Fawcett Premier Book, 1968), pp. 16–17. Originally published in 1903.

from bondage. It was the "Christian" element in black religion that helped African-Americans to reorient their African past so that it would become useful in the struggle to survive with dignity in a society that they did not make.

Although the African and Christian elements have been found throughout the history of black religious thought, the Christian part gradually became dominant. Though less visible, the African element continued to play an important role in defining the core of black religion, thus preventing it from becoming merely an imitation of Protestant or Catholic theologies in the West.

Of course, there are many similarities between black religious thought and white Protestant and Catholic reflections on the Christian tradition. But the *dissimilarities* between them are perhaps more important than the similarities. The similarities are found at the point of a common Christian identity, and the dissimilarities can best be understood in light of the differences between African and European cultures in the New World. While whites used their cultural perspective to dominate others, blacks used theirs to affirm their dignity and to empower themselves to struggle for justice. The major reason for the differences between black and white reflections on God is found at the point of the great differences in life. As white theology is largely defined by its response to modern and post-modern societies of Europe and America, usually ignoring the contradictions of slavery and oppression in black life, black religious thought is the thinking of slaves and of marginalized blacks whose understanding of God was shaped by the contradictions that white theologians ignored and regarded as unworthy of serious theological reflection. In this essay, I will analyze black religious thought in the light of DuBois' "warring ideals" that emerged out of the struggle for justice—beginning with its origin in slavery and concentrating mainly on its 20th century development in the civil rights and black power movements, culminating with the rise of black theology.

ROOTS OF BLACK RELIGIOUS THOUGHT: SLAVERY

The tension between the "African" and "Christian" elements acted to reorder traditional theological themes in black religion and to give them different substance when compared to other theologies in Europe and America. Five themes in particular defined the character of black religious thought during slavery and its subsequent development: justice, liberation, hope, love, and suffering.

No theme has been more prominent throughout the history of black religious thought than the justice of God. African-Americans have always believed in the living presence of the God who establishes the right by punishing the wicked and liberating their victims from oppression. Everyone will be rewarded and punished according to their deeds, and no one—absolutely no one—can escape the judgment of God, who alone is the sovereign of the universe. Evildoers may get by for a time, and good people may suffer unjustly under oppression, but "sooner or later, . . . we reap as we sow."[2]

The "sooner" referred to contemporary historically observable events: punishment of the oppressors and liberation of the oppressed. The "later" referred to the divine establishment of justice in the "next world" where God "gwineter rain down fire" on the wicked and where the liberated righteous will "walk in Jerusalem just like John." In the religion of African slaves, God's justice was identical with the punishment of the oppressors, and divine liberation was synonymous with the deliverance of the oppressed from the bondage of slavery— if not "now" then in the "not yet." Because whites continued to prosper materially as they increased their victimization of African-Americans, black religious thought spoke more often of the "later" than the "sooner."[3]

The themes of justice and liberation are closely related to the idea of hope. The God who establishes the right and puts down the wrong is the sole basis of the hope that the suffering of the victims will be eliminated. Although African slaves used the term heaven to describe their experience of hope, its primary meaning for them must not be reduced to the "pie-in-the-sky," otherworldly affirmation that often characterized white evangelical Protestantism. The idea of heaven was the means by which slaves affirmed their humanity in a world that

---

[2] A concise statement of the major themes in black religious thought, during and following slavery, is found in a 1902 sermon of an ex-slave and Princeton Theological Seminary graduate, Francis J. Grimke: "God is not dead,—nor is he an indifferent onlooker at what is going on in this world. One day He will make restitution for blood; He will call the oppressors to account. Justice may sleep, but it never dies. The individual, race, or nation which does wrong, which sets at defiance God's great law, especially God's great law of love, of brotherhood, will be sure, sooner or later, to pay the penalty. We reap as we sow. With that measure we mete, it shall be measured to us again." (See C. G. Woodson [ed.], *The Works of Francis J. Grimke, I* [1942], p. 354) Grimke's statement was undoubtedly influenced by the slave song, "You shall reap jes what you sow."

[3] For an interpretation of the slaves' idea of justice and liberation, see my *The Spirituals and the Blues* (New York: Seabury, 1972), especially chapter 3. See also Albert J. Raboteau, *Slave Religion* (New York: Oxford University Press, 1978); Vincent Harding, *There Is A River* (New York: Harcourt Brace Jovanovich, 1981); and Gayraud S. Wilmore, *Black Religion and Black Radicalism* (Maryknoll, NY: Orbis Books, rev. 1983).

did not recognize them as human beings.[4] It was their way of saying
that they were made for freedom and not slavery.

> Oh Freedom! Oh Freedom!
> Oh Freedom, I love thee!
> And before I'll be a slave,
> I'll be buried in my grave,
> And go home to my Lord and be free.

Black slaves' hope was based on their faith in God's promise to
"protect the needy" and to "defend the poor." Just as God delivered
the Hebrew Children from Egyptian bondage and raised Jesus from
the dead, so God will also deliver African slaves from American
slavery and "in due time" will bestow upon them the gift of eternal
life. That was why they sang:

> Soon-a-will be done with the trouble of the world;
> Soon-a-will be done with the trouble of the world;
> Going home to live with God.

Black slaves' faith in the coming justice of God was the chief reason
why they could hold themselves together in servitude and sometimes
fight back, even though the odds were against them.

The ideas of justice, liberation, and hope should be seen in
relation to the important theme of love. Theologically God's love is
prior to the other themes. But in order to separate black reflections on
love from a similar theme in white theology it is important to
emphasize that love in black religious thought is usually linked with
God's justice, liberation, and hope. God's love is made known through
divine righteousness, liberating the poor for a new future.

God's creation of all persons in the divine image bestows sacredness upon human beings and thus makes them the children of God. To
violate any person's dignity is to transgress "God's great law of love."[5]
We must love the neighbor because God has first loved us. And
because slavery and racism are blatant denials of the dignity of the
human person, God's justice means that "He will call the oppressors
to account."[6]

Despite the strength of black faith, belief in God's coming justice
and liberation was not easy for African slaves and their descendants.
Their suffering created the most serious challenge to their faith. If
God is good, why did God permit millions of blacks to be stolen from

---

[4] For a fuller discussion of the idea of heaven in slave religion, see my *The Spirituals
and the Blues*, chapter 5. See also John Lovell, Jr., *Black Song* (New York: Macmillan,
1972), especially pp. 310–312, 315–374.

[5] *Works of Grimke*, p. 354.

[6] *Ibid.*

Africa and enslaved in a strange land? No black person has been able to escape the existential agony of that question.

In their attempt to resolve the theological dilemma that slavery and racism created, African-Americans turned to two texts—the Exodus and Psalms 68:31.[7] They derived from the Exodus text the belief that God is the liberator of the oppressed. They interpreted Psalms 68:31 as an obscure reference to God's promise to redeem Africa: "Princes shall come out of Egypt, and Ethiopia shall soon stretch forth her hands unto God." Despite African-Americans reflections on these texts, the contradictions remained between oppression and their faith.

BLACK RELIGIOUS THOUGHT, THE CIVIL RIGHTS MOVEMENT, AND MARTIN LUTHER KING, JR.

The withdrawal of the black church from politics and its alliance with the accommodation philosophy of Booker T. Washington created the conditions that gave rise to the civil rights movement: the National Association for the Advancement of Colored People (NAACP) in 1909, the National Urban League (NUL) in 1911, and the Congress for Racial Equality (CORE) in 1942. These national organizations, and similar local and regional groups in many parts of the U.S., took up the cause of justice and equality of blacks in the society. They were strongly influenced by ideas and persons in the churches. Civil rights organizations not only internalized the ideas about justice, liberation, hope, love, and suffering that had been preached in the churches; they also used church property to convene their own meetings and usually made appeals for support at church conferences. The close relations between the NAACP and the black churches has led some to say that "the black church is the NAACP on its knees."

Due to the de-radicalization of the black church, progressive black ministers found it difficult to remain involved in the internal affairs of their denominations. Baptist ministers, because of the automony of their local congregations, found it easier than the Methodists did to remain pastors while also being deeply involved in struggle for black equality in the society. Prominent examples included Adam Clayton Powell, father and son pastors of Abyssinian Baptist Church in New York. Adam, Jr. made his entree on the public stage by leading a four-year nonviolent direct-action campaign, securing some ten thousand jobs for Harlem blacks. In 1944 he was elected to Congress.

Adam Clayton Powell, Jr., embraced that part of the black religious tradition that refused to separate the Christian gospel from the

[7] "For an interpretation of these texts, see Albert J. Raboteau, " 'Ethiopia Shall Soon Stretch Forth Her Hands': Black Destiny in Nineteenth-Century America," *The University Lecture in Religion at Arizona State University* (January 27, 1983).

struggle for justice in society. In his influential *Marching Blacks*, he accused the white churches of turning Christianity into "churchianity," thereby distorting the essential message of the gospel which is "equality" and "brotherhood."

> The great loving heart of God has been embalmed and laid coolly away in the tombs we call churches. Christ of the Manger, the carpenter's bench, and the borrowed tomb has once again been crucified in stained-glass windows.[8]

Other influential thinkers of this period included Howard Thurman and Benjamin E. Mays. Howard Thurman wrote twenty-two books and lectured at more than five hundred institutions. He also served as dean of Rankin Chapel and professor of theology at Howard University; the dean of Marsh Chapel and minister-at-large of Boston University; and as minister and co-founder of the interdenominational Fellowship Church of San Francisco. His writings and preaching influenced many, and *Life* magazine cited him as one of the twelve "Great Preachers" of this century. Unlike most black ministers concerned about racial justice, liberation, love, suffering, and hope, Thurman did not become a political activist; he took the "inward journey" (the title of one of his books), focussing on a "spiritual quest" for liberation beyond race and ethnic origin. He was able to develop this universalist perspective without ignoring the urgency of the political issues involved in the black struggle for justice.[9]

Benjamin E. Mays, ecumenist and long-time president of Morehouse College, also made an important contribution to black religious thought through his writings and addresses on the black church and racism in America. He chaired the National Conference on Religion and Race in 1963.[10] Mays was an example of a black religious thinker who found the black church too limiting as a context for confronting the great problems of justice, liberation, love, hope, and suffering. Like Thurman and Powell, Mays regarded racism as anti-Christian, an evil that must be eliminated from the churches and the society.

No thinker has made a greater impact upon black religious thought or even upon American society and religion as a whole than

---

[8] Adam C. Powell, Jr., *Marching Blacks* (New York: Dial Press, 1945; rev. 1973), p. 194.

[9] Some of Howard Thurman's most influential writings include *Deep River* (1945), *The Negro Spiritual Speaks of Life and Death* (1947), *Jesus and the Disinherited* (1949), and *The Search for Common Ground* (1971).

[10] For an account of that conference, see Mathew Ahmann (ed.), *Race: Challenge to Religion* (Chicago: Henry Regnery, 1963). Influential works by B. E. Mays include (with Joseph W. Nicholson) *The Negro's Church* (1933), *The Negro's God* (1938), *Seeking To Be Christian In Race Relations* (1957), and *Born To Rebel* (1971).

Martin Luther King, Jr. The fact that many white theologians can write about American religion and theology with no reference to him reveals both the persistence of racism in the academy and the tendency to limit theology narrowly to the academic discourse of seminary and university professors.

Much has been written about the influence of Martin King's graduate education upon his thinking and practice, especially the writings of George Davis, Henry David Thoreau, Mahatma Gandhi, Edgar S. Brightman, Harold DeWolf, G. W. Hegel, Walter Rauschenbusch, Paul Tillich, and Reinhold Niebuhr.[11] Of course, these religious and philosophical thinkers influenced him greatly, but it is a mistake to use them as the primary basis for an interpretation of his life and thought. Martin King was a product of the black church tradition; its faith determined the essence of his theology.[12] He used the intellectual tools of highly recognized thinkers to explain what he believed to the white public and also to express the universal character of the gospel. But he did not arrive at his convictions about God by reading white theologians. On the contrary, he derived his religious beliefs from his acceptance of black faith and his application of it to the civil rights struggle.

In moments of crisis, Martin King turned to the God of black faith. From the beginning of his role as the leader of the Montgomery bus boycott to his tragic death in Memphis, Martin King was a public embodiment of the central ideas of black religious thought. The heart of his beliefs revolved around the ideas of love, justice, liberation, hope, and redemptive suffering. The meaning of each is mutually dependent on the others. Though love may be appropriately placed at the center of his thought, he interpreted it in the light of justice for the poor, liberation for all, and the certain hope that God has not left this world in the hands of evil men.

Martin King often used the writings of Tillich, Niebuhr, and other white thinkers to express his own ideas about the interrelations of

[11] See especially Kenneth L. Smith and Ira G. Zepp, Jr., *Search For The Beloved Community: The Thinking of Martin Luther King, Jr.* (Valley Forge: Judson, 1974); John J. Ansbro, *Martin Luther King, Jr.: The Making of a Mind* (Maryknoll, NY: Orbis, 1982.)

[12] The importance of the black religious tradition for King's theology has not received the attention that it deserves of scholars. See my "Martin Luther King, Jr., Black Theology—Back Church," *Theology Today*, January 1984. See also the important essay of Lewis V. Baldwin, "Martin Luther King, Jr., The Black Church, and the Black Messianic Vision," *Journal of the Interdenominational Theological Center* (forthcoming). David Garrow's definitive biography on Martin King is soon to be published under the title of *Bearing the Cross: Martin Luther King, Jr., and the Southern Christian Leadership Conference, 1955–1958*. It will show the important role of the black church tradition in his life and thought.

love and justice. But it was his internalization of their meaning in the black church tradition that helped him to see that "unmerited suffering is redemptive." While the fighters for justice must be prepared to suffer in the struggle for liberation; they must never inflict suffering on others. That was why King described nonviolence as "the Christian way in human relations" and "the only road to freedom."[13]

To understand Martin King's thinking, it is necessary to understand him in the context of his own religious heritage. His self-description is revealing:

> I am many things to many people; Civil Rights leader, agitator, trouble-maker and orator, but in the quietness of my heart, I am fundamentally a clergyman, a Baptist preacher. This is my being and my heritage for I am also the son of a Baptist preacher, the grandson of a Baptist preacher and the great-grandson of a Baptist preacher. The Church is my life and I have given my life to the church.[14]

The decisive impact of the black church heritage upon King can be seen in his ideas about justice, liberation, love, hope, and suffering. Martin King took the democratic tradition of freedom and combined it with the biblical tradition of justice and liberation as found in the Exodus and the prophets. Then he integrated both traditions with the New Testament idea of love and suffering as disclosed in Jesus' cross, and from all three, King developed a theology that was effective in challenging all Americans to create the beloved community in which all persons are equal. While it was the Gandhian method of nonviolence that provided the strategy for achieving justice it was, as King said, "through the influence of the Negro church" that "the way of nonviolence became an integral part of our struggle."[15]

As a Christian whose faith was derived from the cross of Jesus, Martin King believed that there could be no true liberation without suffering. Through nonviolent suffering, he contended, blacks would not only liberate themselves from the necessity of bitterness and feeling of inferiority toward whites, but would also prick the conscience of whites and liberate them from a feeling of superiority. The mutual liberation of blacks and whites lays the foundation for both to work together toward the creation of an entirely new world.

In accordance with this theological vision, he initially rejected black power because of its connotations of hate, and he believed that

[13] See Martin Luther King, Jr., "Non-Violence: The Christian Way in Human Relations," *Presbyterian Life*, February 1958; "Nonviolence: The Only Road to Freedom," *Ebony*, October 1966.

[14] King, "The Un-Christian Christian," *Ebony*, August 1965, p. 77

[15] See his "Letter From Birmingham Jail," in his *Why We Can't Wait* (New York: Harper, 1963), pp. 90–91.

no beloved community of blacks and whites could be created out of bitterness. King said that he would continue to preach nonviolence even if he became its only advocate. It is significant that King softened his attitude toward black power, shortly before his assassination, and viewed its positive elements as a much needed philosophy in order to eradicate self-hate in the black community, especially as revealed in the riots in the cities. He began to speak of a need to "teach about black culture" (especially black philosophers, poets, and musicians) and even of "temporary separation",[16] because he realized that without self-respect and dignity, black people could not participate with others in creating the beloved community.

A similar but even more radical position was taken in regard to the war in Vietnam. Because the Civil Rights Act (1964) and the Voting Rights Bill (1965) did not affect significantly the life-chances of the poor, and because of the failure of President Johnson's War on Poverty, King became convinced that his dream of 1963 had been turned into a nightmare.[17] Gradually he began to see the connections

[16] The best sources for King's affirmative emphasis on black power and pride are his unpublished speeches on the "Pre-Washington Campaign," recruiting persons for the Poor People's March to Washington. See especially his addresses at Clarksdale, Miss. (March 19, 1968), p. 7; Eutaw, Ala. (March 20, 1968), p. 3; Albany, Ga. (March 22, 1968), p. 5f. In Albany, he said: "We are somebody. We're going to teach our young people something about their heritage. We're going to let them know that Plato and Aristotle were not the only philosophers that came through history, but W. E. B. DuBois, a black man was a political philosopher" (6). Most of King's unpublished papers, addresses, and sermons are found at the Martin Luther King, Jr., Center for Nonviolent Social Change, Atlanta, Georgia.
    In an interview article, King affirmed the need for "temporary segregation": "I must honestly say that . . . there are points at which I see the necessity for temporary segregation in order to get to the integrated society. . . . Often . . . the Negro is integrated without power. . . . We want to be integrated with power. . . . And this is why I think it is absolutely necessary to see integration in political terms, to see that there are some situations where separation may serve as a temporary way-station to the ultimate goal which we seek. . . ." "Conversation with Martin Luther King," *Conservative Judaism*, vol. xxii, no. 3, Spring 1968, pp. 8, 9.
[17] On many occasions, Martin King talked about his dream of 1963 being turned into a nightmare. The most informative reference in this regard is his "Christmas Sermon on Peace," delivered in Ebenezer Baptist Church at Atlanta, December 24, 1967. In that sermon, he said: "In 1963 . . . in Washington, D.C., . . . I tried to talk to the nation about a dream that I had had, and I must confess . . . that not long after talking about that dream I started seeing it turn into a nightmare. I remember the first time I saw that dream turn into a nightmare, just a few weeks after I had talked about it. It was when four beautiful . . . Negro girls were murdered in a church in Birmingham, Alabama. I watched that dream turn into a nightmare as I moved through the ghettos of the nation and saw my black brothers and sisters perishing on a lonely island of poverty in the midst of a vast ocean of material prosperity, and saw the nation doing nothing to grapple with the Negroes' problem of poverty. I saw that dream turn into a nightmare as I watched my black brothers and sisters in the midst of anger and understandable outrage

between the failure of the war on poverty and the expenditures for the war in Vietnam. In the tradition of the Old Testament prophets and against the advice of many of his closest associates in black and white communities, King stood before a capacity crowd at Riverside Church and condemned America as "the greatest purveyor of violence in the world today."[18] He proclaimed God's judgment against America and insisted that God would break the backbone of U.S. power if this nation did not bring justice to the poor and peace to the world. Vicious criticisms came from blacks and whites in government, civil rights groups, media, and the nation generally as he proclaimed God's righteous indignation against the three great evils of our time—war, racism, and poverty.

During the severe crises of 1966–68, King turned, not to the theologians and philosophers of his graduate education, but to his own religious heritage. It was the eschatological hope, derived from his slave grandparents and mediated through the black church, that sustained him in the midst of grief and disappointment. This hope also empowered him to "master [his] fears" of death and to "stand by the best in a evil time."[19] In an unpublished sermon, preached at Ebenezer Baptist Church, he said:

> I've decided what I'm going to do; I ain't going to kill nobody . . . in Mississippi . . . and . . . in Vietnam, and I ain't going to study war no more. And you know what? I don't care who doesn't like what I say about it. I don't care who criticizes me in an editorial; I don't care what white person or Negro criticizes me. I'm going to stick with the best. . . . Every now and then we sing about it: 'If you are right, God will fight your battle.' I'm going to stick by the best during these evil times.[20]

_____

... turn to misguided riots to try to solve that problem. I saw that dream turn into a nightmare as ı watched the war in Vietnam escalating, and as I saw so-called military advisers, 16,000 strong, turn into fighting soldiers until today over 500,000 American boys are fighting on Asian soil. Yes, I am personally the victim of deferred dreams, of blasted hopes . . . ." (See King, _The Trumpet of Conscience_ [New York: Harper, 1967], pp. 75–76) See also similar comments at an Operation Breadbasket Meeting, Chicago Theological Seminary (March 25, 1967) and also during his appearance on Arlene Francis Show (June 19, 1967). (King Center Archives)

[18] See Martin Luther King, Jr., "Beyond Vietnam," a pamphlet published by Clergy and Laity Concerned, 1982 reprint of his April 4, 1967 speech at Riverside Church in New York City, p. 2.

[19] The most reliable sources for Martin King's theology are the unpublished sermons at the King Center Archives. They include: "A Knock at Midnight," All Saints Community Church, Los Angeles, Ca. (June 25, 1967); "Standing By The Best In An Evil Time," Ebenezer Baptist Church, Atlanta, Ga. (Aug. 6, 1967); "Thou Fool," Mount Pisgah Baptist Church, Chicago, Ill. (Aug. 27, 1967); "Mastering Our Fears," Ebenezer (Sept. 10, 1967).

[20] "Standing By The Best In An Evil Time," p. 7.

It was not easy for King to "stand by the best," because he often stood alone. But he firmly believed that the God of black faith had said to him: "Martin Luther, stand up for righteousness. Stand up for justice. Stand up for truth. And lo, I will be with you, even until the end of the world."[21]

Martin King combined the exodus-liberation and cross-love themes with the message of hope found in the resurrection of Jesus. Hope for him was not derived from the optimism of liberal Protestant theology but rather was based on his belief in the righteousness of God as defined by his reading of the Bible through the eyes of his slave foreparents. The result was the most powerful expression in black history of the essential themes of black religious thought from the integrationist viewpoint.

> Centuries ago Jeremiah raised a question, 'Is there no balm in Gilead? Is there no physician?' He raised it because he saw the good people suffering so often and the evil people prospering. Centuries later our slave foreparents came along and they too saw the injustices of life and had nothing to look forward to, morning after morning, but the rawhide whip of the overseer, long rows of cotton and the sizzling heat; but they did an amazing thing. They looked back across the centuries, and they took Jeremiah's question mark and straightened it into an exclamation point. And they could sing, 'There is a balm in Gilead to make the wounded whole. There is a balm in Gilead to heal the sinsick soul.'[22]

---

[21] "Thou Fool," p. 14. This quotation is taken from King's account of his "conversion experience," that is, his existential appropriation of the faith he was taught during his childhood. There is no doubt that the "kitchen experience," as it might be called, was the turning point in King's theological development. During the early stages of the Montogomery bus boycott, the constant threats of death to him and his family (about 40 telephone calls per day) eventually caused him to admit that he was "weak, . . . faltering, [and] . . . losing [his] courage." In that crisis moment when the fear of death engulfed him, he said: "I pulled back on the theology and philosophy that I had just studied in the universities, trying to give philosophical and theological reasons for the existence and reality of sin and evil, but the answer didn't quite come there" (p. 13). The answer came in his dependence on the God of black faith. "Don't be a fool," he said in his climactic conclusion to this sermon. "Recognize your dependence on God. As the days become dark, and the nights become dreary, realize that there is a God, who rules above. And so I'm not worried about tomorrow. I get weary every now and then, the future looks difficult and dim, but I'm not worried ultimately because I have faith in God" (p. 14).

[22] This is an often used conclusion of many of King's sermons. This quotation is taken from "Thou Fool."

BLACK RELIGIOUS THOUGHT, BLACK POWER, AND BLACK THEOLOGY

From the time of its origin in slavery to the present, black religious thought has been faced with the question of whether to advocate integration into American society or separation from it. The majority of the participants in the black churches and the civil rights movement have promoted integration, and they have interpreted justice, liberation, love, suffering, and hope in light of the goal of creating a society in which blacks and whites can live together in a "beloved community."

While integrationists have emphasized the American side of the double consciousness of African-Americans, there have also been nationalists who rejected any association with the U.S. and instead have turned toward Africa. Nationalists contend that blacks will never be accepted as equals in a white racist church and society. Black freedom can be achieved only by black people separating themselves from whites—either by returning to Africa or by forcing the government to set aside a separate state in the U.S. so blacks can build their own society.[23]

The nationalist perspective on the black struggle for freedom is deeply embedded in the history of black religious thought. Some of its prominent advocates include: Bishop Henry McNeal Turner of the A.M.E. Church; Marcus Garvey, the founder of the Universal Negro Improvement Association; and Malcolm X of the religion of Islam. Black nationalism is centered on blackness, a repudiation of any value in white culture and religion. Nationalists reversed the values of the dominant society by attributing to black history and culture what whites had said about theirs. For example, Bishop Turner claimed that "We have as much right biblically and otherwise to believe that God is a Negro, . . . as you . . . , white people have to believe that God is a fine looking, symmetrical and ornamented white man."[24] Marcus Garvey held a similar view:

> If the white man has the idea of a white God, let him worship his God as he desires. . . . We Negroes believe in the God of Ethiopia, the everlasting God—God the Father, God the Son and God the Holy Ghost, the One God of all ages.[25]

[23] For an excellent introduction to black nationalism, see Alphonso Pinkney, *Red, Black, and Green: Black Nationalism in the United States* (Cambridge: Cambridge University Press, 1976). See also John H. Bracey, Jr., August Meier, and Elliott Rudwick (eds.), *Black Nationalism in America* (Indianapolis: Bobbs-Merrill, 1970).

[24] Edwin S. Redkey (ed.), *Respect Black: The Writings and Speeches of Henry McNeal Turner* (New York: Arno Press, 1971), p. 176.

[25] Amy Jacques-Garvey (ed.), *Philosophy and Opinions of Marcus Garvey*, Two Volumes in One (New York: Arno Press, 1968), p. 44.

The most persuasive interpreter of black nationalism during the 1960s was Malcolm X who proclaimed a challenging critique of Martin King's philosophy of integration, nonviolence, and love. Malcolm X advocated black unity instead of the "beloved community," self-defense in lieu of nonviolence, and self-love in place of turning the other cheek to whites.[26]

Like Turner and Garvey, Malcolm X asserted that God is black; but unlike them he rejected Christianity as the white man's religion. He became a convert initially to Elijah Muhammad's Nation of Islam and later to the world-wide Islamic community. His critique of Christianity and of American society as white was so persuasive that many blacks followed him into the religion of Islam, and others accepted his criticisms even though they did not become Muslims. Malcolm pushed civil rights activists to the left and caused many black Christians to reevaluate their interpretation of Christianity.

> Brothers and sisters, the white man has brainwashed us black people to fasten our gaze upon a blond-haired, blue-eyed Jesus! We're worshiping a Jesus that doesn't even *look* like us! Now, just think of this. The blond-haired, blue-eyed white man has taught you and me to worship a *white* Jesus, and to shout and sing and pray to this God that's *his* God, the white man's God. The white man has taught us to shout and sing and pray until we *die*, to wait until *death*, for some dreamy heaven-in-the-hereafter, when we're *dead*, while this white man has his milk and honey in the streets paved with golden dollars right here on *this* earth![27]

During the first-half of the 1960s, Martin King's interpretation of justice as equality with whites, liberation as integration, and love as nonviolence dominated the thinking of the black religious community. However after the riot in Watts (Los Angeles), August 1965, some black clergy began to take another look at Malcolm's philosophy, especially in regard to his criticisms of Christianity and American society. Malcolm X's contention that America was a nightmare and not a dream began to ring true to many black clergy as they watched their communities go up in flames as young blacks shouted in jubilation, "burn, baby, burn."

It was during the James Meredith "march against fear" in Mississippi (June 1966, after Malcolm's assassination, February 1965) that some black clergy began to question openly Martin King's philosophy of love, integration, and nonviolence. When Stokely Carmichael proclaimed "black power," it sounded like the voice of Malcolm X.

---

[26] The best introduction to Malcolm X's philosophy is still *The Autobiography of Malcolm X*, with the assistance of Alex Haley (New York: Grove Press, 1965).

[27] *Ibid.*, p. 222.

Though committed to the Christian gospel, black clergy found themselves moving slowly from integration to separation, from Martin King to Malcolm X.

The rise of black power created a decisive turning point in black religious thought. Black power forced black clergy to raise the theological question about the relation between black faith and white religion. Although blacks have always recognized the ethical heresy of white Christians, they have not always extended it to Euro-American theology. With its accent on the cultural heritage of Africa and political liberation "by any means necessary," black power shook black clergy out of their theological complacency.

Separating themselves from Martin King's absolute commitment to nonviolence, a small group of black clergy, mostly from the North, addressed the black power movement positively and critically. Like King and unlike black power advocates, black clergy were determined to remain within the Christian community. This was their dilemma: How could they reconcile Christianity and black power, Martin King and Malcolm X?

Under the influence of Malcolm X and the political philosophy of black power, many black theologians began to advocate the necessity for the development of a black theology, and they rejected the dominant theologies of Europe and North America as heretical. For the first time in the history of black religious thought, black clergy and theologians began to recognize the need for a completely new starting point in theology, and they insisted that it must be defined by people at the bottom and not the top of the socio-economic ladder. To accomplish this task, black theologians focussed on God's liberation of the poor as the central message of the gospel.[28]

To explicate the theological significance of the liberation motif, black theologians began to re-read the Bible through the eyes of their slave grandparents and started to speak of God's solidarity with the wretched of the earth. As the political liberation of the poor emerged as the dominant motif, justice, suffering, love, and hope were re-interpreted in its light. For the biblical meaning of liberation, black

---

[28] For an account of the origin of black theology, see my *For My People: Black Theology and the Black Church* (Maryknoll, NY: Orbis, 1984). See also Gayraud S. Wilmore and James H. Cone (eds.), *Black Theology: A Documentary History, 1966–1979* (Maryknoll, NY: Orbis, 1979). The best narrative history of black theology by one of its creators is Gayraud S. Wilmore, *Black Religion and Black Radicalism* (Maryknoll, NY: Orbis, rev. 1983). My *Black Theology and Black Power* (New York: Seabury, 1969) and *A Black Theology of Liberation* (Philadelphia: Lippincott, 1970) were the earliest published books on black theology. They were followed by J. Deotis Roberts, *Liberation and Reconciliation: A Black Theology* (Philadelphia: Westminster, 1971) and Major Jones, *Black Awareness: A Theology of Hope* (Nashville: Abingdon, 1971).

theologians turned to the *Exodus,* while the message of the *prophets* provided the theological content for the theme of justice. The *gospel story* of the life, death, and resurrection of Jesus served as the biblical foundation for a re-interpretation of love, suffering, and hope in the context of the black struggle for liberation and justice.

As black theologians have re-read the Bible in the light of the struggles of the oppressed, the idea of the "suffering God" has become important in our theological perspective. Our theological imagination has been stirred by Jurgen Moltmann's writing about the "Crucified God" as well as Luther's distinction between the "theology of glory" and the "theology of the Cross." *But* it has been the *actual suffering* of the oppressed in black and other Third World communities that has been *decisive* in our reflections on the cross of Jesus Christ. As Gustavo Gutierrez has said: "We cannot speak of the death of Jesus until we speak of the real death of people." For in the deaths of the poor of the world is found the suffering and even the death of God. The political implications of Luther's insight on this point seemed to have been greatly distorted with his unfortunate emphasis on the two kingdoms. Many modern-day Lutheran scholars are even worse, because they turn the cross of Jesus into a theological idea completely unrelated to the concrete historical struggles of the oppressed for freedom. For most Lutheran scholars, the theology of the cross is a theological concept to be contrasted with philosophical and metaphysical speculations. It is a way of making a distinction between faith and reason, justification by faith through grace and justification by the works of reason.

But when the poor of the North American and the Third World read the passion story of the cross, they do not view it as a theological idea but as God's suffering solidarity with the victims of the world. Jesus' cross is God's election of the poor by taking their pain and suffering upon the divine person. Black slaves expressed this theological point in such songs as "he never said a mumblin' word" and "were you there when they crucified by Lord."

> They nail my Jesus down,
> They put him on the crown of thorns,
> O see my Jesus hangin' high!
> He look so pale an' bleed so free:
> O don't you think it was a shame,
> He hung three hours in dreadful pain?

Modern-day black theologians make a similar point when they say that "God is black" and that "Jesus is the Oppressed One." Our rejection of European metaphysical speculations and our acceptance of an apparently crude anthropomorphic way of speaking of God are black theologians' way of concretizing Paul's saying that "God chose what is foolish in the world to shame the wise, God chose what is weak in the world to shame the strong, God chose what is low and despised in the world, even the things that are not, to bring to nothing the things that are" (I Cor. 1:27–28 RSV).

Another characteristic of black theology is its de-emphasis, though not complete rejection, of the western theological tradition and its affirmation of black history and culture. If the suffering of God is revealed in the suffering of the oppressed, then it follows that theology cannot achieve its Christian identity apart from a systematic and critical reflection upon the history and culture of the victims of oppression. When this theological insight impressed itself upon our consciousness, we black theologians began to realize that we have been miseducated. In fact, European and North American theologians have stifled the indigenous development of the theological perspectives of blacks by teaching us that our own cultural traditions are not appropriate sources for an interpretation of the Christian gospel. Europeans and white North Americans taught us that the western theological tradition as defined by Augustine, Aquinas, Luther, Calvin, and Schleiermacher is the essential source for a knowledge of the Christian past. But when black theologians began to concentrate on black culture and history, we realized that our own historical and cultural traditions are far more important for an analysis of the gospel in the struggle of freedom than are the western traditions which participated in our enslavement. We now know that the people responsible for or indifferent to the oppression of blacks are not likely to provide the theological resources for our liberation. If oppressed peoples are to be liberated, they must themselves create the means for it to happen.

The focus on black culture in the light of the black liberation struggle has led to an emphasis upon *praxis* as the context out of which Christian theology develops. To know the truth is to do the truth, that is, to make happen in history what is confessed in church. People are not poor by divine decree or by historical accident. They are *made* poor by the rich and powerful few. This means that to do black liberation theology, one must make a commitment, an option *for* the poor and *against* those who are responsible for their poverty.

Because black theology is to be created only in the struggles of the poor, we have adopted *social analysis*, especially of racism, and more recently of classism and sexism, as a critical component of its methodology. How can we participate in the liberation of the poor from poverty if we do not know *who* the poor are and *why* they live in poverty? Social analysis is a tool that helps us to know why the social, economic and political orders are arranged as they are. It enables us to know not only who benefits from the present status quo, but what must be done to change it.

In our struggle to make a new start in theology, we discovered, to our surprise and much satisfaction, that theologians in Asia, Africa, and Latin America were making similar efforts in their contexts.[29] The same was true among other ethnic minorities in the First World and among women in all groups.[30] Black theology has been challenged to address the issues of sexism[31] and classism in a global context, and we have challenged them, especially Latin Americans and feminist theologians of the dominant culture, to address racism. The focus on liberation has been reinforced and deepened. What many of us now know is that a turning point has been made in the theologies of black and Third World communities as radical as were Luther, Schleiermarcher, and Barth in the 16th, 19th, and 20th centuries in Europe. Let us hope that the revolution in liberation theology will change not only how we think about God, but more importantly what we do in this world so that the victims might make a future that is defined by freedom and justice and not slavery and oppression.

[29] For an account of black theologians dialogue with theologians in Africa, Asia, and Latin America, see *Black Theology: A Documentary History*, pp. 445–608; *For My People*, pp. 140–156. See also my essays in the volumes that have been published from the conferences of the Ecumenical Association of Third World Theologians: "A Black American Perspective on the Future of African Theology" in Sergio Torres and Kofi Appiah-Kubi (eds.), *African Theology en Route* (Maryknoll, NY: Orbis, 1979); "A Black American Perspective on the Search for Full Humanity" in Virginia Fabella (ed.), *Asia's Struggle for Full Humanity* (Maryknoll, NY: Orbis, 1980); "From Geneva to Sao Paulo: A Dialogue Between Black Theology and Latin American Liberation Theology" in Sergio Torres and John Eagleson (eds.), *The Challenge of Basic Christian Communities* (Maryknoll, NY: Orbis, 1981); "Reflections from the Perspective of U.S. Blacks," in Virginia Fabell and Sergio Torres (eds.) *Irruption of the Third World: Challenge to Theology* (Maryknoll, NY: Orbis, 1983); "Black Theology: Its Origin, Method, and Relation to Third World Theologies" in Sergio Torres and Virginia Fabella (eds.), *Doing Theology in a Divided World* (Maryknoll, NY: Orbis, 1985).

[30] The dialogue between black theology and other ethnic theologies in the U.S. has taken place in the context of the Theology in the Americas. For an interpretation of this dialogue, see *For My People*, chapter vii; see also Sergio Torres and John Eagleson (eds.), *Theology in the Americas* (Maryknoll, NY: Orbis, 1976) and Cornel West, Caridad Guidote, and Margaret Coakley (eds.), *Theology in the Americas: Detroit II Conference Papers* (Maryknoll, NY: Orbis-Probe, 1982).

[31] See especially *Black Theology: A Documentary History*, pp. 363–442; J. Cone, *My Soul Looks Back* (Nashville: Abingdon, 1982); *For My People*, chapter vi.

CATHOLICISM AND MODERNITY

GABRIEL DALY*

Reinhold Niebuhr records in his notebook for 1927 the experience of being present as a young minister at an open forum which met in a high school in Detroit. One man asked him when he thought the Lord would come again; another tried to get him to agree that all religion is fantasy. Reflecting on these two widely divergent positions, Niebuhr wrote: "How can an age which is so devoid of poetic imagination as ours be truly religious?"[1] A year earlier, Paul Claudel, reflecting on the situation in eighteenth and nineteenth century Catholicism, had written: "The crisis . . . was not primarily an intellectual crisis . . . I would prefer to say it was the tragedy of a starved imagination".[2] In these two reflections we have an indication of a frequently neglected area of encounter between Christianity and modernity, namely, the imagination.

Facing modernity, as Catholics have had to do during the last quarter century, has meant severe institutional, intellectual, and spiritual stresses and strains. In the course of this paper I shall be considering some of these stresses and strains; but I hope that I can manage to convey, however indirectly and impressionistically, my conviction that the remedy lies at least as much in the realm of imagination as in the realms of institution, doctrine, or moral practice.

I shall begin with some reflections on the institutional background, not because I think that the institution holds the key to the rest, or because I attach importance to ecclesiastical power-play, but because, as a matter of historical fact, *aggiornamento* in the Catholic Church originated at an institutional level and only later developed an impetus of its own. The Second Vatican Council, convoked by John

*An Augustinian Priest and Lecturer at Trinity College in Dublin, Dr. Daly presented this paper as a 75th Anniversary Lecture at the 1984 Annual Meeting of the American Academy of Religion.

[1] Reinhold Niebuhr, *Leaves from the Notebooks of a Tamed Cynic* (New York, 1957), pp. 166–7.

[2] P. Claudel, *Positions et Propositions* (Paris, 1926), I, p. 175; cited in A. Dru and I. Trethowan, *Maurice Blondel: The Letter on Apologetics and History and Dogma* (London, 1964), p. 21.

XXIII, was given the specific task of bringing the Church up to date. Any idea that it was going to be a brief and purely cosmetic exercise was quickly dispelled when the Roman Curia lost effective control of events during the first session in 1962. With hindsight we can now see that those events presaged a massive surgical operation carried out without anaesthesia on a patient who thought he was in the best of health.

THREE ATTEMPTS AT AGGIORNAMENTO

On the eve of Vatican II very few Roman Catholics would have attached importance to, much less felt threatened by, the claims of modernity. In 1950 Pope Pius XII, having been made aware of certain theological stirrings in France, responded with an encyclical letter, *Humani Generis,* in which he remarked sternly that

> ... it is apparent that some [Catholic teachers] today, as in apostolic times, desirous of novelty, and fearing to be considered ignorant of recent scientific findings, tend to withdraw from the sacred Teaching Authority and are accordingly in danger of gradually departing from revealed truth and of drawing others along with them into error.[3]

The encyclical was accompanied by the visitation of one or two French theological institutes and the prescription of a change of air for one or two distinguished theologians.

The *Nouvelle théologie* of the 1940s was the last of three attempts made in the century preceding Vatican II to persuade the Catholic Church to come to terms with the post-Enlightenment world. The first had occurred in the 1860s, mainly in Germany. Its central event was a congress of Catholic intellectuals which met at Munich in 1863 under the presidency of the celebrated historian Ignaz von Döllinger who gave the keynote address in which he made a plea for academic freedom, especially from Roman interference, and proclaimed that scholasticism was dead and should now be replaced by critical theology.[4] Pius IX responded with a letter, *Tuas Libenter,* to the archbishop of Munich-Freising in which he condemned the ideal of freedom as put forward by Döllinger. The Pope also laid it down that Catholic scientists were bound to keep revelation before them as a

[3] Pius XII, *Encyclical Letter, "Humani Generis", Concerning Some False Opinions Which Threaten to Undermine the Foundations of Catholic Doctrine* (Vatican, 1950), p. 5. The passage is omitted from Denzinger-Schömetzer, *Enchiridion* (Barcelona, 1967).

[4] For an informative and fully documented account of the Munich Congress see John P. Boyle, "The Ordinary Magisterium: History of the Concept", I, *The Heythrop Journal,* XX, no. 4 (1979), pp. 380–98; 2, *ibid.,* XXI, no. I (1980), pp. 14–29.

guiding star (a remark which shocked John Henry Newman).[5] He further enjoined that Catholic teachers and writers were bound not merely by the infallible judgement of the Church but also by the "ordinary magisterium ... dispersed throughout the world" and exercised by the Roman dicasteries. Pius made it very clear that the teachings of this magisterium were closely tied to the philosophy and theology of "the old school".[6]

This letter, commonly known as the Munich Brief, extinguished, or drove underground, all contemporary Catholic attempts to come to terms with the modern world. It was subsequently overshadowed by the notorious *Syllabus of Errors* which was issued in the following year and which contained the ringing condemnation of the proposition that "The Roman Pontiff can and should reconcile himself and reach agreement with 'progress', Liberalism and recent departures in civil society".[7] Five years later the First Vatican Council was summoned to copper-fasten the Catholic Church's radical opposition to modern thought.

In 1879 Pope Leo XIII imposed the philosophico-theological system of St. Thomas Aquinas upon the whole Church.[8] This was an unprecedented act, and its significance is often underrated. (Its centenary went virtually unnoticed five years ago.) Even the most despotic of popes in the past had accepted the convention of not interfering in matters of legitimate theological difference between the schools. Yet here was a pope with something of a liberal name, breaking with that convention by making the philosophical system of one school mandatory for the whole Church. Leo's act did a serious disservice not merely to his Church but also to a great medieval Christian thinker. I belong to a generation many of whom were Thomist by conscription rather than by conviction. I now find myself psychologically, as distinct from intellectually, incapable of profiting from the genius of Aquinas. I suspect that other Catholic theologians of my generation find themselves similarly affected. One does not return to chains even if the chains are golden.

I have referred to the challenge of the 1940s and to the challenge of the 1860s. Sandwiched between these two was the most significant challenge of the three—that of modernism, a movement which occurred between ca. 1890 and 1910. The term "modernist" was in fact first employed not by the modernists themselves but by the authorities who condemned them with particular ruthlessness. The condemnation of modernism in 1907 signalized a complete victory for Cath-

---

[5] W. Ward, *The Life of John Henry Newman* (London, 1912), I, p. 641.

[6] Denzinger-Schönmetzer, *Enchiridion*, nos. 2875–2880. See also Boyle, art. cit.

[7] Denzinger-Schönmetzer, no. 2980.

[8] Encyclical Letter, *Aeterni Patris, Acta Sanctae Sedis*, 12 (1879–80), pp. 97–115.

olic fundamentalism. Many of the anti-modernists were happy to describe themselves as *integralists*—a title which was extremely revealing of how they saw the Church and its ideology.[9] The integralists believed that Catholic orthodoxy is expressed in, and bound up with, a logically organized system of interconnected doctrines each of which goes to make up a divinely guaranteed whole. This view was stated with admirable clarity by Joseph Lemius, the man who drafted the major part of the papal document which condemned modernism root and branch in 1907. Lemius wrote,

> In a system of doctrines so rigorously connected and linked as is the system of Aristotle and the Angelic Doctor, no single point can be detached from the others, [since] the light of truth which illumines each individual part is the same as that which illumines the whole.[10]

Integralism was the form in which Catholic fundamentalism expressed itself. In many ways it was a self-sealing system which made a positive virtue of fending off the challenges of modernity. It worked all too efficiently and was, as we have seen, still in evidence during the pontificate of Pius XII.

The integralists at Vatican II knew what they were doing when they fought for the preservation of the system as system. Integralism, like other kinds of fundamentalism, is more a state of mind than a corpus of beliefs. It is a *way* of approaching those truths which are perceived to lie at the heart of one's religious faith.

There is one feature which was common to all three attempts to bring the Church face to face with modernity between 1860 and 1960: Each had tried to break the Scholastic hegemony over Catholic theology, and each had been defeated by a reimposition of that hegemony by Church authority.

THE WALLED VILLAGE

There were two serious defects in Leo XIII's strategy of imposing Thomism on the whole Church. The first is that intellectual movements cannot be authentically brought about by decree. The second is that faith has no business allying itself exclusively to any one culture, still less to a culture which was six hundred years old. What Leo did was to use the authority of his office, newly enhanced by the First Vatican Council, arbitrarily to create a medieval cultural enclave with the express purpose of keeping modernity at bay. As a method of ideological control Leo's design was strikingly successful. Neo-

[9] On integralism see G. Daly, *Transcendence and Immanence: A Study in Catholic Modernism and Integralism* (Oxford, 1980), p. 187.
[10] Daly, *op. cit.*, p. 184.

thomism rapidly became a criterion of Catholic orthodoxy and acted as a bastion against the encroachments of modernity. As one integralist put it in 1903, "To the cry . . . 'Back to Kant' let us answer defiantly with the cry of Leo XIII, repeated by Pius X, 'Back to Thomas' ".[11]

In the period between the two Vatican Councils the Catholic Church resembled a village encompassed by a high wall which separated the villagers from the surrounding jungle. An effective system of taboos and cautionary tales severely discouraged them from venturing beyond the wall which both protected and imprisoned them. This artificial village had been specifically designed to preserve the last remnants of a classical and medieval culture which, outside its walls in the surrounding terrain, had long since yielded to the advancing jungle of post-Enlightenment life and ideas.

The Second Vatican Council breached the wall at several points and thus ended the seclusion so carefully fostered by several generations of village rulers. For some of the villagers it was an immensely exhilarating experience; for others it was a deeply disturbing one. Questions from which the majority of Catholics, including theologians, had been sheltered by their education now poured in upon them. The main safeguard of pre-conciliar Catholicism was its seclusion. It had its peace, its certainties, its clarities, its regimentation and its carefully forged chain of command; but it had them often at the price of relevance, vitality, courage, and occasionally even of truth and justice. It met its problems not by discussion or open investigation but by decree. Many Catholics saw this as the distinguishing feature of their faith and Church, and they actually liked what they saw. Many still do. Most, however, have given the changes a welcome which ranges from the enthusiastic to the wary.

There seems to be a fairly unanimous sociological agreement on what tends to happen when a tightly-structured and deeply authoritarian body like the Roman Catholic Church opens itself to change and liberalization. Sociologists tell us that as liberal and humane scholars they of course approve of the reforms, but they then go on to ask with innocent solicitude if we realize that these reforms will be socially catastrophic and that the conservatives are quite right, according to their lights, to oppose them. The ultramontane integralists were probably unaware of the sound sociological sense of what they were doing when they controlled the instruments of power in the Catholic Church. Their integralism was based on theological conviction, though it is of course possible to interpret the theological arguments as rationalizations supporting an essentially political position. The

[11] A. Fumagalli, "Le insidie di una nuova scienza", in *La Scuola Cattolica*, 31 (1903), p. 400.

growth of papal power after Vatican I was phenomenal by any standards, and the Roman Curia missed no opportunity of fostering a theology to support it. Paradoxically, the pope himself, as John XXIII discovered, was to a considerable extent the prisoner of the fortifications erected in his name. The Roman Curia has, since the Conciliar movement of the 14th and 15th centuries, traditionally distrusted general councils. What made Vatican II different from previous councils was the phenomenon of a pope colluding with a council in its challenge to the power of his own bureaucracy. It was this fact which broke the integralist stranglehold over the Church, since no integralist can plausibly deny the doctrine that a pope in council takes precedence over a pope acting alone. I mention this point because it may be the key to any future implementation of the doctrine of collegiality, which, though theoretically accepted by Vatican II, has still to be put into effective practice.

Paul VI explicitly and sadly recognized that the papacy remains the foremost obstacle to Christian unity. Yet, on the evidence of Agreed Statements which have already appeared, many Lutheran and Anglican ecumenists are ready to accord it an important role in any future united Church, but only under extensively changed conditions of operation. This is not the occasion to go into the matter, but I do wish to comment briefly on one curious phenomenon. The papal office continues within Catholicism to exercise a powerful mystique which paralyses the will among Catholics to discuss the conditions of its reform. This taboo is rarely broken. It governed the proceedings of Vatican II. As is now widely recognized, a dialectical coincidence of opposites runs through many of the conciliar documents, leaving the interpreter to decide on his or her relational centre. We all have our own canon within the canon. This dialectic is particularly noticeable in the matter of pope and Church. Medieval and Renaissance Christians could speak with impunity and without embarrassment about reforming the papal office; but not even the exceptional élan of the 1960s was able to generate enough energy and will to break the strongest taboo in the Catholic Church.

In the period preceding Vatican II there were three main agencies of centralized government in the Church. The first was a conception of Catholic orthodoxy stemming from the Neo-scholastic system and exercising a hegemony over all branches of mainline theology. The second was the 1917 Code of Canon Law which was given executive expression by the Roman dicasteries. The third was administration, with particular reference to the appointment of bishops and other Church officers. Vatican II broke the hegemony of scholasticism over theology. The new Code of Canon Law is, as an instrument of control, but a pale shadow of its predecessor, largely because the supernaturalism of Church law has been greatly attentuated. As a consequence of these developments administration has now become the principal instrument of control in the Church, with particular emphasis on episcopal appointments. It is perhaps not without significance that many conservatives are now choosing to fight their battles on the field of morality rather than on that of doctrine. Now that the concept of intellectual obedience has lost its former credibility and power, the argument from authority tends to be brought to bear increasingly on moral and administrative, rather than on strictly theological, matters. In an atmosphere of unscheduled pluralism in theology, and in the absence of one mandatory philosophical system to serve as a criterion of orthodoxy, the official teaching body today finds it increasingly difficult to translate instinctive dislike of this or that theological position into a credible condemnation. It therefore attempts to treat certain topics, such as the papal office, ministry, and sexual morality, as off-limits to any commentators who wish to question the party line. This raises the question of how theology relates to Church life in general and to Catholic life in particular.

CRITICAL THEOLOGY AS DARK NIGHT

David Tracy has noted that from a sociological standpoint theology can be said to have three distinct but overlapping publics, namely, society, academy, and Church.[12] Although, as Professor Tracy remarks, every theologian "implicitly addresses all three publics", it is probable that he or she will address a book or article to one public in particular. In the period between the two Vatican Councils the greater part of Catholic theological writing was addressed to the Church, or, to put it more accurately, to other Catholic theologians; and the whole operation was controlled by an omnipresent censorship. Only the most specialized and non-controversial writings were addressed to the wider reaches of academy. A concept of theology of and for the world lay in the future. Today the situation is very different. Catholic theologians now write freely, though not always with ecclesiastical impunity, for all three publics. Their Church has been brought face to face with modernity. In short, they have won the right to be as cognitively miserable in the modern world as any other reflective believers.

It is of course difficult to assess the extent of spiritual or intellectual discomfort among the non-theologically-minded clergy and laity, but it would seem to fall well short of misery. One can speak with no assurance on these things, but it seems probable that only a relatively

[12] D. Tracy, *The Analogical Imagination: Christian Theology and the Culture of Pluralism* (London, 1981), pp. 3–46.

small minority in any Church is forced by circumstances and mental honesty to undergo this ordeal. It is of its nature a lonely journey of which many believers are unaware and from which many shrink for the very good reason that they instinctively fear for their faith and even for their psychological health. Protestants have greater experience of it than do Catholics.

When Carl Jung gave the Terry Lectures at Yale in 1937,[13] he observed that Catholics protected themselves against "immediate religious experience"[14] by their reliance on the authority, creeds, and symbolic rites of the institutional Church. Protestants, he thought, could, though with far greater difficulty, seek a similar protection by an appeal to faith and the evangelical message. Occasionally one of Jung's patients would insist on making the journey towards real authenticity, a journey which the psychotherapist regarded as a psychological risk, since it would leave the patient "defenceless against God," "no longer shielded by walls or by communities," but which, in spite of these hazards, would offer him "the unique spiritual chance of immediate religious experience."[15] I realize of course that the Jungian process of individuation is not a specifically theological one, but I would wish to argue that the spiritual dimensions of the journey into contemporary critical theology are analogous to those which Jung has described. Protestant theology and spirituality, with their greater reliance on individual and personal religious experience, have more effectively conditioned their adherents to face these rigours than traditional Catholicism has done.

Cognitive misery does not rank high on the pastoral agenda of Catholic Church officers and is unlikely to figure in official communications, if only because public recognition of its existence might "disturb the faithful." The Congregation for the Doctrine of the Faith does not burn with obvious compassion for the plight of those who are suffering from post-Enlightenment blues. One can only hope that increasing experience of modernity will lead to greater pastoral concern for the spiritual needs of those who have to make the stark choice between a critically aware faith and no faith at all.

From questions of ecclesiastical polity I turn now to matters of actual theological experience. I shall select some aspects of the encounter with modernity and ask whether there are characteristic if subtle differences between the Protestant and Catholic ways of approaching it. I need hardly say that I make no claim to comprehensiveness. I also take for granted the degree of ecumenical progress

[13] C. G. Jung, *Psychology and Religion* (New Haven and London, 1938).
[14] Jung, *op. cit.*, pp. 52–3.
[15] *ibid.*, p. 62.

which allows us to contemplate Catholic and Protestant sensibilities equably in the knowledge that any future united Christianity will need both.

MODERNITY IN SEQUENCE

Modernity is not what it used to be. Facing up to it in the late twentieth century is significantly different from doing so over a period of more than two centuries. Protestants have received and absorbed their shocks in comparatively small doses and over an extended period. Thus when Protestant theologians exhort their Catholic colleagues to learn from Protestant experience, they clearly mean well, rather in the manner of a father who addresses his son with the time-honoured admonition "When I was your age . . ." This gambit may, however, invite the irritable and doubtless defensive response, "You were never my age." Catholics are having to recapitulate (in the Irenaean sense) all the stages of post-Enlightenment cultural experience and to do so in the space of a few years. This telescoping is as inevitable as it is disorientating. The context of modernization is no longer the spacious and leisurely culture encountered by Protestants in the 18th and 19th centuries but the hectic and radically secular environment of the late 20th century. When Schleiermacher addressed the cultured despisers of religion in Germany nearly two hundred years ago, he was able to do so in the knowledge that his book would be read pensively by a fairly restricted circle of interested people. Harnack, a hundred years later, had to contend with a much wider readership when he published his *Das Wesen des Christenthums*, but the pace was still leisurely. Catholic theologians today who wish to alert their coreligionists to the challenges of modernity are constrained to write for all three of Tracy's publics. Moreover they have to do so in a fast-changing world which conducts its communications at electric speeds. These conditions do not make for tranquil reception of a difficult and disturbing message.

More importantly, both Schleiermacher and Harnack could count on a secular culture which still had residual religious components, however vague these components might have become. Nineteenth century Liberal Protestantism may indeed have reduced theology to anthropology, as Barth alleged, but the anthropology was still recognizably if only vestigially religious (a point which, admittedly, would not impress Barth). That hopeful age came to an end with the first World War. By the time the second World War broke out the crisis had deepened. Modernity as Dietrich Bonhoeffer seems to have seen it in his last years, was now posing the question of a much more radical secularity. Bonhoeffer's answer was in many respects a holding operation, an interim expedient: Christians were to live in the world *etsi Deus non daretur*. That "esti" maintained a tenuous link with a provident if non-interventionist God. Twenty years later Secular Christianity removed the "etsi" and replaced it with an "eo quod". Christians must now live in the world not *as if* there were no God, but in the knowledge that the God of traditional Christianity had died. This was the moment chosen by the Catholic Church to enter the modern world.

Langdon Gilkey has made the interesting and challenging observation that Catholicism has not yet "tasted the real gall of modernity."[16] Professor Gilkey's thesis is that there are two levels to *aggiornamento*. The first level is concerned with updating the inherited ecclesiastical system of doctrines, rites, laws, and so on. This can be an exhilarating business, a sort of ecclesiastical happy hour when everything looks rosy and full of hope for the future. The hangover, he suggests, comes later when the carefree modernizer finds himself or herself on the second level and has to ask "whether *any* religious existence, thought, or goals in the world are viable in the modern age."[17] Gilkey argues that these "two levels or aspects of the crisis of modernity interact on each other, making the situation more confusing and more bitter."[18]

He is surely right to indicate the initially unsuspected and hazardous depths in any unconditional approach to *aggiornamento*, as he is right to argue that the two levels interact on each other: many of one's ecclesiological assumptions are radically altered by a facing of modernity on the second level. Reform has an inner logic of its own, a dynamic which carries it forward, sometimes in despite of its initiators. This can happen at both of the levels indicated by Gilkey. At the first level, it is probably true to say that most of the bishops at Vatican II were taken considerably further than they wanted to go by the determinism of the council's own drive. Many of them saw the council as an end, a moment of tremendous energy and achievement, after which the Church would need to pause for a long time and take stock of all that had happened. To an increasing number of theologians, however, it soon became apparent that the council marked not an end but a beginning, not an interlude but a prelude. The clash between these two views continues to affect Catholic life today.

While the official ecclesiastical magisterium appears to operate mainly on the first level, many Catholic theologians have progressed to the second level, where Professor Gilkey locates "the real gall of

[16] L. Gilkey, *Catholicism Confronts Modernity: A Protestant View* (New York, 1975), p. 114.

[17] *ibid.*, p. 39.

[18] *ibid.*, p. 34.

modernity." There is, of course, pluralism even among gall-drinkers, and no consensus about which cognitive miseries are the most intense. Perhaps the Feuerbach-Freud thesis of God as the projection of human desire on to an infinite screen presents the sharpest challenge to contemporary Catholic theology.

I specify Feuerbach here because his shadow falls over the work of all transcendental theologians, and because transcendental thought of one sort or another is a prominent feature in much contemporary Catholic philosophy and theology. Nearly all the Catholic modernists had recourse to transcendental experience as an alternative to scholastic essentialism. They accepted Kant's critique of metaphysics without, however, accepting either his moralism or his ban on divine-human communication. Instead they resorted to the basically Augustinian position on unsatisfied aspiration. Friedrich von Hügel, because he was the one most sensitive to what he saw as the dangers of immanentism, appreciated the need to respond to Feuerbach.[19] Von Hügel in effect repeated von Hartmann's very reasonable observation, "It is quite true that nothing exists merely because we wish it, but it is not true that something cannot exist if we wish it."[20]

The modernists are especially relevant to our subject because they exemplify a truncated but characteristically Catholic response to problems that had hitherto troubled only Protestants. The major modernists, including Alfred Loisy, refused to travel the road taken by Feuerbach. What they did was to divert attention and emphasis away from the Catholic pre-occupation with dogma as conceptual expression and place it instead on pre-conceptual experience. Most of them rejected both scholastic Catholicism's obsession with revelation as statement and Liberal Protestantism's reduction of it to moral experience. "Morality divorced from mysticism is a lean sort of religion" was how George Tyrrell put it.[21] In the opinion of Lucien Laberthonnière Liberal Protestantism offered faith without belief, while Catholic scholasticism offered belief without faith.[22] Both offerings suffer from a tragic lack of mysticism, or, if you prefer, of real religious sensibility operating through a baptized imagination.

---

[19] F. von Hügel, *Eternal Life: A Study of Its Implications and Applications* (2d ed., Edinburgh, 1913), pp. 233–244.

[20] Hans Küng reiterates the point and quotes von Hartmann in *Does God Exist? An Answer for Today* (London, 1978), p. 210.

[21] Tyrrell to Petre, Brit. Lib. Add. Ms 52,367.

[22] L. Laberthonnière, "Dogme et theologie," *Annales de philosophie chrétienne*, 5 (1908), p. 511.

CATHOLIC AND PROTESTANT APPROACHES

Catholic experience of confronting modernity, while having much in common with Protestant experience, nevertheless manifests some characteristic differences which extend beyond considerations of period and pace. The challenge issued to faith by modernity is obviously the same in both cases, but the shock-waves it sets up are not exactly similar. I should like to dilate a little on this contention. In 1962 F. J. Leenhardt published a fascinating study, *Two Biblical Faiths: Protestant and Catholic*.[23] Leenhardt was then Professor of New Testament in the University of Geneva. In his book he reflects as a Protestant ecumenist on the characteristic differences between Catholicism and Protestantism. He finds Abraham to have been the archetypal Protestant and Moses the archetypal Catholic. Abraham affirms the liberty of God and his own total incapacity. "The God of Abraham is the God of absolute beginnings." "He is, only in the act of his speaking. . . . He is not present in what He has said, but in what He says."[24] Leenhardt then goes on to draw the interesting conclusion: "Hence faith of the Abrahamic type tends to remove any confusion of the word of the promise with anything human, earthly, factual, historical. It aims at pure interiority."[25] On the other hand the revelation made to Moses is much more concrete and external; it "brings into play a bush, a mountain, and a storm." "The God of Moses is revealed by means of instruments which are raised to the dignity of efficacious signs."[26]

"Abraham. . . . Moses. . . . Two figures, two aspects of Biblical revelation. But also two styles of piety, two types of spirituality, two universes, each with its own internal logic, its implications, its consequences."[27] Leenhardt the biblical theologian is here making something like the case which Paul Tillich makes as a systematic theologian contemplating Catholic substance and Protestant principle. I believe it to be an important hermeneutical key to any future united Christianity. Here, however, I invoke it merely as a way of appreciating the two approaches to modernity. "Catholic spirituality," says Leenhardt, "assigns to the notion of presence the same part as protestant spirituality assigns to the notion of the word."[28] If we take this thesis a stage further than Leenhardt has done, we find that its implications for confronting modernity are interesting.

[23] F. J. Leenhardt, *Two Biblical Faiths: Protestant and Catholic* (London, 1964).
[24] Leenhardt, *op. cit.*, p. 64, 66.
[25] *ibid.*, p. 66.
[26] *ibid.*, p. 67.
[27] *ibid.*, p. 74.
[28] *ibid.*, p. 96.

Protestantism perishes if it allows linguistic positivism to lay down the ground-rules of all discourse, including discourse about God. Catholicism perishes if it capitulates before pan-scientific reductionism. In the one case Abraham ends up on the psychiatrist's couch persuaded that he has been having delusions. In the other, Moses is constrained to take an extra-mural course in climatology and the physics of combustion. Feuerbach and Freud adopted precisely this scenario. Karl Barth, disposing of Feuerbach rather too easily, claimed that he "does not deny either God or theology," he is "merely affirming God's nature as man's true nature" and thus "he is merely affirming anthropology as the true theology."[29] This conversion of theology into anthropology began, according to Barth, "from the moment when Protestantism itself, and Luther in particular, ceased to be interested in what God is in himself and became emphatically interested in what God is for man."[30] Barth's answer to Feuerbach's radical humanism was a defiant reaffirmation of God's radical transcendence. Barth, however, did not attempt to refute Feuerbach; he merely annexed his position in an act of audacious theological imperialism.

German thinkers have been given to standing other German thinkers on their head, thus starting a new school. Following this hallowed precedent, Barth manages to suggest that one has only to stand Feuerbach on his head in order to return to theological health: Man is God's desire projected on to a temporal screen. Barth, in his history of nineteenth century Protestant theology, accords Feuerbach only six pages. Schleiermacher, who is not susceptible of being thus upended, gets the full treatment of nearly fifty pages.

When Bultmann employed existentialism as a cultural medium for expressing his theology of faith, he was adopting a measure which was in keeping with his Lutheran experience and which allowed him to bypass *both* the Kantian interdict on essentialist metaphysics *and* the various liberal stratagems for dealing with that interdict. Roman Catholic theologians have toyed with this expedient of converting the accusative into the vocative and the indicative into the imperative, but one senses that, in spite of their intellectual respect for what was going on, their heart was not really in it. For all its epistemological attractiveness, it does not go far enough towards accommodating their instinctively sacramental mode of thought. Leenhardt puts his finger on one of the principal reasons for this: ". . . catholicism always tends to give the self-contradictory appearance of a spirituality which is

[29] K. Barth, *Protestant Theology in the Nineteenth Century: Its Background and History* (London, 1972), p. 535.
[30] *ibid.*, p. 536.

indissolubly linked to the "physical", the natural, and which at the same time is anxious to affirm the "metaphysical", the *supernatural*."[31] Leenhardt made this observation in respect of pre-Vatican II Catholicism but, when allowance is made for far-reaching reform in the theology of the supernatural, it still retains a good deal of its validity.

WORD AND PRESENCE

Leenhardt's earlier observation that Catholicism attaches greater importance to divine presence than to divine word has interesting heuristic possibilities. I should like here to explore two of them in the light of the challenge posed to faith by modernity.

(1) Official Catholicism's stubborn resistance to post-Enlightenment culture lasted until the revolution of the 1960s. Regrettable as this last-ditch stand was, it was by no means all loss, nor was it simply devoid of intellectual value. If it postponed the day of critical reckoning, it at least promoted the conviction that there are forces in the world which are inimical to all, even the most critically aware, expression of Christian faith, and that these forces have to be resisted through allegiance to the crucified Christ. What it totally failed to appreciate was the notion that at least one element of crucifixion in the modern world is intellectual. The totalitarian concept of intellectual obedience demanded a *sacrificium intellectus* which looked, to the outsider at least, more like suicide than a courageous and painful encounter with the challenge of modernity. While suspicion of science is obscurantist, protection against the spiritual ravages of pan-scientistic reductionism is an absolute requirement for contemporary faith. Blaise Pascal had actually led the way in advance of the Enlightenment by his celebrated distinction between the *esprit de géométrie* and the *esprit de finesse* and by his rejection of the former as an instrument of religious sensibility. Pascal the scientist was in an excellent position to indicate the limits of scientific method in the things of the spirit. It is no accident that he was execrated both by the Enlightenment and by Neo-scholastic Catholicism.[32]

Protestant honesty in facing the challenges of post-Enlightenment thought gave birth to modern Christian theology. We are all, Catholics included, beneficiaries of that great intellectual effort. But we are all also legatees of its defensive and concessionary mentality. It fought a brilliant rearguard action against what it saw as an advancing and apparently insatiable adversary. It conceded large tracts of allegedly untenable ground so that it could fortify more securely the ground it

[31] Leenhardt, *op. cit.*, p. 93.
[32] Some Neo-thomists liked to refer to "le funeste Pascal".

saw as defensible. Religious faith, however, cannot exist indefinitely on concessionary techniques. The good news of salvation cannot with impunity be shredded into illimitable sops to be thrown to Cerberus. If critically responsible Christian belief refuses to take a stand in spite of its cognitive difficulties, it will simply hand over its inheritance by default to the fundamentalists—which would surely be the final *trahison des clercs.* I believe that Catholicism can make a significant contribution to this stand, not by a newly enhanced recourse to authority (which is itself a form of fundamentalism), but by re-appropriating a long-neglected heritage sometimes loosely described as mystical. The term is notoriously imprecise and, into the bargain, suspect to many Protestants. I shall contend not for the term but for one of the realities it seeks to label. That reality is a way of approaching the world, a readiness to find God mysteriously, i.e., sacramentally, present in the same cosmos as that observed by scientists, who approach it quite properly with the *esprit de géométrie,* as Pascal the scientist did. Is it not, however, the province of the theologian to point out that the same cosmos can be approached with the *esprit de finesse,* as Pascal the Christian believer did? Teilhard de Chardin reflected the *esprit de finesse* when he wrote that "research is adoration; adoration is research."

And lest the point be thought too restrictively Catholic, let me quote William Blake.[33]

> Mock on, mock on, Voltaire, Rousseau:
> Mock on, mock on: 'tis all in vain!
> You throw the sand against the wind,
> And the wind blows it back again.
>
> And every sand becomes a gem
> Reflected in the beams divine;
> Blown back they blind the mocking eye,
> But still in Israel's paths they shine.
>
> The atoms of Democritus
> And Newton's particles of light
> Are sands upon the Red Sea shore
> Where Israel's tents do shine so bright.

Since I am not competent in the field of Eastern religions, I must leave it to specialists to indicate the possible relevance of Eastern mysticism to what I am trying to argue. I shall restrict my comments to Western culture.

We have in the West perhaps for too long fought the battle exclusively on the plane of *discursive* reason. I emphasize the word

[33] Conveniently available in H. Gardner (ed.), *The Faber Book of Religious Verse* (London, 1972), p. 232.

"discursive" here, because there are other functions of the mind which operate not against but alongside the merely logical and scientific. We can call such functions "imaginative", "affective", or "intuitional", if we dislike the term "mystical". Scholastic Catholicism disliked the package they seek to label; but scholastic Catholicism has had its day as the official criterion of orthodoxy. What contemporary Catholicism is slowly and painfully learning is that while the formulas in which the Church has cognitively enshrined its beliefs are of continuing importance, they are not comprehensive of all that is important in Christian faith; and indeed they may fail to comprehend what is most important. They derive from experiences which take precedence over them, and these experiences are approachable by means other than that of the speculative intellect. The institutional Church may seek to control the formulas, but it has absolutely no control over the experiences from which they derive. (This fact I take to be a crucial embodiment of the Protestant principle.) If Catholicism is to engage with modernity as critical Protestantism has done, it will have to abandon what Alfred Loisy called "the cult of the formula."[34] This does not mean abandoning its doctrinal inheritance but rather re-evaluating the role of doctrine in the life of the Christian.

The theological crisis brought on by contemporary secularization occurs in the first instance on the plane of direct and pre-reflective experience. As Owen Chadwick has pointed out, "the problem of secularization is not the same as the problem of enlightenment. Enlightenment was of the few. Secularization is of the many."[35] The Catholic Church, however, has been accustomed to conduct its engagements with modernity on the conceptual plane. I am not denying the importance of such conceptual engagement. I am merely observing that to conduct the engagement exclusively on the conceptual plane is to by-pass the *primary* interface between faith and culture. Secularization is an undifferentiated experience before it is a conceptual threat to doctrinal tradition. It is salutary to recall that the very notion of experience was virtually excluded from Catholic theology by the condemnation of modernism in 1907 and that it has been generally repatriated only since the reforms initiated by Vatican II. It will take another generation before the Church as a whole can come to terms with the implications of this change. The Catholic magisterium continues to think and act primarily on the conceptual plane, whereas the crisis is occurring primarily on the plane of

[34] A Loisy, *Autour d'un petit livre* (Paris, 1903), p. 208.
[35] O. Chadwick, *The Secularization of the European Mind in the Nineteenth Century* (Cambridge, 1975), p. 9.

pre-conceptual experience. In this respect Protestantism has been in a better position to confront modernity. Catholicism, with its strong metaphysical inheritance, does not find it easy to respond positively to Schleiermacher's claim that "Christian doctrines are accounts of the Christian religious affections set forth in speech."[36]

It is possible to take refuge from the theological implications of secularization by concentrating on its practical or "pastoral" implications. An authoritarian Church, the majority of whose members are located in the Third World, may be tempted to adopt this stratagem and may even be helped to do so by the regional theologies which are developing there. The present *contretemps* between the Vatican and the Liberation theologians may not last long if Rome comes to see that theology as a possible ally against liberal tendencies in the Northern hemisphere.

(2) This brings me to my second reflection on Leenhardt's contention that Catholicism is more sensitive to presence than to word. I refer to the growth of political consciousness in post-conciliar Catholicism. At first blush this phenomenon would seem to tell against Leenhardt's thesis; for is Liberation theology not prophetic and therefore a theology of the word? On further reflection, however, it can be seen to be a theology of presence by virtue of its central conviction that God is actually revealed in the plight of the poor and the oppressed, and that faith is primarily exercised by action on their behalf. By transferring attention from the intellectual and fiducial aspects of faith in its performative aspect (to use Avery Dulles's terminology),[37] political theology diverts attention away from the somewhat narcissistic and self-pitying posture in which Northern theology has allowed itself to be placed by its wrestle with modernity. I hasten to add that this is merely an unintended by-product of a programme of praxis and reflection which cares little for the cognitive plight of bourgeois theology. Latin American theologians show themselves to be quite aware of the problems we have been considering, but they clearly believe that these problems fade into insignificance when placed alongside the struggle for justice and human rights.[38] The fact that political theology is exciting extensive interest in the Catholic Church today is perhaps a pointer to how one significant strain of Catholicism is facing modernity in its less cognitive guises. In some respects political theology might be seen as an unplanned

---

[36] F. Schleiermacher, *The Christian Faith* (Edinburgh, 1928), p. 76.

[37] A. Dulles, "The Meaning of Faith Considered in Relationship to Justice." In *The Faith That Does Justice: Examining the Christian Sources for Social Change.* pp. 10–46. Ed. by J. C. Haughey. (New York, 1977).

[38] See for example G. Gutierrez, *The Power of the Poor in History* (London, 1983), *passim,* but especially pp. 169–221.

and late response to the Kantian critique. By setting out to find God in
political and social action on behalf of the poor, it adapts Kantian
moral individualism to the needs of society, thus supplying a communal dimension which was lacking in Kant's critique.

I can touch only briefly here on the substantive issues raised by
political theology. Theology after Auschwitz, or in the Third World,
resists peripheral treatment. My purpose here is to focus attention on
the strictly theological conviction of the political theologians that
socio-political action is constitutive, and not merely the moral con-
comitant of a faith which derives its revelatory authenticity solely
from cognitive and fiducial sources. Nevertheless Charles Davis
seems to me right in expressing a certain impatience with what he
sees as a lack of theoretical rigour in the stance of some political
theologians.[39] Just as mysticism without politics is false consciousness, so politics without mysticism is "mere business."[40] We could
with profit attend to Davis's claim that "it is only when Christians as
Christians engage in politics that they experience the transcendent
reality of God as limiting the political."[41] The argument is Augustine
suitably modified: "Thou hast politicized us for thyself, O God, and
our political ambitions remain unsatisfied until they rest in thee".
This argument, a particular form of the limit situation, meets the
Kantian critique and offers a new, or rather, neglected, locus of divine
presence.

Some such theological expedient as Davis suggests seems necessary if political theology is not to capitulate before "Culture Christianity" and thereby to incur precisely, if ironically, the charge which
Neo-orthodoxy brought against 19th century liberal Christianity,
namely, that it baptized what it saw as the best elements in contemporary culture. Baptizing the political revolution is, of course, a good
deal less comfortable and, in Latin American countries at least, calls
for a degree of heroism and self-sacrifice not demanded of 19th
century liberal theologians. Nevertheless, by its somewhat exclusive
concern with certain elements in Judaeo-Christian experience, it runs
its own risk of losing that balance of ingredients within Christian
belief which the Scholastics used to call the "analogy of faith". It is
one thing to see liberation as a process of paramount importance in
Latin America and other Third World countries; it is quite another to
view the theological analysis of that process as normative for all
Christian theology.

Political theology, including Liberation theology, is well aware of

[39] C. Davis, *Theology and Political Society* (Cambridge, 1980), p. 60.
[40] *ibid.*, p. 181.
[41] *ibid.*, p. 68.

the modern critical problems which have to be faced by reflective Christians everywhere. To charge it with fundamentalism is, I think, unwarranted. If it is anti-liberal, this is more for politico-economic than for theological reasons. Latin American impatience with the Northern world's critical anxieties is altogether understandable, and it puts the Northerners in a difficult position. Dialogue between political theologians of any kind and their less politicized colleagues is always uncomfortable for the latter, if only because moral passion normally upstages academic detachment. In this respect certainly, political theology shares a psychological advantage with fundamentalist orthodoxy. One instinctively quails before a prophet conscious of possessing a just cause who advances upon one with the light of rectitude in his or her eyes, proclaiming in a loud and peremptory voice: "We talk, you listen." The whole point of prophecy is that it should be uncomfortable; but, as Paul indicated, the discomfort should lead not to irritation or despair, but to metanoia. However, one source of discomfort often anaesthetizes another: a toothache can make you forget your backache, but it does not remove the causes of your backache, as a visit to the dentist will quickly demonstrate. So then, the critical problems remain and have to be faced by all theologians, political or not; and no amount of necessary political struggle can remove them, though it may well teach a valuable lesson in how to see them in perspective and how to live with them patiently and constructively.

LANGUAGE AND THE NIGHT BATTLE

The fact that traditional religious language can be understood in a radically secularist sense should perhaps alert us to what may be the most serious of our contemporary problems: the partial collapse of language as an agreed currency in religious thinking. Feuerbach could repeat with approval the classical patristic dictum that "God became man so that man could become God," while understanding it in a way which the Fathers would have repudiated with horror. We must sometimes wonder whether we use such words as "transcendent", "supernatural", and "secular" in a manner which has sufficient univocity to maintain them as instruments of truthful discourse or honest communication. It is not God who has died but rather the human power to name him. I am optimistic enough to believe that this linguistic collapse may be a necessary and chastening experience which is preparing us for an as yet undisclosed future. (This I take to be the cognitive dimension of Christian hope.)

We are paying for the sins of our confident and sometimes garrulous theological ancestors. They named not only with confidence but with abandon, and they have left us a heritage which both enriches and embarrasses us. They have left us a game to be played as they played it, but we are no longer sure that we are playing on the same field, with the same ball, or under the same rules. In these straitened circumstances Wittgenstein has enjoined silence upon us; but not even the most apophatic of theologians could accept this death sentence passed on their trade.

Instead, theologians are constrained to work with words that have grown tired, concepts that have become flaccid with constant bending, and images that are now tarnished with age and indiscriminate use. We must therefore hope that our successors will find it possible to create new languages in newly developing cultures. In the meantime the least we can do is refrain from incontinent charges of heresy and reductionism. We could, I submit, do more. We could recognize explicitly that we are using words in contexts which demand what David Tracy has called the analogical imagination. We need to recognize that there is an isomorphic relationship not merely between God and humankind, but also between each of us human beings. On the one hand, Humpty Dumpty cannot be allowed to get away with his "Words mean what I want them to mean;" on the other hand, we have to accept that dictionaries are tendentious instruments and that words have a built-in equivocity—theological words most of all. John Henry Newman put it succinctly in a celebrated passage from his tenth University Sermon.

> Half the controversies in the world are verbal ones; and could they be brought to a plain issue, they would be brought to a prompt termination. Parties engaged in them would then perceive, either that in substance they agreed together, or that their difference was one of first principles. This is the great object to be aimed at in the present age, though confessedly a very arduous one. We need not dispute, we need not prove,—we need but define. At all events, let us, if we can, do this first of all; and then see who are left for us to dispute with, what is left for us to prove. Controversy, at least in this age, does not lie between the hosts of heaven, Michael and his Angels on the one side, and the powers of evil on the other; but it is a sort of night battle, where each fights for himself, and friend and foe stand together. When men understand each other's meaning, they see, for the most part, that controversy is either superfluous or hopeless.[42]

Newman's "night battle" is nowhere more apparent than in disputes over transcendence and immanence, where sensitivities are often tender and where accusation and counter-accusation often abound. Much that has happened in Protestant theology over the past

[42] J. H. Newman, *University Sermons* (3d ed., London, 1871), pp. 200–1.

two centuries can be interpreted in terms of the dialectical tension between transcendence and immanence. In general, the claims of modernity have effected a further swing of the pendulum towards immanent, historically expressed, human experience of the divine. The swing continues in spite of the Barthian interlude.

A significant element in Catholic thought had begun to come to terms with the claims of immanence during the modernist period. The philosopher Maurice Blondel deliberately set out to do for Catholic thought what Kant had done for Protestant thought.[43] However, the condemnation of modernism in 1907 outlawed all attempts to give Catholic fundamental theology an immanent point of departure. When I was a theological student in Rome in the late 1940s, my teachers openly ridiculed the idea that religious experience could constitute a datum for serious theological discourse. One left that sort of thing to Protestants. Theology was about revealed truth, which was seen as "objective", meaning not only that it had reference to a supernatural realm, but also, and consequently, implying a conceptual view of revelation as supernatural knowledge qualitatively different from either rational (natural) or historical knowledge. Experience on the other hand was seen as "subjective" and conceptually peripheral. This attitude was of course closely tied in with the pre-critical Neo-scholasticism which then prevailed. Since Vatican II the change has been remarkable and astonishingly effortless. There have been no condemnations or rumours of condemnations of it. Today's theological text-books simply assume the methodological primacy of experience.

Much of the credit for this bloodless revolution must go to transcendental Thomists like Rahner and Lonergan who have been able to give currency and credibility to the new thinking by their familiarity with the old. One must wonder, however, whether the old and patched wineskins will continue to be able to contain the new wine; but they have certainly performed a most valuable interim holding operation. Furthermore, it is doubtful whether the full implications of this revolution have been recognized and taken on board by the Catholic Church at large. Protestantism was able to do so more easily, since the immanent dimension of Christian thought was in harmony with the guiding principles of the Reformation. Catholicism, on the other hand, had, as George Tyrrell pointed out nearly eighty years ago, constructed its system of Church government upon a concept of transcendence which was in effect deistic, incorporating as it did "the notion of a sort of direct 'telegraphic' communication

---

[43] M. Blondel, *Lettres philosophiques* (Paris, 1961), p. 34.

between Heaven and the rulers of Church and State,"[44] an absent God making his will known through the words and instructions of his appointed representatives. It would appear that many Catholics of conservative instincts continue to rely on this theory of extrinsically mediated transcendence. They think of God, in Tyrrell's phrase, as a sort of arch-pope.

Authoritarian heteronomy can therefore rightly be seen as the Catholic form of fundamentalism, in that it treats the ecclesiastical magisterium in the same manner as the Protestant fundamentalist treats the Bible.[45] Tyrrell's diagnosis and remedy are straightforward: Our forefathers "knew nothing of that fatal discord which arises when religion is derived from outside and civilization from inside. To their belief we must return in a better form, and derive both one and the other from God, but from God immanent in the spirit of man."[46] This modern retrieval of an earlier Christian belief implies, not a capitulation to the secular world, but a recognition that transcendent being is to be encountered in secular forms. To quote Tyrrell again, "The transcendent is not the spiritual as opposed to the phenomenal; but the whole as opposed to an infinitesimal fraction of possible human experience."[47] This wise insight seems to me to be what Paul Tillich meant, in part at least, by theonomy. Any natural or cultural phenomenon can embody and manifest the transcendent; and it is no attenuation of transcendence to claim that in historical conditions it is always encountered in phenomenal manifestations. If the secular mind is to be queried, it is not about the wholeheartedness of its turn to the world or to human experience of that world, but rather about the apparent scientism and historicism of its epistemological assumptions. These assumptions, if and when they are present, deny the analogical and isomorphic character of what is going on by decreeing that one must either speak univocally or else keep silence. This assault on the poetic imagination may indeed be rightly described as reductionism—perhaps the worst kind of reductionism—but one ought to be slow in detecting it in the words of men and women who continue to wrestle with the meaning of God in today's world.[48]

[44] G. Tyrrell, *Through Scylla and Charybdis: Or The Old Theology and the New* (London, 1907), p. 360.

[45] Peter Berger questions this identification in "Secular Theology and the Rejection of the Supernatural: Reflections on Recent Trends," *Theological Studies* 38 (1977), pp. 54–5.

[46] Tyrrell, *Through Scylla and Charybdis*, p. 383.

[47] G. Tyrrell, *Christianity at the Cross-Roads* (London, 1909), pp. 207–8.

[48] See J. Coulson, *Religion and Imagination* (Oxford, 1981) for a stimulating discussion of the role of imagination in matters of faith. Coulson's book is a fine exemplar of interdisciplinary work in the field of literature and theology. The author summarizes his thesis thus: "The argument of this book is that the real assent we make to the primary

I began this paper with some words of Reinhold Niebuhr on the role of imagination in religious sensibility. Let me conclude by returning to that perceptive entry in his notebook: "Fundamentalists have at least one characteristic in common with most scientists. Neither can understand that poetic and religious imagination has a way of arriving at truth by giving a clue to the total meaning of things without being in any sense an analytic description of detailed facts."[49] Niebuhr's correlation of scientism with fundamentalism prompts one last question.

How does one account for the rise of fundamentalism and its continuing ecclesiastical vitality? Liberally-minded theologians are often puzzled and sometimes dispirited by the failure of rationally disposed religion to command a popular following. Does not the same thing, however, happen in other spheres of human experience, notably in politics? Liberally-minded citizens have today in many countries to live under reactionary governments which draw their strength and support from deeply conservative electorates. Much that is done in the name of such citizens by their governments outrages some of their deepest and most passionately held convictions. In addition, if they are religious, they have sometimes to endure the invocation of God in support of policies which they detest as profoundly immoral.

The existence of a fundamentalist movement in all historical faiths is a phenomenon which should neither surprise nor disturb the reflective believer. It is, in part at least, a protest against the intimations of lost innocence. Instead of dwelling on the theological defects of fundamentalism, I should like to sound a more subversive note. The ecumenical instinct to entertain and where possible to respond positively to the truth in the position of others should extend also (if unilaterally) to fundamentalism. An attitude of academic contempt achieves nothing, if only because intellectual sophistication in matters of faith is precisely what many fundamentalists most despise and condemn. (It is appropriate to recall that A. C. Dixon was chosen as editor of *The Fundamentals* on the strength of an attack he made in a sermon against "one of those infidel professors in Chicago.")[50]

From Tertullian on, there has always been some degree of protest in Christianity about what intellectuals are alleged to do to the purity and strength of the faith. Not all of that protest can be simply dismissed as irrationalism. It poses an important question, at least for

---

forms of religious faith (expressed in metaphor, symbol, and story) is of the same kind as the imaginative assent we make to the primary forms of literature" (p. 145).

[49] R. Niebuhr, *Leaves from the Notebooks of a Tamed Cynic*, pp. 166–7.

[50] G. M. Marsden, *Fundamentalism and American Culture: The Shaping of Twentieth-Century Evangelicalism: 1870–1925* (New York, 1980), p. 118.

Church-affiliated theologians. How is it that when religious belief and practice are brought into harmony with the reasonable requirements of the secular world, so often they lose their power to attract and to satisfy? It sometimes seems that a Church which squares up to modernity loses precisely that "Dionysian" element which fundamentalism so often preserves. Nietzsche saw Socrates and his agent Euripides as the destroyers of classical tragedy: At their hands, Nietzsche alleged, logos emasculates mythos.[51] The sensible rationality of Apollonian religion somehow fails to satisfy the deeper receptors of religious symbol in the human psyche. The Kantian ideal of "religion within the limits of reason" is in the end the most unreasonable aim of all, because it neglects an element in human nature which is both necessary to spiritual health and impervious to the censorship of reason. Perhaps the most rational act of all is to recognize the existence and legitimate demands of pre-rational experience. As Bishop J. V. Taylor has put it, "There is more of Dionysus than Apollo in the Holy Spirit."[52] Popular religion, even in its most superstitious, anti-intellectual, or emotionalist manifestations may be telling us something we do not want to hear in Academe. Just as cigarette manufacturers are compelled to display the warning "Smoking may damage your health," so perhaps faculties and departments of theology might be profitably compelled to display in their lecture rooms the warning "Dionysus always strikes back"—which is only another way of expressing the New Testament conviction that the Spirit breathes where he wills.

[51] This is a central thesis of Nietzsche's *The Birth of Tragedy*. Ed. by W. Kaufmann (New York, 1967).

[52] J. V. Taylor, *The Go-Between God: The Holy Spirit and the Christian Mission* (London, 1972), p. 50.

ARCHAEOLOGY & SYMBOLISM IN AZTEC MEXICO: THE TEMPLO MAYOR OF TENOCHTITLAN

EDUARDO MATOS MOCTEZUMA*

The excavations of Templo Mayor in Mexico City between 1978–1982 have provided important archaeological data which, combined with the ethnohistorical data, greatly broaden our knowledge of the Templo Mayor of Mexico-Tenochtitlan, the capital city that controlled the Aztec Empire between 1425–1521. My interpretation of the symbolism of the Templo Mayor is based on the combined archaeological and written resources associated with the ceremonial center of the Aztec capital. In my view the Templo Mayor is a precise example of the Mexica views of the cosmos, consisting of sacred mountains which constitute the fundamental symbolic center of the vertical and horizontal cosmos of the Aztec universe. The twin temples of Tlaloc and Huitzilopochtli situated on top of the pyramidal base are replicas of this cosmic order.

As an archaeologist committed to understanding the relationship of economic structures to ideological forms, I am attempting to uncover the interrelationship of the material and symbolic character of the Great Aztec Temple. In what follows, I will describe the material record of the major portions of the excavation and offer my interpretation of the symbolic order of the Temple.

*Professor of Archaeology at the Centro de Investigaciones y Estudios Superiores en Antropologia Social in Mexico and Director of the excavations of the Templo Mayor of Tenochtitlan, Dr. Moctezuma presented this paper as an illustrated slide lecture at the 75th Anniversary Annual Meeting of the American Academy of Religion. The Editor expresses the gratitude of the Academy to Professor David Carrasco and his Assistant, Ms. Joan Goertoffer, of the University of Colorado, Boulder, for their generous assistance toward the present form of the paper. We are also grateful to Professor Jose Cuellar of Stanford University for his translation of Professor Moctezuma's lecture at the Academy Meeting. Professor Moctezuma requested that footnoting be omitted, given the informal character of his address. Readers interested in pursuing the scholarly apparatus of the paper are advised to consult the forthcoming work of Professors Moctezuma and Carrasco, *The Great Aztec* (University of California Press, 1986).

DISCOVERY!

On the night of February 21, 1978, the workers of the Mexico City electric-power company were digging at the corner of Guatemala and Argentina streets when they encountered a huge, round stone covered with Aztec reliefs. The Office of Salvage Archaeology of the National Institute of Anthropology and History led a team of archaeologists in excavating the 3.25 meter wide stone disc. On the upper surface of the disc was sculptured the representation of a female deity: nude, decapitated and with her arms and legs separated from her torso, and decorated with snakes, skulls and earth monster imagery. This was without a doubt the representation of Coyolxauhqui, sister of the Aztec patron god, Huitzilopochtli. In the written sources, Coyolxauhqui was a lunar deity who was slain and dismembered by her brother after a battle on the sacred hill of Coatepec (Snake Mountain).

The chance discovery renewed interest in excavating the ancient Great Temple of the Mexicas: the people of the Aztec city of Tenochtitlan. As the initial excavation revealed, the monumental sculpture of Coyolxauhqui formed a part of the temple platform which led up to the shrine of Huitzilopochtli. Under the authority of the President of Mexico, Miguel Lopez-Portillo, a full scale excavation of the site was planned and carried out under my co-direction. The project, entitled Proyecto Templo Mayor, involved a number of scientific and cultural problems which were continuously discussed throughout the excavation. One important dimension of the Great Temple Project for social scientists was the opportunity to demystify our pre-Hispanic past. In general the pre-Hispanic past has been the object of a distorted vision based on certain ideological principles which picture the ancient world as one of grandeur, marvelous architecture, superb astronomy, excellent in everything. This vision of the pre-Hispanic world ignores a more integrated view of the pre-Columbian societies which should present evidence of the many components of Mesoamerican social life and the complex interrelationships of groups and cultures.

In the case of the Great Temple Project, we were aware that we faced a unique opportunity to study a fundamental part of the Aztec state which reflected the dynamic interplay of different peoples, ideologies and economic patterns. We approached the excavation with the goal of understanding all spheres which composed the society represented at the Templo Mayor.

The people who founded the Templo Mayor arrived in the lake of Mexico and established their temple around 1325 A.D. The historical sources say that the first thing the Aztecs did was build a rush and reed temple for their deity, Huitzilopochtli, who had led them on a long pilgrimage to the site. It is this temple that served as the center of the society that struggled to establish a stronghold in the world of competing city-states of 14th century Mexico. In this manner the temple began to constitute the midpoint of the whole cosmovision of Aztec society.

MORPHOLOGY

In our study of the history and structure of the Templo Mayor we have essentially two types of information. On the one hand we have a) 16th century chronicles and pre-Conquest pictographs, and b) on the other hand we have the complex archaeological data which have been periodically uncovered since the 18th century.

Among the existing documents we have one that indicates the precise moment of the founding of Aztec society. The frontispiece of the document known as the Codex Mendocino illustrates the foundation of the city under the guidance of Huitzilopochtli. The drawing shows that the city of Tenochtitlan was originally divided into four sections with the image of a great eagle perched in a cactus growing from a stone in the center of the lake. It was on this spot that the first temple was built. In this manner we see the immediate establishment and separation of the sacred landscape from the surrounding territory.

Various written sources tell us that the ceremonial center was approximately 400 meters on each side, contained about 78 temples, and had several entryways aligned to cardinal directions. We know for certain that there was one at the north, south and west side. Some historical sources indicate that there was one on the east as well which would be most logical.

The Great Temple occupied the center space and consisted of a large high platform of four or five stepped levels, facing toward the west with two steep stairways leading up to the top level. At the top were two structures: the sanctuaries of Tlaloc (the god of water, rain and fertility) and of Huitzilopochtli (the god of war and of the sun). It was in front of these two imposing sanctuaries that massive human sacrifices took place.

The 16th century Franciscan, Bernardino de Sahagun, writes of Tlaloc: "This god called Tlaloc Tlamacazqui was the god of rain. They said he gave them the rains to irrigate the earth and that these rains caused all the grasses, trees, fruits and grains to grow. It was he who also sent hail and thunder and lightning and storms on the water and the dangers of the rivers and sea. The name Tlaloc Tlamacazqui means that he is the god who resides in the terrestrial paradise and gives to men the subsistence necessary for life."

Sahagun researched Aztec religion for 30 years in the central valley of Mexico while attempting to convert the Indians. His work revealed the great power of Huitzilopochtli: "The god called Huitzilopochtli was another Hercules, exceedingly robust, of great strength and very bellicose, a great destroyer of towns and killer of people. In warfare, he was like living fire, greatly feared by his enemies . . . While he lived this man was highly esteemed for his strength and prowess in war."

The prominence of these two deities reflects the fundamental needs of the Mexicas: their economy was based on agricultural production (hence the importance of water and rain) and on tribute collected by conquest of the many towns and cities in central Mexico (hence the importance of war). Thus we expected that all the elements associated with the Great Temple, such as offerings and sculptures, would in some way be related to these two fundamental themes.

It is absolutely clear that the Great Temple of Tenochtitlan was the place, real or symbolic, where Mexica power was centered. It is significant that the shrines to the two great deities related to the economic structure of the Mexica state were located at the top of temple: Tlaloc, god of rain, water, and agricultural production; and Huitzilopochtli, god of war, conquest and tribute. Their presence at the Great Temple indicates a coherent relationship between structure and superstructure. Let me summarize briefly my use of these terms. The "structure" refers to everything relating to the economic base of the group: productive forces, including habitat and natural resources, and man as an active component who uses these forces and transforms them with his tools in the process of production. Structure also includes the relationships that are created between those who exercise power and those who are subject to the controlling group, including the people conquered by the Mexica. As for the "superstructure," it is made up of such aspects as art, philosophy, religion (ideology), etc: all of this under the control of the governing class known in Aztec society as the pillis.

Concerning these vital relationships we can propose the following general postulates: (1) the archaeological context associated with the Great Temple such as offerings, sculpture, architecture, has an ideological content which probably reflects the ideology of the dominant group and indicates how it uses two apparatus of the state, the repressive and the ideological, to maintain its hegemony and assist in its reproduction. The first apparatus acts by using force and the second is expressed through religion, art, education, the family and the political system and (2) the different discoveries including sculpture, murals and offerings, probably reflect both internal and external Mexica control, through the presence of their own materials (Mexica) and of other groups (tribute).

In order to be able to understand what the Great Temple signified, it is necessary to refer to two categories which will help us in the process of our investigation: *phenomenon* and *essence.*

Our research begins with the study of a collection of phenomena related to the Great Temple, and these phenomena allow us to penetrate the essence which produced them. To analyze scientifically this motley collection of phenomena, we must use the two general categories which play an important role in the process of acquiring knowledge. The first refers to the outward appearance of objects and the processes of its objective reality, which moves and changes. "Essence," the more stable of two categories, is the internal aspect of process that is contained within and manifested through a phenomenon. Scientific knowledge would be directed not only to the study of phenomena, but to the study of internal processes, of the essence that produces these phenomena.

The phenomenal aspect is what we generally know as the presence of Tlaloc and Huitzilopochtli at the Great Temple, the symbols and elements proper to each deity, the rituals of the various festivals and their characteristics. This includes everything which is manifested and present before the priest and the participants, with all its religious complexity.

The essence is what is not directly present but which, nevertheless, acts as the basis of this process. For us, this is the ideological presence of the two deities at the Great Temple. First, there is Tlaloc, an ancient god of water and rain for agricultural peoples such as the Mexica, and second, there is Huitzilopochtli, a tribal god, solar god, god of war and domination over other groups. This domination required the generous payment of tribute from conquered areas. Tenochtitlan used this tribute to provide itself with a whole series of products necessary to its economy: loads of corn, beans, cacao, cloth, feathers, objects; raw materials like skins, stones, lime, etc. In other words, the presence of these two gods and not others, at the top of the temple is a reflection of the economic and political base of Tenochtitlan.

ORIGINS AND ORIENTATION

The Mexica were the last Nahua group to penetrate the Valley of Mexico during the middle of the 13th century. Guided by their titular god, Huitzilopochtli, they left Aztlan, place of the purple heron, and traveled until they arrived, many years later, at the promised island where they settled, prospered and finally disappeared, annihilated several centuries later in the Spanish conquests. A beautiful Nahua text has survived which tells us of their original journey.

And as the Mexica came,
it was clear they moved aimlessly,
they were the last who came.
No one knew their faces.
So they could settle nowhere,
they were always cast out,
they were persecuted everywhere.
Then they came to Chapultepec
where many people settled.
The rule of Lord Azcapotzalco already existed,
but Mexico did not yet exist.
There were still fields of rush and reed
where Mexico is today.

A number of historical chronicles relate how the Mexica arrived in the valley of Mexico after many hardships and found the different city-states engaged in intense military struggles for control of the valley and its resources. The Mexica eventually submitted to the Tepanec lord of Azcapotzalco who extracted tribute from them in exchange for the right to settle on the edges of their territory which was a marshy island in the middle of the lake. This occurred in the year 2 House or 1325.

It was here, in the middle of the lake, where the Mexica began to construct their first temple. One chronicle tells us:

Seeing that everything
was filled with mystery,
they went on, to seek
the omen of the eagle
and wandering from place to place
they saw the cactus and on it the eagle.
When the eagle saw them, it bowed to them,
nodding its head in their direction.
Now we have seen what we wanted,
now we have received what we sought.
"My children, we should be grateful to our god
and thank him for the blessing he has given us.
Let us all go and build at the place of the cactus
a small temple where our god may rest."

During the ensuing decades, the Mexica enlarged their temple, the Great Temple, numerous times by utilizing previous stages as the foundation for the larger structure. Our excavation shows that the temple was enlarged seven times on all four sides and on top, while the main facade received a number of partial enlargements. We will now describe what the Great Temple was like, referring to both the archaeological data and reports from historical sources.

Until recently, our fundamental sources of information about the Great Temple were the chronicles written in the 16th century. Now that we have the excavated temple before us we see that the historical descriptions were faithful to what the Spaniards saw and what they had learned from native sources. Also, the project has uncovered very ancient stages of the Great Temple built around 1390 (designated as Epoch II) which even the last generations of the Mexicas were not familiar with. This earliest stage was completely covered by the many superimpositions built during the 15th century. We are only able to observe the uppermost part of the earliest temple because 3/4s of the temple is still below the ground. We were not able to uncover it because it is now covered by the natural water of the lake of Mexico.

After excavation, we can now confirm that the last Mexica construction epoch of the Great Temple had been razed to its foundations by the Spanish. We found only traces of the edifice on the stone-slab pavement of the great plaza. On the north side of the plaza only about a meter of the platform wall remains. The earliest construction epochs, however, were better preserved: they were older, smaller and had sunk farther below the present street level.

In placing our archaeological findings against the background of historical accounts, we know that the Great Temple was oriented with its principal facade toward the west. As stated, it was built on a large platform which supported a foursided structure with two stairways leading upward to the two shrines of Hutizilopochtli and Tlaloc. Huitzilopochtli's shrine was on the south side, while Tlaloc's was located on the north side.

The temple was enlarged many times for different reasons. On the one hand the city of Tenochtitlan suffered periodic floods which required the raising of the base of the structure. The Temple also had structural defects due to the sinking of the unstable earth beneath it. On the other hand, the historical sources tell how some of the rulers ordered the construction of new temple on top of existing ones, creating a pattern of superimposing new stages of the Great Temple. These reconstructions accompanied the enthronement of a king or the major expansion of Aztec territory.

STRUCTURE

Let me give a general picture of each stage of the Great Temple by utilizing a system of Roman numerals which designate total enlargements of the four-sided structure. A Roman numeral accompanied by a letter refers to the additions on the main facade only.

Epoch I refers to the first temple structure which historical sources indicate was a small hut made of perishable materials. No excavation is possible.

Epoch II is the earliest excavated epoch of the Great Temple; it was found almost intact and dates from about 1390 A.D. It provides us with startling information about the symbolism of Templo Mayor. We could only excavate the uppermost parts of this building and the remains of the two sanctuaries on top which were constructed of stone with some of the stucco still covering the surfaces (a mixture of lime and sand). In front of the entry to Huitzilopochtli's shrine we found the notorious stone of human sacrifice.

The pattern of twin temples and sacrifical stone which we found intact at this earliest stage is similar to the reports of Spanish chronicles and priests, eyewitness accounts of the final stage of construction in 1520.

Of the temple itself, Sahagun writes: "In the center and higher than the (other temples of the city) the principal (temple) was dedicated to the god Huitzilopochtli, or Tlacauepan Cuexcotzin. This (pyramid) was divided at the top so that it looked like two; it had two (sanctuaries), the principal one, stood the statue of Huitzilopochtli . . . also called Ilhuicatl Xoxouhqui; in the other was the image of the god Tlaloc. In front of each one of these statues was a round stone like an executioner's block, called techcatl, where they killed all those whom they sacrificed in honor of that god. From the block to the ground there was a pool of blood from those who were killed on it, and this was true of all the (temples). They all faced west and had very narrow and steep steps leading to the top."

Bernal Diaz describes what he saw; "On each altar were two giant figures, very tall and very fat. They said that the one on the right was Huichilobos (sic), their war-god." He adds: "At the very top of the (pyramid) there was another concavity, the woodwork of which was very finely carved, and here there was another image, half man and half lizard . . . They said that the body of this creature contained all the seeds in the world, and that he was the god of seedtime and harvest."

Discussing sacrifices in honor of Xipe Totec, Sahagun adds: "Having brought them to the sacrificial stone, which was a stone three hands in height or a little more, and two in width, or almost, they threw them on their backs."

It is interesting that we found a sacrificial stone, the obvious symbol of Mexica power and where captives of war were sacrificed in front of the 1390 sanctuary of Hutizilopochtli. It is a slab of black volcanic rock, and its dimensions conform with those given by Sahagun. The stone, which was found in situ embedded in the floor near the stairs (two meters away) measured 50 centimeters by 45 (20 inches by 18).

On the Tlaloc side of the top level of the 1390 temple we found a polychromed statue, known as a chacmool, also in situ and in the same position as the sacrificial stone in relation to the sanctuary of Huitzilopochtli. The find confirms the historical interpretation of the role of the chacmool: it is an intermediary between the priest and the god, a divine messenger. Both elements—the sacrificial stone and the chacmool—in front of the sanctuaries can be considered as dual symbols, the first symbol related to war and the second to a more "religious" idea: the divine messenger.

We discovered that two large stone piers framed the entrance of the sanctuary of Tlaloc. The surfaces of the piers that faced outward were painted with a row of black and white circles representing the eyes of Tlaloc; just below the circles were three horizontal bands, one blue and two red. The lower halves of the piers were decorated with alternating vertical bands of black and white. In the interior of the structure we discovered the bench on which the image of Tlaloc probably sat. We consider this stage to be prior to 1428, the year in which the Mexica liberated themselves from Atzcapotzalco and began their climb to dominance. It may correspond to the reign of the Aztec ruler Huitzilhuitl.

In front of the sacrificial stone on Huitzilopochtli's side, on the last step leading up to the platform and on an axis with the sacrificial stone, we found the sculptured face of a person with the glyph two rabbit carved above. This year sign is equivalent to the year 1390 A.D. In the interior of the shrine, behind the sacrificial stone we discovered a stone bench which runs north-south. In the middle there is a small altar which apparently supported a statue of the deity Huitzilopochtli. Following this stage, we found partial remains of superimpositions IIa, IIb, IIc, which show a deficient system of construction on the western facade of the temple.

Epoch III: This stage reveals finely made steep stairways bordered by vertically constructed foundations. Most significant, we found eight impressive sculptures of life-size standard bearers reclining on the stairway leading to Huitzilopochtli's shrine. These figures were probably located at symbolic locations around the building before they were gathered together on this stairway when the next stage was constructed over them.

This structure has the glyph 4 reed carved into the rear platform wall of Huitzilopochtli's stairway. It is equivalent to the year 1431, which corresponds to the rule of Itzcoatl.

Stage IV: This stage is one of the richest in its elements. The large general platform is adorned with braziers and serpent heads on each of its four sides. The braziers on the side of Tlaloc (in the rear, for example) show the face of this god while braziers on the side of Huitzilopochtli have only a bow which symbolizes that deity. Beneath the braziers and serpents were found various offerings of which you can still see the cists. Stage IVb is an addition to the main facade (on the west) which has yielded a great series of significant objects. It includes the great platform which the Great Temple rests upon, a platform which contains stairways at both ends. Next to the stairways we found enormous serpents whose undulating bodies and great heads still carry some of the original pigment which covered them. The wide flight of steps to the platform is only interrupted by a small altar with two frogs resting on top of small pedestals. These sculptures are found in line with the middle of the stairway which leads to the upper part of Tlaloc's temple. On the side of Huitzilopochtli, in front of the stairway which leads to his shrine, we found a stone serpent 2.50 meters long which forms part of the fourth stairway of the platform.

The pedestal forming the base of the stairs which led to the upper part supports 4 serpent heads, two located at the extreme ends of the pedestal and two in the middle, which mark the union of both buildings. At the center of the Huitzilopochtli side of the platform we found the monumental stone sculpture of Coyolxauhqui, who is the dismembered sister of the war god. In Aztec myth, these two deities fought at the hill of Coatepec and together they constitute a major portion of the symbolism of the Great Temple. On this platform, we found various offerings, some around the Coyolxauhqui stone, others between the two serpent heads and others in the middle of the stairway to Tlaloc. All of these offerings were found beneath the platform while chambers 1 and 2 were found behind the stairways in the exact middle of each one of these buildings.

At the extreme north and south of this platform were found the remains of rooms with colored marble floors. Also, on the Tlaloc side was found a small stairway leading to a tiny altar within which were discovered two extremely impressive offerings. One contained more than 42 skulls and bones of children, finely covered masks and delicately painted funerary urns full of small sea shells perhaps representing human hearts. Below this rich offering we found another offering called chamber III. Both were dedicated to Tlaloc.

Chronologically, we think that much of stage IV corresponds to the reign of Moctezuma I because we discovered a glyph 1 rabbit on the Huitzilopochtli side of the platform which is equivalent to the year 1454. The additional elements of Coyolxauhqui and the serpents could well correspond to the reign of Axayacatl, for another glyph on the south side of the structure carries the symbol 3 House which is the year 1469 coinciding with the ascent to the throne of that king.

Epoch V: We have only found the general platform of stage V, covered with stucco as well as part of the floor of the great ceremonial enclosure formed by slabs which were joined by stucco.

Epoch VI is the penultimate one which formed part of the great platform previously discussed. The principal facade reveals a wall with three serpent heads facing west, a decorated beam and a stairway.

THE OFFERINGS AND THEIR SYMBOLIC ORDER

Perhaps the most exciting and intellectually significant aspect of the entire excavation was the unexpected discovery of more than 100 offerings buried at or near the Great Temple. Some were discovered as offerings in the smaller shrines adjacent to the Templo Mayor.

As for the location of these rich caches, generally, they were placed along certain axes. On the main facade there were three main axes: the first two beneath the floor of the platform facing the middle of each of the two stairways; the other closer to the junction of the stairways leading up to the twin temples of Tlaloc and Huitzilopochtli. They were also located at the corners of the Temple as well as along the north-south axis approximately halfway down the structure. There are also three axes at the back part: at the middle of each of the buildings and at their junctions. Some of the offerings were placed around the base, equidistant from each other.

In general, it can be stated that the placement of objects within the offerings was made according to a symbolism which we must decode. This means that the objects and their placement have a language. For example, there are materials which usually occupy the lower part of an offering on the bottom, just as others always occupy the upper part. We have also observed that the materials are oriented in a certain way. Both the offerings on the west side (main facade) and in the back part of the Temple are oriented toward the west, in the direction of the setting sun, while those that are found halfway down the Temple on its northern and southern facade are oriented in those directions. Another interesting aspect is that the placement of objects within an offering also follows a plan. Offerings 7 and 61, the first of which is located halfway down the southern side of the structure, the other on the northern side, both have the same distribution of materials. On the bottom, strombus mollusks are oriented north to south; over them were placed crocodiles. On top were placed the seated gods whom we have denominated Xiuhtecuhtli, since they represent old people. On the right side of these gods we have marine coral and on their left a clay vessel with an effigy of the god Tlaloc. Could this distribution mean that the strombus represent the sea and the crocodiles an earthly level and Xiuhtecuhtli and Tlaloc a heavenly level? The same thing occurs with offerings 11 and 17, the first of which is located on the main facade between the two serpent heads which marks the junction of the shrines of Tlaloc and Huitzilopochtli and the other located at the back part of the junction of both edifices.

The material obtained from the 100 plus offerings associated with the Great Temple is abundant and varied. More than 7,000 objects have been uncovered including pieces which are clearly Mexica and others which definitely came from tributary areas. The great majority of the tribute objects came from the present states of Guerrero, from the Mixteca (Oaxaca), and the Gulf Coast (Puebla). Interestingly, not one single object came from the Tarascan culture in the west (which, as we know, was not under Mexica control). The same thing pertains to other areas, such as the Maya, from which there are no materials. Among the Mexica materials, the most numerous objects are sculptures of seated old men, probably Xiuhtecuhtlis, dressed only in their "maxtlatl" or loinclothes and wearing headresses characterized by two protuberances. Xiuhtecuhtli was the father of the gods located at the center of the universe and of the home.

Other Mexica representations are numerous effigies of the god Tlaloc, carved out of "tezontle" (volcanic rock) and other kinds of stone; some coiled serpents; representations of rattlesnake heads made of obsidian; stone braziers with knotted bows.

There are other remarkable pieces from the tributary areas revealing the geographical expansion and limits of the empire. There are a great quantity of Mezcala masks and figures of different kinds of sizes from the Southwest region. There are also alabaster pieces from the Puebla region, such as deer heads and finely carved arrows and seated deities. From the Gulf Coast we have two magnificent funerary urns of orange ceramic, inside of which were found fragments of burned bones, necklaces and other materials. The great variety of snails and shells, fish, swordfish swords, and corals come partly from the Gulf Coast and partly from the Pacific. The same thing is true of the crocodiles and jaguars, which came from Veracruz, Tabasco or Chiapas. These objects reflect the style and ecological forms of the Aztec peripheries.

Another group of objects includes those which clearly belong to societies which long preceded the Mexica. Such is the case with the magnificent Teotihuacan masks and the beautiful Olmec mask which were excavated. The latter came from the region which lies within the borders of the states of Puebla, Oaxaca and Guerrero, according to the petrographic analysis which has been made.

All of the material is under study but a preliminary analysis reveals that the majority of the objects represents Tlaloc or symbols associated with him, such as all of the objects of marine origin, canoes and art forms. We also have objects associated with Huitzilopochtli such as the braziers with the knotted bows; skulls of the decapitated victims, "tecpatl" sacrificial knives with eyes and teeth of shell, and the presence of objects which came from tributary areas, the products of military conquest. Significantly, no stone image of Huitzilopochtli has been found.

The foregoing tends to confirm our hypothesis that the Mexica were, of necessity, an agricultural and militaristic people whose sustenance depended on both agriculture and tribute, water and war, life and death, and all of this was integrated in the Great Temple of Tenochtitlan. Moreover, the Templo Mayor represents the concentration of Mexica power and their control over the destiny of conquered peoples, just as Huitzilopochtli conquered and took control of the "anecuyotl" (destiny) of his brothers. On a symbolic level this is important, for it shows how the Mexica continue the mission initiated by their titular god. They not only take control over the "destiny" of the conquered peoples but also control their agricultural production.

THE SYMBOLISM OF THE GREAT TEMPLE

We shall now discuss an extremely important subject: the symbolism of the Templo Mayor. As we shall see, this symbolism was based partly on the myth of the struggle between Huitzilopochtli and Coyolxauhqui on the hill of Coatepec. Also, research has revealed the historical basis of the myth, which helps us understand the tie between the historical conquest and cosmological conquest in Aztec life.

On many occasions real historical events are converted over the course of time into myths. Several world religions offer us examples of this assertion. As the history of religions teaches us, there are many cases when an individual, because of his special qualities is deified after his death. The same thing happens with places at which a transformative event occurs. These places are made sacred by the society which experienced the event and it becomes the center for future orientation. Once the place is made sacred or the individual is deified, it becomes necessary to reproduce what took place in what has now become "mythic time". Therefore, the need emerges to ritually re-enact the mythic event. Hence it is indispensable to explore the deeper significance of rituals, since behind each rite there generally is a myth. Occasionally, there is behind the myth a real, historical fact. We can summarize the process of ritual formation in this way: (a) historical, real fact is told in (b) myth, which is (c) re-enacted in ritual. This process of ritual formation is clearly reflected in the Aztec traditions associated with the Templo Mayor.

If we study carefully the myth of the struggle between Huitzilopochtli and his sister Coyolxauhqui we can see how the aforementioned steps have been followed and how the Templo Mayor is the re-enactment of the myth, all of this based on a real, historical fact.

The sixteenth century chroniclers, Alvarado Tezozomoc and Diego Duran tell us how in the process of the migrations from Aztlan, the Mexicas arrived at a place called "Coatepec" (Hill of the Serpent), where they settled. However, they were part of a group, the Huitzna-hua, who disobeyed their leader Huitzilopochtli, who then attacked them and killed a woman warrior, Coyolxauhqui, decapitating her. The Huitznahua were defeated and their hearts taken out.

Some authors have interpreted this account to mean that histori-cally a significant struggle occurred at a hill called Coatepec. It seems certain that part of the group, made up of people from the barrio of Huitznahua, opposed the forces of Huitzilopochtli. The Huitznahua were led by a woman, Coyolxauhqui, the woman with bells on her cheeks, and they lost the confrontation. This rebellion signifies the attempt to usurp the power and control of the larger group. It is a matter, then, of an internal power struggle. Nevertheless, this event provided the basis for the appearance of the myth which was reported to the Franciscan friar, Sahagun, who used old Indians as informants in the writing of his *Historia General*. At the time of Sahagun, 1550–1570, it was believed that Huitzilopochtli was born on the hill of Coatepec, while in the historical version we find that he arrived there after a pilgrimage. What happened at Coatepec held great importance to the Mexica, who believed that the tutelar god was born there.

The "divine song" told to Sahagun tells that:

> On Coatepec, in the direction of Tula,
> a woman by the name of Coatlicue,
> the mother of the four hundred Southerners,
> and of a sister of one of them
> named Coyolxauhqui,
> was sweeping when some plumage
> fell on her . . .
> From that moment Coatlicue was pregnant . . .
> When the four hundred Southerners saw
> that their mother was pregnant,
> they became very angry . . .
> And their sister Coyolxauhqui
> said to them:
> Brothers, she has dishonored us,
> we must kill our mother . . .
> When the four hundred Southerners were resolved
> to kill, to destroy their mother,
> then they began to move out,
> Coyolxauhqui guided them . . .
> At that moment Huitzilopochtli was born,
> He dressed himself in his finery,
> he took out the serpent made of candlewood . . .

Then with it he wounded Coyolxauhqui,
he cut off her head,
which was left abandoned
on the slope of Coatepetl.
The body of Coyolxauhqui
rolled down the slope,
it fell apart in pieces,
her hands, her legs, her torso
fell in different places . . .
Then Huitzilopochtli raised up,
he pursued the four hundred Southerners,
he kept on pursuing them, he scattered them
from the top of Coatepetl,
the mountain of the serpent.

Before we begin our discussion of matters related to the re-enactment of the myth and how the Templo Mayor is the living myth, it will be helpful to summarize several major aspects of Aztec cosmology related to the Great Temple.

For the Mexica, the Universe consisted of two fundamental planes, one horizontal and one vertical. The first was made up of the four cardinal directions, each with its characteristic color, its own sign and the god who ruled it. This was also the plane where the earth (the Cem-anahuac) was located, symbolized by a portion of earth completely surrounded by water. In the center from which the four directions radiated was located the Great Temple. The Temple was intersected by the vertical plane, characterized by nine lower levels of a netherworld, a place through which the dead must travel in order to arrive at the ninth and deepest level: Mictlan. The upper levels consist of thirteen heavens which lead to the highest level: Omeyocan, the Place of Duality, in which resides the Dual Lord and Lady, Ometecuhtli and Omecihuatl.

The Mexicans tried to symbolize this cosmological structure in the Great Temple, in their ceremonial precinct and in their city.

It is not surprising, for example, that the Temple of Ehecatl-Quetzalcoatl, god of the wind, is located opposite the Templo Mayor facing east. Let us recall that in the myth of the emergence of the sun and of the moon in Teotihuacan, the assembly of deities were confused as to where the new sun would rise. Quetzalcoatl looked toward the east and the rising sun appeared above the horizon. Quetzalcoatl's shrine is located with its main facade oriented toward that cardinal point of the equinox sunrise. We also wish to point out that exactly north of the Templo Mayor we located three shrines during our excavations. We have named the center one a "tzompantli" or skull rack altar, since it is decorated with more than two hundred forty carved skulls. Its relationship to death is evident and, contrary to our expectation that a shrine similar to this might appear on the southern side of the Great Temple, no equivalent temple was found. This reminds us that the Mictlampa (the place of the dead) is located in Mexican cosmology in the northern quadrant.

From the earliest construction stages we have uncovered, we find present the idea of duality: there exist two bases built on a common platform with their respective shrines in the upper part, the shrine of the god of water and that of the god of war. A review of the mythology suggests that both represent sacred hills or sacred mountains revered in Mexica tradition.

The temple on the southern side, corresponding to Huitzilo-pochtli, is a specific symbol of the mountain the Aztecs called the Templo Mayor, Coatepec. If we analyze the placement of deities we see that the god Huitzilopochtli is located on high, while his sister, Coyolxauhqui, represented in the great stone, lies conquered at the foot of the hill-temple, on the platform, decapitated and dismem-bered. The temple stairway and Coyolxauhqui were not placed randomly, but in precise places assigned to them by myth. Also on the platform supporting the Coyolxauhqui stone are the serpent heads which adorn and give their name to the hill-temple: Coatepec (Hill of the Serpent).

We believe that in the third construction stage the material which forms the base of the temple is composed of projecting stones with no representations in order to give a better idea of a hill. They simply have their natural form and they jut out from the walls. In the same period, eight anthropomorphic sculptures were found leaning against the stairway leading up to Huitzilopochtli's temple. The sculptures may represent the Centzonhuitznahua, the enemies of Huitzilo-pochtli, whom he annihilated in the myth. In this way, the Templo Mayor, on the southern side, represents the real-mythical place of the combat of Huitzilopochtli and his siblings. The chronicles tell us that in the festival of Panquetzaliztli dedicated to Huitzilopochtli, every-thing that happened in the myth was repeated in elaborate rituals culminating in sacrifice, on the top of the Templo Mayor, of warriors conquered and captured for that purpose. Their hearts were taken out and their bodies were thrown down the stairway, where the bodies were divided among those who had captured them. That is the way Coyolxauhqui is depicted in the magnificent sculpture which is located at the foot of the hill-temple: dead and dismembered. This allows us to reflect upon that cosmic struggle between the sun and the moon, between light and nocturnal powers. The moon in various religions is associated with the feminine, while the sun is masculine. It is not surprising that in the historical record Huitzilopochtli constantly had problems with Malinalxochitl and Coyolxauhqui during the pilgrimage, which also might be related to the problems of the patriarchy or even a change from the lunar to the solar. Further research may tell us more about this aspect of the symbolism.

For its part, the Tlaloc side of Templo Mayor also represents a hill. We know from several chronicles that homage was also rendered to this god on the tops of sacred hills and at special locations in the lake. One hill in particular, known as Mount Tlaloc in Spanish times was the site of major ritual pilgrimages of Aztec kings. At the ceremonial center on Mount Tlaloc child sacrifice was carried out to renew the agricultural forces of the Aztec world. As expected, it was on the Tlaloc side of the temple that we found the remains of child sacrifice beneath the platform floor. In the *Codex Borbonicus*, Tlaloc is shown several times with his shrine on top of a hill. The distinctiveness of Tlaloc's hill at the Templo Mayor is suggested by the different kinds of serpents which adorn the half of the platform that belongs to him.

What is important to note here is that both hills are the living presence, made visible, of myths which were important to the Mexicas. On one side, the myth of their tutelar god, who was born to fight, and on the other the hill of sustenance, the place of Tlaloc, where the food that is used to sustain man is obtained. In a broader sense, we are in the presence of a significant duality: the Great Temple is the place or symbol of life (Tlaloc) and death (Huitzilopochtli). It also appears that the Templo Mayor's vertical symmetry indicates the different levels of the cosmos as well. We believe that the general platform on which the Temple rests may well represent the earthly level. This platform is characterized by having a single common stairway on which is located the altar of the frogs, an aquatic symbol associated with the waters of the earth. The braziers which surround the four sides of the Temple are also on the platform and represent fire. On the main facade are the serpents which indicate the horizontal earth. The stepped sides of the Templo represent diverse heavens or levels of ascent until one arrives at the upper level where the two shrines in which the gods are located represents the Dual Heaven, Omeyocan, from which all creation emerges.

What is described here does not belong exclusively to the Mexicas of Tenochtitlan, but also with their own variations and characteristics, to a number of people who had a socio-economic development similar to that of Tenochtitlan.

My intention has been to present a general panorama of what has been obtained from the Templo Mayor during four and a half years of work there and to suggest what the Templo Mayor of Tenochtitlan symbolizes: a place of glory for the Mexicas and of misfortune for those who were in their power.

RELIGION AND POLITICAL CULTURE IN AFRICA

ALI A. MAZRUI*

As the European colonial period was coming to an end in the 1950s, calculations were made about the balance of religious forces in the African continent. In the year of Ghana's independence (1957) the Paris Academy of Political and Moral Sciences received some pertinent estimates. The Academy was informed that between the years 1940 and 1946 the annual increase of professing Muslims in the French African colonies was nearly a quarter of a million every year. Between 1931 and 1951 Muslims in the whole of Africa had risen from 40 million to 80 million in comparison with a Roman Catholic rise of from 5 million to 15 million.

Of the total black population estimated at the time as being 130 million in Africa south of the Sahara, 28 million were Muslim, 30 million were Catholics, 4 million were Protestants and 85 million still followed primarily their own traditional indigenous religions. Islam in Africa as a whole, including Arab Africa, commanded the allegiance of approximately 40 per cent of the continent's population.

ISLAM: REGIONAL DIFFERENCES

Islam had entered the continent quite early in the Hijra (Islamic) era. The Arab conquerors snatched away Egypt from the Byzantine Empire in the 7th century within a few years of the Prophet Muhammad's death. We can certainly say that the Islamization of North Africa took place primarily through *political* means (conquest, control and suzerainty).

On the other hand, Islamization in Black Africa has tended to occur primarily through *economic* means (trade and economic migration). Islam came to Black West Africa on horseback across the Sahara,

*Research Professor at the University of Jos (Nigeria) and Professor of AfroAmerican and African Studies at the University of Michigan, Dr. Mazrui presented this paper as a 75th Anniversary Lecture at the 1984 Annual Meeting of the American Academy of Religion.

mainly as part of economic traffic between the northern societies of the continent and the western.

Islam came to East Africa on dhows, usually with the monsoons. Again, the dhow traffic from the Arabian peninsula and the Gulf areas was essentially economic, involving trade in both directions. Muslim traders were often also part-time missionaries and informal proselytizers.

In the continent as a whole the distribution of Islam has taken the shape of an inverted crescent. Islam is strongest in North Africa, West Africa along the bulge of the continent, and in Eastern Africa including the Horn of the continent. Islam in the middle of the continent is relatively weak, and in Southern Africa it is very thin indeed. The nature of the European impact on Africa had something to do with the distribution of Islam. The spread of Islam in Eastern and Southern Africa, for example, was effectively arrested by the consequences of European colonization. If Islam spread north of the Sahara through conquest, so did Christianity spread south of the Sahara by the same means. If north of the Sahara Islam spread by the sword, south of the Sahara Christianity spread by the gun. As a British poet once put it:

Whatever happens we have got
The Maxim gun and they have not.[1]

But in spite of the importance of the gun in the consolidation of Christianity south of the Sahara, the European influence was not even. Islam in West Africa continued to conquer in spite of European colonization, while in Eastern Africa it was held in check by European colonization. The question arises, why the difference?

One possible explanation for the greater vigour of Islam in West Africa could be its greater degree of indigenization and Africanization. Islam had ceased to be led by the Arabs and had acquired an independent dynamism in Western Africa. The great leaders and religious preachers, the great warriors of Jihad like Usman dan Fodio were themselves indigenous Africans. This contrasted quite sharply with religious leadership in many parts of Eastern Africa, where immigrant Arabs or visiting Arabs played a disproportionate role. Throughout much of the colonial period East Africa under British rule allocated positions of Kadhis and chief Kadhis disproportionately to Islamic jurists of Arab ancestry. This was particularly so in Zanzibar, Tanganyika (now mainland Tanzania) and Kenya. The fact that Muslim leadership in these countries was disproportionately in the hands of immigrant Arabs helped to reduce the dynamism of Islam in

[1] The couplet is from the English writer, Hilaire Belloc.

Eastern Africa, and contributed to the slowing down of the spread of Islam during the colonial period.

Another factor behind the arrest of Islam's expansion in Eastern and Southern Africa was the high visibility of the European presence in those sub-regions. The prestige of European civilization within Africa was reinforced by the actual physical presence of European settlers in those areas. Quite often a white settler presence in one African country had ramifications and a conspicuous profile in the sub-region as a whole. Thus the white settlers in Kenya exercised considerable influence over the destiny of the neighbouring countries, especially Uganda, Tanganyika and colonial Zanzibar.

In Southern Africa the white profile was even more conspicuous, and the aggressive exclusivity of European civilization helped to close the gates of any further Islamic expansion southwards. This was very different from the situation in West Africa where the absence of white settlers and the Africanization of Muslim leadership ensured for Islam a substantial measure of local authenticity and sheer vibrancy.

But even in West Africa the impact of Islam varied considerably from one African society to another, one African culture to another. Islam among the Hausa in Nigeria, for example, is very different from Islam among the Yoruba in the same country. For one thing, Yoruba Islam is significantly less politicized than Hausa Islam. In their political behaviour the Yoruba can often be as volatile and even violent as any other Nigerians. But the Yoruba are more likely to explode in defence of ethnic interests rather than in pursuit of religious concerns. Religious explosions in Nigeria tend to be located in the north among the Hausa and their neighbours, rather than in the South among the Yoruba. When elections go wrong in Nigeria, and tempers run high, it is the ethnic organ which tends to show in Yorubaland, rather than the religious limb.

On the other hand, both religion and ethnicity can get very political among the Hausa in Nigeria. Periodic religious explosions have occurred involving Muslims of different denominations in the north of the country, sometimes costing a lot of lives. The Jihad tradition among Nigerian Muslim northerners is latent and potentially revivable. The links between religion and politics among the Muslims of northern Nigeria are deeper and more durable than such links among the Muslims of southern Nigeria. The major reason is that historically the pre-colonial Hausa city-states often attempted to enforce the Shari'a (Islamic law) and fused church and state. Yoruba states and kingdoms before European colonialism tended, on the other hand, to be based on indigenous Yoruba customs and traditions, rather than primarily on the Shari'a. Yoruba Islam in these post-colonial times remains less Arabized and less subject to politicization than Hausa Islam has tended to be. It is because of these considerations that Yoruba Muslims have sometimes been regarded as Yoruba first and Muslim second—while Hausa Muslims have been perceived as the reverse.

THE CRESCENT AND THE CLOCK

But whatever the precise combination and weight between indigenous loyalty and Islamic allegiance, the Muslim presence in Nigeria has deep roots. And the number of Muslims in the country is greater than the number of Muslims in any Arab country, including Egypt. In other words, Islam in Nigeria has more followers than Islam in any single Arab country, mainly because Nigeria itself is of course much larger than any particular country in the Arab world. There have been occasions when Nigerians going on pilgrimage to Mecca constituted either the largest or the second largest contingent of pilgrims from any part of the Muslim world. In 1981, Nigerian pilgrims once clocked the one hundred thousand mark, the largest contingent from any Muslim country. The decline of the number of pilgrims in subsequent years was due mainly to foreign exchange problems in Nigeria. This resulted in greater control of numbers of pilgrims permitted to go by the federal government. The inhibitions of the modern state system and the constraints of the world economy were now intruding more decisively into Islamic calculations in post-colonial Africa.

But in a sense these new international horizons within Africa are themselves an extension of a process which was initiated by Islamization in some parts of Africa. Islam introduced a new understanding of distance and space, as well as a new understanding of time and duration. The obligation on every Muslim to go on pilgrimage to Mecca at least once in his or her lifetime was itself an extended perception of distance. Africans newly converted to Islam were forced to think of a far away place called Mecca not simply as the birthplace of the Prophet Muhammad but as a target for their own travelling in their own lifetime. What is more, Mecca was prevented from becoming too vague by the requirement that five times every day a Muslim should face Mecca in his or her prayer. The combination of facing Mecca five times a day, and the aspiration to go on pilgrimage to Mecca at least once in a lifetime and sometimes several times, transformed perceptions of space and distance among African communities which in some cases had previously been confined to villages and constrained by rural perspectives.

In the centuries of Islam many Africans marched overland over many months, not running away from pestilence or drought, not seeking new worlds to conquer, but simply in quest of Mecca.

Reportedly there are two million Nigerians in the Sudan who are descended from pilgrims who either never made it to Mecca but stopped in the Sudan or, more likely, stopped in the Sudan on their way back and never made it to their homes in Nigeria ever again. The grand trek to the twin cities of Islam, Mecca and Medina, was itself a kind of annual Bantu migration, a new revolution in mobility for many sectors of African society.

But Islam also introduced its own disciplines of time in societies which previously felt less pushed by considerations of punctuality. Again, Islam's discipline of time was related to the five prayers of the day. These prayers were spaced out across the twenty-four hours with a good deal of precision. Each prayer had to be performed within its own allocated time during the day. It was normally a sin to postpone the prayer unless there were exceptional and compelling reasons. Sensitivity to the time of the day was a pre-condition for avoiding the sin of ritual procrastination.

It is a common sight in Muslim Africa to see a trader or hawker at the road side interrupting his business in order to perform a particular prayer of the day. The prayer had to be *done* (not just "said") at that particular time. In many indigenous African societies such a pre-occupation with exact time was a significant social revolution.

What all this means is that the ethos of punctuality in much of Africa did not come initially with Western culture and its obsession with precision in time. That ethos initially came with Islam. But did both imported civilizations fail to tame Africa into the discipline of punctuality? The answer is that Islam succeeded in promoting punctuality in the religious sphere, but failed to extend it to the secular domain. Muslims do observe their five prayers each day, usually within the prescribed times allocated to those prayers. Muslims search the skies for the sight of the new moon in order to ensure that the rituals of the different lunar months are satisfactorily observed. The fast of Ramadhan, from the hours before dawn to sunset, is prescribed with precision. It is a sin to eat at dawn, so one has to be sure precisely what time it is. It is also a sin to eat before the sun has gone completely down, and this also requires a sensitivity to minutes and seconds, and not just to hours. As for the pilgrimage to Mecca, it has a precise week in the year, and the different steps are carefully timed within the rituals of the *Hajj*.

Strictly speaking, Islam was all set to inaugurate a revolution in time among its converts in Africa, as well as in the Arab world. The revolution in the discipline of time succeeded strictly within the religious domain. Both the Arab world and Africa have had to await the greater impatience of Western civilization before the ethos of punctuality could be secularized. Even then the West has failed to make Africa observe the clock with the same attentiveness with which it observed the clock under Islamic stimulation. Appointments with visiting businessmen and professors in transit in African cities are sometimes broken with impunity or at any rate subjected to delay. But appointments with God are a different case. That is why the Muezzin calling believers to prayer is a more compelling alarm-clock in Muslim Africa than all the chimes of Big Ben and the Greenwich time signal.

The most important prayer of the week in Islam is of course the mid-day prayer on Friday. Only certain mosques are used for that prayer in order to encourage believers to assemble in a limited number of places and thus ensure a higher level of collective worship on Friday. Most of the remaining mosques are closed for that particular prayer.

The mosques chosen for the Friday prayer are sometimes not large enough to accommodate the huge crowds which turn up. Many such a mosque in African witnesses great overflows of believers, sometimes into the streets, bringing traffic to a standstill during that hour and a half of worship. Non-Muslim Nigerians have been known to complain about this disruption of traffic, but since Muslim Nigerians are forced to observe Sunday as the Sabbath instead of Friday in spite of the fact that there are more Muslims than Christians in Nigeria, their grievances probably cancel each other out.

THE LANGUAGE OF GOD

The Friday prayers are preceded not only by the Muezzin calling believers to prayer, but also by a sermon. In many parts of Africa the sermon is still entirely in Arabic, although the bulk of the congregation south of the Sahara might not understand the Arabic language. In Zanzibar since the 1964 revolution some degree of Africanization of the Friday ritual has taken place, including the introduction of a Swahili section to the Friday sermon. The rest of the sermon is still in Arabic, notwithstanding the language of the congregation.

The actual prayer itself, involving bowing to God, kneeling and prostrating before God, is usually accompanied by oral recitations from the Qur'an. Again, the words recited throughout the actual formal prayer are entirely in Arabic.

This brings us to a striking paradox concerning Islam in relation to Christianity in Africa. Strictly from the issue of the language of worship, Islam has been less compromising than Christianity. It is as if the God of Islam understood only one language, Arabic. Formal prayer and ritual in Muslim Africa, as well as in the bulk of the rest of the Muslim world, is conducted almost entirely in the Arabic language. Most Muslim children have to learn the art of reading and reciting the Qur'an even if they do not actually understand what the words they are reciting really mean. That is why many Muslim schools in Africa are referred to as Qur'anic schools, emphasizing the actual verbal mastery of the Holy Book. Most of the hymns in the mosques in Africa are in the Arabic language, which are memorized and recited, not necessarily with a command of their meaning. It is in this sense that Islam in Africa is linguistically uncompromising, demanding due conformity with the language in which God communicated with humankind.

In contrast, Christianity has quite often communicated with Africans in the language of their own societies. The Bible was translated into indigenous African languages quite often decades before the Qur'an was. Services in African churches are often conducted in indigenous African languages. Hymns, though sometimes originating in Europe, have been translated quite early and are often sung in indigenous African tongues. At least at the level of language, Christianity has made more concessions to Africa than Islam has done.

And yet in other respects Islam has appeared to be more accommodating to the wider culture of Africa, more ready to compromise with African ancestral customs and usages. For example, the use of the drum in certain Muslim ceremonies in Africa contrasts with the stricter disapproval of the drum in comparable Christian ceremonies. Islam has also been less militant against certain practices which are both un-Islamic and un-Christian. One illustration is female circumcision. European Christianity has often taken a strong position against this custom which is practiced by a minority of African societies. The most dramatic confrontation between Christian churches and this particular African custom was in Kenya during the colonial period. And even more recently Christians under European leadership have regarded female circumcision as abhorrent and, in some important respects, un-Christian.

It is possible that by the canons of orthodox Islam female circumcision is equally alien and un-Islamic. And yet such deeply Muslim societies as Somalia and Northern Sudan practice female circumcision on a relatively wide scale. Islam has interfered less with this preexistent African custom than Christianity has sometimes done.

There is also the issue of areas of accidental similarity between Islam and traditional Africa. A widely discussed area of congruence is attitudes to polygamy, the marrying of more than one wife. Islam has a limit of four wives, whereas traditional Africa has an open ended policy. Normally African Muslims have not been tempted to go beyond four wives in any case. It has been widely suggested that part of Islam's success in Africa is precisely its greater toleration of polygamy as compared with monogamous Christianity.

But this kind of argument overlooks other disciplines which Islam imposes and which Christianity does not. Among these is Islam's prohibition of alcohol. Many traditional African societies used alcohol for a variety of cultural and ritual ceremonies. African Islam has not made concessions on this issue. At least until Western influence entered the scene, African Muslim societies were relatively strict in avoiding alcohol. The revival of alcoholic drinks in Muslim Africa is not because of a revival of indigenous African alcoholic pastimes, but is more due to Western alcoholic penetration.

On the whole, while it is indeed true that Islam in Africa had gained from not being monogamous, Christianity in its turn has gained by not being opposed to alcohol. Africans being courted by the two religions have had to choose between the discipline of being satisfied with only one wife and the discipline of being satisfied with only soft drinks. In many instances the choice has not by any means been easy.

But on the wider spectrum of comparison, it remains true that Islam has been more accommodating to indigenous African customs and traditions than European Christianity has been. I use the term "European Christianity" to distinguish between the religion which came with the European missionaries in the 19th and 20th centuries, on the one hand, and the Christianity of Ethiopia and North Africa, on the other. Ethiopian Christianity has certainly accommodated itself with female circumcision in traditional Ethiopia. A fusion of Christian and pre-Christian Ethiopian ways has occurred. The precise mixture has been unique.

But why has Islam combined linguistic intolerance in the mosque with a wider cultural accommodation? Why has it insisted on the primacy of Arabic as a medium of prayer with a spirit of compromise towards the wider aspects of African traditions and lifestyles? Let us take the two parts of the question separately in turn—linguistic intolerance on one side and wider cultural compromise on the other. Islamic theology has divided the world conceptually into *Dar el Islam* and *Dar el Harb* (the Abode of Islam as against the Abode of War). The Abode of Islam is of course the Muslim world as a whole, the lands where Islam is supreme as a way of life if not as a system of law. The Abode of War is the rest of the world, but only in the sense in which Thomas Hobbes, the English philosopher, meant by "a state of war". Both Islam and Thomas Hobbes are really referring to a situation where there is no recognised central authority, and where everyone is for himself with the possibility of war constantly on the horizon.

Within the Abode of Islam there is an official language—just as every African country in the second half of the 20th century has had an official language. The official language of Islam is Arabic. This is because Arabic is the language in which the Qur'an was revealed to the Prophet Muhammad. The fact that the holy book of Islam is actually available and read in the original language in which it was revealed has a lot to do with the possessiveness with which Muslims treat Arabic. There is no Christian equivalent of that language. Only a few scholars ever read the Bible in the language in which it was originally written. Indeed, the evidence would seem to suggest that the language in which it was written is now dead. And certainly very few Christians recite anything from the Bible in the language in which Jesus himself spoke.

This is in sharp contrast to Islam, where the words of the Qur'an are precisely the words that the Prophet Muhammad used to communicate to his followers what he felt was the message of God.

GODS IN EXILE

What all this means is that the Bible has from very early times been primarily a work of translation. Afterall, Christianity did not triumph among the people to whom it was first revealed—the ancient Hebrews. Christianity has its greater successes away from its own cradle. It became preeminently the religion of the foreigner, the religion of the gentiles. By becoming the religion of the stranger, it entered into the realm of translation almost from the beginning.

This is the history of the estrangement of Christianity. The message of Jesus started as a sect of Judaism. Early Christians accepted Jewish rituals, and the Jerusalem church insisted on circumcision and saw itself as operating under Mosaic Laws.

It was the Christian Jews of the diaspora who started the trend towards universalism. The first such Christian Jew, Stephen, demanded the abrogation of the Mosaic Code. He was taken before the Jewish Sanhedrin, the arbiter. He denounced official Judaism as unreceptive to the Holy Spirit. Stephen was stoned to death—the first Christian martyr.

Persecution of liberal Christian Jews followed, and many had to flee to Antioch. The Antioch Christians began something which was to transform the world—they began to convert gentiles and to insist that gentiles did not have to circumcise. The Antioch Church of young Christianity then started to send missionaries to neighbouring provinces.

Paul was probably the first to preach a thorough-going and complete Christian universalism. As he declared in his letter to the Romans "there is no distinction between the Jew and the Greek; the same Lord is Lord of all and bestows his riches upon all who call upon him."[2]

The imperative of translation was beginning. Between the years 48 and 58 A.D. Paul travelled through much of Asia Minor and Greece, preaching to Jews and Gentiles alike. Christianity began to penetrate the Eastern Provinces of the Roman Empire. Even Rome itself was to witness before very long a small Christian community. Multi-lingualism was beginning to be a feature of the new Gospel. The Christian religion was spreading, becoming indeed internationalized, but at the same time becoming isolationist in a contradictory manner. It was internationalized in the sense of making converts among new cultural groups and across provincial frontiers. But Christianity was also isolationist in the sense of living apart and refusing the pagan worship of the God-Emperor. Christians regarded emperor worship as idolatory. The Roman government in turn regarded Christian refusal as treason punishable by death. Christians prayed in secret—and many were thrown to the lions.

The next major divide in the history of Christianity came in the 4th century. Christianity had grown to such an extent that recognition by the Roman Emperor seemed politically desirable. The Edict of Milan was proclaimed in 313 A.D. by Emperor Constantine I, giving toleration to Christianity on an equal footing with other religions.

Why did Emperor Constantine do it? According to one legend, he called on the God of Christians in a critical battle and saw the sign of the cross in the sky with the words *In hoc signo vinces* ("in this sign thou shalt conquer").

Emperor Constantine delayed his own formal conversion to Christianity until rather late in his life. And at least on the eastern part of his Empire he never abandoned the concept of God-Emperor, but he did lay the foundations of Christianizing the Roman Empire. And that foundation served as the genesis of European Christianity, and the origins of the estrangement of the message of Jesus away from the people among whom it was initially revealed, and moving towards a fundamental condition of translation.

Islam had no such experience in estrangement. The people from among whom it was first revealed were converted overwhelmingly to that religion. It is true that only a fraction of the Muslims of the world today are in fact Arab. The population of Muslim Indonesia alone is almost the equivalent of the population of the Arab world as a whole. The Muslim population of the Indian peninsula or South Asia (Muslims of Pakistan, Bangladesh and India itself) outnumber the population of the Arabs in the world. The Muslim population of the African

---

[2] *Romans X*, 12, Revised Standard Version.

continent is greater than the Arab population *outside Africa* by a ratio of two to one.

But while it is indeed true that Islam has expanded beyond the Arabian peninsula, and far beyond the Arab world, the Arabs themselves are overwhelmingly Muslim in allegiance.

Two factors have maintained Arab centrality in the fortunes of Islam, the Arabic language and Mecca. There is little doubt historically that the Qur'an as it exists today was the Qur'an of the days of the Prophet Muhammad and were the words in which the Prophet communicated the message of God to his followers. That degree of authenticity is assured in Islam to a degree which is far greater than what can be guaranteed with regard to the authenticity of the Christian New Testament. But in addition the major capitals of Christianity for Africa in the 20th century are places like the Vatican in Rome and Lambeth Palace in London. It is very doubtful that Jesus Christ visited either Rome or London. The estrangement of Christianity is captured in that very contradiction. Indeed, until Pope Paul was elected Pontiff, the Papacy had been dominated by Italians for several centuries. Christian leadership on a world scale was an exercise in estrangement and Eurocentrism.

It is against this broader background that we can understand why it is that in Christian churches in Africa today there is readiness for linguistic accommodation and compromise, acceptance of foreign languages as media of communication with the Almighty. Where would European Christians be if they could not communicate with God in languages other than those used by either Jesus or his Apostles or the writers of the Gospels?

On the other hand, the Abode of Islam could rightly take pride in an official language, bequeathed in entirety across the centuries from the pulpit of Muhammad himself. Indeed, the Qur'an has been the greatest stabilizing factor behind the Arabic language itself, preventing literary Arabic from too drastic a departure from the style of the Qur'an.

It is a major principle of Islam that the Qur'an cannot be imitated. This is the doctrine of the Qur'anic inimitability. And yet, by a curious twist of fate, no book in human history has served as a greater model of imitation than the Qur'an has done to Arabic literature throughout the ages.

It is against this wider background of principles of authenticity and linguistic uniqueness that we have to understand why in the mosques of Black Africa, from Dakar to Dar es Salaam, the Arabic language has been permitted to reign supreme in spite of the fact that the majority of the congregation do not understand it. It is the official language of Muslim communication with God. But that is because it is also the authentic language of Islam's communication with its own ancestry, its own dawn.

But why is it that the religion which is linguistically monopolistic should at the same time be more tolerant on a wider scale? Why should Africans, on the one hand, be expected to pray to God in the Arabic language, and on the other hand be permitted to uphold female circumcision and the use of the drum in at least certain areas of worship?

This in turn is related to the origins of Islam before the African phase. To begin with, Islam envisaged itself as being a fusion of three religions and ways of life—Judaism, Christianity and the religion fostered by the Prophet Muhammad. Islam's trinity was not a trinity of God but a trinity of religion—a linkage among the three most important Semitic religions, Judaism, Christianity and Islam. And so doctrinally, almost from the beginning Islam had the seeds of multiculturalism, an acceptance of at least three different peoples of the book—Jews, Christians, Muslims.

And then soon after the Prophet Muhammad's death in the year 632 A.D. Islam took on the challenge of non-Arab parts of the world. Islam conquered Syria in the year 636 A.D., Iraq in the year 637 A.D., Mesopotamia in the year 641 A.D., Egypt in the year 642 A.D. and Persia (or Iran) in the year 651 A.D. The twin processes of Arabization (bequeathing the Arabic language as a native language) and Islamization (bequeathing Islam as the official religion) got underway in most of these conquered territories. Indeed Syria, Iraq, Mesopotamia, and Egypt got Arabized linguistically as well as Islamized religiously. Persia (or Iran) got Islamized religiously but not Arabized in identity.

Arab imperialism fostered the spread of Islam beyond the Middle East. New religions had to face the Islamic challenge. Of course Zoroastrianism in Persia tried to fight off Islam, fled to some extent to India in the form of the future Parsees, and retained a small presence in Iran. Hinduism in India had to accommodate some Islamic presence, losing many followers to Islam, but retaining a Hindu majority. Christianity in Egypt and the rest of North Africa was on the defensive with the coming of Islam. Indeed, North Africa is one area where Christianity really suffered severe setbacks as a result of Islamic conquest. The bulk of North Africa was dis-Christianized permanently.

In a way the success of Islam against North Africa was more profound than the success of Christianity against Islam in Africa south of the Sahara. While Islam in North Africa earlier in history effectively replaced it as the dominant religion, Christianity south of the Sahara in the 19th and 20th centuries at best only arrested the spread of Islam and seldom replaced it altogether.

The origins of cultural accommodation in Islam go back not only to the conquests we referred to earlier but also to the shift quite early in Islam from the Umayyads in Damascus to the Abbasids in Baghdad. The Umayyad empire after the death of the Prophet was still primarily Arab. The ruler Muawiya assumed authority in the year 650 A.D. Islam was still an Arab democracy in essence, with power based on a federation of Arab tribes.

But then came the Abbasid revolution in Baghdad, and the consolidation of authority from the year 744 A.D. to the year 754. This was the period when the Arab factor in Islam had to confront the non-Arab factor in terms of a primordial social conscience. The question of the equality of Arab and non-Arab Muslims was put to its most direct test during the Abbasid Caliphate. The great division between Sunni Islam and Shiite Islam remained unresolved. Most Arabs are Sunni Muslims; most Shi'a Muslims are non-Arab. The stage was set for a sectarian divide which was to last the bulk of the remaining period of Islamic history.

But behind that very mixture of culture and orientation was a predisposition towards syncretism. Islam was ready to accommodate divergent customs and cultural orientations. Sometimes these new elements enriched Islam, quite fundamentally. Certainly the Persian contribution to the artistic and cultural wealth of Islam has been inestimable. Many of the stories of the Arabian Nights are really Persian or Iranian stories, rather than Arab legends. The Moghul Empire of India has also been a major enriching experience in Islamic history, Islamic architecture and Islamic art. After all, the Taj Mahal is one of the great architectural monuments to Islamic civilization.

It is against this background that we can say that Islam in Africa has been culturally accommodating, in spite of being linguistically monopolistic.

COMPARATIVE ORGANIZATION AND STRUCTURE

But there are other factors as to why Islam in Africa was less subject to acculturation and dis-Africanization. The fact that the Islamic religion is not under a formal priesthood, and not subject to formal structures of decision making, has been a major element in the cultural flexibility of Islam. There is no priestly hierarchy, no Vatican, in Islam's infrastructure. Much of the business of the religion has been completely decentralized. To that extent Islam, unlike Catholicism, does not have to look to a fountain-head of authority, to legitimize particular departures from mainstream ritual. The decentralization of Islam in terms of church organization has been a major element behind its accommodationist inclination.

This is really another irony in the history of the two religions. After all, Muhammad was to all intents and purposes a head of state when he died. Islam had become substantially centralized politically before its founder left the scene. Mecca and Medina constituted a tale of two cities, two capitals of a new and expanding civilization. A new political community had come into being, complete with its own juridical system under the Shari'a, a tax system based on the Islamic Zakat, a constitutional order based on Islamic theocracy. Muhammad died virtually as a head of state, presiding over a centralized social and political order.

And yet the same religion which produced a founder of Islamic centralism also produced an order of missionary decentralization. The priesthood was not formal or specialized. The missionary activity was neither organized nor institutionalized. The religion which had produced a centralized political order did not produce a centralized missionary order. Muslim missionaries had been disproportionately individual, informal and almost casual. I myself converted two or three followers of indigenous African religions to Islam.

Curiously enough, I bequeathed my name to them. Each of them began to have two fathers, biological and religious. I was their religious father. In one case, the man was older than me. He became Ramadhan, son of Ali (meaning myself) although I was at least a decade younger than him. Why was he named Ramadhan? Because, almost masochistically, he embraced Islam on the eve of the fasting month of Ramadhan. He therefore had to undergo the discipline and relative agonies of self-denial during the fasting month.

I named one of the other converts to Islam Hassan, after one of the grandsons of the Prophet who were martyred. I kept in relative contact with my religious offspring for as long as I remained in East Africa before my departure for higher studies in England. When I got lost in the new civilization of Huddersfield, Manchester, New York and Oxford, I lost all contact with my "children"—especially Ramadhan and Hassan. Indeed, they were my first "children". I had religious offspring before I ever had biological children.

During the same period I knew of an Indian missionary in Africa, a follower of the Aga Khan. He had taken a vow to convert at least a thousand Africans to Islam. Curiously enough, his ambition was not to create more followers of the Aga Khan in Africa. He realized that the majority of African Muslims were Sunni. The Aga Khan followers were a branch of Shiite Islam. In spite of the sectarian difference, the Indian missionary was dedicated to the conversion of a thousand Africans to Sunni Islam, avoiding the potential cleavage across the sectarian divide. The Aga Khan himself approved of this discriminating fastidity. Indeed, the Aga Khan had conferred upon his African missionary the title of *El'Afriqi*, meaning the One of Africa.

In general the most striking thing about proselytism in Islam is precisely its basically decentralized nature and its essentially informal characteristics. The religion which had produced a relatively centralized government seemed to be unwilling to produce formal centralized missionaries.

On the other hand, the religion which had produced the underdog on the cross, the man who could pronounce neither temporal legislation nor temporal taxation, the man who was tried by the laws of others, could at the same time inspire a relatively centralized church and a hierarchical system of authority. Christian denominations, especially Roman Catholic, Greek Orthodox, and to some extent Anglican, have been denominations of more centralized authority than anything within the missionary activity of Islam. Whatever may have happened in the 7th century in terms of Islamic centralization, Islam has become a religion of informal conversations with God. On the other hand, whatever may have happened in the crucifixion of Jesus and the denial of Christian power to the founder of the religion, Christianity has since become a language of cultural hegemony and a structure of church authority and hierarchy.

It is once again against this broad background that we have witnessed Islamic linguistic intolerance, on the one side, and Islamic cultural compromise, on the other. It is against the same background that we had witnessed the reverse phenomenon—Christian linguistic toleration, on the one side, and the narrow-minded Christian response to Africa's cultural customs, on the other.

But Christian missionary activity in Africa has always been prepared to dig its own secular grave. Christian schools in the African continent have been among the major carriers of secularism in the total African experience across generations. All Christian schools were simultaneously carriers of Western secular skills and values. The missionary schools taught mathematics as well as religious studies. Sometimes philosophy as well as catechism, social studies in the here and now as well theology about the hereafter. Young Christians like Kwame Nkrumah, products of missionary schools, once considered becoming actual priests—only to change their minds and become politicians with a rendezvous with history.

It is one additional irony of African history that Christianity, so often identified with European imperialism, should at the same time have produced so many African nationalists. The struggle against imperialism, as well as the struggle for imperialism, owes a good deal to the Christian impact upon Africa.

What all this means is that Christian missionary schools were ambivalent, while Muslim schools were single minded. Christian schools split allegiance between Western Christianity and Western secularism, whereas Muslim schools concentrated allegiance to Islam on its own. The schooling wing of Islam never undermined the belief structure of Muslims. But the schooling wing of Christianity often undermined religiosity through secularism.

In a sense this is the masochistic side of Christianity which goes along with its theme of estrangement. At least in Africa Christianity has come with a death wish, an orientation towards self-nullification. I suppose this is because by the time Western interests emerged in Africa, Western secularism was beginning to gain ascendancy over Western Christianity. The results from an African point of view was an African Christian masochism, promoting the Gospel by destroying it, inculcating faith by promoting secularism, creating a new religious order by building a new secular order. It has been one of the more bizarre orientations of religious history ever.

One result has been the remarkable irony that Christianity has been both an ally of colonization and a partner in liberation. African nationalists who are products of missionary education include not only Kwame Nkrumah of Ghana, but also Julius Nyerere of Tanzania, Kenneth Kaunda of Zambia and Robert Mugabe of Zimbabwe. Some of these missionary products have actually flirted with the possibility of going into the priesthood itself. It is one of the more remarkable features of African nationalism that some of the more dynamic nationalistic leaders should in the past have considered the priestly option, for better or worse.

The fear of the clock is still part of the general scene. The time of the pilgrimage to Mecca remains suitably predictable. The strand of the triple heritage is still discernible.

As for the actual distribution of Islam in Africa, the more deeply and historically durable is of course Arab Africa itself, which is highly Islamized. The significant minority in Egypt is religious, the Copts, whereas the significant minority in the Maghreb is linguistic, the Berbers.

Next to Arab Africa are those Black African societies which have a clear Muslim majority. These include such countries as Senegal, Mali, Guinea, Niger and Somalia.

Countries with Muslim plura'ities (where Muslims are the largest single group but not necessarily the majority) include Sierra Leone, Chad and perhaps Liberia.

African countries with approximately as many Muslims as Christians include Tanzania, Ethiopia and Nigeria.

African countries with Muslim minorities, who have sometimes produced the ruler of the nation, include Uganda and Gabon.

African countries with Muslim minorities without likely pretensions to power include Ghana, the Ivory Coast and Cameroon. It is conceivable that the Ivory Coast has a Muslim plurality but for the time being a Christian supremacy seems inevitable.

Christian countries are in reverse proportion. Christianity is definitely a minority religion in North Africa, and an ambivalent religion in Western and Eastern Africa and struggling to become a majority religion in Central and Southern Africa. One is not to be surprised if the presidents of such countries as Nigeria, Senegal, Mali, Somalia, Niger, Gabon, the Gambia, Sudan, Mauritania, as well as other sectors of African society are Muslim by affiliation or at least responsive to the call of Islam. But of course there are countries where Islam is over-shadowed by the Christian presence—countries like Ghana, Zambia, Zimbabwe, and much of the rest of Southern Africa. The distribution of the two semitic religions has been profoundly affected by the balance of rivalry between them across the generations.

TOWARDS AFRICANIZING NEW GODS

As a matter of fact, there are at least two main ways by which both Christianity and Islam have been Africanized. One is through relatively blind social forces at work across time, causing cultural mixture and sometimes synthesis. The other mode of Africanization is through a prophet or social reformer, intent on giving greater native meaning to the imported religions or seeking to close a cultural and psychological gap which Christianity and Islam have sometimes created in Africa.

So far we have discussed indigenization through blind social forces leading to cultural mixture. Let us now take a closer look at the phenomenon of indigenization through prophetic intervention and purposeful religious reform.

In the middle of the countryside in Central Africa, quite far from any major city, there stands a startling structure. It is a temple of the Kimbanguist religious movement, mainly based in Zaire. The founder of the movement was Simon Kimbangu. The Congo, as the country was then called, was still under Belgian rule when Simon Kimbangu began to challenge the white monopoly of religious leadership in the country. There were Congolese who were already framing the question in racial terms. If God wanted to communicate with the black races, would he have chosen the white man to serve as His messenger? Such worries have sometimes affected Christian Africans from generation to generation. But in the case of Simon Kimbangu's followers, the answer was at last clear. This prophet was at least African; this messenger was black.

But was this a case of merely Africanizing the messenger without necessarily Africanizing the message? Has the message of Jesus changed as a result of channelling it though Simon Kimbangu?

Although the symbol of the cross has not completely disappeared in the Kimbanguist church, it plays a significantly more modest role than it does in the rest of Christianity. Indeed, the huge Kimbanguist Temple at Nkamba has no cross within the building. To that extent the building is startlingly unChristian within.

But there is a theological reason for the low profile of the symbol of the cross in the Kimbanguist church. After all, the Almighty had always warned his people to beware of graven images and idolatry. A cross with an actual statuette of Jesus came pretty close to a graven image, according to Kimbanguist theology. But even a cross without a figure of Jesus should not be elevated too highly lest it becomes yet another version of the graven image, yet another form of idolatry.

The people from among whom the Kimbanguist church emerged were matrilineal, tracing descent through the mother. The matrilineal tendencies of the wider traditional society helped to enhance the role of women in the Kimbanguist church. Women in this church can become pastors and deacons. Debates in Europe and America about whether women can become priests had not even gathered momentum when the Kimbanguist church gave women a firmer role. Female pastors in the church are just an extension of the mother symbol in indigenous matrilineal culture. Indeed, female religious figures and reformers are more likely to emerge from indigenous traditions than from either orthodox Islam or European versions of Christianity. The range of major female religious reformers in Africa is from women in pre-colonial Ashanti to Alice Lenshina in colonial and post-colonial Zambia, leading her Lumpa Church.

Sometimes African women have shown enormous courage and readiness for martyrdom in defence of religious ideas. Way back in the year 1706 a woman in Central Africa was burnt at the stake holding her baby son. This was Donna Beatrice, otherwise known as Kimbaveta. She too was in the tradition of trying to Africanize Christianity. Some of the changes she espoused were quite fundamental, perhaps more fundamental than those of the Kimbanguist church. For example, she argued that many of the Apostles of Jesus were not Hebrew at all—they were Africans. She insisted that the Patron Saint of Portugal was an African. She argued that Jesus Christ never prohibited polygamy. But her most controversial assertion was that a virgin birth was not a monopoly of the mother of Jesus—that an

African woman was as capable, with God's help, of having a virgin birth as any woman in Bethlehem or Nazareth.

These were of course very radical assertions. And when Donna Beatrice tried to demonstrate the virgin birth theory by having a baby son of her own, it was almost too much for those converted to Europeanized versions of Christianity. The Portuguese missionaries and Portuguese officials advising the old Congo Kingdom set to work, persuading the converted rulers of the Kingdom to take action against this female messiah. And so she was burnt at the stake holding her son. Out of those ashes arose new movements struggling once again to narrow the gap between African cultural realities and Christian doctrine. One such movement, as we have indicated, is the one which Simon Kimbangu initiated.

Kimbangu himself was also a martyr. The Belgians arrested him after a while, again partly instigated by Western missionaries in the new Congo of the colonial period. Kimbangu spent almost as long in jail as Jesus Christ spent on earth. Kimbangu entered a series of Belgian cages when he was just a young man, and died more than three decades later at a relatively advanced age. His own martyrdom was not on the cross; it was in a cage.

Today the Kimbanguist Church in Central Africa claims some four million followers. It may not sound like many, but when you think about it, that is more followers than Jesus Christ had in the first three centuries of the Christian era.

What about efforts to Africanize Islam through prophetic intervention? In reality heretical prophets in African Islam have been relatively few and far between, partly because Islam has responded more readily to informal Africanization except on the issue of the language of worship. The recent case of Muhammadu Marwa, otherwise known as Maitatsine in Nigeria, is pertinent here. Though of Cameroonian origin, Maitatsine succeeded in arousing the enthusiasm of Nigerian Muslims in their hunger for an African prophet of Islam. In a sense the Maitatsine movement was a quest to dis-Arabize Islam. But the movement was paradoxically infused with the Jihad militancy. A number of violent eruptions between Maitatsine's followers and other Nigerian Muslims occurred in northern cities of the country, including one in 1980 which resulted in the death of the African prophet himself. Further confrontations with security forces occurred later on, including in the year 1984 when the Maitatsine zealots killed a police unit which went to investigate or arrest some of their followers. And a number of other policemen were subsequently killed when reinforcements arrived. A massacre of the zealots occurred later on when the tables were turned. The cost of prophetic Africanization of Islam in Nigeria has been exceptionally high.

It should be borne in mind that dis-Arabization of Islam is not necessarily the Africanization of Islam. One of the best organized movements in Muslim Africa is the Ahmadiyya sect, operating in both East and West Africa. The founder of the sect was Mirza Ghulam Ahmed of old India under the British Raj. Doctrinally the movement seems to uphold the position that the Prophet Muhammad of Arabia was the most important of God's prophets but not the last. This is a major departure from mainstream Islam which insists that Muhammad was both the greatest and the last of all the prophets.

The Ahmadiyya movement has quite extensive missionary activity in Africa. It is often bitterly opposed by Sunni Africans, who are the great majority in the continent. My own father wrote a number of passionate essays against the Ahmadiyya movement, and was constantly at loggerheads with the Indian-derived sect.

In East Africa the Ahmadiyya movement was also the first to translate in full the Qur'an into the Swahili language, the most widespread indigenous language in the continent. Again Sunni Muslims strongly reacted against the Ahmadiyya translation. My father as Chief Kadhi of Kenya once again took the leadership in this reaction. He started translating the Qur'an himself, and made some progress, but he never lived to complete the job. His fragment of the translation was published posthumously.

Later on, another Chief Kadhi of Kenya, Sheikh Abdullah Saleh Farsy, provided a more complete Qur'an in Kiswahili.

The central charge against the Ahmadiyya movement, which still commands many followers in Eastern and Western Africa, remains that of claiming the status of a new prophet after Muhammad. But the fact that the new prophet, Mirza Ghulam Ahmed, was an Indian attempted to shift the focus of Islam away from the Arabian peninsula. To that extent the Ahmadiyya movement has in part been an effort to dis-Arabize Islam to some limited extent, but not actually to Africanize it as yet. It has taken people like Maitatsine to embark upon a more complete attempt to Africanize Islam.

But not all Messianic African movements under Islam are necessarily heretical. Islam has a concept of the Mahdi, a renewer and reviver of religion, but not necessarily a full scale prophet in the technical Islamic sense itself. Perhaps the most famous and most enduring Mahdist movement has been in the Sudan. A substantial section of Northern Sudan was aroused in the 19th century against British penetration and to some extent against Egyptian overlordship. Again the movement took the form of the Jihad, and initiated military action against the foreign intruders. Gordon from Britain was killed in the Battle of Omdurman. The Mahdist movement has itself continued in more peaceful forms to the present day, but it has retained a considerable political orientation.

Less militant in the military sense have been the *Mourides* of Senegal, an Islamic brotherhood that grew out of the Qadiriyya movement of the Sufi branch of Islam. The *Mourides* came into being in the second half of the 19th century under the leadership of Amadou Bamba. Like the Mahdist movement in the Sudan, the Mourides were responding to an external threat. In the latter case it was the reaction to French imperialism and the social environment which resulted from French penetration.

Amadou Bamba acquired a widespread reputation of supernatural power and grace, a capacity to perform miracles in response to persecution by the French. A Mouride picture poster exists in the modern period. It shows Amadou Bamba jumping off the ship which was taking him to exile. He spread out his mat and prayed on the waves. The French guards had forbidden him to pray on board the ship. He bid the waves be tranquil so that he could pray on them.

Exile is itself a major Islamic institution. The Prophet Muhammad himself twelve centuries earlier had been forced into exile from the city of Mecca to the city of Medina. So important is this act of migration in Islam that the entire Islamic calendar begins not when Muhammad was born, nor when Muhammad first sensed revelation and became a prophet at the age of forty, nor indeed from the moment when Muhammad died. The entire Islamic calendar begins from the moment Muhammad migrated into exile. That is why the calendar is called the Hijra, the movement into exile. But the fundamental aspect of an Islamic exile is that there is a day of return, a day of religious conquest, a day of God's triumph. There was such a day when Muhammad returned to Mecca as military victor and political ruler.

A more recent illustration in Shiite Islam was the return of Ayatollah Khomeini from exile in France, to assume supremacy in a new revolutionary Iran after the fall of the Shah. Once again exile was temporary, sealed with the promise of ultimate triumph.

So indeed was the exile of Amadou Bamba of Senegal, as he tried to deal with a foreign conquering power. Bamba was neither as militaristic as the Mahdi in the Sudan nor as revolutionary as the Ayatollahs of Iran, but he alarmed the French enough to induce them to exile him twice for a total of twelve years.

There has indeed been a final triumph in some sense. Although Amadou Bamba was not an organizer, the movement grew around him. Some claim that up to three-quarters of the population of the country are now Mouride, though that estimate may be exaggerated. What is clear is that the Mouride movement has had a major impact on both the economy and the politics of Senegal. The capital of the brotherhood is Touba, a three-hour drive from Dakar, and founded by the brotherhood. The town is dominated by a giant mosque.

> The giant mosque is a towering symbol of Mouride unity and strength, a proof of the devotion of the Talibes [disciples] and of their capacity for hard work. The central minaret is 86 metres high (almost 300 feet), apparently the highest in Africa, and it is even provided with a . . . lift. There are four other minarets, fourteen domes and two ablution baths . . . The size of the building is most impressive, and in the flat-land around Touba surrounded by single-story dwellings, it seems all the more immense.[3]

Touba as a town is growing. A palace for the Khalifa-General or successor to Amadou Bamba is about to be completed. An Islamic university and a major Islamic library are also under construction. Touba has become virtually another Mecca to the Mouride Muslims of Senegal. Indeed, there are some who believe that a pilgrimage to Touba could, under certain circumstances, substitute for a pilgrimage to Mecca, but this is a heretical point of view. Certainly during the major festival of the Great Magal, now tending to be held in December every year, many thousands of people converge on this town, reminiscent of the early days of Mecca when the Muslim community was limited to the boundaries of the Arabian peninsula. The celebrations in Touba today are as spectacular as those of ancient Mecca (contemporary Mecca is even more overwhelming by the scale of the number of pilgrims, sometimes up to three million in a year). When the Khalifa-General appears at the Great Magal, all are silent. The African Khalifa has arrived. The spirit of Islam lives on in the Black World. But the struggle for further Africanization of the religion of the crescent continues.

CONCLUSION

Long before the religion of the crescent or the religion of the cross arrived on the African continent, Africa was at worship, its sons and daughters were at prayer. Indigenous religions had a concept of divinity which was decentralized. God is not in heaven, or on a throne, or necessarily in the shape of man (anthropomorphic). The concept which some indigenous Eastern Africans call *Jok* is primarily the process of being the essence of universal power, which inheres in life as a force in its own right. In indigenous religion, man was not created in the image of God; nor must God be conceived in the image

[3] D. B. Cruise O'Brien, *The Mourides of Senegal* (London: Oxford University Press, 1971).

of man. The universe and the force of life are all manifestations of God.

Totemism in Africa led to groups identifying themselves with objects or other animals. Clans among communities like the Baganda adopted totemic symbols which established a sense of continuity between nature and man. Indeed, many African belief systems still include the so-called animistic tendencies, which blur the distinction between man and nature, between the living and the dead, between the divine and human, between the natural and the supernatural. The belief systems of indigenous Africa did not assert a monopoly of the soul for the human species alone. Could a tree have a soul? Could a mountain have a soul? Could a river, in spite of its flow, retain a soul?

And then came Christianity and Islam with a greater focus on man as being in the image of God, and with a God often defined and described in the image of man. In the case of Christianity, God even had a begotten son.

Africa has both the oldest forms of Christianity, such as those of Egypt and Ethiopia, and some of the newest forms of Christianity, such as those of the Kimbanguists. But sometimes the balance of power has shifted. In Egypt Islam has dominated the Coptic Church. In Ethiopia the Coptic Church has dominated Islam. In Egypt Islam has been more hostile to the Pharaonic legacy of Ancient Egypt than Coptic Christianity has been. In Ethiopia both Christianity and Islam have accommodated three semitic religious practices. But all over Africa the processes of both synthesis and dissonance continue. Three visions of God seek to capture the soul of a continent.

PSYCHOANALYSIS AND RELIGIOUS HEALING: SIBLINGS OR STRANGERS?

SUDHIR KAKAR*

Traditionally, psychoanalysts have tended to view the conflict between religion and their own discipline in terms of an ultimate divide between a scientific and a pre- or non-scientific vision of human experiences. Equipped with a specific model of man's deepest motivations and a method of genetic analysis which uncovered them, early analysts, following Freud, felt confident in dissecting the various elements of the religious vision against an emerging psychoanalytic image of what constitutes a fulfilled human life.

Religious ideas, especially the Judeo-Christian cosmogonies which received the greatest attention from Freud (1927; 1930; 1939), became illusory wish-fulfillments, their strength derived from man's infantile helplessness in the face of overwhelming powers of nature and a threatening external world on the one hand and the child's ambivalent feelings towards a father who is both a source of protection and fear on the other. The religious attitude or feeling, which Freud called "oceanic", was interpreted as a regression to the infant's earliest state of unity with the mother and as the feeling of limitless narcissism pervading that blissful state when the individual ego was not yet separated from the world of objects (Freud, 1930).

Religious practices and rituals received an even more scathing treatment in being labelled with psychiatric diagnostic categories. Freud compared the practices of the devout to the self-imposed restrictions of the obsessional neurotic and the world of their religious belief to amentia, a state of blissful hallucinatory confusion (Freud, 1907; 1927). Franz Alexander (1931), applying psychoanalysis to stages of meditation in Buddhism, discerned in them successive

*Sudhir Kakar is a Senior Fellow at the Centre for the Study of Developing Societies in New Delhi, maintains a private psychoanalytic practice in New Delhi, and was a Member of the School of Social Sciences, Institute for Advanced Studies, at Princeton (1983–84). He presented this paper as a 75th Anniversary Lecture at the 1984 Annual Meeting of the American Academy of Religion.

clinical pictures of melancholia, catatonic ecstasy, apathy and schizo-
phrenic dementia. For him the Buddhist meditator attempted to
regress even further than in Freud's theory of "oceanic feeling" to a
condition of intra-uterine existence. Even today, the tendency among
psychoanalysts to move the religious world with the lever of psycho-
pathology has not completely disappeared. For instance, in a recent
study (Masson, 1980) much of Buddhism has been seen as a manic
defense against depression and the Hindu tantric's desire for stillness
traced to early fears of sexual excitement.

Many contemporary analysts, though admiring the boldness of the
pioneering generation in applying psychoanalytic models to social
and cultural phenomena, would wince at the reductionistic, "nothing-
but" approach of some of the early efforts. What they find especially
puzzling (and I know it puzzles me) is the harshness which marked
the analysis of religious expression and ideas. This harshness is
absent from psychoanalytic studies of other cultural phenomena, for
instance, of art. The respect accorded to art and the mixture of
benevolence and admiration with which artists are regarded in psychoanalytic writings, even while their underlying motivations are
being uncovered, are strikingly absent from most analytic treatments
of religion and the *homo religiosus*.

Here, I would only like to mention rather than discuss in detail
the possible reasons for the psychoanalytic antagonism toward religion in the early years of its establishment as a discipline. The
self-understanding of psychoanalysis as a science in the sense of
nineteenth-century positivism, with its roots going back to the ratio-
nalism of Enlightenment, was certainly one source of the hostility
against the religious world-views.

Another reason may lie in the historical evolution of the psychoanalytic method which arose at a time in the history of European
imagination when the older techniques of introspection and self-
interrogation which drew their sustenance from religion had largely
withered away. As George Steiner puts it, "It (psychoanalysis) provided a secular, though heavily mythological surrogate for an entire
range of introspective and elucidatory disciplines extending from
private meditation to the metaprivacies of the confessional" (257). It
then becomes understandable that during its fledgling years, psychoanalysis sought sharply to demarcate its boundaries and differentiate
its methods from comparable religious techniques which antedate it
so vastly in the history of human consciousness.

Yet another, third reason may well lie in the person of the founder
of psychoanalysis and his own complex relationship to the religion of
his fathers. Freud's identification with the Jewish religious tradition
as a child, the breaking up of the identification with the help of his

new psychology, and a return to religious tradition, now through the medium of his psychological writings, as an old man (Homans, 1984), need to be studied in detail if the relationship between psychoanalysis and religion is to be ever fully understood.

Freud's emphasis on the difference between the epistemological assertions of psychoanalysis and religion, his castigation of Judeo-Christian instructions and prohibitions, all of which led him to call religion the chief enemy of science (Freud, 1933) and thus implicitly of psychoanalysis, has masked the essential similarity between the two in what I consider to be their core function: healing. It is in healing, in what the *Oxford English Dictionary* defines as "to restore (a person, etc.) from some evil condition or affection (as sin, grief, disrepair, unwholesomeness, danger, destruction); to save, purify, cleanse, repair, mend", that I see the central expression of both psychoanalysis and religion. They are, then, rivals rather than enemies who, as I attempt to show below, use much the same processes and mechanisms of the psyche as they go about their pivotal concern. The example I take, that of a religious-mystical cult, is from India where the healing concern of religious activity and religious leaders— the *sadhus, swamis, matas, babas, maharajs, bhagwans*—is strikingly more apparent than in contemporary Western societies. In fact, I would speculate that at the beginning of this century when psychoanalysis was taking its place among the healing arts in Europe, the rivals of the new healers for the cure of hysterical and other neurotic disorders were not the unfeeling physicians and *Nervenaerzte* wrapped up in the coldness of their physiological theories, as has been depicted in the psychoanalytic lore. The rivals, I suspect, were to be found more in religious shrines, cults and faith healers of various kinds living at the fringes of the orthodox churches.

The Radhasoami Sect

The historical beginning of the Radhasoami Sect can be dated to 1861 when the mystic Shiv Dayal Singh or Soamiji as he is known among the members of the sect established an organization with that name in the city of Agra. Somaiji's new sect was very much in the mainstream of Indian devotional mysticism as expounded by such venerated medieval saints as Kabir and Nanak, the founder of the Sikh faith. The two main pillars of the cult are guru *bhakti*—the devotion to the guru—and a particular kind of mystical discipline known as *surat shabad yoga*—literally, the joining (*yoga*) of the spirit or soul entity (*surat*) with the Divine Sound or Word (*shabad*). According to the tenets of the Radha Soami cult, with proper guru *bhakti* and the practice of *surat shabad yoga* the individual soul can become attached to the sound current which pulls it up through the various "mansions of the soul" till it reaches the highest realm of consciousness.

In practice, in the lives of a vast majority of the sect members, the meditational regimen of the *yoga* takes a secondary place to guru *bhakti* which is not a matter of mere intellectual acceptance and respect for the guru as a teacher or guide. For one, the guru referred to is the *Satguru* ("True Master") who is the "embodiment of the divine and is in fact the Supreme Being himself". A *Satguru* can take his devotee to the highest realm where the disciple is redeemed from the cycles of birth, life and death.

The idea of the Satguru and the need to achieve a complete surrender and develop an intense love for him are the patrimony of many medieval Hindu saints, as also of the Muslim mystics, who have highlighted the emotional and ecstatic aspects of the devotees' surrender. Another notion connected with the Radha Soami institution of *Satguru* is the importance placed on *Satsang* ("True Association") where devotees congregate in the holy service conducted by or under the authority of the *Satguru* and where they can partake of the guru's presence (*darshan*) in person or through a large photograph that presides over the meeting.

I attended my first *Satsang* at Beas, a small township in Punjab and the headquarters of the sect, on the feast day of the founder. On this particular December day, the congregation was especially large, numbering well over fifty thousand. Swaddled in rough woollen blankets and huddling close together for warmth, the crowd was impressive in its silent orderliness.

As I made my way through the patiently squatting men—the women were sitting on the other side—my strongest impression was of a pervasive friendliness, bubbling over into welcoming smiles and the low-murmured cultic greeting of "Radha Soami!" While we waited for Maharajji, as the *Satguru* of the sect is called, we sang. The mellifluous voice of a *panthi*—the chanter of scriptures—drifted out of the loudspeakers strung out on the grounds as he sang of man's spiritual longing for *Satguru*. The crowd joined in the refrain at the end of each familiar and well-loved verse, fifty thousand voices merging into one deep-throated chant. To anyone sitting within the vast belly of the crowd, a choir of fifty thousand feels like an elemental sound of nature—of high wind and torrential rain which has been shaped into a musical pattern. Here I am deliberately emphasizing my subjective experience of the Satsang, on this day as on the following days, and the fantasies that bubble up to the forefront of consciousness as one sits ensconced in the warmth and closeness of thousands of bodies. At first there is a sense of unease as the body, the container of our individuality and the demarcator of our spatial boundaries, is sharply wrenched away from its habitual mode of experiencing others. Distances and differences—of status, age and sex—disappear in the fierce press of other bodies in an exhilarating feeling (temporary to be sure) that individual boundaries can indeed be transcended and were perhaps illusory in the first place. Of course, touch is only one of the sensual stimuli that hammers at the gate of individual identity. Other excitations, channelled through vision, hearing and smell, as also the more subliminal exchanges of body heat, muscle tension and body rhythms, are very much involved (Greenacre, 1972). In short, a friendly crowd's invitation to a psychological regression—in which the image of one's body becomes fluid and increasingly blurred, controls over emotions and impulses are weakened, critical faculties and rational thought processes are abandoned—is extended in a way that is both forceful and seductive.

It was in such a mild state of "altered consciousness", pervaded with a feeling of oneness and affection for every member of the congregation, that I waited for Maharajji to appear at the high podium from where he would hold the Satsang. A majestic figure with a long white beard and neatly tied white turban covering his head, Maharajji that day was dressed in cream colored robes with a beige shawl wrapped around his shoulders. With a brisk tread belying his sixty-three years, Maharajji mounted the podium and sat down cross-legged on the chair, pulling the microphone in front of him closer. The silence continued, broken occasionally by a cough, while Maharajji sat there impassively, slowly turning his head from one side to the other in a wide sweep, surveying his flock from under bushy white eyebrows and through slightly hooded eyes.

The people around me were transfixed, overwhelmed by the presence of the Satguru who to a Satsangi is God made flesh, divine made human. This was *darshan*, "viewing" in its most intense form. There were tears of emotion running down the cheek of the middle-aged man sitting next to me, merging with drops of saliva dribbling out of the corner of his mouth, and I had the distinct feeling that my neighbours were visually feasting on Maharajji's face.

Maharajji finally cleared his throat and began to talk. His voice was soft and low, the tone intimate, the diction full of assurance and easy authority. The contents of his discourse, which lasted for more than an hour and which he repeats at all Satsangs, are familiar from many mystical traditions, Indian as well of other societies. To list some of these repetitive elements: there is the derogation of the perceived real world and an emphasis on its painful, withholding nature; there is the suggestion of mystical withdrawal as a solution to the individual's psychic needs and life problems; there is the offer of the sect's system of psychological and physiological practices by which a person can deliberately and voluntarily seek detachment from the everyday external world and replace it with a heightened awareness of inner reality.

Emotionally, to an Indian, the familiarity of the message, repeated often enough since the beginning of childhood, constitutes its greatest strength and attraction. Once again the men and women were transported to the time when their small hands clutched in those of older family members, they had sat up late into the night, in the midst of a group of neighbours and kinsmen, sleepily listening to wandering *religiosi* expound the mysteries of life. It was familiar from the many after-death ceremonies where they had listened to the priest and the family elders talk of the laws of karma, the cycles of birth, life and death and the mukti or liberation that was every being's goal. Maharajji's talk was then a murmur from the past—both individual and collective—that had suddenly become audible.

In meetings with smaller and more intimate groups, Maharajji rarely speaks and confines himself to *darshan*. The *darshan* itself does not take too much time. Without any preliminaries, he looks steadily for a couple of minutes at one section of his small audience, regally turns his face and stares unblinkingly at another section—a virtuoso use of look and silence. The transformation of the disciples' faces as their eyes look into his is remarkable. The eyes glaze over as they drink in his visage. Visibly, their brows smoothen out, the jaw muscles slacken and a beatific expression slowly spreads on their faces. The whole transformation is startlingly similar to that of the nursing infant when he takes the breast into his mouth and the milk begins to spread its soothing warmth, generating those good feelings that gradually obliterate all the earlier unease, the tension and the plain anxiousness.

Radhasoami teachings lay a great stress on the mutual viewing in *darshan*, the locking of glances between the guru and the devotee, as a precondition for the devotee's salvation. Dreams and visions of the guru are common and are regarded as signs of grace while it is believed that at the time of death, a true devotee will once again have the guru's *darshan*. The viewing in large congregations is no hindrance since each devotee experiences the guru as gazing at him personally. "We join glances as I stand facing him", says the poet devotee and "Satguru casts on me the glance of compassion." It is the *daya-dirshti*, the glance of compassion and benevolence, which enables the cult member to achieve his spiritual goals and, for us, is also essential in the restoration of his psychic well-being.

In my interviews with the Satsangis (Kakar, 1982), I found that many of them shared a common pattern in their lives that had led them to a search for the guru and to initiation in the Radha Soami cult.

Almost invariably the individual had gone through one or more experiences that had severely mauled his sense of self-worth, if not shattered it completely. In contrast to the rest of us, who must also deal with the painful feelings aroused by temporary depletion in self-esteem, it seems that those who came to the Radha Soami cult grappled with these feelings for a much longer time, sometimes for many years, without being able to change them appreciably. They had been on the lookout for someone, somewhere, to end a persistent and painful internal state. This "someone" eventually turned out to be Maharajji and the "somewhere" the Satsang at Beas, to which the seekers were led by events—such as a vision of Maharajji—which in retrospect seemed miraculous. Perhaps a few vignettes from life histories will illustrate this pattern more concretely.

K. was a fifty year old woman from a rich business family who had been deserted by her husband when she was thirty-five. She did not remarry and, unable to "plant another garden of love" around her, she had busied herself with the running of the household (which in any case was efficiently managed by the servants) and with her grown-up children, who needed her less and less. Gradually, she lost whatever interest she had been able to summon up in life after the shock of her husband's desertion. She attended a couple of Satsangs, heard Maharajji speak and was deeply impressed though she did not take the initiation. One day, sitting alone in a hotel room in a strange city, she was overwhelmed by the hopelessness of her situation and felt that she had come to the end of her tether. She had closed her eyes in utter weariness, she says, when she felt Maharajji's presence in the room and had the distinct sensation of a hand squeezing her shoulder like that of a kind father. She says she knew at that moment that if she went to Maharajji for protection all her problems would be resolved.

H. was the youngest of four sons in a Sikh peasant family who had tilled their own land for many generations. As the "baby" of the family, H. had been much indulged during childhood, especially by his mother. She had died when he was eighteen and ever since her death, he said, a peculiar *udasinta* (sadness) had taken possession of his soul. Though he had all the comforts at home, enough to eat and drink and an abundant measure of affection from his father and elder brothers, the *udasinta* had persisted. For fifteen long years, he said, his soul remained restless, yearning for an unattainable peace. His thoughts often dwelt upon death, of which he developed an exaggerated fear, and he was subject to crippling headaches that confined him to the darkness of his room for long periods. Then, suddenly last year, he had a vision in a dream of Maharajji (he had seen his photograph in a Satsangi home in his village), who told him to come to Beas and take initiation. He had done so. The *udasinta* disappeared, as did his fear and headaches, and he felt the loving omnipresence of the Master as a protection against their return. I may add here that depressions and depressive disorders seem to play a significant role in the life histories of many members of the other mystical cults I studied.

Initiation into the Radha Soami cult undoubtedly restored a sense of well-being to many whose emotional lives had been marked by starkly depressive features. Psychoanalytically speaking, the healing takes place through the establishment of a massive unconscious identification with and an internalization of the idealized guru. The cult's group activities such as the Satsang, its philosophy as expounded in the cultic literature, by senior disciples and by the guru himself in his discourses, all propel idealization to its culminating point, where the guru can be experienced as a powerful, utterly compassionate, omnipresent inner object. The guru himself actively drives these processes forward. In his discourses, Maharajji, for instance, emphasizes his dependability and his assumption of total responsibility for the disciple's welfare throughout eternity. To the disciple's feeling of insignificance he offers his omnipotence and miraculous powers. To the disciple's feeling of crippling inertness, Maharajji offers his energy: "We are in a deep, deep sleep. We are all dead. We need somebody to put life into us. We need somebody to give us that eye with which we can see inside, we need somebody to give us that ear through which we have to hear, somebody to give us that living water by which we have to come back to life again, from death." To the disciple's feeling of limitation and circumscription he offers his all-pervasive presence.

Identification with and internalization of the guru is also fostered by the cult's philosophy and practices prescribed for the initiated member. The disciple must strive for a oneness with the Master which, the guru assures him, is vital for his rebirth and reemergence. As a poem by Kabir (which I heard often at Beas) puts it:

> When I was there, then the Master was absent
> When the Master was there, then I was not
> The lane of love is narrow,
> There is room only for one.

Even the daily meditative practice of the *surat shabad yoga*, with Maharajji's face as the prescribed object of meditation, further cements the internalization of the guru since he is daily experienced as the benevolent protection against the anxieties that arise during the meditative process. These anxieties may well have to do, as Shafii (1973) has suggested, with the re-experiencing, on a silent and non-verbal level, of the minute traumas of the separation and individuation phase of early childhood.

This model of healing, through an internalization of an ideal healer who also represents the values of the patient's cultural and religious tradition, is necessarily foreign to the therapeutic model of traditional psychoanalysis based on drive psychology. The patient's illness in this model is due to an inner conflict because for one reason or other the aims of infantile impulses, arising from sexual and aggressive drives, have not been adequately subordinated to the ego's domination. Psychoanalysis heals by making the infantile aims and the defenses used against them conscious and thus replaying old conflicts under the watchful eye of the adult ego. Though the analysis may be experienced as beneficial in cathartic or supportive ways, knowledge and insight alone are curative as they make the unconscious conscious. In other words, psychoanalytic cure only takes place once conscious choice replaces unconscious defense and the ego is strengthened against infantile drive demands. Religious healing and classical psychoanalytic therapy are thus, inevitably, wary strangers.

The picture, however, changes if one looks at some significant innovations within psychoanalysis of the last thirty years. Though the innovators—Klein and Fairbairn, Mahler and Jacobson, Erikson and Kohut, to mention only a few names—differ considerably among themselves and on the relationship of their theories to the classical drive psychology model, they share a common focus in that they highlight the "relational" rather than the biologically based drive as the prime motivation of human existence. In Margaret Mahler's vision of the conflicts of childhood, for instance, the child is less a creature struggling with the demands of his instinctual drives and more a person torn between a powerful push for independent and autonomous functioning and an equally strong pull toward surrender and a reimmersion in the enveloping maternal fusion from which he has just emerged.

"For the relational theorist," as Greenberg and Mitchell (1983) put it, "all people struggle to establish and maintain relationships with other people, from their earliest efforts to reach their parents to their current efforts to consolidate safe and meaningful intimate relationships in their adult lives. Clinical work is filled with other people, these analysts argue: parents who are unavailable, who have to be shared with siblings, who can never provide the attention desired" (404). For the more relational oriented analysts, images of oneself in relation to significant others, fantasies of oneself and of ideal others, internal voices born in real and imagined experiences, are the stuff of the self. In other words, crucial exchanges, in reality or in fantasy, with significant others in one's life are internalized and shape subsequent perceptions, attitudes and behaviour. Thus disorders of the self in these models are primarily disorders of internalized relationships—deficiencies and failures of a facilitating environment as Winnicott would put it.

Similar to the supreme importance of the guru-disciple relationship in religious healing, the quality of the analytic relationship is fundamental for cure in these approaches. Like the guru, the analyst in the relational models needs to be experienced and internalized as a real, benign figure who is different from the patient's bad internal objects or the rejected parts of his self. Without going so far as the guru who actively encourages the process of idealization, the analyst at least allows himself to be idealised by the patient as he enters the patient's closed world of archaic and destructive object relationships in order to open it to new relational possibilities. The analyst's engagement is vital, his interpretations are as much acts of empathy (which is therapeutic by and in itself) as they are communications of knowledge. Like the guru with his talk of rebirth for the disciple, the analyst too provides a kind of developmental second chance, the transmuting internalization of the analytic relationship building the core of a "new" and compensating structure of the self (Kohut, 1977). The guru-healer of the religious tradition and the analyst of the newer relational approaches are therefore certainly not strangers but siblings, with recognizable features of a common ancestry in development of the self as a locus of relationships.

For the relational theorist, the silent looking of *darshan*, the most important form of interaction between the guru and the disciple, the chief healing technique if one would like, has a meaning other than the one it possesses for the classical psychoanalyst. Traditionally, the understanding of the self and an insight into its workings in the analytic situation is through verbalization. Words are the carriers of the knowledge that heals. Silence and quiescence are often interpreted as resistance, defensive inhibition, or an ego disturbance of a shorter or longer duration (Shafii, 1973). In the other analytic model, where the avoidance of a sense of estrangement and abandonment is deemed to be one of the primary motivational thrusts in the individual, the identity giving powers of the eyes that *recognise* are at least as crucial, if not more, as the words that explain and integrate diffuse experience. In the silent affirmation of *darshan,* the individual reexperiences the caretaker of his "prehistoric" era, of the time before speech and verbal meaning, and the mutuality of their recognition which Erikson (1976) calls "the first knowledge, the first verification and thus the basis of hope". The *darshan,* in deepening the bond with the guru and in its brief but regular fulfillment of the profound human need for mutual affirmation, is therefore truly charged with the therapeutic power of what Erikson terms the *numinous,* the sense of hallowed presence, which pervades man's first and dimmest affirmation (Erikson, 1976). Psychoanalysts thus may be going astray in their misplaced emphasis on the "oceanic feeling" produced by Yoga, Zen and other Eastern practices as the chief attraction of what is loosely called mysticism. In the real world of mystical cults, the attractions of "mysticism" for a vast majority of the members seem to lie in the deeply healing relationship with the guru rather than in any promises held out by esoteric psycho-physiological practices associated with a particular cult.

The effectiveness of *darshan* as a therapeutic technique is of course immeasurably enhanced by the Indian cultural symbol system. Hindus, it has been observed, not only want to see their deities but want to be seen by them (Babb, 1981). Perhaps nothing indicates this more clearly than the iconographic importance given to the eyes. Even the crudest representations of a god or a goddess, a flat stone slab, a stone pillar as a *lingam*, are likely to have eyes painted on them even if all the other facial features are absent. Eyes, moreover, are associated with the life (and I would add, life-giving and life-affirming power) of the image. The consecration of the idol takes place, in part, through the creation or opening of its eyes (Eck, 1981). The image is infused with divinity, becomes a deity to be worshipped when it can *see* its worshippers. The eyes of the gurus who are the living deities are frequently accentuated in photoiconography as well as in accounts of their followers where they single out a disciple, light on him.

Similarly, I suggest, the silence of the *darshan* and the quiescence of the meditative practice prescribed by a particular mystical sect are reinforced in a positive fashion by the caretaking patterns of the culture. In most Western societies, a large part of reassurance against the separation anxiety of childhood is provided by the mother's voice, for instance, at bed time. Sleep itself means darkness, silence and—in most middle class sleeping arrangements—separation from the mother so that silence becomes associated with the fear of her absence. In India, on the other hand, the child is almost constantly carried on the mother's body and sleeps at night with the mother in the same bed. Silence and quiescence may well be associated with the mother's presence and a union with the deep rhythms of her body.

The symbolic system of the culture in which religious healing is enveloped and which propels the healing process may often appear as bizarre or incomprehensible to the alien observer. Yet the cultural garb should not obscure the fact that perhaps the central healing mechanism, the relationship between the patient and the healer, with the *guru* in our specific case, is common across cultures and therapies. It is, after all, based on what evolution has created: human development embedded in a web of human connectedness.

WORKS CONSULTED

Alexander, F.
1931   "Buddhistic Training as an Artificial Catatonia." *Psycho-analysis* 19: 129–145.

Babb, L. A.
1981   "Glancing: Visual Interaction in Hinduism." *Journal of Anthropological Research* 37: 387–401.

Eck, D.
1981   *Darsan: Seeing the Divine Image in India.* Chambers-berg, Pa.: Anima Books.

Erikson, E. H.
1976   *Toys and Reasons.* New York: W. W. Norton.

Freud, S.
1907   *Obsessive Acts and Religious Practices.* Standard Edition, 9. London: The Hogarth Press.
1927   *The Future of an Illusion.* Standard Edition, 21. London: The Hogarth Press.
1930   *Divilization and its Discontents.* Standard Edition, 21. London: The Hogarth Press.
1933   *New Introductory Lectures on Psycho-Analysis.* Standard Edition, 22. London: The Hogarth Press.
1939   *Moses and Monotheism.* Standard Edition, 23. London: The Hogarth Press.

Greenacre, P.
1972   "Crowds and Crisis." *The Psychoanalytic Study of the Child* 27: 136–155.

Greenberg, J. R. & Mitchell, S. A.
1983   *Object Relations in Psychoanalytic Theory.* Cambridge, Mass.: Harvard University Press.

Homans, P.
1984   "Once Again, Psychoanalysis East and West: A Psycho-analytic Essay on Religion, Mourning, and Healing." *History of Religions* 24: 133–154.

Kakar, S.
1982   *Shamans, Mystics and Doctors.* New York: Alfred Knopf.

Kohut, H.
  1977   *The Analysis of the Self.* New York: International Universities Press.

Masson, J. M.
  1980   *The Oceanic Feeling: The Origins of Religious Sentiments in Ancient India.* Dordrecht: D. Reidel.

Shafi, M.
  1973   "Silence in Service of the Ego." *International Journal of Psychoanalysis* 54: 431–443.

Steiner, G.
  1976   "A Note on Language and Psychoanalysis." *International Review of Psychoanalysis* 3: 253–258.

COMING AND GOING: THE AGENDA OF AN ANNIVERSARY

LEO J. O'DONOVAN, S.J.*

Gathering between December 8 and 11, 1984, at the commodious old Palmer House in Chicago, the American Academy of Religion and the Society of Biblical Literature had in many ways their most successful Annual Meeting to date. In their regular joint meetings each year since 1971, our two societies have drawn a smaller attendance than do conventions of political scientists or philosophers, not to mention the Modern Language Association. Still, almost 4,000 scholars and students crowded the Palmer House and overflowed into adjoining hotels last December, an increase of 700 over the largest previous meeting (3,200 at the New York Hilton in 1982). In a year when religion and politics was a major topic in the presidential election, such an assembly deserves attention not only for its importance to American education but also for its possible significance to civil society at large. Cultural and religious issues that appeared in Campaign '84 may have deeper roots and likelihood of growth than the electoral machine could allow to appear.

The SBL celebrated its 100th anniversary at the joint convention held at Dallas in 1980, while 1984 marked the AAR's 75th anniversary year. Devoted to critical study of the classical biblical literatures, the older society supports the various disciplines—ancient languages, textual criticism, history, and archaeology—concerned with the literatures and religions of the ancient Near Eastern and Mediterranean regions. Our own younger society, a more sprawling and diversified organization, currently numbers some 5,222 members (990 of which are institutional members and 1,186 of whom also belong to SBL) who are engaged in the study of religion at private and state universities,

*Professor of Systematic Theology at Weston School of Theology (Cambridge, Massachusetts), Visiting Fellow at Woodstock Theological Centre (Georgetown University, 1984–85), Past President of the Catholic Theological Society of America, Chair of the AAR Program Section on Theology and Religious Reflection (1982–), Dr. O'Donovan was commissioned by the Editor to write this overview of the 75th Anniversary Annual Meeting of the American Academy of Religion.

colleges, seminaries and divinity schools. The annual meeting of the two societies usually comprises about 55% AAR and 45% SBL members. In view of the AAR's 75th Anniversary celebration, and also considering that our members are typically (though not uniquely) concerned with a wider range of topics that bear on religion in society today, I shall concentrate here on the AAR part of the Chicago program.

While the Academy's Board of Directors was meeting in the Loop, William J. McCready, program director of the National Opinion Research Center at the University of Chicago, was elsewhere in the city presenting an analysis of American religious attitudes and values to a group of philanthropists. Dr. McCready noted a strong perdurance of religious feeling in the nation accompanied by a decisive shift away from its primary expression in organized religion. For an increasing number of people, a search for basic meaning in life has supplanted obedience to religious authority as the central religious experience. Such a shift belies the frequently expressed view that our culture is entering a postreligious age. The culture may be postmodern, but it is by no means necessarily postreligious, as Harvey Cox and Richard John Neuhaus have also argued from quite different points on the ideological spectrum. A significant reshaping of traditional American religiosity seems to be taking place, a transformation that may be interpreted as maximizing the values of freedom, conscience and personal association. "The transition is not from authority to anarchy but to conscience," McCready said. This view of our current religious situation, however, should not encourage complacency among religionists. No turn to conscience is without its cost. If a new appropriation of faith is under way in the United States, we shall need guidance in understanding the experience and courage in learning how it may be socially constructive. The American Academy of Religion is, of course, the largest single professional association for students of religion who might contribute to meeting this need.

ORIGINS

In 1909 the founders of the AAR had more modest but quite specific goals. In that year Prof. Ismar J. Peritz of Syracuse University, a German-born convert to Christianity, convened his colleagues Irving Wood (Smith College), Raymond C. Knox (Columbia University), and Olive Dutcher (Mount Holyoke College), to generate the "Association of Biblical Instructors in American Colleges and Secondary School." Four goals were clearly stated: to exchange the results of scholarship, to increase the standards of research, to develop fellowship among colleagues, and to promote publication in the field. (The delicacy of the age would not have mentioned providing an opportunity to hire new faculty, even had that been an early concern.) The Association began yearly meetings in 1910 and in December 1922 changed its name to the National Association of Biblical Instructors (NABI, its acronym, being also the Hebrew word for *prophet*). Due largely to Prof. Peritz's insistent suggestion, the *Journal of the NABI* began to appear biannually in 1933. Renamed the *Journal of Bible and Religion* in 1937, it then became a quarterly.

Over the years, as the organization grew in breadth and representation, there was concern to express its identity more adequately. In December 1963, following the recommendation of a self-study committee which had been supported by a grant from the Danforth Foundation, the name was changed to the American Academy of Religion. "American" was to indicate the inclusion of members from Canada, the United States and Mexico; "Academy" served to indicate that all levels of academic rank (not merely instructors) were involved; and "Religion" was considered more comprehensive than any other available term. In previous years, the central reality defining the association had been the Bible; the symbol of Scripture had seemed easily and comprehensively to fit the temper of religious studies in America, "the nation with the soul of a Church," as Sidney Mead has called us. But gradually a broader, more objective and intercultural perspective on religion had begun to emerge, an approach already in fact proposed as early as 1902 by Morris Jastrow, Jr.'s *The Study of Religion*. For all its continuity with the past, then, the newly named AAR of the mid-60's moved rather typically, as Charles H. Long observed at the 75th Anniversary banquet, "from the clarity of the Book to the chaos of discourse about religion."

The NABI Self-Study Committee of 1963 helped to establish an agenda for twenty years. In 1966 the name of the association's publication was changed to the *Journal of the American Academy of Religion*. A pattern of smaller regional meetings coupled with the national Annual Meeting was firmly established. Drawing on the experience of shared meetings in 1964 and 1965, the larger stepchild began in 1971 at Atlanta to gather jointly with its parent organization SBL. In 1972 this combined meeting became the unprecedented International Congress of Learned Societies in the Field of Religion, which almost burst the seams of Los Angeles' gleaming Century Plaza Hotel. Scholars Press had been founded at the University of Montana (which also hosted the national offices of SBL and the editorial offices of *JAAR*) and was regularly publishing AAR series and individual titles. An ever growing number of scholars and their graduate students were participating in the Academy's meetings and reading its publications, and the Academy could now state its purpose quite simply: "to stimulate scholarship, foster research, and promote learning in the complex of disciplines that constitutes religion as a field of inquiry."

But larger meetings and more numerous publications do not guarantee the quality and critical contribution that many members of the Academy desired. Accordingly, in preparation for the 1984 Annual Meeting, the Executive Director, James Wiggins, obtained a grant from the Lilly Endowment and the Board of Directors created a Task Force on Governance and Development. One result of this self-evaluation will be seen in a series of new standing committees—on education, on long-range planning and development, on research (now separated from publications)—committees intended to help carry the Academy's goals forward in a reinvigorated way. A program to honor excellence in scholarly publication has also been instituted, with awards designated in three categories: constructive reflective thought, historical studies, and analytic or descriptive texts. President Ray L. Hart secured grants from the Henry Luce Foundation and the Exxon Education Foundation to assist in the planning for and execution of the anniversary meeting, whose rich program proved a powerful stimulus for the new agenda and at the same time gave a general indication of the disciplinary challenges which have emerged for the scientific study of religion today.

CELEBRATION

The 1984 meeting itself was arranged according to the usual pattern of plenary sessions and various smaller sections, groups and consultations. It also featured an outstanding series of 75th Anniversary lectures. The banquet celebrated previous officers of the Academy and, in a special way, our incomparable historian of religions, Mircea Eliade, in whose honor a quartet for piano, oboe, violin and cello was commissioned from Frank Burch Brown and an original sculpture from Isamu Noguchi. The implied theme holding the overall program together was at once retrospective and prospective, an historical evaluation of where we've been in religious studies and where we might be going. As such, the program represented so many exercises of imagination recalling the past and rendering the present in order to take stock of religion's relation to culture.

In this welter of arrangements and wealth of scholarship, of course, one can name but a few of the speakers and topics that addressed the Academy's renewed agenda. The energy and commitment of Prof. Ray L. Hart of the University of Montana at Missoula shaped the meeting more than any other person or committee of persons. In his presidential address he pointed to the de-constructing incursion of negation, or the "not," into our thought and experience and insisted on its paradoxical importance for a specific grasp of human existence.

A hushed and moving plenary session by Paul Ricoeur meditated on the challenge suffering and evil pose to philosophy and religion. Tracing the permutations of the problem from the earliest mythic and biblical approaches to the later stage of theodicy in European philosophy, Ricoeur suggested that current views generally surrender the ambition to explain suffering theoretically and address instead the task of redressing it wherever possible. But Langdon Gilkey gave perhaps the most comprehensive diagnosis of our current religious situation. With ringing urgency he contrasted the quest for transcendence in an age of anxiety, on the one hand, and, on the other, emerging forms of idolatry expressed in the rise of unconditional nationalism, the new Religious Right, and the religion of nuclearism. These latter developments suggest the threat of heteronomy and absolutism; they are also strangely accompanied by a new experience of relativity borne in on Western consciousness through its encounter with the great world religions and, even more, the plurality of world cultures. Such a situation calls for "a relativized theology," Gilkey argued, one which can learn to find the absolute dialectically in the relative, the infinite in the finite. To seek God, in other words, in all things—and only there.

Many speakers clearly aimed to contexualize their theology or religious analysis; they emphasized that one discovers the genuine religious promise of texts and experiences and events only by entering into their particularity. The more theology is pursued in context, recognizing its local situation and limits, the better it can assure a relative but real responsibility for religion and culture on a global scale. Only a truly local theology can hope also to be global, making its own real contribution towards a shared, more human future. The international dimension of religious studies had certainly been a concern of the meeting from the start and distinguished scholars from abroad had been invited to address it: Fritz Buri from Switzerland, Sudhir Kakar from India, Philip Shen from Hong Kong, Eduardo Matos Moctezuma from Mexico, Ali Mazrui from Africa, Gustavo Gutiérrez from Peru. But our own national neglect of opportunity had been addressed even before any of the visitors shared their horizons with us: William Bennett, formerly Chairman of the National Endowment for the Humanities and now Secretary of Education, tantalized the audience of the first plenary session with his lecture on "Relentless Suboptimization and the Art of Soulcraft."

In various forms art figured largely in the proceedings. John Dillenberger, newly elected Vice-President of the Academy who will become its President in 1986–87, spoke on "Theological Method and the Artistic Mode: Theology, the Arts, and the Visual Arts." The renowned literary critics Northrup Frye and Wayne Booth each gave major presentations. Frye proposed metaphor as the way to live in an ever-expanding world. Booth unmasked "the passion for righteousness" in much contemporary computer science and cosmology. In addition, one of the program's regular sections is devoted to Arts, Literature, and Religion, and a group has formed to study Narrative Interpretation and Christian Theology. Imagery, poetry, and literary criticism are also concerns of the SBL's annual program, of course, and many AAR members regularly cross over to attend biblical papers and discussions.

For the sheer use of imagination and the mastery of vivid rhetoric, however, few speakers at the Palmer House could match the performances of three representatives of current liberation movements: James Cone, Gustavo Gutiérrez, and Rosemary Radford Ruether. Cone vividly traced the origin and development of black theology and analyzed its place as a force for renewal in American religion. Gutiérrez moved an overflowing audience deeply as he spoke of recognizing the presence of the poor in history and learning from the suffering of the innocent how to speak truly of God. In a powerful address that received standing applause from men and women alike, Ruether anatomized the androcentrism and misogyny of patriarchal culture. She continued by showing the growth of feminist theology through three stages: 1. the early critique of masculine bias; 2. the search for alternative traditions affirming the autonomous personhood of women; 3. present tentative efforts to restate the norms and methods of theology. She made it clear that with other religious leaders in feminist thought she does not conceive the movement as pitting women against men but rather as inviting partners to be mutually opposed to a system of exclusion. The call is not to create a new sect, but to join in rebuilding the center of faith from which the whole of its hope may be perceived.

OPPORTUNITIES

After so many words and so much analysis, it was no wonder that many guests at the Palmer House escaped to stroll beneath the dance of Christmas lights along the Miracle Mile of Michigan Avenue or to slip off for "A Day in the Country," the exhibition of Impressionism and the French landscape at the Art Institute. But the days of the meeting itself did show how strong the Academy's health is—and how well it is supervised by Executive Director James B. Wiggins. The riches of the program and the breadth of participation from institutions across the continent indicate strong development in the study of religion. The meeting serves as an occasion for frequently awkward but nonetheless necessary job interviews. It offers religious publishers a concentrated opportunity to present their latest offerings, and it serves indispensably to reunite friends and colleagues on both a private and an institutional basis. This year, predictably, there were also special computer exhibits and demonstrations. As the Academy mourned revered and recently deceased members like William Clebsch of Stanford, a former president, it was invigorated by new young members joining the ranks. (The deaths of Karl Rahner and Bernard Lonergan in 1984 have recently been commemorated in *JAAR*.) Perhaps most significant of all is the continued association and collaboration with the Society of Biblical Literature; and the national recognition of AAR's coming of age, signaled by its admission to the American Council of Learned Societies in 1979. And it was heartening to learn that Scholars Press had published almost 100 titles in the past year, a good number of them under contract with the AAR.

The growing participation of Catholic scholars as well as students of Catholicism reflected the rising current of Catholic thought in the mainstream of religious studies in the United States and Canada. For quite a few members of the audience, no more eloquent or searching address was given this year than Gabriel Daly's. An Augustinian priest from Dublin who now lectures at Trinity College, Daly spoke on "Catholicism and Modernity" and analyzed in a stark but bracing way the cognitive misery of a critically aware faith after the Enlightenment. With a rare blend of eloquence and vigor he contrasted two aspects of biblical faith, the Abrahamic alertness to absolute beginnings revealed in the word and the Mosaic sense for signs and presence seeded throughout the world. Exploring the implications of the two types, Daly urged that Catholicism should try to reappropriate the mystical tradition of seeking God in the world sacramentally. It should also recognize, he continued, the new sense of presence which has come to light through heightened political concern after Vatican II and the conviction that socio-political engagement can be constitutive of authentic faith. His sober but moving presentation could well set the topic for many a future conference on how—or whether—Catholicism will indeed confront modernity.

CHALLENGES

For the Academy at large, the breadth, depth and quality of participation at this Annual Meeting do indicate that the study of religion is prospering in America. And yet there are clear challenges in the situation as well. Some are more organizational: how, for example, to relate the AAR effectively to other national or local professional organizations, or how, a perennial problem, to relate its own regional and national activities. More substantively, challenges arise from the very conception of religion that is dominant in our culture. A typically Durkheimian functional theory of religion looks for it to fulfill an integrating role in society, bonding disparate elements together through fundamental values and symbols. A more interpretative theory, as in the work of Clifford Geertz, sees religion as a way of identifying oneself and one's place in the world through a general interpretation of existence. However, when one recalls the social criticism often voiced by religion and then the present crises of our society, neither of these approaches alone seems sufficient. Rather, one must look to relate both of them to still a third view of religion's place in culture, a perspective which emphasizes its power to convert, energize, and involve people in the prospects for a renewed creation. Depending on *how* one understands religion itself, then, one may expect our American Academy of Religion to be more— or less—challenging to the society in which it exists and to be more— or less—concerned for the unity of purpose among members who are both citizens and believers.

No single emphasis at this year's annual meeting seemed to me so promising in this respect as the frequently heard insistence that religious inquiry, theology, and ethical reflection must all be contextual: particular, empirical, resolutely aware of both common *and* unique historical circumstances

Only if religious thought recognizes the limitations of its time and place will it be local in a way that can aspire also to be global, rooted in its own condition with a realism that can truly contribute to the more universal human condition. Many consequences can be expected to flow from such self-awareness, both for particular questions in religious studies and for their overall program. No longer for example, would one expect to pursue the history of doctrine apart from the history of religions; indeed, one would probably place the history of doctrine precisely within the history of world religions. (And this one notes just as the recent writings of William H. McNeill, J. M. Roberts and Hugh Thomas have begun to make the task of "world history" again respectable.) Further, less than ever could the Academy excuse indifference to the situation of a world-wide Christianity which is tragically divided; the continuing importance of ecumenism in the narrower sense suggests that meetings such as ours in Chicago can ill afford to neglect ecumenical documents as significant as the Lima Statement on Baptism, Eucharist and Ministry. Finally, a contextual approach to religious studies seems to argue for the usefulness, indeed the necessity, of a social agenda. If religious identity, integration and involvement are to bear on actual life, some sense of the key issues in our culture seems required, not only for ethical reflection but for the imaginative appreciation of the real world in which we live and the resources that religion may bring to it.

Such an agenda has been sketched in various ways, of course, by documents from the World Council of Churches and by Vatican II's Pastoral Constitution on the Church in the Modern World. An American version of it is being proposed by the Roman Catholic bishops' courageous efforts to address the threat of nuclear war and the inequities of our economic system. Religionists at large would do well to consider their own versions of the agenda. In the lecture already mentioned, Langdon Gilkey reflected wisely for us all on the issues of nuclearism and unbridled relativism. In my view, it would be not merely imcomplete but a serious distortion if one were to exclude two further major issues from such an analysis of our religious situation. The first is the realms of oppression—racism, sexism, anti-Semitism— to which the emancipatory power of religion must respond today. The second is the real poverty within America with reminds us of the greater poverty outside the nation, an international poverty from which we ourselves profit in many ways. Without concern for these issues, too, neither Christianity nor any other religion today is likely to be a socially constructive movement in faith, hope, and charity. With its instinct and organization for presence at the personal, local, and global levels, Catholicism should have something special to contribute to the effort.

Speaking to the philanthropists in Hyde Park, William McCready of NORC had noted that more people today seem to express their religious faith in mythic, imaginative and reflective forms. He added that more people also seem desirous of going beyond mere church membership to identify with a living ecclesial heritage. Whether the academic study of religion can respond to this social situation will surely be a matter of concern for its largest professional organization when it meets again next year at the Anaheim Hilton just before Thanksgiving. Will the grand contemporary sculpture of Chicago— Calder and Picasso and Miró—be replaced in a dispiriting way by Disneyland? Next year we will again be searching for images that travel well, images that even bear transcendence. If our study of religion is genuinely concerned for its cultural context, then there should be time enough for a good-humored visit to the Enchanted Kingdom. But if we pursue religion for our own sakes alone, then the Meeting will pass by emptily. Next fall in California, it seems, there will be another opportunity to see which face of religion will be uppermost, the timelessly trivial or the historically transcendent, the giddiness of self-centered human ceremony or the true joy that accompanies God's pleasure in creation.

DATE DUE